AUSTRALIAN STUDIES

A SURVEY

Edited by

JAMES WALTER

OXFORD

Melbourne
Oxford   Auckland   New York

OXFORD UNIVERSITY PRESS AUSTRALIA

Oxford   New York
Athens   Auckland   Bangkok   Bombay
Calcutta   Cape Town   Dar es Salaam   Delhi
Florence   Hong Kong   Istanbul   Karachi
Kuala Lumpur   Madras   Madrid   Melbourne
Mexico City   Nairobi   Paris   Singapore
Taipei   Tokyo   Toronto
and associated companies in
Berlin   Ibadan

OXFORD is a trade mark of Oxford University Press

© This collection James Walter, 1989.
Contributors retain © in respect of their own contributions.
First published 1989
Reprinted 1991, 1995

This book is copyright. Apart from any fair
dealing for the purposes of private study,
research, criticism or review as permitted under
the Copyright Act, no part may be reproduced,
stored in a retrieval system, or transmitted, in
any form or by any means, electronic, mechanical,
photocopying, recording, or otherwise without
prior written permission. Enquiries to be made to
Oxford University Press.

Copying for educational purposes
Where copies of part or the whole of the book are
made under Part VB of the Copyright Act, the law requires
that a prescribed procedure be followed. For information, contact
the Copyright Agency Limited.

National Library of Australia
Cataloguing-in-Publication data:

Australian studies.

> Includes bibliographies and index.
> ISBN 0 19 554773 X.
> 1. Australia — Social life and customs. 2. Australia —
> History. 3. Australia. — Civilisation. 4. Australia —
> Politics and government. I. Walter, James, 1949 –

994

Designed by Steve Randles
Typeset by Kasia Graphics
Printed Impact Printing Pty. Ltd.
Published by Oxford University Press,
253 Normanby Road, South Melbourne, Australia

CONTENTS

Preface vii

Notes on Contributors ix

PART I STUDYING AUSTRALIA: REASONS AND
APPROACHES *James Walter* 1
Introduction 3
1 Why Australian Studies? 5
2 Studying Australia: A Review of Approaches 9
3 Defining Australia: A Case Study 18
References 40

PART II SETTLEMENT AND SOCIETY 45
Introduction 47
4 Australia: A Settler Society in a Changing World
Malcolm Alexander 49
5 Regionalism *Chilla Bulbeck* 70
6 Nineteenth-Century Urbanization *Gail Reekie* 84
References 97

PART III SHAPING CULTURAL INSTITUTIONS 105
Introduction 107
7 Institutions of Australian Literature *David Carter
with Gillian Whitlock* 109
8 Nationality and Australian Literature
Patrick Buckridge 136
9 Australian Film and Television *Albert Moran* 156
References 175

PART IV ORDER AND CONFLICT   183
   Introduction   185
   10 Aboriginal History *Stephen Garton*   189
   11 Labour, Class and Culture *Mark Finnane*   206
   12 From Women's History to a History
       of the Sexes *Judith Allen*   220
   13 Poverty in Paradise *Stephen Garton*   242
   References   258

PART V POLITICAL IDEAS AND INSTITUTIONS
        Brian Head   271
   Introduction   273
   14 Political Dependency and the Institutional
       Framework   275
   15 Political Ideologies and Political Parties   284
   16 The Role of State Intervention   295
   References   304
Index   310

Acknowledgement

The editor and publishers are grateful to Angus & Robertson Publishers for permission to reproduce the extract from 'Clancy of the Overflow' by A. B. Paterson from *The Collected Verse of A. B. Paterson*, © Retusa Pty Limited, 1921, in chapter 8 of this book.

PREFACE

This book consists of a series of linked interpretative chapters. Each chapter serves as a general introduction to contemporary discussion in its area and offers a list of references. This is not only to assist students working in these areas but also to interest the general reader. To this end, and in the light of common aims, the authors have worked as a collective.

The book has been produced by a group whose primary interest is in research on and teaching about Australian culture and society. It has grown out of this group's own wrestling with the questions of how to approach Australian studies: What materials are available? How are they best deployed in teaching and research? What methods are best suited to making the problems of Australian studies accessible to an audience (whether students or the readers of research papers)? But the perspective is broader than just 'the Australian'. Our purpose is to present Australian studies as an innovative means of casting a series of the key questions of contemporary humanities and social sciences by studying a particular society.

We argue that it is in the nature of 'new' societies to demand a degree of self-conscious attention to national, institutional and cultural formation not common in 'traditional' societies, and that this throws general problems of culture and society into particular relief. Discussion in disparate areas of this book is bound together by recurrent reference to the difficulty of reconciling a parent culture ('metropolis') and its offshoot ('periphery') in looking at literature, politics, economy and history. While readers are drawn into immediate consideration of how 'Australian' constructions of these subjects have been arrived at, this is shown to constitute an introduction to broader debates. It is assumed that readers will the more readily recognize and enter into such debates because they are placed in a familiar context.

In practical terms, then, this book provides for beginning researchers, teachers, students and interested readers generally a number of guidelines. First, it provides initial direction towards sources and resources in particular areas of Australian studies. Second, it suggests that the way to begin the analysis of culture and society is to generate a series of questions or problems relating to a particular society and to see how different sorts of academic investigation address such questions. Thus we learn both about that society and about academic methods of investigating society. Each part of this book illustrates the application of this approach. Third, it argues for the utility of constructing a dialogue (rather than a narrative) as the most appropriate means of acquiring knowledge about our society. Fourth, it insists on the importance of Australian studies to all students, teachers and researchers pursuing their work in Australia.

This book relates primarily to work in the humanities and social sciences because the members of the group that produced it themselves work in these fields. It might be argued that the humanities and social sciences encompass the enterprises where the questions of how and why a society or culture evolves in a particular way are most consciously addressed (at least more so than in, say, chemistry or engineering) and that therefore this is where Australian studies should be rooted (see, for instance, Turner & Patience 1985). But there are powerful arguments for suggesting that Australian studies should be pursued in every area of learning, whether pure or applied (see, in particular, CRASTE 1987). We accept those arguments, and hope that other books will be produced in other areas.

Among many debts which should be acknowledged, the first is to the students who have passed through the Australian studies courses at Griffith University. Their enthusiasm and demands led to the growth of the area from a single course to a major sequence in two degree programmes, and their queries and responses shaped the approaches adopted in this book. Lyndall Ryan was a farsighted contributor to the initiation of Australian studies work at Griffith University and a significant influence on the debates pursued in these pages. I would like to thank two supportive colleagues and friends, Stephen Garton and Judith Allen, for their assistance through some difficult patches with this enterprise. The Division of Humanities, Griffith University, provided financial support via its Research Committee. Lisa Neville, Carmel Black and Dianne Ward provided research assistance. The stenographic staff of the Division of Humanities collectively gave unstinting service in deciphering and retyping our manuscripts. We are grateful to Louise Sweetland at Oxford University Press for getting this project on the road in the first place, and to Ev Beissbarth for helping us to bring it to fruition. Finally, I would like to thank my fellow contributors for their interesting and stimulating responses to

Preface

my demand for essays that would serve the disparate ends of introducing and surveying their fields, identifying fundamental questions and methods of analysis and suggesting agendas for future enquiry.

James Walter
October 1988

NOTES ON CONTRIBUTORS

All contributors have taught in the Division of Humanities at Griffith University.

Malcolm Alexander teaches comparative sociology and history. His major research interest is the comparative history of settler societies as an aspect of modern world history and world politics. He has been particularly involved in comparative studies of Australia and Canada and is currently co-editor (with Gillian Whitlock) of *Australian-Canadian Studies*.

Judith Allen was foundation convenor of the Women, Gender and Society programme at Griffith University and is now the Professor of Women's Studies. She has published widely on historical aspects of gender, criminology and feminist theory. She is the author of *Sex and Secrets: Crimes Involving Australian Women Since 1880* (1989), and is currently writing a history of Australian 'first wave' feminism centred on the work of Rose Scott.

Patrick Buckridge teaches Australian and comparative literature. He has research interests in literary history and theory, and is currently working on an intellectual biography of the writer and editor Brian Penton.

Chilla Bulbeck has taught interdisciplinary social sciences at Murdoch University and at Griffith University. She has published (with Colleen Heath) *Shadow of the Hill*, a biography of a Pilbara unionist, and is author of *One World Women's Movement* (1988). Her present research interests are in the areas of women and the law, western and Third World feminism, and the experiences of expatriate women in Papua New Guinea.

David Carter teaches Australian and comparative literature. He is currently writing a study of the literary and political careers of Judah Watern.

Mark Finnane has published books and articles on Australian and Irish social and political history, and recently edited *Policing in Australia: Historical Perspectives* (1987).

Stephen Garton has taught Australian social history at Griffith University and now lectures in Australian history at the University of Sydney. He is the author of *Medicine and Madness* (1987) and has written widely on the history of incarceration, asylums and social reform.

Brian Head has taught politics, policy and social sciences. He has edited six volumes on Australian public policy issues. His recent books include *Intellectual Movements and Australian Society* (1989) (with James Walter), and *From Fraser to Hawke* (1989) (with Allan Patience). He has also written on European social and political theory, and is currently working on the history of Australian political thought and a book on power in Australia. He is currently working in the Premier's Department of the Queensland State Government.

Albert Moran lectures in film and media studies. His books on Australian film and television include *Images and Industry: Television Drama Production in Australia* (1985) and *A Country Practice: Quality Soap* (1986), and he co-edited *An Australian Film Reader* (1985). He is currently working on studies of government documentary film and Australian book publishing.

Gail Reekie teaches in Australian Studies and Women, Gender and Society. She has researched topics in Australian women's history (feminism, sexuality, war, work) and has written a doctoral thesis on the development of mass marketing in Sydney's big stores 1880-1930.

James Walter has taught politics and Australian studies and is the author of *The Leader: a political biography of Gough Whitlam* (1980) and *The Ministers' Minders: personal advisers in national government* (1986). He has edited a number of books, including *Intellectual Movements and Australian Society* (1988) (with Brian Head), and has published widely on aspects of leadership, political psychology, Australian studies and political history. He is currently the director of the Sir Robert Menzies Centre for Australian Studies at the Institute of Commonwealth Studies in London.

Gillian Whitlock teaches Comparative Studies and Women's Studies at Griffith University. She has edited (with Russell McDougall) *Australian and Canadian Literatures in English: Comparative Perspectives* (1987) and edited *Eight Voices of the Eighties* (1989). Her present research interests are post-colonialism and feminism.

PART I

Studying Australia: Reasons and Approaches

James Walter

Introduction

Part I is organized around three themes. It asks, first, why undertake Australian studies? Second, it offers a review of distinctive approaches—the discipline-based and the problem-oriented—and the questions they address. And third, it presents a case study for discussion: the problem of 'defining Australia'.

1 WHY AUSTRALIAN STUDIES?

Discussion commences by looking at the history of those periods in which, like the present, a concern with understanding Australian culture and society came to the forefront of community attention. It is argued that crisis provokes such concern but that it can lead us to understand that the urge for community self-awareness is always present—and should be attended to. What can we learn from how this has been done in the past?

2 STUDYING AUSTRALIA: A REVIEW OF APPROACHES

The systematic study of Australia has been relatively short-term. Historical and literary studies are taken as central and analysed to see how disciplines have examined Australia. It is shown that assuming there *is* an object, 'Australia', whose history and literature are readily to be examined, can produce problems, and that disciplinary approaches which take such a stance are question-begging. Instead, therefore, a problem-oriented approach is canvassed, one that starts from such questions as: How do we define 'Australia'? Is 'Australia' different? What are its characteristics? It is then argued that attention to the specifics of Australian society can be elaborated into the general discussions of culture and cultural production that are the fundamental concerns of the humanities and social sciences. Can this be demonstrated?

3 DEFINING AUSTRALIA: A CASE STUDY

Chapter 3 asks what do we mean when we talk about Australia? It shows that at ceremonial 'moments', such as on Australia Day, many different meanings of 'Australia' are in play. It goes on to show that scholars, examining Australia from different perspectives, arrive at answers that have been influenced by the assumptions they started with. In the course of discussion, ideas of 'the nation', 'derivative' and 'new' societies, 'tradition', 'metropolis' and 'periphery', and attendant debates about the cultural fragment, the cultural cringe, and the Australian legend are discussed. Methods of analysis characteristic of the humanities and social sciences are found to be integral to such debates.

CHAPTER ONE

WHY AUSTRALIAN STUDIES?

The study of Australia has become a matter of broad public interest in the past decade. This interest is manifest in the proliferation of local history groups and genealogical societies; the publishing boom in Australiana; the formation of an Australian Studies Association; and the popularity in educational institutions of courses about Australia. In the educational sphere, one attempt to give a focus to this trend was the Commonwealth government's establishment, in 1984, of an Australian studies project, with committees to inquire into Australian studies at secondary and tertiary levels. This book is itself a product of course developments which began at Griffith University in the late 1970s.

The first question to ask is why this upsurge of interest in things Australian? The Bicentennial reminded us that part of the impulse is nationalistic. But the spread and longevity of the boom (with its current origins some eight years prior to the Bicentennial) suggest that there is more to it than this. One way to obtain a view is to stand back and try to see this latest phase in the 'Australianist' cycle in historical perspective. There have been other such swings of interest: in the 1840s, the 1890s, the 1930s, the 1970s and now in the 1980s.

There was a radical-nationalist-tempered polity in Sydney in the 1840s, whose polemicists (one of whom, for instance, was the writer Charles Harpur) found a ready outlet in Sydney's fifty newspapers. In the face of economic decline some felt that the colony's best interests would be served if control lay in local hands rather than being dictated from Britain. The time seemed ripe for independent nationhood. But then the gold-rushes arrived, solving the economic malaise but swamping the colonists with an influx of new immigrants for whom Australianism was not important. The 1890s and 1930s were both periods of depression when there was intense and divisive debate about how Australia was to resolve current problems and how it was to face its future. The 1890s saw the flowering of the Heidelberg school of Australian painting (Astbury 1985), the ascendance of the *Bulletin*, whose professed bias, significantly, was 'offensively Australian' (Lawson 1983), and the prominence of poets (Lawson, Paterson, O'Dowd) and novelists (Furphy, Rudd) who, it was later claimed, spoke for the essentially Australian. The 1930s saw the emergence of distinctively Australian social-realist novelists and artists—women writers in particular found a voice at this time (Modjeska 1981)—and provided the seed-bed of the radical-nationalist temper which was to dominate historical writing from that time until the late 1950s, the most influential expression of this theme being Russel Ward's *The Australian Legend* (1958). The 1970s and 1980s again have been times of economic hardship and transition for Australia, initiated by the short-lived hope and assertive nationalism of the Whitlam government (1972–75), and characterized thereafter by a variety of governments, all of which have claimed to be setting a new direction for Australia in the modern world. And in parallel there has been, as we have seen, a general resurgence of 'Australianism'.

It is clear that all of these periods encompass times of crisis, the sort of crisis that appears to demand an attempt at national self-definition and self-knowledge. One self-definitional ploy is to appeal to a myth of Australian character and to try to assert cohesiveness around the supposed attributes of such a character. This is a powerful impulse behind the nationalism politicians favour at such times, encouraging us to forget differences and to emphasize commonality. Unfortunately, such nationalism can stand in the way of analysis and understanding by obscuring the fact that differences may be important, that the nation-state is and will remain the site for conflicts of interests, and that an understanding of community problems will not be achieved if this is ignored. Allied with such nationalism therefore (and sometimes in conflict with it) is an urge to know ourselves as the first step in understanding our place in the world. And hence arises the sentiment which prefaces one of the main reports from the Commonwealth Australian studies project: 'Australians want their education to give them a firmer and sharper sense of their own place and culture' (CRASTE 1987:ix).

This historical digression explains the popularity of Australian studies now, but a specific lesson should be drawn from it: if it is important at times of difficulty to be self-aware, surely it is important to maintain that impulse. Surely a secure understanding of the world must originate in a firm understanding of one's starting point—and the starting point for all of us is a particular local context. Such sentiments became central to an analogous investigation of Canadian studies in 1975:

> The most valid and compelling argument for Canadian studies is the importance of self-knowledge, the need to know and to understand ourselves: who we are; where we are in time and space; where we have been; where we are going; what we possess; what our responsibilities are to ourselves and others. But before the quest for such knowledge can begin, an individual or a collectivity must first be conscious of being Canadian. Unless Canadians recognise their distinctiveness . . . what motivation is there for self-study? [Symons 1975:12]

The more such issues are pursued the more significant they become. An early work in the relatively new area of cultural studies forcefully made the point: 'The key to any description is its starting point: the particular experience that is seized as determining. In general, in thinking about a society, we start from *these* people in *this* place . . .' (Williams 1961:121). The author went on to develop the thesis: 'Since our way of seeing things is literally our way of living, the process of communication is in fact the process of community: the sharing of common meanings and thence common activities and purposes . . .' To put this in another way, we understand the world in a certain way because we are Australian. Donald Horne (1986:4) talks of this as 'the hypotheses about existence we learn from our culture, the repertoires of collective thinking and acting that give meaning to existence'. It follows that we cannot stand outside the society which shaped us; we must be alert to our 'ways of seeing' (Turner & Bird 1982). If we are not, our understanding of the world at large will certainly be deficient.

Let us translate this argument into practical terms, related to ways of learning. Traditionally, at the upper levels of secondary schooling and in tertiary institutions we are introduced to disciplines—social sciences, history, literary studies—and to the methods of study appropriate to those disciplines, as ways of pursuing knowledge. This is important work, but it has the danger of appearing abstract and limited. One might learn, for instance, to write critical essays on Shakespeare's plays, but have no notion of how to translate those skills to work in the larger society. Or one might learn the technical skills of, say, engineering, but have little sense of what effects putting those skills into operation can have on the environment and community. The issue is to put the abstract skills of disciplinary analysis into a context that makes their practical applications evident. And the way to do this is to start from the local context. To recommend this is not to recommend an insular, inward-looking approach:

a truly liberal education consists in following a problem through all its ramifications, wherever it might lead you. Taking the starting problems from Australian experience should not lead to students who know nothing of the rest of the world. Quite the contrary. To understand an explorer like

Leichhardt, one needs to know about German romanticism; the experience of Australian settlers can be illuminated by comparison with the settlers of South Africa or New Zealand; the organisation of labour in Australian factories needs to be understood in the light of British and American experience. Australia was settled by Europeans and is part of an increasingly interdependent world...Australian studies will introduce students to ideas and events far beyond Australia. [Brett 1985:26]

One metaphor that illuminates this strategy is to talk of pursuing Australian studies as a 'window onto [the] world' (CRASTE 1987): understanding our society gives us a secure vantage, a particular 'window', from which we can look to understand the world at large. Australian studies, then, must not be parochial, but must lead out into the broader study of culture and society.

CHAPTER TWO

STUDYING AUSTRALIA: A REVIEW OF APPROACHES

It is useful to begin this chapter by asking: How has Australia been studied in the past? The preoccupation with asking questions about Australia and what it means was part of the culture brought here by European settlers 200 years ago. The indigenous peoples belonged to the country and their Dreaming told them all they needed to know; European settlers, in contrast, brought with them the conviction that knowledge was a matter of investigation and classification. One of the features of their taking possession of this country was to classify it anew (it was named Australia in 1814 by the man who had first circumnavigated it, Matthew Flinders). But because they *were* Europeans the nature of their enquiry about Australia took directions that impeded their understanding of the new country.

For natural scientists Australia's unusual conditions and abundance of new flora and fauna made it a treasure trove. It was also, in their view, a place sufficiently unspoiled by civilization to provide a perfect laboratory for testing all sorts of theories that were then popular (White 1981:1–15). Some of this curiosity and enthusiasm lay behind the great journeys of exploration that characterize our nineteenth-century history. For the same reasons explorers' journals were very popular when published in Europe. So scientists showed a very early interest in studying Australia, but they found it difficult to understand on its own terms. The approach to farming, for instance, owed much to expectations and 'scientific' principles developed in the (very different) conditions of Europe, and these expectations were inappropriate here, so the early settlers' experiences were of failure even though they did the 'right' things. Thus, according to Manning Clark ([1979] 1980), white Australians began to feel there was some fault in themselves. Scientists further confused matters by taking, or sending, their major discoveries back to Europe because they felt that was where the significant work of research and classification was done. But this made it most difficult for later researchers to carry on their work in Australia because now crucial pieces of evidence and links were missing, scattered throughout overseas institutions. George Seddon, who has looked closely at the consequences of this, concludes: 'In many ways the sciences in Australia have been distorted—and generally retarded—by European perspectives. Australian researchers have tended to work within theoretical frameworks from Europe and . . . mainly appropriate to European experience' (Seddon 1982:446).

When it came to questions that were not on the agenda of the natural sciences, questions about culture and society, Australia was hardly considered at all. That is because the settlers persisted in seeing themselves as transplanted Europeans, and so treated questions about society, culture, literature and history as questions about European society, culture, literature and history. There was, after all, no 'history' in this new society was there (Macintyre 1987:1)? The Aborigines were ignored:

The residue of that situation was found in the view that Australia wasn't of much importance and that in the words of one of the many expatriates . . . 'primary reality' lay elsewhere—in London, Paris or New York. The institutions of Australian cultural and intellectual life until recently saw themselves as . . . defined by their attempts to 'reach' the 'standards' found in the older institutions of Britain, Europe and the US on which they modelled themselves. [Alomes & Grant 1984:5]

We will see in later chapters of this book the sorts of reasons—geographic, demographic, economic, political, eventually nationalistic—that arose to complicate the colonial relationship between Australia and the parent societies of Europe, and impelled the realization that it was essential to ask such questions about Australia itself. The practical outcome, though, has been that the history of studying Australia has been very recent. Descriptions of the colonies were published in the nineteenth century, stretching back as far as W. C. Wentworth's *A Statistical, Historical and Political Description of New South Wales*, published in 1819. But the first university course in Australian history was taught at Stanford University in California in 1907–08. Australian historical overviews (such as Scott 1916) and social science analyses (such as Northcott 1918) began to appear in the first decades of the twentieth century, but in Australia the first Australian history course was not taught until 1927 at the University of Melbourne, and did not become a regular annual course until 1946 (Alomes & Grant 1984:6). (For a broader overview see Bourke 1988.) Australian texts had been studied in university English courses since the 1920s, and significant critical studies of Australian literature appeared then (Palmer 1924; Green 1930). But the first full courses in Australian literature did not appear until the 1950s, the first major work of scholarly analysis (Green 1961) appeared a decade later, and it was not until the 1970s that separate units in Australian literature became common (Grant 1983:39; CRASTE 1987:71). Attempts to offer Australian studies courses that are more broadly based than the individual disciplines are even more recent; they are a product of the 1960s and 1970s (Alomes & Grant 1984:7).

In summary, the study of Australia is recent, the questions asked are still fresh, and the issue of which approaches are most productive is still a matter of vigorous discussion. Which approach best suits your purposes might depend on what problem or question you wish to investigate, but in general it will help to have an overview of these approaches. They can be generalized as either disciplinary or problem-oriented approaches, though it will be productive to note further categories (for instance, comparative studies, regional studies) within these major headings.

Disciplinary approaches

The organization of the pursuit of knowledge in most Australian tertiary institutions is of separate departments of scholars specializing in discrete disciplines: literature, geography, political science, history, economics, and so on. These institutions (where teachers are trained and textbooks are written) have flow-on effects in the way learning is organized in the rest of society, particularly in schools.

The intellectual history of this disciplinary approach has emerged only in the period since European occupation of Australia. Australia's universities are even more recent; universities at Sydney and Melbourne were founded in 1852 and 1853 respectively and, despite universities established in Adelaide (1874), Hobart (1890) and Brisbane (1909), they functioned as our major tertiary institutions until the 1950s. The real growth in numbers of universities and in the size of each, and the proliferation of other tertiary institutions, has occurred only in the last thirty years. The disciplinary perspective was taken as integral to these developments, and so has rarely been challenged.

Not surprisingly then, when questions about Australia at last were admitted to the agenda, they were seen as questions to be dealt with in terms already familiar in the disciplines. It was just a matter of adding research and courses in Australian literature in English departments, and Australian politics in government departments, as the brief history above shows. There is not sufficient space here to consider the effects of these new courses in many disciplines, but it is worth noting the central examples of historical and literary studies.

Why are history and literature central cases? Because it has been widely assumed that to understand people's behaviour now entails examining the history of how they have behaved in the past. Similarly, to see if people have anything distinctive to say, one must search for its expression in their literature. When we come to consider Australian studies more broadly we will consider criticisms of these assumptions, but it should be stated here that history and literature have led the field in the debate about Australia.

To introduce Australia into historical and literary studies, however, has not been as straightforward as it might appear. How should it begin? For one thing, historians have not been able to agree on why European settlement of Australia took place (G. Martin 1978). And what place should white settlement assume in the historical record? Where does 'Australian' history start? Until recently, white historians had assumed that it started with the imposition of European civilization on this continent, and constructed a history starting in 1788. But what about the Aboriginal people, whose land this has been for possibly as long as 120 000 years (White & Lampert 1987; Ward 1987)? Where does 'their' history fit into 'our' history? And even if one concentrates on the Anglo-Saxon majority, what does the British settlement of 1788 mean for the descendants of the many waves of non-British immigrants since, especially after the mass-migration of the 1950s? As for Australian literature, what texts should be included? Books by the Australian-born? (What if the author spent most of his working life overseas, as did Morris West?) Books about Australia? (Does this make the English author D. H. Lawrence's book *Kangaroo* a part of Australian literature?) Books written in Australia? (What if they are by foreign-born or merely visiting authors and do not mention Australia?) Almost analogous questions can be generated for any other discipline. The point is that if one is going to make a start on Australian literature, history or anything else, a stand must be taken on such issues.

One group of writers of historical and literary studies did take a stand in an attempt to solve such problems. Because of their pro-Australian stance they came to be called the radical nationalists. Among their most prominent exponents were Brian Fitzpatrick, Vance Palmer, Ian Turner, Russel Ward and Geoffrey Serle (historians), and Nettie Palmer, A. A. Phillips, Stephen Murray-Smith and Tom Inglis Moore (literary critics). They decided that the history of Australia was the history of those influences that produced what they saw as an 'essentially' Australian character, and that truly Australian literature was that which gave expression to this character. The issue, therefore, was to decide what were the typical features of the Australian character, and then put together the story of the origins of these traits. The most widely-read version of this argument was Russel Ward's *The Australian Legend*:

The Australian Legend . . . advances in four stages. Firstly, Ward argues that there is something identifiably Australian, a proletarian 'mystique' . . .

Secondly, this mystique evolved out of bush life, especially out of the conditions of labour and leisure of the nineteenth century nomadic bushmen . . . Thirdly, this set of values was transferred to city people by osmosis, especially through the fiction of popular writers such as Lawson and Furphy. Finally, the advent of socialist ideas . . . after about 1880 was accepted by these men quite quickly, since mateship—an integral part of the mystique—was a 'natural socialist ethos' . . . [Pascoe 1979:52]

The radical-nationalist project has been described as historicist and evolutionary because it postulates a set of historically evolving circumstances that, at a certain point, produced the essentially Australian attributes (Docker 1984; Wells 1988). (The 'legend' was usually seen as fully flowering in the 1890s.) This approach has been called contextualist because it seeks to evaluate literature on the basis of how representative or expressive it is of the society it portrays (Docker 1984; Buckridge 1988).

There has been a strong stream of radical-nationalist writing in the disciplines of literature and history, and it has shown a capacity to create powerful myths and memorable narratives. But it has also generated controversy and opposition. It has been said that radical nationalism, with its emphasis on the bush tradition and the digger, leaves women, Aborigines and urban dwellers out of the picture. It has concentrated on the working class, where the tradition's values are allegedly embodied, to the exclusion of understanding how the powerful monied classes affect society and history. It has accentuated particular narrow characteristics at the expense of saying anything of value about experiences universal to humankind. It has valued social-realist depictions of life in literature at the expense of abstract and expressionist modes, and has concentrated so much on the context of literary works that it has overlooked entirely the intrinsic literary merits of texts:

The chief weakness of this body of writing lies in its unexamined assumptions, its narrow range of reference, its tendency to draw on the same repeated examples of national character or national literature, its failure to recognize the wider historical context, its tendency to interpret historic figures and texts unhistorically, confounding topical significance with universal value, its didactic and doctrinaire tone. [Colmer 1978:246]

The most fundamental flaw is that it tends to assume as a starting-point what might be expected to be proved at the end of the enquiry, that is, the existence of an Australian character.

The above discussion indicates some of the potential dangers of assuming that there is an object, 'Australia', that can be studied in a straightforward way using traditional (disciplinary) methods. One means of gaining a perspective is to see that Australia is not an object *sui generis*, but that it bears important similarities to other societies:

Its historical development follows patterns and enacts situations that can be paralleled by other colonial and ex-colonial nations, particularly former settler societies like the United States, Canada, New Zealand and South Africa . . . The colonising experience imposes structurally similar or homologous experiences so that study of Australian society can be illuminated in every significant area of class, race relations, male–female relationships, and so on, by a horizontal examination of comparable societies. [Docker 1978:23–4]

Comparative studies have become an important stream within Australian studies (Hartz 1964; Denoon 1983). Comparative studies have been championed as a means of honing disciplinary methods and widening the boundaries of disciplinary analysis (Reid 1979). Perhaps a broader approach leads to more self-consciousness about the focus of studies, and perhaps the comparative method is more likely to expose distinctions between stereotypes and fluid norms. There is still the danger that cross-cultural comparisons will involve 'the attempt to delineate "national" identities as if these were unique, fixed or all-inclusive categories' (Reid 1979:36). Certainly this criticism could be levelled at some of the most influential works in the genre (for instance, Pye & Verba 1965; Almond & Verba 1963). Perhaps, therefore, comparison should be an element within a more inclusive approach to Australian studies. And perhaps one should ask more preliminary questions about the object of study, and let the answers to those questions indicate what methods of enquiry (disciplinary, comparative, or something other) look most promising.

Problem-oriented approaches

In important respects Australia defies academic attempts to depict it as an entity with certain unifying characteristics that can be dispassionately analysed. We should start here by noting the sorts of differentiation inherent within Australia. The inhabitants of the nation–state are not all in the same boat; there are economic differences between wage-labourers and entrepreneurs, and between manufacturers and farmers (Connell & Irving 1980); differences of value between the Anglocentric mainstream and the multitudes of non-English immigrants since the 1950s (and cultural differences between various ethnic immigrant groups) (Burnley, Encel & McCall 1985); differences between states with more or with less diversified economies (Head 1986); rivalry between leading cities (Davidson 1986); and differences between urban areas (where most Australians live) and the country (where most of our myths allegedly originate (Davison 1978).

It has been argued that the diversity Australian studies must encompass is registered by regional studies (Docker 1978; West 1986a). To take an instance, Queensland has a distinctive economic base in comparison with most other states: it relies much more than Victoria or New South Wales on service, primary and extractive industries than on processing, finance or manufacturing industries (McQueen 1982; Mullins 1986). This primary industry bias leads to demographic differences: it is the only state where a majority of the population lives outside the capital city; Queenslanders generally have a lower level of education than people from other states; and there is a much smaller professional and managerial sector (McQueen 1982:112). These features in turn are said to have led to a distinctive political culture: tolerant of authoritarian government, committed to rural verities, conservative and chauvinist (Smith 1985). This is only an instance of a much more general phenomenon. Holmes and Sharman (1977:46ff) provide evidence of strong regional identities throughout Australia, and argue that 'the regional diversities which shaped our federal system at the turn of the century still flow through our political processes' (1977:16). McQueen (1982) has provided further substance to this by filling out the state-by-state picture (see also Galligan 1986; Head 1986). Others have argued for the importance of studying regional writing (Whitlock 1984). And of course an extended study of the famous Melbourne–Sydney split is available (Davidson 1986). All of this reinforces the importance of the comparative method; it is clear that comparison must be intra- as well as international.

Does this recognition of differentiation, however, mean a fragmentation of Australian studies into small area studies? It has been argued that 'regional studies can be microcosmic, involving overall aspects of "civilization" in the very study of local problems' (Docker 1978:23). Such a stance assumes that something general arises out of the study of the particular. If that general thing is not 'Australia' itself (and the radical nationalists show the problems of attempting that path), what is it to be? The answer comes from recognizing that what we are searching for is not 'Australia' but an understanding of how general principles of cultural formation are manifest within Australia. These general principles might be expressed very broadly in this way: societies or communities seek means of self-definition and of explaining reality; they do this through 'inventing' a self-image and a rhetoric (for instance, founding myths) and symbolic action (for instance, celebration of national days) which justify and explain this image. This 'imagined community' determines the structure of the community's institutions (at least at the level of ideals) and the result is the production of a culture (Anderson 1983; Horne 1986). Thus, in Australian studies, we are analysing the production and maintenance of cultures.

A direct means of commencing such analysis is to ask not about categories of social product (history, literature, politics, economics) as disciplines typically do, but to ask a series of fundamental questions which disciplines might then be used to address. Such an approach treats problems as central (note the problem-defining titles of the chapters in this book), but also serves to introduce academic methods of enquiry and to situate these within the community in which they might eventually be put into practical effect. More importantly, one should thus learn about the continuing concerns at the heart of the humanities and social sciences. This can be demonstrated by a practical elaboration.

The elaboration can commence by going back over the discussion so far, bringing out the recurrent questions, and seeing how they mobilize disciplinary insights, and can lead in turn to more fundamental problems of cultural formation. Clearly one of the main issues encountered above has been: What are we talking about when we talk about Australia? Let us therefore pose the question: *How can we define Australia?* A moment's reflection will show that this raises a series of subsidiary questions, all of which relate to more traditional studies through disciplines, and thence to more fundamental concerns. These questions might include:

Does 'Australia mean 'the nation'? Where does the idea of 'a nation' come from? (history of ideas)

What has nationhood meant in the contemporary world? (history and politics)

Can 'Australia' be understood best in terms of the history of settlement of this continent? (history and economics)

How can 'Australia' be differentiated from other nations—both the 'parent' societies of Europe, and other regions of recent settlement like Canada or New Zealand? (history, economics and comparative studies)

Where do our social institutions come from, and do they function in ways unique to Australia? (political science and sociology)

Where do our cultural institutions come from? How, for instance, do we define what is Australian literature, film, television? (literary and media studies)

In what ways is contemporary Australian society like and unlike societies of similar countries? (sociology, social studies, economics)

Is Australia best understood in terms of what is unique to the country? (geography, environmental studies)

Can Australia be understood in terms of the myths and images generated here? Is there an 'Australian legend'? (history of ideas, history, literary studies)

Who are the 'Australian' people? (histories of indigenous peoples, immigration, settlement; the debate on multiculturalism)

Seen thus, Australian studies can bring together diverse facts, materials and ideas, and the disciplines that help us to understand them, in a coherent way. The coherence comes from the unifying questions at the heart of the project, questions which at base amount to: What does it mean to be Australian? (How is the 'imagined community' to be understood?); How have we come to be this way? (How has the symbolic complex of cultural practices been produced?); How does this appear in the society around us? (In what ways do our institutions manifest underlying cultural dynamics?) Not only does the attempt to answer these questions draw attention to practical applications of the methods of history, political science, literary studies, geography and other disciplines, but it also highlights the central concerns that generated these disciplines in the first place: How are societies formed? How are they maintained? How do they evolve? How are institutions developed?

This approach, informed by fundamental questions, provides a systematic theoretical core for our work, helping to avoid the common misunderstanding that 'Australian studies are a "ragbag"—a bit of history, a bit of music, a bit of geography, and a lot of literature—without any specified overview or framework or informing theory' (Anderson 1985:28; see also Turner & Bird 1982).

Australian studies are particularly useful in directing attention to such fundamental questions. Settler societies like Australia are forced to make choices about issues crucial to the nature of culture and society: choices about how to relate to indigenous peoples; what can be learned from them; what to retain, jettison or adapt from parent cultures; and how these choices sit with the experience of living in the new land. The underlying features—complex interaction with an initially strange environment, the fact of white invasion of Aboriginal land, the experience of a long colonial period of British economic, social, cultural and political influence, diverse waves of migration (cf. Alomes 1985; Docker 1978)—deeply influence those choices (reminding us of Marx's great maxim: 'men make their own history, but not under terms of their own choosing'). It might be argued that in older societies such matters are obscured in the mists of history; they simply do not appear as matters for choice and debate.

In summary, it is in the nature of new societies such as Australia to demand a degree of self-conscious attention to national, institutional and cultural formation not common in 'traditional' societies, and this throws the general problems of culture and society into particular relief. There are, therefore, special advantages for students of humanities and social sciences in pursuing Australian studies, and in adopting the problem-oriented approach. An additional benefit is that debates about society will appear more germane when the leading questions are placed in a familiar context. An outcome should be not only knowledge about Australia, but also an appreciation of the relevance of academic concerns, and a confidence about applying the techniques of academic enquiry to one's own society, and to work outside educational institutions.

CHAPTER THREE

DEFINING AUSTRALIA: A CASE STUDY

In the remainder of part I the project of 'defining Australia' mooted in chapter 2 as an example of generating problem-oriented enquiry is taken up as a case study of methods of discussion in Australian studies. There is not space to consider all of the questions conjectured on p. 16, and in any case some of the issues raised there are the subject-matter of later parts in this book: settlement and regional studies in part II, the cultural institutions of literature and the media in part III, social history and the nature of society in part IV, and political institutions in part V. Of the remaining questions, perhaps those most central to a beginning on Australian studies are those to do with 'the nation' and 'nationalism', so they are considered here.

The purpose is to establish dialogue on these questions by looking at how they have been tackled by various writers. On one level, therefore, this chapter serves as commentary on those who have broached such issues, while it remains alert to matters of method and purpose and always concerned not only with the object but also with the nature of enquiry.

It is instructive to start by asking: Are we dealing with a real problem?

Defining Australia: is there a problem?

One way of starting to think about defining Australia is to see what people say about Australia at a time when they are explicitly encouraged to think about what it means. Australia Day, which is supposed to serve such a function, provides a good starting point. Australia Day, 26 January, intended as a day of national celebration and a focus for collective Australian consciousness, always gives rise to a flurry of newspaper commentary. Press coverage of this day for any year shows uncertainty about both the nature of the ceremony and exactly what it is that is being celebrated. The debate was particularly intense at the start of the Bicentennial year, and some striking examples of journalistic approaches to the issue can be found in the major metropolitan newspapers of 23-26 January 1988.

One theme common to such passages is that the commentators are wrestling with how to arrive at a sense of ceremony and of 'Australia' that will have a meaning for all Australians. The impulse of the debate is unity, the rhetoric is that of 'the nation', and the goal is the establishment of boundary distinctions, a community distinct from others, a clear idea of what is Australian and what is not. But there are considerable difficulties:

Let us consider whether the day marking the anniversary of British settlement of the penal colony of NSW has relevance as a national day, given that the Aboriginal people were here long before, that other States celebrate different founding days—and that a very large proportion of Australia's . . . population has no link with Britain's long-gone colonial activities. Looked at from those aspects, January 26 has more divisive than nationally unifying properties. [Editorial, *Australian*, 1 February 1982]

There is, as this passage notes, the problem of what this celebration means to the Aborigines:

We have to remember that to the Aborigines, the first settlement was straight-out invasion. [Fred Daly, *Age*, 23 January 1981]

I used to hate history . . . Aborigines were given only a few derogatory mentions in the books . . . When they [the white community] say this is a grand nation they are liars. Certainly some don't know. It's been very well-hidden. I think the Bicentenary should be an occasion not to celebrate, but for Australia to face its history. Until they face it, we won't have harmony. [Eve Fesl, OA, *Age*, 27 January 1988]

If we who have arrived in the past two centuries are to identify with this land, we must also identify with those who, for perhaps as long as 60,000 years have been the repositories of its wisdom and secrets, its human presence. To deny them is to deny ourselves . . . ['Shadows behind the celebrations', *Age*, 27 January 1988]

Taking a historical viewpoint, it is evident that the Australia of the Aborigines (with their unique visions of country and society) was a different Australia from that understood by predominantly British settlers (with their European visions of country and society) between 1788 and 1988.

Even within the white community, understandings of Australia may have altered radically, for instance after about 1830 when free-born immigrants began to supersede convicts and their administrators, roughly after 1890 when the native-born outnumbered immigrants, and again after 1950 with the large influx of immigrants from diverse, non-English speaking cultures.

[The Australia Day Committee] . . . is emphasising the arrival of the First Fleet as *one* of Australia's three big waves of immigration. First came the Aborigines, then the British settlers, many of them in chains. Finally, there was the flood of migrants after World War II. Australia Day, the Committee says, must include them all. [*Age*, 23 January 1981]

From a contemporary perspective it seems that distinctive views of Australia may be held by different cultural groups. It may make sense to talk of the Aboriginal-Australian Australia, the Italo-Australian Australia, the Anglo-Celtic Australia, and so on. Even within the dominant cultural group, whites of British descent, there is a distinction between those who see 26 January 1788 as the primary event in our national life and those who would rather celebrate another event (the proclamation of the Commonwealth on 1 January 1901 and Anzac Day on 25 April are popular contenders: the first alleged to be the birth of the nation, the second said to represent our 'coming of age'):

today is not an anniversary of nationhood, for it commemorates the foundation of a British convict colony, not the formation of a free and independent nation. We have another 13 years to wait before we can celebrate . . . the centenary of federation and the creation of the Commonwealth of Australia . . . 1901 was the peaceful birth of a nation. [editorial, *Age*, 26 January 1988]

Those who would stay with the British founding moment presumably see Australia in terms of links with an older culture, a dependent component in a broader British cultural grouping. Those who would prefer to celebrate nationhood or 'coming of age' presumably wish to emphasize Australia as something unique, having distinctive qualities and an independent cultural life. Such attitudes, too, arguably imply different Australias.

The underlying issue here is that a national day must have a unified meaning, yet if Australia means different things to different people it is not surprising that there continues to be so much debate about Australia Day. What is important to our discussion here is to consider how to come to terms with the definition of Australia at all if it is subject to such variation. Australia Day alerts us to this larger issue, and indicates that defining Australia does present a real problem.

Does 'Australia' mean 'the nation'?

Discussion of Australia's national day—even if only as a means of introducing the problematic status of 'Australia'—brings the issue of Australia as a nation to the fore, and goes back to one of the initial questions: Does 'Australia' mean 'the nation'? That suggests a preliminary question: Where does the idea of 'the nation' come from?

One writer who has attempted to clarify the process of debate about culture and society by drawing attention to the history of the meanings of words is Raymond Williams. He elaborates the framework of ideas and the historical context of 'nation':

Nation . . . has been in common use in English from the late 13th century, originally with a primary sense of a racial group rather than a politically organized grouping . . . It is not easy to date the emergence of the predominant modern sense of a political formation . . . Clear political uses were evident from the 16th century and were common from the late 17th century . . . There was from the early 17th century a use of the nation to mean the whole people of a country, often in contrast, as still in political argument, with some group within it. The adjective *national* (as now in *national interest*) was used in this persuasive unitary sense from the 17th century. The derived noun *national*, which is clearly political, is more recent . . . *Nationality*, which had been used in a broad sense from the late 17th century, acquired its modern political sense in the late 18th and early 19th centuries.

Nationalist appeared in the early 18th century and *nationalism* in the early 19th century. Each became common from the mid-19th century. The persistent overlap between racial grouping and political formation has been important, since claims to be a *nation* and to have *national rights*, often envisaged the formation of a *nation* in the political sense, even against the will of an existing political *nation* which included and claimed the loyalty of this grouping . . . In practice, given the extent of conquest and domination, *nationalist* movements have as often been based on an existing but subordinate political grouping as upon a group distinguished by a specific language or by a supposed *racial* community. *Nationalism* has been a political movement in subjected countries which include several races and languages (as India) as well as in subjected countries or provinces or regions where the distinction is a specific language or religion or supposed *racial* origin . . . [Williams 1976:178-9)

Look first at the matter of dating. 'Nation' and 'national', like much of the terminology used to discuss culture and society, were first used in a political sense in the seventeenth and eighteenth centuries. Coincidentally, these developments parallel the first settlement. Keep this in mind and ponder how the emergence of the distinctively modern ways of thinking about society generally affected the development of particular ideas about modern Australia.

Second, note that the idea of nationalism became common in the mid-nineteenth century, that is to say at roughly the same time as the number of white, native-born Australians came to equal the number of immigrants (the native-born became numerically dominant in the 1890s). Around this time both the native-born, and those who felt their future to be bound up with the new country, began to seek a means of distinguishing colonial society in a positive way from the British mainstream. The tool that came to hand for this purpose was nationalism.

There is a paradox here, since those who identified with the colony were looking for a way of making a break from 'the old country' in a distinctively Australian way, and yet the means of doing this came not from something particular to Australia, but through concepts that were current in Europe at that time. Something supposedly new, an indigenous culture, could only be understood through dependence on a shared western framework of ideas (White 1981:viii–x).

Most of the contemporary discussion of Australia as a nation has been in terms of a political formation (that is, a politically organized and unified grouping) which Williams notes is the predominant modern sense. But the sense of a racial group should not be ignored—persistent emphasis on 'British stock', the arrival of the first fleet as the moment of our birth, the exclusion of the Aboriginal population from political participation in the society and the denial of their rights, the White Australia policy from the 1890s until the early 1970s—all suggest the importance that has been given to the racial (indeed racist) connotations of nationalism.

Williams refers to the uses of the concepts of nation and nationalism as a means of politically mobilizing subject groups within a country. These concepts have been used to persuade people in a country controlled by an outside political grouping (say, India by the English in the nineteenth century) that they have unified common interests and should resist such outside control. Such uses remind us of the impulse fostered by Australian nationalists to assert a distinctive identity in the face of British (or, after the Second World War, American) dominance. But perhaps more important has been the sense of the nation to mean *the whole* people of a country, given that Australia is a federation of formerly discrete colonies. Hence the growing debate over Australian nationalism in the nineteenth century included attempts to persuade the people of all the colonies that they had shared interests that transcended colonial boundaries. Indeed, contemporary emphasis on nationalism can be understood as reasserting this argument. It is reasserted because first, states' rights issues (for instance in Queensland, where Queensland rights versus Canberra's encroachments is a familiar topic) and, second, the many identities existing in national life, are seen as antagonistic to the 'whole people, common interests' concept.

When people talk of 'the nation' to imply the whole people of a country—without reference to the many identities or diverse interests within it—they are encouraging acceptance of what Williams calls 'the persuasive unitary sense' of the nation: much discussion of Australia Day exemplifies this attempt to get people to forget their differences. The problem is to decide whether such persuasive unitary uses have positive or negative effects. This will depend very much on personal opinion. From one point of view, nationalism may be regarded positively when it is seen as a way of persuading a group within a country (or political formation) to oppose external control or oppression to protect its national rights. Western newspaper commentators, for instance, represent Polish nationalism as a virtue and as justifying a move against the government of that country, which is seen as under the control of the Soviet Union. Similarly, nationalism may be a movement which opposes imperialist exploitation. Or, as in Australia, the sense of being the whole people of a country may be a step towards overcoming the economic inefficiencies of colonial fragmentation, and a step towards cultural distinctiveness as against simple derivativeness (second-hand Britishness); at least these uses of the term 'nationalism' are familiar in discussions of Australian history.

Alternatively, 'nation' and 'nationalism' may be used in ways intended to invoke exclusivist, even racist, attitudes. They may also be used to persuade people to subordinate the particular interests of their own group to the common interests of the whole country. Nationalism calls on people to give such allegiance to the broad political grouping that there is reluctance to question the status quo. Although some groups are always better served by the status quo than others, the disadvantaged groups are prevented from realizing this fully by their sense of allegiance to the nation; to question the status quo would be divisive, implying that the nation is *not* the whole people. Hence most of the people in a country are easily persuaded that the claims of particular, identifiable groups within a country are merely sectional and selfish and against the national interest, as Williams points out.

Nationalism has been central to the modern political order. To understand why this has been so, we need not only Williams's etymology, but also a more extensive theoretical and historical understanding of the uses of nationalism in the world.

Benedict Anderson offers a helpful interpretation of the rise of nations and nationalism in his *Imagined Communities* (1983). A nation, suggests Anderson (1983:11–16), can be thought of as an 'imagined community', with limited boundaries, a sovereign state which is the nation's emblem, and a sense of fraternity. The turning point of Anderson's concept of the nation is the notion of a community which is tied not by religion (as in medieval Christendom) or by kin (as in tribal or some types of peasant society), but by its 'imagined' status. Why imagined? 'because the members of even the smallest nation will never know most of their fellow-members, meet them, or even hear of them, yet in the mind of each lives the image of their communion' (Anderson 1983:15).

Why and how did these imagined communities arise? An essential precondition was the breakdown of the medieval world order and the decline in the authority of established religions. In the west this meant the decline of Christendom and the deterioration of the link between church and state. This made a legitimating ideology of secular authority necessary. An investment in 'the nation' became that legitimating ideology. It was also the tool for a new society. Vernacular nationalisms mobilizing populist appeal were used to challenge decaying absolutist dynasties and paved the way for the new capitalist order. Three emergent tendencies—of challenging *ancien régimes* with the new order, populist appeal to 'the people', and appeal to a particular glorious history to justify action—came together in the French and American revolutions of the late eighteenth century, and were then pirated through new print technologies as nationalist models for the rest of the world.

The role of nativist intelligentsias (that is, intelligentsias identifying with their communities of origin) became important in the articulation of national entities in the nineteenth century, particularly in the new societies created by capitalism's global imperialist expansion. In the settler societies the nativist intelligentsia was excluded from the heights of the colonial career structure, which was dictated by and dominated by functionaries from the European metropolis. Colonial intellectuals none the less learned of nationalist ideology in Europe through pilgrimages to the metropolises (Lisbon, Madrid, London) for education and experience. They were to use this ideology to contest their exclusion from influence at home, and to foster the emergence of new nations ('imagined communities' separate from the colonial empire). Thus the many states which emerged from the wreckage of the European empires were led by nationalist intelligentsias. The result: in the twentieth century the nation–state has become the legitimate international norm.

Anderson suggests the reasons for 'the *attachment* that people feel for the inventions of their "imaginations" '. The appeal of the nation is that it is without interests, like the family 'a domain of disinterested love and solidarity'. Solidarity, 'contemporaneous community', is established through language (for instance, the singing of national anthems). The nation is simultaneously 'open and closed', since it is both a *'historical* fatality' (one can be *naturalized*, one can join the nation) and a 'community imagined through language' (it possesses a privacy which is impervious to outside speakers).

Looking back at Williams's discussion on nationalism suggests some qualifications to Anderson's argument. Williams remarks:

claims to be a *nation* . . . often envisaged the formation of a *nation* in the political sense, even against the will of an existing political *nation* which included and claimed the loyalty of this grouping . . . *nationalist* movements have . . . often been based on an existing but subordinate political grouping . . . [Williams 1976:178–9]

The imagined community may therefore not be as cohesive as Anderson implies. As shown below, there have always been groups *contending* to represent Australia's nationhood. Equally, we should not forget that we belong to communities that operate at a sub-national level (Australians are sometimes encouraged to see themselves as Queenslanders or Victorians rather than Australians, for example). Still, there is little doubt that Anderson is right in suggesting that as an *ideal* the nation (always represented as cohesive) is the most dominant form of imagined community in contemporary life.

How does such an approach accord with the questions already raised about Australia, and with the way the 'nation' has been discussed in the Australian context?

The birth of a nation? History and political economy

Those radical-nationalist historians who concentrated on 'the Australian legend' were very much involved in the construction of an 'imagined community'. While criticisms of the radical nationalists have been noted, it is illuminating to look at the features of their argument in more detail in the context of Anderson's analysis. Ward's version of the argument (Ward 1958) has been discussed above (see p.12-13: we will look here in comparison at other exponents of the legend.

First, why was the legend seen as important? R. M. Crawford (1955) argues that it provides a self-picture that enables Australians to act with confidence. It is perhaps an idealized picture, but as it encapsulates positive values it gives Australians something to live up to. It was inevitable that this picture would derive from the bush ethos. When Australians turned from Britain in search of some element unique to life in this country, and in particular when artists sought inspiration from distinctively Australian sources, where could they find them, argues Crawford, but in the bush? The bush ethos was *distinctive*, not *representative*. Artists, particularly the writers of the *Bulletin*, made the bush accessible and gave it expressive meaning for all Australians. Thus, because it filled an imaginative need, it entered the Australian consciousness and *became* the Australian legend. And the values that had their basis in the experience of bush life—self-reliance, egalitarianism, mateship—were encapsulated in the national character.

Vance Palmer ([1954] 1966:9) deals with another aspect of this argument, suggesting that the Australian people in the latter half of the nineteenth century were united in their ideals and aspirations, and that they were consciously isolationist, determinedly working at an imagined community of their own devising and rejecting outside influences: 'there is no doubt that . . . the Australian people were acutely aware of their isolation, and were determined to turn to account the freedom it gave them by building up something like an earthly paradise for the common man' (Palmer [1954] 1966). Writing in the early 1950s, Palmer was reacting to the divisions and bitterness of the post-war world; he sought to heal the rift by harking back to a prototype of fellowship that had supposedly thrived in less sophisticated times, uncorrupted by cities and untainted by outside influences. His message is that under those conditions, Australians were fused in a common dream of the future. Palmer seeks to formulate a common experience (albeit one in the past) to serve as a point of reference for the present. That is, he does not argue that we could or should resurrect the 1890s (he refers to that period as a 'dreamtime'), but rather that reference to the legend can help us transcend contemporary divisions, to recognize that we are 'a people' and can again share a common dream, build a common culture.

The radical nationalists provide an exemplary case of nationalist historiography as we might identify it from Anderson's argument. Their history builds a picture of a society (imagined community) characterized by unity, consensus, solidarity and fraternity: 'the nation is always conceived as a deep horizontal comradeship' (Anderson 1983:16). Certainly the radical nationalists locate those characteristics in the past, in the 1890s, but their purpose in invoking the legend is, as Vance Palmer shows, to regenerate just such an imagined community in the present (see also Turner 1979:2). That is, their history is not a *description* of nation-building, but a part of the *process* of nation-building. The question is, was our society, even in the 1890s, so unified?

Our earlier review of criticisms of the radical nationalists noted that one problem in their method was their failure to account for groups and values that were at odds with the bush ethos. They took no account of contending versions of the imagined community. Manning Clark was a pupil and then colleague of Crawford's, emerged from much the same background as the radical nationalists, and shared their concerns. Yet even while they were working on their histories he sounded a discordant note. His 'A letter to Tom Collins' ([1943]1980) is a direct challenge both to the bush ethos, and to the picture of unity advanced by Palmer. In his letter Clark addresses Tom Collins (the pseudonym of Joseph Furphy, whose novel *Such is Life* was taken by many to express the values of the 1890s) as the representative of 'mateship'. But Clark shows mateship to be a thin base for culture, indeed a source of vulgarity. Mateship did serve as a comforter in a foreign environment, but it also served as a blind to conceal the way in which European man in Australia turned to ravaging the land. It is as if, bereft of the 'civilized' values of the European heritage, the pioneers went on a rampage of exploitative destruction—and then erected the gaudy monuments of Australian society to hide their guilt and despair. There is much to be unhappy about, but the unhappy want us to confess our failure, to embrace the 'old faith' (in other words, renounce 'Australia' and resurrect the 'old faith' of the British heritage). The élite, scornful of the vulgarity of mateship, did embrace the old faith, and continued to emulate the European conventions, while the people aped the mate's ideal; there was a rift in national life.

Manning Clark returned to fill in the detail of this rift in a later essay, 'The quest for an Australian identity' ([1979]1980). He attempts to

Defining Australia: A Case Study 27

explain the factors which shaped the colonial quest for self-definition, and how these impinge on the contemporary nation. He argues that a fundamental experience for the white settlers was the vastness and strangeness of the land itself, which seemed so much at odds with the purposes of civilized humans (understood purely in terms of European conditions) that it quite dismayed the first observers. Clark suggests that the apparent uselessness of the land and the fact that its European inhabitants felt compelled to apologize for it instilled an initial sense of inferiority in them. The material backwardness and isolation inevitable in a pioneering community contributed further to their feeling of being second-rate. Impotence in the face of the intractable land led to doubts about their power to effect change. This was consolidated by the religious views of the time which indoctrinated them with the sense of God's omnipotence, and their impotence in the face of His designs. At the social level, the absence of careers open to native talent (all the top positions being held by British administrators) seemed to imply a lack of ability in the native-born. The British demand for primary products from its colony condemned Australia to being a 'sheep-run' rather than a civilized, progressive society, and this accentuated inferiority.

Such experience, Clark suggests, is the lot of all colonial people. What is important for the sort of culture produced is the way colonists react. In his view, Australian colonists reacted either by rejecting European ideas and standards to reassure themselves that they were a unique breed, or by claiming to be no different from the British mainstream. Those who adopted the first mode denied inferiority through absurd boasting, cruel mockery of the depraved and corrupt dandies of civilization, and a refusal to accept responsibility for their circumstances. The others tried as much as possible to be the same as those at the centre of civilization, and became the toadies and flunkies of the British, aping their life-styles and values. These reactions may be seen as the grounding for what would later be the assertive 'ocker' style, versus the precious Britishness of some of the middle class and some intellectuals. Thus instead of unity, Clark emphasizes a rift, and introduces the important qualification that there are sub-national groups in contention over the 'imagined community'.

What may seem especially striking to the contemporary reader of these debates about the origins of nationalism is their gender blindness. Both the radical nationalists and the historians who engaged with them at the time, like Clark, wrote histories of *man*'s experience in Australia as if that were the whole story. The radical nationalists concentrated on male mateship. Clark, for his part, marked his initial difference from them by revealing mateship to be a species of self-deception, but then elaborated what Lake (1986) and Allen (1987) would rightly describe as a 'masculinist' quest for identity. This is not to criticize the nationalist historians, but to establish the nature of the cultural assumptions that dominated the period in which they wrote. Such debates show the implicit claims of men to be the arbiters of cultural meaning, claims that are now increasingly contested. And to engage with the bush legend is to beg the questions of whether women's experiences were the same as men's, what women's roles were in the saga of nation-building, and what such notions as national identity can possibly have meant for women. While these issues are discussed at greater length in part IV, it is useful to note here some relevant themes in feminist reinterpretations of Australian nationalism.

A central theme is how women systematically came to be excluded from the myths of national identity. It is not, after all, that women were absent from the political or literary scene in that allegedly nationalist period, the 1890s. The contributions of such women as Louisa Lawson (editor), Barbara Baynton (writer) and Rose Scott (reformer) are starting now to be analysed alongside such well-recognized male counterparts as J. F. Archibald, Henry Lawson and Alfred Deakin. Equally, the extraordinary flowering of women writers and artists in the 1930s—Miles Franklin, Eleanor Dark, Nettie Palmer, Margaret Preston and Katharine Susannah Prichard (see Modjeska 1981)—was perhaps more culturally significant than the work of such male peers as Frank Wilmot, Louis Esson, Vance Palmer and Frederick Sinclair (see Walker 1976). But why have such women been comparatively invisible? In addressing such questions, historians have sought to define the whole cultural construction of woman's role, taking up such strands as demography, class and ideas of respectability in Australia.

On the demographic front, gender ratios on the Australian frontier have been seen as a significant formative influence. The legacy of the colonial imbalance between (many) men and (few) women has been a misogynist culture (Summers 1975; Dixon 1976). The relative paucity of women led in the nineteenth century to official anxiety about the availability of women to fill men's needs, great pressure on women to marry young into unequal relationships and to bear children (with a corollary limitation on other economic options open to them), and the expectation that women would serve 'order' and restrain the licence granted to men by being the upholders of tradition and culture (Summers 1975; Dixson 1976; Kingston 1986; Lake 1986).

This last expectation equated bachelorhood (and mateship) with freedom, and marriage with servitude, with the idealization of the bushman representing a rejection of the cult of domesticity (cf. Lake 1986:117). This led to sex antagonism, as figures on domestic violence against women suggest (Allen 1987). This may have been class-linked: at moments when working-class men confronted the fact of their oppression (for example in the depression and defeated strikes of the

1890s), they turned their bitterness against the only people subordinate to them, their wives.

These factors had an impact on women's ascribed image and self-image: dogged by low self-esteem (Dixson 1976), troubled by an intensely felt colonial status (Kingston 1986) and forced as the bearers of culture to assume the burden of denial of the convict stigma, women took refuge in stereotypical idealizations of 'gentlemen' and 'ladies' and in a cult of 'ultrarespectability' (Kingston 1986; Dixson 1986). Such a cult privileged bourgeois ideology, and so John Rickard (1976) 'found class consciousness in the late nineteenth century running into the sands of a shabby gentility, largely described and sustained by female persons', as Kingston (1986:39) says.

Much now suggests a bitter campaign between masculinism and feminism in the 1890s (Lake 1986; Allen 1987). But the emphasis on the desired qualities of the colonial bourgeoisie had a debilitating effect on colonial politics. While the impetus for social reform was never merely the drive for respectability, women were forced to mount campaigns for a better position *vis-à-vis* men in terms of the imperatives of domestic life and issues of nurturance and welfare: 'such privatization severely constricted and in many ways diminished women at the very time bourgeois men were opening up the non-domestic or public arena in an unprecedented way' (Dixson 1986:18).

Such circumstances produced the context in which the contributions of women were seen as less relevant to the 'public' agenda of nation-building than those of men. And they generated the culture in which nationalist writers were able to conflate a distinct set of male cultural practices with a national tradition which devalued (and did not describe the experiences of) women.

Political economy approaches

Another approach which avoids essentialist idealization (such as that encouraged by the bush legend) is one that looks closely at the politics of nationalism at transitional points in our past. To focus on politics and economics is still to engage with the public rather than the domestic world, but it does avoid over-investment in 'individual/typical' (and, as we have seen, usually male) experience.

The debate about federation in the last decade of the nineteenth century is frequently represented as such a transitional point. Charles Blackton (1961) is one who has taken up the theme of Australian nationalism and of federation as a decisive break with the past. His representation of the contesting groups in the federation debates is an interesting parallel with Clark's depiction of 'currency' versus Anglophile trends, but Blackton, in tracing the emergence of his groups through close attention to politics and economics, relies on different sorts of evidence.

Blackton looks hard at the socio-economic aspects of nineteenth-century politics and identifies three streams of colonial opinion: the radicals (egalitarian, materialistic, republican, socialist, intent on opposing Empire loyalty and the influence of the mother country), the middle-class nativist moderates (conscious of their identification with the environment and of a native outlook, intent on the unity of the colonies as a nation, seeing independence as the change from an autonomous British colony to British ally), and the Anglo-Australian loyalists (at the social and economic apex, ready to declare their Australianism but acknowledging a higher Empire loyalty, ambitious for British honours conferred 'at Home', preferring a responsible élite under the wing of the British Crown, regarding egalitarian nationalism as almost treasonous). These differences were the product of different social and economic circumstances—that is, class differences—which led to different purposes. The radicals sought a more equitable society for the working class; they found their strength in the mass of bush and industrial workers, although with middle-class leadership and the participation of the new intelligentsia. The nativist moderates were essentially of the cautious middle class but, as urban entrepreneurs and professionals, sought to challenge the influence of the old landed élite. The Anglo-Australian loyalists were from the educated gentry, commanding the large pastoral holdings (the squatter was their touchstone), controlling the financial centres, clubs, universities and entrée to Government House. These divisions Blackton shows to be related to divergent views on every issue, from landholding to democracy, the economy, the role of labour, participation in foreign wars, and federation.

Federation was the middle-class road to nationhood. The Anglo-Australian gentry became anachronistic with the rise of the cities and industrial and entrepreneurial capital in the late nineteenth century. Radicals opposed federation for many reasons—among them being that the scheme proposed did not lead to the creation of a republic but of a federal government which still had constitutional links with Westminster and gave reserve powers to the monarch's representative, the governor-general. But the radicals were in disarray in the 1890s. There were philosophical divisions in their ranks. Most importantly, the labour movement had been fragmented by the defeat of a series of strikes in the early 1890s, at the start of a depression. The resulting loss of momentum and disunity seemed only to be overcome with the emergence of the Labor Party, but this was a party committed to working within the existing political system to achieve reforms for the working class. It was not a republican party. Leadership on nationalist issues therefore passed to the moderates of the middle class; it was their vision of Australia which was to be decisive in forming the federal compact.

Blackton shares with Clark the view that in the nineteenth century there were divisions of opinion in national life. However he posits a resolution to these rifts achieved by the middle-class domination of the federation debates, and suggests that this provided a sound basis on which to build a future autonomy. Blackton's championing of the moderate proto-nationalists is at odds with the radical nationalists' celebration of the common man. Yet he shares with Palmer the view that the pressure towards integration came from 'native drives' rather than external stimuli. Is this persuasive?

Humphrey McQueen, a scholar who also stresses political and economic dimensions of explanation, thinks not. In the article discussed here (McQueen 1973) much of his argument is captured in the title 'The suckling society'. This is a metaphor of dependence and immaturity pointedly at odds with the radical nationalists' depiction of the nation evolving to maturity and impelled by a people working in isolation with their own resources. Indeed, McQueen argues that Australia is not a society in its own right and can never be understood by looking for a 'genuine essence'. His thesis is that Australians have enjoyed an economically privileged position, but only because of a relationship with larger powers, and that hence we have remained passive, dependent and imaginatively subservient to those larger powers.

The basis of our privileged position has been the reliance of the economy on primary products which brought high returns for low investment. We have depended on major capitalist imperial powers to buy these products (first England, then the United States, now Japan), but none the less have been able to maintain the life-style of a developed western country without suffering the dislocation, privations and social division that the older countries experienced to get there. Strong central administration (a hangover from colonial days) and 'tame cat' unionism resulting from relatively good conditions have led to social passivity. The effect has been a strongly anti-theoretical streak in national life. The fact that rewards flowed on smoothly meant that theory never became an issue: 'People become interested in theory when they encounter problems that cannot be resolved . . . in practice' (McQueen 1973:8). Australia's relative immunity from the ravages of war and economic privation has meant that Australians have avoided prolonged periods of self-questioning. The result: we are ill-equipped to think about social problems, tend to rely on rules rather than reason (and punish deviance from rules), and resort to piecemeal social tinkering rather than reform when problems are encountered.

In consequence, McQueen argues, Australia is derivative, dependent and closed:

derivative—derived from another society and place in such a way as to seriously impede the evolution of an appropriate relationship with our geographic and political surroundings;

dependent—flows on from the derivativeness, in the sense of seeking innovations from outside our environment rather than through creative adaptations to it;
closed—indicates the absence of an internal critique and is based on the repressively homogeneous nature of Australian society. [McQueen 1973:5]

Australia in McQueen's view is more an imperialist outpost than a colony. Because we look back to the metropolis which dictates every economic development we are insufficiently attentive to the local context and environment. Dependence stops us from taking initiatives—we look for innovations from outside, from 'the old country' (or from 'great and powerful friends') to solve local problems. Because the society has been repressively homogeneous (dominantly Anglo-Celtic, free of the conflictive class relations produced by economic turmoil in the old countries, and intolerant of divisions) it is closed to the sort of currents that would give rise to an internal critique. Indeed, these problems have been accentuated because we speak English. Sharing the language of the major powers of the nineteenth and twentieth centuries (England, then the United States), we had no barrier to stave off direct penetration, nothing to prevent permeation by every influence from the metropolitan centres. Cut off from the ferment that produced major critiques in those countries, we were yet swamped by every vogue of the English and American mainstream and so precluded from producing anything unique and resilient of our own.

A history of ideas?

In each case considered above there are arguments about the need or pressure for nationhood, and the interests it served. Positions might be clarified by asking: Who gave expression to those needs? Further, if we are to resolve the issue of whether ideas emerged from 'native drives' (the radical nationalists, Blackton 1961) or were simply part of the metropolitan tidal wave by which we were swamped (McQueen 1973), it will help to look more closely at the history of those ideas.

The radical nationalists do have an argument about how ideas of the essential Australia were expressed and transmitted: they were carried from the real experience of the bush to the cities by artists (balladeers, poets, short-story writers, novelists, painters) who, for the sorts of reasons Ward (1958) and Crawford (1955) discuss, were seeking local reference points. There is, however, reason to question this thesis. Graeme Davison (1978) argues persuasively that the genesis of the Australian legend may have come from the city rather than the bush, and that the materials from which the legend was fashioned were derived at least as much from British literary fashions as from bush experience.

Davison shows that the artists on whom the radical nationalists relied were urban intellectuals. They were members of the emerging modern intelligentsia whose existence was made tenable by the growing audience for newspapers, periodicals, pulp-fiction, popular illustration and so on. Yet theirs was still a precarious and marginal existence; they were hit hard by the depression of the 1890s, and forced into the poorest areas of the cities. Because of their alienation they came to treat the city as a symbol of misery, while idealizing the bush as the place of happiness, freedom and genuine Australian values: 'careful attention to the chronology of their writings discloses the connection between their increasingly dismal view of the city and the rise of the bush ideal' (Davison 1978). Yet their treatment of the bush was shaped by then dominant British literary styles—of Charles Dickens, ballad conventions, and the tradition of rhetorical, quasi-religious verse in which the city became an almost apocalyptic symbol of corruption and exploitation.

The picture can be amplified to show that the self-consciously bohemian intelligentsia was not only élitist, but also decidedly misogynist, associating 'feminine' values with the respectability bohemians scorned, and women's artistic interests with amateurism at a time when these men were striving to protect their professional interests (White 1981:ch. 6, esp. 101). Here then was the spur for those masculinist writings of the 1890s discussed earlier.

In a more extended study, Leigh Astbury (1985) shows the complicated relationship between European art movements and colonial traditions in the much-vaunted nationalism of the Heidelberg painters:

while the Heidelberg artists made a conscious effort to reveal an Australian national identity in their pastoral figure subjects, an equally important inspiration lay in their growing awareness of European art movements. The French and English realist painters held a deep reverence for nature and emphasized the moral, universal dimensions of their subjects: the simple dignity, the hardships and humble rewards of the peasant's or labourer's life close to the soil which gave him sustenance. Changes in the Heidelberg artists' treatment of the bushman were as much a response to recent developments within European realism as a spontaneous reaction to local events. [Astbury 1985:2]

Such detailed study suggests qualifications both to the determined isolationism depicted by the radical nationalists, and to the subservience to the metropolis indicated by McQueen. Clark is closer to representing the dilemma of choice between the Australian and the European; what actually happens, as Davison and Astbury show, is a process of negotiation over which element of the local and the metropolitan to accentuate. The intelligentsia will play its role in articulating the terms of choice but, as this discussion shows, other factors will play their part: the struggle of an élite to dominate the people (Clark [1979]1980; cf. Anderson 1983); socio-economic factors (Blackton 1961; McQueen 1973); rivalry between contending interests (Blackton 1961); and economic relations with great powers (McQueen 1973).

An overview which provides a framework for the interrelation of most of these factors is provided by Richard White's *Inventing Australia* (1981:viii–x). White's argument can be summarized in four propositions:

- 'Australia' is not primarily a place, it is a system of ideas, an intellectual construct;
- the core of this construct is a 'national identity' supposed to capture the essential meaning of national life, and invented by an intelligentsia (writers, artists, journalists, historians, critics) in terms of a framework of *western* ideas particular to European history at a specific time;
- the intelligentsia is influenced in this process of invention by owing patronage to powerful economic interests (a broad ruling class) whose purposes are best served by preservation of the current status quo;
- the process of invention is continuous: because groups outside the ruling class can develop alternative images, and because (more importantly) the ruling class itself is not always united but contains powerful competing economic interests, 'the national identity is always being fractured, questioned, and redefined'.

Because of this process of redefinition there will be a succession of different Australias reflecting the fluctuations in influence of competing political and economic groups. As manufacturers, say, gain dominance over pastoralists, pressure to stress those features of national life that are closest to their interests will be translated into new ideas or images of Australia by the intelligentsia.

What does this mean in practice? To continue the example, for much of Australia's history pastoralists relied on exporting their products to British markets. Politically and economically it served their purpose to stress Australia's links with the Empire, and to encourage images that would promote Empire loyalism (Australia as a 'dutiful daughter' for instance). Manufacturers, in contrast, sought to protect their position in the local market by erecting tariff barriers to prevent their relatively smaller industries being swamped by the products of the much larger British industries. Hence, they encouraged images of autonomy and independence—Australia as a 'youngster' breaking maternal bonds to make a place in the world (White 1981:ch. 7).

The intelligentsia played a special part in all this (see White 1981:esp. ch. 6). The late nineteenth century saw the professionalization of the intelligentsia. The community had developed to a state where there was a market, albeit marginal, for what they produced. In consequence, the writers, artists, journalists, historians and critics assumed the leading role as image makers. The intelligentsia had to make their efforts pay, hence their reliance on the patronage of political and economic élites. They were also intent on popularizing and promoting the nationalist image, that is, they wanted to protect the local cultural industry, creating the artefacts of a national culture (as saleable commodities), emphasizing distinctiveness (they represented themselves as purveyors of the authentic 'Australian' article), excluding competition (entailing efforts to exclude European influences) and, connected with all of these, self-promotion.

In the late nineteenth century the intelligentsia found their reference point and a means of expressing their revolt against the old British-oriented cultural establishment by projecting their values onto the bush (which was the real issue suggested by Crawford 1955). That the bush represented an imaginative refuge from the constraints and the anonymity of the city made it a powerful symbol (and here White's argument compares closely with Davison's). It was none the less a city-dweller's vision of the bush, informed by generational conflict and popular literature, containing the values of urban bohemia (values which were misogynist in effect).

White's argument perhaps goes too far in suggesting that national identities are inventions:

There is no 'real' Australia waiting to be uncovered. A national identity is an invention. There is no point in asking whether one version . . . is truer than another, because they are all intellectual constructs . . . and necessarily false . . . [White 1981:viii]

This implies that they are illusory or arbitrary, that it is open to anyone to construct the Australian character or way of life in any way they please. This is not the case. Astbury, for instance, shows that the 'city bushmen' of the Heidelberg school were not only influenced by European art movements, but also 'that a keen and informed acquaintance with earlier colonial traditions in art played a vital role . . . ' (Astbury 1985:2). The images of Australia and Australian-ness produced in the past operate as a cultural force in the present, constituting a repertoire of national images and identities, which newly proposed images must take into account if they are to gain effective influence. Further, as Anderson (1983) shows, the fact that nations are imagined communities does not mean that they exist solely as inventions; the imagined community does have its correlation in the nation as a specific cultural organization in space and time. White's notion of invention might also be criticized as being élitist: an intelligentsia hands down an image which is uncritically accepted by the people. This ignores the role which ordinary people play in culture—at the least, whether they will accept the image being sold.

Surely the determination of how ideas gain currency is more complicated than that.

Yet White (1981) does offer a useful synthesizing framework by showing how three major areas of influence on the nation—the European heritage, the intelligentsia and the economically dominant classes—might be integrated in terms of material interests. Most of the other writers considered here have discussed different components in the cultural production of national identity. White works not only with the components (connections with the metropolitan culture, local interests and material circumstances) which must be taken into account when analysing cultural production, but also with a *model* of cultural production.

In chapter 2 it was mooted that Australia might offer special advantages to the student of cultural production. Does the discussion of 'nation' bear this out?

We have seen that the rise of the concept of nationalism in Europe meant that the national culture was a ruling concern in many countries at the time of the consolidation of a settler society in Australia. None the less, much of the reading discussed here suggests that there was a special edge to this preoccupation in Australia. One lead is in a remark by Ken Inglis:

National days are a preoccupation of new states and new regimes . . . Ask an Englishman what his national day is and he can afford to smile. Having so many generations of national existence uninterrupted by revolution, England has a calendar only faintly marked by history. [Inglis 1967:22]

Continuity gives a confidence that allows nationhood to be taken for granted. But the disruption, above all the fresh start of establishing a new colony, creates problems. For a time settlers may continue to stress their heritage, to assert that they are (in the Australian case) simply transplanted Britons sharing the continuous British heritage. But the experience of living in the new land will be different, not only physically (as Clark [1979]1980, stresses) but also at the social level. The whole structure of the mother country will not have been imported—there will be no aristocratic élite, no hereditary ruling class. Inevitably, the nature of social relations will be different. Indeed, perhaps the most basic relations of all, those between men and women, can differ in striking ways on the frontier, giving a particular inflection to the emerging culture of a settler society. Cultural products, as artists and writers wrestle with such questions as whether to emulate the metropolitan mainstream and how to represent their new environment, will change (as Astbury 1985, for instance, shows). Eventually the native-born, whose images of the mother country are second-hand and perhaps distorted, will outnumber immigrant generations. Such differences will make the assertion of continuity increasingly difficult. When combined with a recognition that the mother country itself regards the colonials as secondary (if not second-rate), this will provide an incentive to discover something more appropriate to the experience of life in the new society, and something which will reaffirm for colonials their distinctive worth.

In terms of the political debate of the nineteenth century (or at least the way that debate has been represented in our reading) terms that came to hand for expressing and then resolving these problems were those of 'identity' and 'the nation'. If we are not British, who are we? Well, we are Australians. But what does it mean to be Australian? How does being Australian resolve the problem of blending elements of the British heritage with elements originating in the local community? As we have seen, different groups advocated mixing these elements in different proportions, and accordingly arrived at different images of Australia (see Clark [1979]1980 and Blackton 1961 in particular). But the debate, taking up more universal issues of the time, took place around the concept of the nation, and of nationalism and the national type.

To return to the original question, and to Inglis's (1967) lead, people in the mother country, because of the framework of continuous tradition, will never have to confront the questions that colonial peoples must ask themselves. It is this feature of the Australian case that makes the issues of nationhood and Australian identity especially important, and gives a special pressure to the search for images which will make boundary distinctions clear.

Analysing the debate

The writers discussed here have proffered different arguments about Australia. They have also used very different forms of evidence: the radical nationalists mine creative works—ballads, poetry, stories, paintings—as expressive of the Australian character; Clark relies on historical records of reactions to the environment; Blackton looks at socio-economic factors; McQueen looks at transnational economics; Davison works with the demography of the city and with literary conventions; Astbury relies on close reading of art conventions; White looks at frameworks of ideas and at trends in popular literature. Still, there are common features: the concern with who gives expression to or articulates national identity; the dilemma of what weighting to give to external influence as opposed to local experience; the interest in the origin of ideas (metropolitan or colonial), and drives (native and developed in isolation, or the flow-on of European trends); the suggestion that the search is for something distinctive rather than representative. All of these writers parallel Anderson in seeing the nation as an intellectual construct, though there is a spectrum from those who see it having definable, material origins (the radical nationalists) to those who see it wholly as invention (White 1981). This reading suggests that debates over some important issues, such as 'Australia', will never be resolved because there are no right or true answers to such questions as 'What is the 'real' Australia?'. But there *are* processes of cultural production through which versions of Australia are arrived at, and academic enquiry should alert us to these. All of the writers considered offer some insight into varieties of cultural production (the groups involved, their motives and needs, the material circumstances, the origins of ideas), but only White suggests a coherent core: 'When we look at ideas about national identity, we need to ask, not whether they are true or false, but what their function is, whose creation they are, and whose interests they serve' (White 1981:viii).

This points to the importance of the *context* of debate. We have seen that historical period and cultural environment affect the debate. For instance that the debate over Australia in the late nineteenth century was about 'the national type' depended on two features of the context: first, native-born Australians were becoming dominant and looking for a means of explaining their difference from the British colonizers; and second, the nineteenth-century preoccupation with categorization gave rise to the concept of national type at the same time, so that it became available for Australians to construct just such an explanation as was needed. In the context of the 1950s, however, White shows that the concept of national type was less effective in serving such a purpose (White 1981:158-66). It had been discredited by the master race theories of the Second World War, and so people looked elsewhere, to the notion of a 'way of life', to explain what was important about Australia.

It is evident that people enter the debate about Australia with certain intentions. The assumption by the intelligentsia of the principal role in articulating definitions and boundary distinctions since the late nineteenth century has been discussed at length. Their emergence in this role was also to do with context—social circumstances that facilitated their becoming professionals. But, once engaged in the process, White (1981) demonstrates that they pursued clear purposes: career advancement, social change that would enhance their position (the ideal was cultural leadership) and patronage of powerful interests—all of which influenced the images they purveyed.

The issues of context and motive (or intention) should also be read into the academic debate. It is clear that White, Crawford, Blackton, Palmer, Clark and McQueen provide different histories of the debate about Australia. They cannot avoid speaking out of a specific context. For instance, the Clark of 1943 ('A letter to Tom Collins') speaks differently from the Clark of 1979 ('The quest for an Australian identity'): doubt has been replaced by the certainty that we must emphasize 'the Australian' in our cultural goulash. And it is no accident that White, writing at a time when economic problems and theories about them were at the forefront of attention, gives mainly economic reasons as the factors which determine different inventions of Australia. Feminist historians in their turn have alerted us to the gender blindness of much of the historical writing on which we have relied. Motives play their part in all of this, and indeed most of these historians make no secret of them. Crawford and Palmer, for instance, thought Australia had lost its way and that a new consciousness of national identity would help us regain our footing; that is why they tried to revive the debate. Historians of women have been intent on restoring women's part as integral to national history. McQueen and Clark sought to confront us with the origins of our limitations as a precondition for changing our society.

These contexts and motives cannot be avoided. Academic writers are not omniscient beings, able to stand outside society and see it objectively. They write at a particular time in a particular society. They are part of (and not detached observers of) the imagined community, and part of the process of cultural production by which it is constantly being re-presented to its participants.

In the end, although the subject of the debate changes, and the questions raised are always giving rise to new answers, the *nature* of the debate is constant. The search for intelligibility continues. The mark of academic enquiry is continuing dialogue.

References

Allen, J. 1987, 'Mundane men: Historians, masculinity and masculinism', *Historical Studies*, vol. 22, no. 89, pp. 617–28.
Almond, G. & Verba, S. 1963, *The Civic Culture*, Princeton University Press, Princeton, NJ.
Alomes, S. 1985, 'Australian studies: Definitions and directions', *Australian Studies Bulletin*, no. 3, April, pp 28–32.
Alomes, S. 1988, *A Nation at Last? The Changing Character of Australian Nationalism 1880–1988*, Angus & Robertson, Sydney.
Alomes, S. & Grant, D. 1984, 'Studying Australia', *Australian Studies Bulletin*, no. 1, April, pp. 5–7.
Anderson, B. 1983, *Imagined Communities: Reflections on the Origin and Spread of Nationalism*, Verso, London.
Anderson, H. 1985, 'Then and now', *Bulletin*, no. 2 (Committee to Review Australian Studies in Tertiary Education), Canberra, pp. 27–8.
Astbury, L. 1985, *City Bushmen*, Oxford University Press, Melbourne.
Blackton, C. S. 1961, 'Australian nationality and nationalism, 1850–1900', *Historical Studies*, vol. 9, no. 36, pp. 351–67.
Bourke, H. 1988, 'Social scientists as intellectuals: From the First World War to the Depression', in B. Head & J. Walter (eds), *Intellectual Movements and Australian Society*, Oxford University Press, Melbourne, pp. 47–69.
Brett, J. 1985, 'Why Australian studies?', *Bulletin*, no. 2 (Committee to Review Australian Studies in Tertiary Education), Canberra, pp. 25–6.
Buckridge, P. 1988, 'Intellectual authority and critical traditions in Australian literature 1945 to 1975', in B. Head & J. Walter (eds), *Intellectual Movements and Australian Society*, Oxford University Press, Melbourne, pp. 188–213.
Burnley, I., Encel, S. & McCall, G. (eds) 1985, *Immigration and Ethnicity in the 1980s*, Longman Cheshire, Melbourne.
Clark, M. (1943) 1980, 'A letter to Tom Collins', *Occasional Writings and Speeches*, Fontana, Melbourne.
Clark, M. (1979) 1980, 'The quest for an Australian identity', *Occasional Writings and Speeches*, Fontana, Melbourne.
Colmer, J. 1978, 'Australian cultural analysis: Some principles and problems', *Southerly*, vol. 34, no. 3, pp. 243–52.
Connell, R. W. & Irving, T. H. 1980, *Class Structure in Australian History*, Longman Cheshire, Melbourne.
CRASTE (Committee to Review Australian Studies in Tertiary Education) 1987, *Windows Onto Worlds: Studying Australia at Tertiary Level*, Australian Government Publishing Service, Canberra.
Crawford, R. M. 1955, 'Australian national character: Myth and reality', *Journal of World History*, vol. 2, no. 3, pp. 704–27.
Davidson, J. (ed.) 1986, *The Sydney–Melbourne Book*, George Allen & Unwin, Sydney.
Davison, G. 1978, 'Sydney and the bush: An urban context for the Australian legend', *Historical Studies*, vol. 18, no. 71, pp. 191–209.
Denoon, D. 1983, *Settler Capitalism*, Clarendon Press, Oxford.
Dixson, M. 1976, *The Real Matilda: Women and Identity in Australia 1788 to the Present*, Penguin, Ringwood.

References 41

Dixson, M. 1986, 'Gender, class and the women's movements in Australia 1890-1980', in N. Grieve & A. Burns (eds), *Australian Women: New Feminist Perspectives*, Oxford University Press, Melbourne, pp. 14-25.

Docker, J. 1978, 'Australian studies forum (K. Hancock, B. Kiernan & J. Docker)', *Meanjin*, vol. 37, no. 3, pp. 23-8.

Docker, J. 1984, *In a Critical Condition*, Penguin, Ringwood.

Evans, R. 1987, *Loyalty and Disloyalty: Social Conflict on the Queensland Homefront 1914-18*, George Allen & Unwin, Sydney.

Galligan, B. (ed.) 1986, *Australian State Politics*, Longman Cheshire, Melbourne.

Grant, D. 1983, 'To know ourselves: Canada and Australia', *Overland*, no. 93, pp. 39-42.

Green, H. M. 1930, *An Outline of Australian Literature*, Whitcombe & Tombs, Sydney.

Green, H. M. (1961) 1985, *A History of Australian Literature*, 2 vols, Angus & Robertson, Sydney (rev. edn ed. D. Green).

Hartz, L. 1964, *The Founding of New Societies*, Harcourt, Brace & World, New York.

Head, B. (ed.) 1986, *The Politics of Development in Australia*, George Allen & Unwin, Sydney.

Head, B. & Walter, J. (eds) 1988, *Intellectual Movements and Australian Society*, Oxford University Press, Melbourne.

Holmes, J. & Sharman, C. 1977, *The Australian Federal System*, George Allen & Unwin, Sydney.

Horne, D. 1986, *The Public Culture*, Pluto Press, Sydney.

Hughes, R. 1987, *The Fatal Shore*, Collins Harvill, London.

Inglis, K. S. 1965, 'The Anzac tradition', *Meanjin*, vol. 24, no. 1, pp. 25-44.

Inglis, K. S. 1967, 'Australia Day', *Historical Studies*, vol. 13, no. 49, pp. 20-41.

Inglis, K. S. 1988, 'Anzac and the Australian military tradition', *Current Affairs Bulletin*, vol. 64, no. 11, pp. 4-15.

Kingston, B. 1986, 'The lady and the Australian girl: Some thoughts on nationalism and class', in N. Grieve & A. Burns (eds), *Australian Women: New Feminist Perspectives*, Oxford University Press, Melbourne.

Lake, M. 1986, 'The politics of respectability: Identifying the masculinist context', *Historical Studies*, vol. 22, no. 86, pp. 116-31.

Lawson, S. 1983, *The Archibald Paradox*, Allen Lane, Ringwood.

Lippmann, L. 1983, 'A migrant people', in J. McLaren (ed.), *A Nation Apart*, Longman Cheshire, Melbourne, pp. 113-26.

Macintyre, S. 1987, 'The writing of Australian history', in D. H. Borchardt, *Australians: A Guide to Sources*, Fairfax, Syme & Weldon, Sydney, pp. 19-29.

McQueen, H. 1970, *A New Britannia*, Penguin, Ringwood.

McQueen, H. 1973, 'The suckling society', in H. Mayer & H. Nelson (eds), *Australian Politics—A Third Reader*, Cheshire, Melbourne, pp. 5-13.

McQueen, H. 1982, *Gone Tomorrow*, Angus & Robertson, Sydney.

Martin, G. (ed.) 1978, *The Founding of Australia*, Hale & Iremonger, Sydney.

Martin, J. 1978, *The Migrant Presence*, George Allen & Unwin, Sydney.

Modjeska, D. 1981, *Exiles at Home: Australian Women Writers 1925-1945*, Angus & Robertson, Sydney.

Mullins, P. 1986, 'Queensland populist politics and development', in B. Head (ed.), *The Politics of Development in Australia*, George Allen & Unwin, Sydney, pp. 138–62.
Northcott, C. H. 1918, *Australian Social Development*, Columbia University Press, New York.
Palmer, N. 1924, *Modern Australian Literature 1900–1923*, Lothian, Melbourne.
Palmer, V. (1954) 1966, *The Legend of the Nineties*, Melbourne University Press, Melbourne.
Pascoe, R. 1979, *The Manufacture of Australian History*, Oxford University Press, Melbourne.
Prescott, M. 1987, 'Immigration', in S. Aplin, S. G. Foster & M. McKernan (eds), *Australians: A Historical Dictionary*, Fairfax, Syme & Weldon, Sydney, pp. 202–6.
Pye, L. & Verba, S. 1965, *Political Culture and Political Development*, Princeton University Press, Princeton, NJ.
Reid, I. 1979, 'Australian literary studies: The need for a comparative method', *New Literature Review*, no. 6, pp. 34–9.
Reynolds, H. 1982, *The Other Side of the Frontier*, Penguin, Ringwood.
Reynolds, H. 1987a, *Frontier*, George Allen & Unwin, Sydney.
Reynolds, H. 1987b, *The Law of the Land*, Penguin, Ringwood.
Rickard, J. 1976, *Class and Politics*, Australian National University Press, Canberra.
Robinson, P. 1985, *The Hatch and Brood of Time*, Oxford University Press, Melbourne.
Scott, E. 1916, *A Short History of Australia*, Oxford University Press, London.
Seddon, G. 1982, 'Eurocentrism and Australian science: Some examples', *Search*, vol. 12, no. 12, pp. 446–50.
Smith, P. 1985, 'Queensland's political culture', in A. Patience (ed.), *The Bjelke-Petersen Premiership*, Longman Cheshire, Melbourne, pp. 17–32.
Summers, A. 1975, *Damned Whores and God's Police: The Colonization of Women in Australia*, Penguin, Ringwood.
Symons, T. 1975, *To Know Ourselves: The Report of the Commission on Canadian Studies*, Association of Universities and Colleges of Canada, Ottawa.
Turner, B. & Patience, A. 1985, 'The scope of the review', *Bulletin*, no. 2, (Committee to Review Australian Studies in Tertiary Education), Canberra, pp. 26–7.
Turner, G. & Bird, D. 1982, 'Australian studies: Practice without theory', *Westerly*, vol. 27, no. 3, pp. 51–5.
Turner, I. H. 1979, 'Australian nationalism and Australian history', *Journal of Australian Studies*, no. 4, June, pp. 1–11.
Walker, D. 1976, *Dream and Disillusion: A Search for Australian Cultural Identity*, Australian National University Press, Canberra.
Ward, R. 1958, *The Australian Legend*, Oxford University Press, Melbourne.
Ward, R. 1987, *Finding Australia*, Heinemann, Melbourne.
Wells, A. 1988, 'The old left intelligentsia 1930 to 1960', in B. Head & J. Walter (eds), *Intellectual Movements and Australian Society*, Oxford University Press, Melbourne, pp. 214–34.

References 43

West, P. 1986a, Australian studies and Canadian studies: National identity and regional differences, Paper delivered at ACSANZ Conference, Griffith University, Qld, May, mimeo.
West, P. 1986b, 'History and Australian studies', *Journal of Australian Studies*, no. 18, pp. 96–9.
White, P. & Lampert, R. 1987, 'Creation and discovery', in D. J. Mulvaney & J. P. White (eds), *Australians to 1788*, Fairfax, Syme & Weldon, Sydney, pp. 2–23.
White, R. 1981, *Inventing Australia: Images and Identity 1688–1980*, George Allen & Unwin, Sydney.
Whitlock, G. 1984, 'Queensland: The state of the art on the "last frontier" ', *Westerly*, vol. 29, no. 2, pp. 85–90.
Williams, R. 1961, *The Long Revolution*, Chatto & Windus, London.
Williams, R. 1976, *Keywords: A Vocabulary of Culture and Society*, Fontana, London.

PART II
SETTLEMENT AND SOCIETY

Introduction

Part II deals with three levels of analysis of social formation: the constitution of Australia as a unit in the world system, the study of regions and the history of urbanization.

4 AUSTRALIA: A SETTLER SOCIETY IN A CHANGING WORLD

Australia's pattern of settlement and development is examined during the booms and depressions of the late nineteenth and early twentieth centuries. Three important tensions and dilemmas implicit in the characterization of Australia's situation as a settler society are described: the clash between settler and indigenous peoples on the frontiers, the vulnerability of an economy based on specialized primary production and the problems associated with Australia's reliance on British capital. The world economic crises of the 1970s and 1980s are shown to have reopened debate about the fundamentals of the Australian economy and the type of society which can be built on it, and these contemporary debates are examined in the light of the description of the concerns and dilemmas of the earlier period.

5 REGIONALISM

Chapter 5 uses the concepts 'region' and 'regionalism' to question the vision of Australia as one nation. It contrasts the work of several disciplines, identifying the issues of homogeneity and autonomy as central to the identification of regions. Comparison of sociology's use of community in opposition to fragmented society; contributions by press, electronic media and literature to a regional rather than national identity; the writing of local histories within the framework of a national history; discussions of state–federal conflicts in political science; and political economy's identification of regions in terms of a world economic system reveal that both the concept of regionalism and the identification of regions in Australia depend on the approach of the discipline seeking to explore the concepts.

6 NINETEENTH-CENTURY URBANIZATION

Some of the ways in which scholars have approached the history of cities and urbanization in Australia in the nineteenth century are examined in chapter 6. It is asked, first, has the pattern and the process of urban development been different in Australia compared with other countries? A number of explanations for urbanization are looked at, focusing on those that help in understanding what is similar and what is different about the growth of cities in Australia. Second, it is asked what has the city meant to Australians? It is suggested that the experience, meaning and cultural significance of the city has differed according to the political viewpoint of the observer, and to social factors such as sex and class. The apparent paradox between the highly urban nature of Australian society and the persistence of a national identity based on rural values is pointed out.

CHAPTER FOUR

AUSTRALIA: A SETTLER SOCIETY IN A CHANGING WORLD

Malcolm Alexander

Introduction

The image of Australia as a settler society can evoke simple visions of a socially cohesive group: British settlers in Australia, united in the task of opening and settling the Australian continent through the nineteenth century and on until the First World War. Beneath this appearance of pioneer achievement and singular national identity, however, there lies a reality of continuing conflict with the indigenous people, a worrying uncertainty about the vulnerability of Australia's economic base and a nagging ambivalence about the destiny of this outpost of the British Empire. The heyday of settler expansion on this continent was the first decade of the twentieth century, c. 1906–13, when new and varied forms of agricultural production finally allowed the newly federated colonies of Australia to lift themselves out of the trauma of the 1890s depression and stimulated an era of immigration and growth comparable to that generated by the pastoral industry and gold-rushes earlier in the nineteenth century. Examination of the uncertainties and dilemmas of this period provides important insights into the peculiar nature of Australia's economy and the social order which has been constructed on its base. Although Australia's industrial expansion in the 1950s and 1960s seemed to lift the economy away from its nineteenth-century base, the economic crises of the 1970s and 1980s have made economists re-examine the continuing survival of these economic structures. Consideration of the economic nature and social problems of Australia's settler society in its heyday allows us, therefore, to confront the continuing legacy of our history as a settler society.

At the level of world politics the image of Australia as a settler society is not a comfortable one. In the 1960s and 1970s world politics were dominated by concerns about colonialism and racism as the newly decolonized countries of the Third World developed a collective identity and presence in international forums. To speak of Australia as a settler society in this context is to draw attention to our history as a frontier of European imperialism, to emphasize the Europeans' displacement of indigenous peoples and their appropriation of global resources to feed Europe's industrialization. Donald Denoon, who has done most to propagate the idea of Australia as a settler society, locates his own concerns in this context by speaking of Australia as one of the settler, as opposed to one of the tropical, dependencies (Denoon 1983:1-3). Within this context, racism in Australia becomes one chapter in the history of western imperialism and its ideologies.

Comparative analyses of Australia's economic history as a settler society raise questions about Australia's economic vulnerability, an issue dramatically reopened by the crises of the 1970s and 1980s. In the period before the First World War Australia, together with the United States, Canada, South Africa, New Zealand, Argentina, Uruguay and Chile, was a region where the external stimuli of foreign investment, trade, immigration and technology were seen to generate substantial economic and commercial growth and significant social development. From the perspective of later history Latin Americans have wondered why Australia and the other dominions benefited from this external dependency while they, apparently, did not. The paradox of Australia's 'dependent development', the dilemma of balancing internal development needs against the demands of foreign investors, is one of the themes of Australia's economic history as a settler society (Cochrane 1980:ix). Comparative studies go on to highlight the peculiar nature of Australia's external dependency and pattern of growth. Although Denoon (1979;1983) argued that the settler societies were essentially similar economic environments, this was disputed by Fogarty (1981) and the thrust of later comparative analysis is to see Australia's nineteenth-century economy as distinctive, even within the already limited development experience of the settler societies (Schedvin 1987:21-22).

In the heyday of the settler society, however, questions about Australia's position in the world were debated in terms of our racial and historical destiny. For Anglo-Australians Australia's history was integral to Britain's history. Although we were a province or region of Empire, our achievements and needs were presented to the British ruling élites as crucial aspects of imperial policy. Radicals rejected the acceptance of privilege and hierarchy which this deference implied.

They saw Australia as a 'new' society where, like the United States, democracy and equality could flower unfettered by the encumbrances of the Old World (White 1981:ch. 4). Both groups, however, were obsessed by fantasies of racial superiority and racial degeneration promoted by social Darwinism, and debates about the adaptation and mutation of British racial 'stock' in Australian conditions were the lodestone of social and historical commentary in this period.

In the varied contexts of nineteenth-century debates the question of how Australia was different from the parent culture of Britain was always a topic of primary concern. It was the central question for studying Australia in this era and the ideologies of the period resonate in current debates. The settler society reached its apogee in the boom period preceding the First World War, between 1906 and 1914. But the Australian economy was not simply the creation of this powerful development dynamic (cf. ch. 4). It was, rather, a peculiar, variegated and slightly ramshackle structure of different industries created by a succession of resource exploitative booms in the nineteenth century. Similarly, although the establishment of a federal government permitted the development of 'national' policies, the political direction of such policies was still divided between the conservative, Anglo-Australian vision and the radical, populist one. This chapter examines some of these differences and divisions in Australia at the turn of the twentieth century and also comments on how those differences and divisions are still part of debates on Australia's economic and social structure and, hence, current concerns about our potential for strategic adaptation to the changing world of the 1980s and 1990s.

The lucky country in the world economy of the nineteenth century

As in the post-Second World War period, it is possible to argue that Australia's economic growth in the late nineteenth century was the result of fortuitous external circumstances and lucky coincidence. The economic expansion of the settler societies which at first sight was common to Australia and other British dominions in the later nineteenth century is graphically described by Denoon:

> By the end of the century the settler societies had all felt the exhilaration of pulling in capital investment hand over fist, drawing migrants by thousands, laying railway tracks into the remotest interior, shovelling minerals furiously, harvesting grain by millions of tons, slaughtering thousands of stock, and enjoying per caput [*sic*] incomes which were the envy of the world. [Denoon 1983:4]

The economic denominators of this common experience were the 'package of opportunities' provided by European (primarily British) industrialization: markets, the positive stimulation of capital investment, services, transportation and communication networks and an inflow of labour to produce the staple commodities and run the infrastructure of international trade (Denoon 1983:43–8). The tangible indicator of this expansion was not economic growth *per se* (increases in per capita product and income) but population growth (Butlin 1986:7) and the most visible form of population growth was immigration. Furthermore, immigration flows were visible on a day-to-day basis, giving contemporaries an immediate sense of economic prosperity or depression.

Table 4.1 summarizes total immigration for the Australian colonies and for the Commonwealth from the 1860s to the First World War.

Table 4.1 Average Annual Net Migration: Australia 1861–1915

Period	Number (000)	Rate per thousand of total population
1861–65	17.2	13.3
1866–70	16.1	10.7
1871–75	12.3	6.9
1876–80	26.0	12.7
1881–85	44.8	18.2
1886–90	31.7	10.9
1891–95	4.5	1.0
1896–1900	0.5	0.2
1901–05	−3.4	−0.8
1906–10	11.5	2.7
1911–15	27.4	6.2

Source: Jackson 1988:27.

These figures show the explosion of immigration from the mid-1870s through until 1890 and the length and depth of the 1890s depression, which does not lift until after 1905. Year-by-year figures (Vamplew 1987:6) add further details. After a peak in the mid-1860s there is a decade of relative stability until a new plateau from 1874 to 1876 that lasts through the 1880s until 1892, with 1883–84 being an exceptional peak. The impact of the 1890s depression is clearly visible in the figures from 1893 to 1906 and immigration on the scale of the 1880s only resumes briefly from 1909 to 1914. A similar pattern is evident for total gross domestic product (GDP), which reached a peak in 1889 that was not equalled again until 1904 (Vamplew 1987:186). Because of the high levels of per capita income attained in the prosperous years of the gold-rushes and the 1880s, however, Australia's per capita incomes still remained among the world's highest.

Two distinctive phenomena are evident in these figures. On the one hand the periods of boom are clearly visible, as are their tremendous contributions to total growth. They are clearly engines of growth. But this growth was highly specialized. It was largely based on the expansion of the cities as bureaucratic–commercial entities, with little spin-off into rural settlement or indigenous industrialization. It was also regionally specific, laying the basis for the regional divisions that continue within the Australian federation even today. These are aspects of Australian society taken up in the later sections of this chapter. The second phenomenon that needs careful attention is the 1890s depression. It was both severe and prolonged; and it was exceptional in its length and severity, as the United States, Canada and the other settler societies all recovered fairly quickly after 1896 and did not see such a severe curtailment of growth. These phenomena set the conditions for economic and social policy in Australia in the 1890s. They also indicate the vulnerability of the settler society created by Australia's dependence on the nineteenth-century world economy as its engine of economic growth.

The economic and political conditions of Australia's settler society are not separate. Economic stability was linked to the stability of Australia's position in the informal networks of imperial financial collaboration which lubricated the continuing flow of investment funds necessary for the infrastructural investments of settler expansion. The actions of governments were the crucial factor in this. In the language of today's international relations theorists, they had to carefully manage their foreign trade and investment 'regimes'. Of necessity, Australian statesmen were engaged in presenting an image of the colonies to a British audience. What were the raw materials they could draw on to fashion this image? What were the myths they had to counter or, perhaps, could harness to this task?

By the eve of the First World War the Australian economy and society comprised a conglomerate structure which had assimilated and balanced the legacies of the economic tides which had washed over it in the century and a quarter of contact with Europe. There was a legacy of booms but also a legacy of contraction. The wool boom of the early part of the nineteenth century had faltered badly in the 1840s and this uncertainty was dispelled only by the discovery of gold in the 1850s. Gold generated a new dynamic of speculative growth which lasted until 1890. The depression of that decade, however, saw a shift of economic concerns towards urban industrial growth and a greater investment in agricultural rather than pastoral industries. Even in its heyday Australia's economy and society were an assemblage, a collage of distinct components, both rural and urban, with significant regional differences.

Australia's years as an outpost of the British penal system from 1788 to 1853 (to 1868 in Western Australia) left some important traces on Australian society; prior conditions were not 'swept away'. The dominant staple of the early years was wool and the conditions of its production left their mark. The European invasion of Australia's interior began with the rush to exploit the grasslands after Britain established a preferential tariff for colonial wool in 1822. But the first wave of squatters were resource gatherers, not settlers. They treated grasses as a natural resource, something like timber, to be harvested and then left to regenerate while the flocks were moved on to the next available site (Bolton 1981). Penetration of the interior also brought Europeans into direct conflict with Aborigines who used the same areas for their own hunting and gathering. The frontier was therefore a distinct region for the whites; it was an area of danger and adventure where peculiar qualities of resourcefulness and hardiness were needed for survival. Although it was the Aborigines whose prior occupation and management of these areas had shaped the land's exploitable ecology and although it was the Aborigines who taught the frontiersmen most of the bush skills of survival, their claims were brushed aside, as the settlers could only see the frontier as the furthest, but distinctive extension of their own society (Reynolds 1982).

The locus of settlement proper was close to the administrative centres and the ports. The pastoralists and agriculturalists of the areas of early settlement held title to their lands, while the towns were populated by merchants, artisans and the urban professionals. These settlers saw the future of Australian society entangled with the social struggles behind the frontier. The impact of the convict system on the labour market and social structure of the colonies raised questions about the fundamental nature of colonial society, while the colonial administration's dispensation of the major economic resource, land, affected the pattern of inequality and social justice within that order. The social power associated with the control of convict labour created the possibility for state power to become a buttress for the establishment of a colonial gentry, aping the eighteenth-century English gentry, but recreating, in fact, the structure of the 'plantation' economies of the Empire. Although this seemed a possibility during the operation of the convict assignment system, the opposition of bourgeois democratic forces within the towns snuffed it out (Connell & Irving 1980:51–4).

The other area of social conflict related to those zones of European occupation beyond the settled areas controlled as legal or *de facto* leases by the squatters. These 'big men' of the frontier wanted the Crown to grant or give them freehold title. The Crown wanted to sell the land in smaller parcels both for economic reasons (it would raise more revenue), and for reasons of social engineering. Settlement theories still upheld the ideal of a 'sturdy yeomanry' or, following Wakefield's theory, saw the denial of access to land as the only way to establish a viable supply of labour. The squatters' demands seemed urgent in the economic crisis of the 1840s but to prevent any permanent resolution the imperial administration granted 21-year leases only.

Settler views of the world saw the frontier as the cutting edge of their expansion; indigenous peoples' claims did not enter the picture. The convict system and its effects were therefore the principal questions of social policy and political theory for the settlers. Its major strength and legacy were in New South Wales and Tasmania. On the other hand, the main forms of policy and experimentation focused on land policy, and therefore South Australia and Victoria come to be seen as 'free' colonies. These differences also involved different views of pastoralism and agriculture, with South Australia being the colony that most approximated the ideal of a community of small, independent agriculturalists. The Swan River settlement, meanwhile, had been struggling to survive since 1829 and in 1850 introduced convict labour in an attempt to bolster population growth. The first period of European expansion had created, therefore, socially and economically distinctive enclaves of development. In the succeeding decades the gold-rushes of the 1850s and, in particular, the spectacular growth of Melbourne, laid a new element over this assemblage.

It was an ageing and fading English publicist, George Augustus Sala, who, after a visit to Australia in 1885, coined the phrase 'Marvellous Melbourne' (Davison 1979:229–30). The phrase became popular partly because it assuaged the insecurity of Melburnians of the 1880s by giving imperial recognition to their commercial metropolis. It was apt, however, because it reminded hearers of the prodigious rate of growth of the city in the decades after the gold-rushes. The Melbourne of the 1880s had been created within the life-span of a single generation. The gold-rush merchants had participated in the development of a sizeable commercial city by 1880 and in the space of the next decade the social and economic structure was to diversify away from that base to accommodate a new system of retail commerce and real estate development, as well as a growing manufacturing sector (Davison 1979). But British moral economists had less complimentary views of Melbourne's sudden advance. To them it was the site of a pathological mania. The pursuit of gold diverted men from productive pursuits and they feared that the injection of such quantities of gold into the international monetary system would fuel an inflation that would disrupt the foundations of social order. In the men who sought it, and the cities they built, these moral economists saw only the feeding of an insatiable appetite for gambling and speculation (Goodwin 1974:ch. 2).

While a large part of the population increase created by the gold-rushes was deployed in the construction of the urban metropolises of Australia, there was sufficient surplus to generate a consensus that the question of closer settlement, carried forward from the 1840s, was even more urgent. Throughout the 1870s and 1880s the demands to 'unlock the lands' became the political rallying point for liberal reformers among the colonies' political élites. Self-government in the 1850s had laid the ground for this by passing control of land to colonial legislatures which had, by the quirks of imperial politics, more democratic franchises than Britain itself. But the campaigns to unlock the lands were more important as political campaigns than as instruments of real social change. They reinforced the urban liberals' ascendancy over the political representatives of the pastoralists and squatters, but the failure to frame adequate legislation and the doctrinaire blindness to the need to provide support for the small selectors ensured that the major effect of the legislation was for the wealthy squatters to gain freehold title to the land (usually the best land) they already controlled (Macintyre 1985:32–9). In contrast to the North American settler societies, where agricultural settlement led economic development, Australia's drive for closer settlement derived from internal political pressures.

The depression of the 1890s began with the collapse of the Melbourne land boom, but also involved a crisis in the major export industries which escalated into a confrontation between employers and the newly emerging labour movement. It was then capped by a dramatic and prolonged collapse of the financial system in 1893 (de Garis 1974:216–24). Here, it seemed, was the proof for Australia's detractors that its spectacular achievements were built on insubstantial foundations. Later assessments of the period suggest, however, that the colonists responded to the macro-economic constraints, the difficulties created by the economic crisis and the prolonged drought of 1895–1903 by significant diversification of exports, technological improvements in the rural sector and a relatively effective programme of import-substitution. Australian wheat-growing, formerly concentrated in South Australia and Victoria, had always been at the forefront of technological innovation, and the adaptation of new techniques to the establishment of wheat-growing areas in New South Wales in this period permitted wheat to become a major export (de Garis 1974:227–8). The development of significant technical innovation in steam power shortened the sea journey between Australia and Britain and allowed the pastoral industry, particularly in Queensland, to compete in the chilled and frozen meat trade (Blainey 1966:279–81; de Garis 1974:228). On top of these structural changes in the eastern colonies came the new gold finds in Western Australia, which softened the macro-economic constraints.

The varied patterns of settlement within the different Australian colonies defined them as distinctive social and economic regions by the end of the nineteenth century and fostered their continued separation from each other. The experience of growth under the aegis of British capital produced a sufficiently varied mix of agricultural industries and settlement patterns to sustain a sense of regionalism and political difference in each colony as well as a sense of common identity. The same qualifications apply to their political programmes. As Denoon (1983:ch. 5) argues, the settler societies innovated in social and policy areas in ways that drew attention and comment from both reformers and conservatives in Britain, but there was no common blueprint. However, each colony and each settler society tried to justify its policies by reference to a supposedly common Britishness. How Australia figured in this discourse of imperial administration, with its protagonists and detractors, is an interesting story.

Australia and the parent culture: 'new society' or 'citadel of heresy'?

Within the informal networks of imperial collaboration Australia had boosters and detractors. The boosters, who included both *émigrés* and Australian 'natives', extolled the rustic virtues of the frontier society and, late in the nineteenth century, saw aspects of their ideas taken up by the imperial federation movement which was influential throughout the Empire and made a significant impact on British domestic politics. Australia's main detractors were the moral economists in Britain. Not only were they sceptical about the stability of an economy founded on resource exploitation and speculation, they also questioned the effect of such experiences on the nature of Australian society, or, in their terms, the 'Australasian race'. Because of the slippage from moral economy into social Darwinism, their views overlapped with the physiological dimensions of debate. Finally, images of Australia were generated not only in intellectual and social circles but as part of the debates about Australian responses and adaptations of the major policy reforms of the Anglo-Saxon democracies.

Australia's most prominent boosters in the later nineteenth century were, of course, the men behind the Melbourne land boom. The land boomers founded and ran the banks and building societies which attracted funds from all classes of colonial society and from British investors. Many of them were active in political life as well and promoted government spending and borrowing on a gargantuan scale, particularly in railway and urban infrastructure (Cannon 1966:ch. 5). Boosterism was, therefore, an important aspect of the promotion of a flattering colonial self-image although, as Davison suggests, there was also a substantial element of urban modernization underneath the bubble of the land boom (Davison 1979:133–4). Images of Australia's urban development generated by the world's curiosity about Melbourne reflected one side of the dualism of the settler society in Australia; images of the frontier and discussions about the national type reflected the other.

Russel Ward draws attention to the importance of the myth of the noble frontiersman as a compensation and justification for the expansion of imperialism at the end of the nineteenth century. Although his account of this myth-making in Australia focused on it as a component of debates about Australian nationalism, he also suggests that this myth compensated for the brutality of imperialism by sustaining the image that those who selflessly bore the 'white man's burden' made the Empire appear as something that was good for the governed (Ward 1958:253). From the first half of the nineteenth century intellectual fashions had propagated the idea of national or racial types, distinguished by appearance, physiognomy, psychology and destiny. Even before Darwin there was speculation about the new type that would be produced in the new areas of settlement, of which Australia was seen as an unusual example (White 1981:64). Growing from this base, popular thought easily adapted social Darwinism and its attendant quasi-scientific apparatus as a legitimation for the frontier's elimination of indigenous peoples. What was more ambiguous and troublesome to the settler population itself was the argument that it would suffer a degeneration of its racial stock in the debilitating climates and alien conditions of Australia's hot and arid lands. Concern with racial purity demanded, therefore, the exclusion of lesser races. The *Bulletin*, although republican in its political pronouncements, was unswerving in its ideas of racial purity and belief in the virtues of the British character (White 1981:69–71). The 'new' society had the mission of asserting the importance of higher historical loyalties and destinies to the British government of the day.

Australia was not only a place for the location of a new branch of the Anglo-Saxon race, it was also recognized as a significant component in the imperial networks of trade, investment and emigration. A distinctive image of Australia was formed in Britain by the impact of the gold-rushes. The inflow of gold was seen to have potentially disturbing effects on the imperial economy, while the allure of speculative wealth was felt to undermine the basis of the social order and good government in the colonies. The high level of public interest in the colonies led to a major ancillary industry producing pamphlets and books about the Australian colonies (Goodwin 1974:ch. 2). This genesis tended to fix British assessments along lines generally disapproving of colonial innovations. On a range of specific policy matters such as land policy, tariff policy, public finance and urban development, Australia was seen as a citadel of heresy. Dominant British opinion believed that the Australian colonies were deliberately unwilling to heed the distilled wisdom of imperial experience. Their stubbornness also prevented the amalgamation of the colonies, a feature that puzzled the British from Earl Grey onwards (Goodwin 1974:ch. 4).

Although based largely on prejudice and little real knowledge of Australian conditions, these views remained highly influential in framing British analyses of the 1890s depression. There were, however, attempts at intra-imperial enlightenment by colonial leaders themselves (although these were often undermined by detractors from their own social circles) and, when the imperial federation movement helped foster a more favourable climate of opinion, positive images of Australia gained ground. The final achievement of federation and active participation in the Boer War helped these views make some headway (Goodwin 1974:208).

The final aspect of these images of Australia was the gradual moving together of policy reforms in Britain and Australia. On the one hand, Australian colonies did begin to follow Britain in reforming the public service and, in particular, lessening the abuses of patronage and political corruption in the 1880s (Davison 1979:ch. 5; Connell & Irving 1980:108-13). The crisis of the 1890s also created some reform and rationalization of the banking and finance sectors which conformed more to British orthodoxies. Finally, changing attitudes in Britain and the rise of a new liberalism made its politics more open to the possibility of reform along the lines which had been prefigured in the colonies.

By the first decade of the twentieth century the unfavourable British images of Australia generated by the gold-rushes had been moderated by the better understanding of Australia and Australian conditions fostered by the growing sophistication and credibility of colonial representatives in London. Attitudes in London itself were also changing as the narrow orthodoxies of free trade were coming under challenge. The debate was not over, but the greater variety of responses and positions by the end of the 1890s meant that the claims of settlers to be at the forefront of modern trends and their positive self-images could have some credibility in the cauldron of imperial thought that bubbled in London.

This review of the heyday of Australia's settler society has highlighted the varied and conglomerate nature of its economic structure and examined three characteristic dilemmas arising from its particular situation in the British Empire. Its conglomerate economic structure arose from the intensive focus of world economic opportunities on particular staple industries: wool, gold, urban construction, wheat or meat. It was the lack of world market access during the 1890s depression which forced the economy towards a more integrated 'national' mould and fostered a process of economic diversification.

Despite the changes after the 1890s Australia did not escape the legacy of its nineteenth-century development. There were three characteristic dilemmas of its settler society. First, the social and political legacy of a frontier society; the conflict between settler and indigenous rights. Secondly there were the problems of understanding and dealing with Australia's particular form of economic development; the difficulties of dealing with the intense but focused opportunities created by boom conditions without falling into the trap of speculative and unproductive overexpansion. Thirdly there were the dilemmas of dealing with the informal controls exercised by British investment within the 'empire of free trade'.

The severity and length of the depression of the 1890s suggests that this last problem was not easily solved by the Australian colonies after the collapse of 1893. But this issue is not isolated from the other two. British investors could not be reassured unless colonial spokesmen could convince them that they had a good understanding of the nature and dynamics of Australia's social and economic programmes. Debates around the first issue were also important for symbolic reasons as they were an arena where imperial obligations and concerns had to be accommodated to the realities of settler power. But the colonists had to show that they could exercise that power within the demands of imperial policy concerns.

Economic crises and the challenges to Australia's settler society in the 1970s and 1980s

The industrialization and the structural changes created by two world wars and the economic fluctuations of the inter-war period added new elements of an urban, industrial economy to Australia's conglomerate settler economy but did not displace basic structures. Indeed, a few years of prosperity in the 1920s briefly resurrected the economic dynamic of the settler society in the 'men, money and markets' imperial strategy of the Bruce–Page government, before the depression of the 1930s saw British investment and finance dry up once again. There was then a defensive reaction by Australian governments, with the Commonwealth government gaining greater control of fiscal policy-making, but recovery was barely evident when the Second World War intervened. The war saw a decline of British commercial influence on Australia and a shift towards American economic links. The post-war reconstruction plans adopted many of the fiscal innovations generated by Keynesian economics in the heat of Britain's battle for survival and applied these to Australia's new position and potentialities. The result of this was the 'long boom', the first period of sustained growth and development in the twentieth century that could match those of the nineteenth century. Direct investment from the United States came to Australia to establish manufacturing industry behind protective tariffs. The labour needed was supplied by increased immigration in which the usual preponderance of British immigrants was supplemented by Southern Europeans and, eventually, a modicum of Asian immigration. From the early 1950s until the end of the 1960s this economic recipe seemed capable of confirming Australia's place as a lucky country and maintaining its place in the world (Horne [1964] 1977).

The 1970s and 1980s have seen a succession of economic crises that not only marked the end of the long boom but have made Australian economists examine, once again, the fundamentals of Australia's economic structure. These crises began with a brief commodity boom in 1970–71 which generated strong inflationary pressures. These were then compounded by the confusion of international money and commodity markets as they grappled with the dislocations caused by the Organization of Petroleum Exporting Countries' first successful interventions in oil production and pricing and, in Australia, by the policy uncertainties and conflicts of the Whitlam government years. The later 1970s saw little improvement as the new phenomenon of stagflation (persistent high unemployment and economic stagnation) stifled the Australian economy. The sense of obdurate recession began to lift after 1979 when a new rise in oil prices fueled a flurry of speculative investment in Australian resources, but this was cut brutally short by a sudden steep recession in 1982–83. Faced with unprecedented economic conditions (Perkins 1987:47) the Hawke Labor government has restructured economic policy institutions in Australia, particularly with the deregulation of the financial sector and foreign exchange markets. For its first two-and-a-half years of office it was able to claim relative success with its macro-economic strategy and significant co-operation with the union movement through a formal accord with the Australian Council of Trade Unions (ACTU) (Ewer et al. 1987).

In mid-1986 the Australian dollar depreciated very suddenly and Australia's terms of trade also deteriorated substantially. This appeared to belie the government's claim that macro-economic policy was on course and that programmes of restructuring were having an effect. As Bruce Grant observes, the fall of the currency's external value has a potent symbolic importance:

A strong currency is the mark of a particular kind of power and prestige which elites and aspiring middle classes value, in that it enables those who possess it to travel abroad and to change money at favourable rates in foreign countries, a true sign of imperialism. It enables luxuries from abroad to be enjoyed relatively cheaply . . . thus promoting sophistication over provincialism. Australians have enjoyed . . . access to the sophisticated quality of life that more advanced societies have produced. [Grant 1988:12]

Responding to a range of issues associated with the currency's decline, a feeling emerged within the government itself that policies to reverse the balance of payments position should have top, if not sole, priority in policy formulation (Tregillis 1988). Suggestions that Australia could become a 'banana republic' were suddenly taken seriously and economists began to suggest that Australia might have something to learn from the experience of Third World countries, an idea the profession had not treated seriously before (Manning 1988:3).

The economic crises of the 1980s have focused attention on Australia's balance-of-payments difficulties. However, the balance of payments is only the most visible point at which the structures and competitiveness of the Australian economy are measured against world standards. Long-term analyses of the Australian economy indicate that, despite the addition of an industrial sector to the conglomerate structure of Australia's economy in the long boom, the reorientation of Australia's economic institutions to the 'industrial' logic required in the present crisis involves changing development goals that stretch right back to the period of settler society.

Commenting on Australia's present situation in the light of his monumental scholarship on Australian economic trends since the early nineteenth century, Noel Butlin argues that development goals, particularly population growth, were a linchpin of Australian government action from at least the 1850s. Australian colonial governments acted as investors and entrepreneurs, a pattern of 'colonial socialism', and, even from the late nineteenth century, they used micro- and macro-economic regulation to achieve developmental goals. They thus established a pattern of closure and protection with the reasonable belief that the population growth thus generated would serve as the springboard for the development of diversified exports (Butlin 1986:7). The famous Harvester judgement of 1907, which linked tariff protection for manufacturers to the Arbitration Commission's protection of the basic wage to maintain living standards and hence immigration, is the most famous symbol of this complex of policy orientations and developmental goals.

Boris Schedvin, another major economic historian, develops this picture further. He notes the peculiarity of Australia's development task in that, in the twentieth century, it had to industrialize on the basis of already established high productivity in the rural sector. On the one hand this limited, indeed reversed, the usual European pattern whereby transfers of 'factors' (people and capital) from agriculture to industry created an early productivity gain and, secondly, the need to provide the infrastructure for high per capita consumption levels in the cities meant that there was a double demand for capital in the initial stages of industrialization (Schedvin 1970:4). Finally, he suggests, the very success of the wool industry in the nineteenth century established a pattern and expectation of growth through resources rather than labour productivity (Schedvin 1987). According to both these writers the reorientation of policy direction and thinking that the economics profession has been proposing since the early 1970s constitutes a fundamental reorientation of thinking from the basis laid by the nineteenth-century history of Australia as a settler society. A further comment on the urgent nature of these issues comes from Schedvin's analysis of balances and trends in the international economy; this suggests that Australia's export concentration on bulk commodities to complement the needs of growth in the metropolitan economies has gradually broken down and is no longer a suitable basis for economic development strategies. Australia has become marginalized in the network of world trade.

Schedvin claims that the Australian economy and its characteristic institutions are only now on the 'hinge of history'. The last two decades of economic crisis and uncertainty have finally undermined the older dreams of economic development, population growth and settlement, and replaced them with the dream of Australia as an industrially sophisticated, modern economy able to compete with Western Europeans in its levels of innovation and skill. In its recent form this reorientation has been driven by the concern with the balance of payments and the perceived weakness of the Australian dollar. At the medium-term level it is driven by the continuing debate about the structural characteristics of the Australian economy, but at the long-term level it involves a recognition of the continuing legacy of the ideals of the settler society in contemporary Australia and the need to question that legacy.

There is a significant difference between the institutions and structures of the small, modern, industrial society which it is claimed Australia needs to become, and the older institutions and structures of the settler society. This difference is reflected in debates about Australia's self-image and social attitudes. Protagonists of change see these debates as a part of the process of selling the changes and, indeed, a necessary aspect of their successful implementation. Those who value the goals and rationale of the older structures label the calls for change an attack on fundamental aspects of Australian society and seek to revitalize the images that embody and legitimate those goals.

The claim that Australia needs to reorient its export structure comes from the perception of significant and permanent changes in Australia's external environment. The changes which such a reorientation entails are, however, many. There is the need to discover which kinds of products Australia could produce well and competitively; the establishment of 'market niches', and a new reputation for quality, a task that requires reversing our past reputation. Companies need to devote organizational resources to product development rather than cheaper production engineering (that is, product rather than process innovation) and a network of effective sales and service outlets have to be established overseas. Marketing abroad involves changes in Australian industry's reputation and image abroad but there are also significant associated changes in our self-image at home.

This chapter has suggested three particular dilemmas faced by Australia's settler society: the opposition of settler and indigenous rights; the problems of its particular economic development needs and *inter alia* the dilemma of building on resource wealth to create genuine development; and finally, the dilemma of reconciling national development needs with the strictures of informal imperial control. It is possible to see parallels to these dilemmas in current debates and, hence, to recognize the legacies of the settler society in their new guises.

The issue of settler and indigenous rights now revolves around questions of immigration selectivity and multiculturalism. Part of Australia's assertion of its own strategy of empire against the British was the restriction of non-white immigration and a rejection of imperial claims to stewardship and protection of indigenous peoples. The settlers sought to prevent the degeneration of their valued racial stock and any miscegenation, as this would have undermined their claims to an equal place in the Empire based on the informal criteria of 'kinship'. On the other hand it was imperial recognition of subjects of the Crown that gave formal equality to indigenous peoples and non-white inhabitants of imperial domains. Multiculturalism and non-racial immigration policy are a recent recognition of comparable international rather than purely national obligations by the state, as well as a response to ethnic communities created by post-war immigration. These are, however, defensive or reactive legitimations which do not challenge the basic assumptions of the settler society and, in particular, its belief in the necessity of eventual assimilation. If Australia is to present an image of a new, modern society it will have to come to terms with the positive ideals of multiculturalism and give less weight to the implicit claims of the settler 'charter groups' (Castles et al. 1988).

The problem of the particularity of Australia's economic development pattern is posed particularly sharply by the medium and long-term economic analyses described in the last section. The idea that Australia can achieve a significant penetration of foreign markets from the basis of a small but sophisticated and efficient industrial base reverses the vision of development and the dynamic of scale that was implicit in the settler society's fixation on population growth. As Butlin (1986:7) points out, this belief implied that diversified exports would follow from the eventual development of a significant national economy. The expectation of the 1880s, which we now see as a dream, was that Australia could be another United States. The self-image it promoted was that of Australia as a 'new' society, a vital democracy moving ahead of the parent culture of Britain. This belief was not abandoned in the wake of the 1890s or 1930s depressions; it was postponed, and the measures taken to cope with the crises were reactive and defensive rather than actively taking Australia towards a different future. The older vision of our potential as a settler society resurfaced in the post-war reconstruction period, driven to a large extent by the old fear that we must 'populate or perish'. Even in the 1950s and 1960s it was a critical part of Liberal Party ideology (Simms 1982). Present concerns about Australia's military 'vulnerability' re-echo that older mode of thought. The weight given to this concern appears to be diminishing at each reprise, however.

There are contemporary parallels also with the dilemma of wealth and development perceived in the nineteenth century: the problem of creating a basis for long-term growth on the basis of short-term booms. How to deal with the good times as opportunities for strategic structural change is a problem that recurs periodically, with pastoral expansion of the 1820s and 1830s through to the resources boom of 1979–81. Institutional change, particularly central banking and currency control, have created more sophisticated and effective means for government interventions to balance and direct these sudden fluctuations of good fortune. The problems are now perceived as political rather than technical. An electorate would have to be convinced of the reality of the long-term programme to believe that denial of short-term benefits was justified. The technical aspects of the problem relate to the way the excess earnings are gathered and the mechanisms of their redistribution.

Doctrinaire commentaries on these two sets of issues often betray the legacy of nineteenth-century debates. Recent concerns about the 'ungovernability' of democracies question whether popularly elected governments are ever able to resist the temptation to deliver immediate economic benefits to the electorate. The Fraser government was seen as being prepared to buy electoral popularity and back away from the hard line it had followed from 1976 to 1979 once it thought it could increase government spending on the strength of the resources boom (Grant 1988:28; Perkins 1987:41–3). Throughout the nineteenth century the British financial community distrusted American democracy and its endemic localism and corruption and sought to avoid the establishment of similar structures in Australia. In the 1920s and 1930s such tendencies were attributed to populism, but 'financial responsibility' triumphed with the dismissal of Jack Lang's government in New South Wales in 1932. Contemporary doctrinaire rejections of government intervention appeal to these long-standing habits of thought but shed little light on the carefully constructed institutional balance of private banking and public finance. Similarly, concerns that 'excessive borrowing' means that we are 'living beyond our means' carry overtones of the nineteenth-century condemnations of Australian speculation and its implications of the necessary virtues of thrift and parsimony. In these respects the value conflicts of the earlier age continue in the popular simplicities of the present.

The third dilemma of the settler society also dealt with financial questions. In this case it was not bankers' doubts about Australia's moral economy which raised concern, it was the informal imperial control which could be exercised through the power of finance. The difficulties of raising capital after the 1890s collapse and the loan problems of the 1930s forced Australian statesmen to make regular pilgrimages to London. Electronic communication means that the foreign market assessments of policy can now be beamed directly to Australian living rooms, giving the impression that approval of government policy rests in the hands of the young whiz kids of Wall Street's investment firms rather than the local electorate. Furthermore, the volatility of the dollar, again resting, it appears, in the hands of dealers and speculators, undermines that feeling of guaranteed access to world trends described by Grant (1988:28). Although motivated by these short-term considerations initially, the need to sell Australia on world markets would appear to justify such appearances. If nationalism is defensive it will work against the new orientation that economic exigencies demand.

The restructuring that economists call for also involves a reorientation of Australia's geopolitical thinking and self-image. The legacy of the settler society offers one strategy but its historical weight should not be allowed to obscure the alternatives. The strategy of the settler society would involve making ourselves a more active and recognizable entity in the metropolitan societies (in the current situation, the United States and Japan). By establishing some expertise in aspects of industrial development complementary to theirs we might establish market niches in these larger economies. The alternative would be to follow a regional strategy, to seek to be an industrial power in the South-West Pacific and perhaps to enter into some sort of regional economic co-operation. On the whole we seem to be moving towards the first alternative, partly because of the initial bridgehead developed by earlier ties and partly because of the difficulties of an 'Asian future', including that of establishing a genuine multicultural and multiracial society. On balance it appears that we are instinctively following the settler society strategy in the new conditions of the 1980s, defending, as we must, the gains created by our post-war association with the American economy.

The parallels between the current situation and the tensions of the settler society suggest, however, that being a satellite or colonial society is neither the passive nor necessarily the beneficial path its supporters or detractors suggest. There is a constant need to adjust local production to the opportunities and problems created by changing metropolitan policies; there is a need to assert the claims of the smaller powers in world or imperial forums and there is the need to generate a positive national self-image in a situation of dependence. It seems understandable, however, that these familiar and known problems have more appeal than the uncharted alternatives. Furthermore, Europe presents us with an image of modernity we can understand; Asia with a future that may be inscrutable. The duality of the settler vision was, I have suggested, the belief that the settlers alone knew the realities of the frontier but also carried the burden of making the metropolis give due recognition to their achievements and the exigencies of their struggle. This duality continues in the present situation.

In the battle of images, described by Goodwin (1974), between Australia and Britain from the 1850s until the 1930s, the defenders of Australia's reputation had to fight both the misinformation propagated by their opponents in Britain and the disparagement of colonial innovations that were part of the structuring of imperial control. The drive to establish 'British' institutions in Australia, to impose stability and order on the potential chaos of frontier democracy, was the settlers' internalization of this imperial condescension. To a large extent the celebration of settler achievements was a defensive reaction to hostile critics in Britain. One of the long-term consequences of this defensiveness was, however, the 'cultural cringe' in Australian educational institutions and intellectual life which lasted until the 1950s.

This attitude and its associated provincialism were roundly criticized by Donald Horne and others in the 1960s (Horne [1964] 1977). To change the nature of our trade, to send our manufactured goods to metropolitan countries, also means a reversal of this cultural reflex. In this context the self-image of a settler society can impose severe limitations. If it fixes Australia as the *outpost* of a larger collective entity (the Empire, the Anglo-Saxon race, the 'English-speaking peoples') it perpetuates a 'cringe' mentality. However if it disputes metropolitan assessments of the overall imperial strategy, as did the radical nationalism of the 1890s, asserts a leading role for the colonies and seeks to gain metropolitan recognition for their achievements, then it is a positive force. Contemporary attempts to gain international recognition for Australia continue this ambivalence. Willing participation in a major power's colonial or neo-colonial conflicts appeared to be a useful ticket to gain a greater hearing in the imperial capitals even in the 1960s. The American withdrawal from Vietnam and the declaration of the Guam doctrine—which reduced the United States' commitment to 'forward defence' in Asia—forced a reassessment of this strategy. Australia now appears more committed to a middle power strategy with an independent policy stance exemplified, for instance, by its initiatives in the formation of the Cairns Group, a caucus of agricultural-exporting countries within the General Agreement on Tariffs and Trade (GATT).

Conclusion

To refer to Australia as a settler society in the late nineteenth century directed attention to our position as an integral component of the British Empire, linked to it not only by sustained commercial ties but seeing ourselves, and hoping to be seen, as a major province of Britain, not an outpost. Imperial condescension triggered a fear that we would lose our claim to Britishness and the obsessive concern with racial purity was a defensive reaction to this trauma. On the other hand, the claim to be a major province of the Empire meant that Australia also wanted an equal voice in the discussions of long-term imperial policy. These viewpoints overlay, but did not contradict, an earlier, more radical vision of Australia as a 'new' society—another United States. As this radicalism developed we could assume to show Britain, and even the United States, the collectivist institutions of a socialist future. This radical vision, however, did not impress British investors. Although there were many dimensions to this debate, I have suggested that the basic dialectic of (British) imperial assertion and colonial counter-assertion was strengthened by the pattern of economic development increasingly evident in the later part of the century.

To refer to Australia as a settler society in the post-Second World War period is to see us not as an organic fragment of European expansion but rather as an imperialist intrusion into the territory of non-European peoples; a society founded on the same principles that legitimated white rule in South Africa or Kenya but one where the indigenous peoples did not survive as a political force. The prominence of the colonialism issue is generated by Third World activism in world political forums. Nevertheless, it warns against glorifying this frontier heritage or using it as the legitimation for our institutions, although, as the success of the film *Crocodile Dundee* has shown, it is an enduring popular mythology both in Australia and the United States. Internal debates about multiculturalism reflect this conflict between 'mainstream' domestic images of Australia and enlightened 'internationalist' ones. But these difficulties are also reflected in world political forums as the problem of reconciling the principle of national self-determination with the claims of state sovereignty over 'national' minorities within state territories. The cumulation of official policy has been towards some redefinition of contemporary Australian society as a land of immigrants and a focus on the achievement of equality and democracy for all groups, downplaying, it appears, the claims of the Anglo-Celtic majority to be a charter group but also sidestepping the issue of 'historic injustice' to the indigenous peoples.

The second problem that post-war analysis of Australia's history as a settler society raised was that of understanding the commercial and financial mechanisms of our nineteenth-century history that promoted economic development within the framework of imperialism. I have argued that it is essential to distinguish economic development from the modern vision of economic growth associated with 'industrial productivity'. Settler society was triumphant because of mechanisms and structures which promoted the former rather than the latter. In the post-war period we have seen a replay of these trends. The 'long boom' was like the early settler society periods in that Australian growth was propelled by the complementary nature of the Australian economy, and social attitudes and public institutions were moulded by that economic context. The end of the long boom and two decades of economic uncertainty have produced a cumulative reassessment of these social attitudes and public institutions, carrying forward critiques of Australian society begun even in the 1960s. If the economists are right and the marginalization of Australia's traditional commodity exports from world trade is a permanent and not a temporary condition, we are facing an urgent need to generate a new economic dynamic in our institutions and social attitudes and a new set of exports with the commercial and finance networks that they entail.

However in the images of Australia's future there is an ambivalence in the projections of where we can go. While there are elements of change that point towards an independent role for Australia as a major power in the South-West Pacific, there are also signs of an aggressive reassertion of our place as a settler society in the American-dominated Pacific structure. Since it seems unlikely that the former is a viable short-term goal, the latter appears the most likely outcome. The strategic problem of asserting our importance within the structure of the new Pacific economy is different from that of dealing with the British imperial structure. Our commercial complementarity to the United States is not as close as it was to Britain. Japan's claims and needs also have to be understood. As the issues of racism and colonialism show, the formal principles of equality are an important part of the new supra-national network, and in Australia we will have to accommodate our self-image to this. But these are the formal principles. Unfortunately, the success of *Crocodile Dundee* in the United States has kept alive some Australians' secret conviction that the informal recognition of 'kinship' links will be the ones that count in the end!

CHAPTER FIVE

REGIONALISM
Chilla Bulbeck

Introduction

In chapter 4 it was suggested that apparently sovereign nations are caught in a web of international economic and political interdependencies. Nations may be but cogs in the machine of a world system. We might further ask whether the concept of nation does not mask internal divisions as well as external dependencies. In Australia, with its federal system, it seems obvious that there are states within the nation; but even in non-federal systems regions may divide a nation.

As noted in part I, the idea of Australia as one nation may disguise internal and cross-cutting conflicts: conflicts based on race, sex, age, ethnicity, class, residence in the city or the country. These oppositions or differences may outweigh any sense of unity constructed through national identity. Sometimes such conflicts are seen as horizontal: the opposing groups are found in different places, as in the city–country opposition. Alternatively, the oppositions may be seen as vertical: they divide people living in the same city or region, for example divisions based on race or sex. However most categories have both horizontal and vertical dimensions. There are still some working-class suburbs and regional cities, such as Port Adelaide and Wollongong. Redfern is becoming identified as an Aboriginal community, while land rights have given Aborigines control over some of their traditional lands. Some of the (wealthy) aged retire along the coast north and south of Brisbane.

A central concern in the definition of 'region' is the size of the unit and its relationship to other units, both smaller and larger. At the largest level a group of nations may be conceived of as a region: the countries of South-East Asia for example. Most commonly in Australia, region is treated as synonymous with state (for example, see ch. 1, pp.14-15; cf. Holmes & Sharman 1977; Alomes 1988:5, who identifies city with state). This is partly because statistical data published by the Australian Bureau of Statistics is most commonly subdivided by state and territory. Davidson (1986:24) notes the difficulty of compiling comparative statistical tables for Sydney and Melbourne. However, statistical series for statistical divisions within states *are* available. It is the political significance of state governments, as much as the less accessible statistical series based on other units of analysis, that encourages the state-based approach.

In those analyses which do not equate region with state there is little agreement as to the meaning of regionalism. To some extent, various definitions result because each discipline concentrates on different aspects of a region. For sociology it is the notion of a community of shared interactions and beliefs. For politics it is an area administered by a single political unit. For history it is the notion of how events in time unite and identify specific localities. For political economy it is the interaction between the forces of world capitalism and local political responses and resistances. For cultural and literary studies it is the mechanisms which construct a local identity. The different disciplinary perspectives of sociology, cultural studies, literary studies, history, politics, and political economy will be used to explore some of the different meanings of 'region' used in Australian studies.

Benedict Anderson, in his discussion of the nation, attempts to draw on a number of disciplines to discover what makes a nation. He rejects a purely spatial definition for the term 'imagined community'; the nation is 'conceived as a deep, horizontal comradeship' (Anderson 1983:16). The members of the nation share a common identity—their nationality—and that identity arises out of a process of construction or conceiving. For Anderson a shared language is crucial in constructing the national identity. Members of the nation share a language which differs from the language spoken across the border. In Australia there are no longer regions that are conceived and distinguished from their neighbours solely through a shared language. Even ethnic communities, Greek or Vietnamese for example, are not constructed through a tight coupling of space and language. Jock Collins (1988:38–42) notes that non-English-speaking migrants cluster in particular suburbs, thus giving rise to descriptions such as 'Little Italy' (Leichhardt) or 'Vietnamatta' (Cabramatta). Even so, no more than 40 per cent of the population in any local authority in the three southern states was born overseas; immigrants come from a variety of ethnic backgrounds; and, nine years later, the Vietnamese who lived in Cabramatta in 1974 had moved. With perhaps the exception of some Aboriginal groups on their traditional lands, regions in Australia, if they do exist, are not based on a distinction between 'our' language (spoken by all within the geographic area) and the language of outsiders.

Approaches to regionalism

Sociology: the community

The notion of community as used by sociologists perhaps comes closest to Anderson's idea of 'horizontal comradeship'. Toënnies (1957) contrasted the dense social networks of the community (in German *Gemeinschaft* and *Gesellschaft*) with the alienation of association in the city in the nineteenth century. This distinction forms the theoretical underpinning of sociology's community studies. These are detailed analyses, often based on interviews and participant observation, of a specific geographic area, identifying power relations, work and leisure pursuits, and the attitudes and life-styles of the inhabitants. At times sociologists undertaking community studies self-consciously modelled their work on anthropological studies of traditional communities. Sometimes community studies confirmed Toënnies's arguments—for example Lois Bryson and Faith Thompson's *An Australian Newtown* (1972) on the fringe of Melbourne. At other times contrary results were found; Herbert Gans (1962) discovered communities in the suburbs of American cities, particularly ethnic ghettos, while Ron Wild (1974) discovered gossip, conservatism and fierce opposition to outsiders in his study of a rural Australian town.

Anderson rejects Toënnies's opposition of the 'true' community to the alienating association of the city. He argues instead that 'communities are to be distinguished, not by their falsity/genuineness, but by the style in which they are imagined' (Anderson 1983:15). This implies that distinct communities or regions must have local and particular means with which to produce their identities, for example a local newspaper, a regional television station, a regional literature. From where do Australians derive their identity: their nation? their state? their region? And what means are available for reflecting and shaping those identities?

Cultural studies: the dominance of Sydney

White, in *Inventing Australia* (1981) argues that Australia is not primarily a place but a system of ideas, the core of which is 'national identity'. Some writers agree that national identity is more important than regional identity. Denis Murphy (1978) and Peter Ward (1978) argue that there are more things uniting Australians than dividing them into distinct regional tribes: for example 'the relentless conformity' of shops, cinemas, houses, barbecues according to Ward (1978:71). In other words there are national media networks, national transport systems, and a national economy which obliterate regional distinctions. As a result, groups who argue for their local or regional needs are often seen as sectional and selfish. National chauvinism is acceptable, but regional chauvinism can only be justified if it is linked to national goals, for example 'the development of Australia'.

Albert Moran discusses the political and intellectual battles which led to increased 'Australian' content in television shows between the late 1950s and early 1980s. However, he doubts that locally produced television is very different from television shows produced elsewhere or really speaks for and identifies the nation (Rowse & Moran 1984:235–6). In a more recent discussion Moran (1988) notes that our continuing opposition to the 'Americanization' of television may be misplaced. Between the mid-1950s and mid-1960s regional stations throughout Australia were active in the production of variety shows and local dramas. As an example, a Melbourne studio produced dramas such as 'Homicide' and 'Division 4', and Victorian country towns featured in 'Matlock Police' and 'Bellbird'. Today almost all television drama production is located in Sydney, but it is increasingly produced for national and international audiences. As a result the 'contemporary and specific' (Moran 1988:40) references to place are gone. Instead, historical mini-series, 'remote and picturesque', make no links between identity and locality. Moran argues that 'localism' in television production has almost completely disappeared, thus depriving regions of a significant medium for the construction and articulation of their specific identities.

Regional or local newspapers still exist, and in country areas, along with regional radio stations, continue to reflect and shape the political issues and human pursuits of the region. In cities, however, the state or national daily has far more significance than the local suburban newspaper. The concentration of the print media, as with all other media, has reduced the political significance of locality-based newspapers, which had their heyday in the 1890s (Connell & Irving 1980:189). Between 1870 and 1899, 107 labour newspapers alone were established; in 1899 thirteen were locality-based newspapers, six of them, for example, published in various Queensland towns.

Literary studies: parochialism

Regionalism has been something of a dirty word among Australian literary critics. Regionalism is often interpreted as narrow parochialism, to be unfavourably contrasted with the search for the universal and archetypal, the hallmarks of great literature—for example see Leonie Kramer (1980:94–5). Interestingly, Canadian literary critics do not have such a distaste for regional literature. In discussing this difference, Gillian Whitlock (1984) identifies the successful construction of an Australian identity which helped cut the cultural umbilical cord to Europe from the 1890s. This successful deployment of the bush myth, as Russel Ward (1958) describes it, has produced in Australia a focus on the national literary tradition to the exclusion of regional variations in that tradition. This is, as Whitlock (1984:87) and Susan McKernan (1986:548) note, a characteristic of Australian literary criticism, not

Australian writing. It is not that we do not have literary texts that are richly textured by specific localities; it is that the attention of critics focuses on the national or universal characteristics of these texts.

Literary critics who advocate regional literature argue that concrete particularity is valued above abstract generality. Compare this with the much more enticing term 'universalism', used by opponents of regional literature. Regionalism in literature, so its advocates argue, avoids 'pallid anonymity' and the trans-Atlantic style (Shapcott 1978:69). On the other hand, it is almost impossible to identify what factors make an author's writings peculiarly linked to regional characteristics (McKernan 1986:558). For such an attempt see Jim Davidson's (1978:77) analysis of how the environment enters the psyche of the people.

Thea Astley, a strident advocate of a Queensland literature, uses the motif of the tropics to develop the mind/body, civilization/nature split (Whitlock 1984:89). This theme, common in literature, and indeed much of western knowledge, is articulated in *Hunting the Wild Pineapple* through a 'tropic cliché' (Astley 1976:258), in which the value of the terms civilization and nature is at least partially inverted. The strangeness of north Queensland's tropical vegetation, time and space produce strange people, the 'Queensland oddball' or 'humanoids'. But these almost non-human products of nature are to be valued; they are a new and original people. Astley (1976:254), in a response to the universalists, attempts to tie together parochial and cosmopolitan perspectives on literature: 'literary truth is derived from the parish, and if it is truth it will be universal'.

Thus regional writers use wider literary conventions, for example the distinction between mind and body or city and country, to reinforce and produce a regional identity which is anchored in the particularities of the parish. However, as with television programme production, the means of regional literary production must be available. While producing television programmes is an expensive and multifaceted task, even the production of books outside Sydney and Melbourne has become increasingly difficult. Western Australia has responded by establishing the Fremantle Arts Centre Press (Hewett 1979:243) and its own professionally edited literary magazine *Westerly*.

History: changing boundaries

Another way in which Australian regions have been studied is through histories of them. J. W. McCarty (1978) suggests that most regional histories have been studies of formal regions defined by a dominant pursuit, for example pastoralism or mining, which distinguishes them from neighbouring regions. Alternatively, histories have been written of regions defined by the single factor of political control—histories of states or local council areas. Local histories commissioned by councils, perhaps as part of their centenary or other celebrations, are often heavily weighted with the activities of the local authority. This is not merely a response to patronage; it may also reflect the fact that the only unifying characteristic of the area is administration by a local council.

Sometimes the dominant economic pursuit and the political administration are in conflict. Margaret Kiddle's (1961) study of the Western District of Victoria stops abruptly at the South Australian border even though the functional region extends beyond the state line. G. L. Buxton's (1967) study of the Riverina similarly halts at the border of the Murray River. Competing definitions of the region— political unity or economic unity for example—therefore may produce different versions of regional history, depending on the variable used to define regions. Rather than a neat map of Australia separated into its various regions, we may have to envisage overlapping and cross-cutting regions.

For historians time is a crucial element in the telling of history. What may be seen as a region today may have had quite different boundaries in the past. For example Maurice French and Duncan Waterson's (1982) study of the Darling Downs recognizes five different periods of occupation, only the last two of which define the Downs as a region familiar to us. Regional histories thus often read back from the present definition of the region and impose a false unity on the past.

McCarty (1978) suggests that more attention should be paid to functional regions; a region defined by the relationship between two distinct sub-areas, a town and its hinterland, a state and its capital city, for example. Only J. B. Hirst's (1973) study of Adelaide and its hinterland stands as an example of this kind of functional regional history. The regional historian should, according to McCarty, go even further and study the relationship between the locality and the region, the region and the state, the state and the nation.

Histories of groups of regions and their relationship to the total structure of the nation would, according to McCarty, produce a quite different national history. He argues that Australian history is written as a single progressive chronology, the story of our arrival at nationhood. Analysis of the variable development and decay of different regions, the gains in population or economic activity to some regions at the expense of losses to others, 'has the potential to fracture beyond repair the assumptions embodied in general history' (McCarty 1978:104). Such a possibility is envisaged by some of the contributors to *The Sydney–Melbourne Book*, edited by Jim Davidson (1986). In the 1880s 'Marvellous Melbourne' first overtook the older rival. But with the collapse of the building and pastoral boom in the 1890s, Melburnians deserted for the Western Australian gold-fields, the Victorian countryside, and the bohemianism, libertarianism and journalism of Sydney. Manufacturing development from the 1920s gave Melbourne a new lease of life. Melbourne had the appropriate transport systems and infrastructure, especially before the Sydney Harbour Bridge was opened in 1932. As a result, Melbourne still accounts for over half of Australia's imports and exports, while its stock exchange turnover is greater than Sydney's.

However Melbourne's class-based politics and economic activity, appropriate during the long boom up until the 1970s, is no longer attuned to the financial and speculative economic activity of the 1970s and 1980s. Additionally, Sydney business has oriented itself to the Pacific and Asia, while Melbourne's industrial activity remains continental. As a result, in the mid-1980s only two national arts organizations are based in Melbourne, while there are forty in Sydney, and of the 200 largest companies in Australia, 98 had their head offices in Sydney, and only 68 in Melbourne (Davidson 1986:4–16; Wells 1986:64–74; Burnley 1986:123). The Bicentennial celebrations were based in Sydney, which also houses the only national symbols: the Harbour Bridge and the Opera House. The national newspapers— the *Australian Financial Review*, the *Australian*—and the national magazines—the *Bulletin*, the *Women's Weekly*—are produced in Sydney (Spearritt 1980:148–9). Davidson (1986:17) suggests that Melbourne's loss of pre-eminence is permanent: 'Cities, as well as mining towns, rise and fall'. The functionalist history advocated by McCarty, if applied to these two cities, may thus show the rise of one at the expense of the other, rather than the progress of the whole 'Australian nation'.

Political studies: states made equivalent to regions

As noted above, the use of the term 'region' is often synonymous with 'state'. Adapting Anderson's (1983:15) formulation, the state is 'an imagined political community . . . imagined as both inherently limited and sovereign'. The Australian states, while not being sovereign, each have considerable political autonomy as a result of the compact made at federation. The Commonwealth Constitution identified the powers the Commonwealth was to have (for example external affairs, defence, currency, coinage and legal tender), the remaining or residual powers belonging to the states. Most Australians are equally familiar with national and state politics. If Australian academics are not studying the nation they are more than likely studying a state. In political studies this is particularly so, with analyses not just of the politics of each state, but the relations between the states and the Commonwealth.

Jim Davidson (1978:78) suggests that one ingredient usually accompanies regional affiliation—a sense of grievance. He believes this is lacking in Australia, which has no truly poor or backward regions (see also McCarty 1978:100; Higgins 1981:21). Jean Holmes and Campbell Sharman (1977) attribute this greater geographic or horizontal equality in Australia to the operation of the Commonwealth Grants Commission and the Financial Assistance Grants. Once the federal government gained control of income taxation in 1942, most taxation revenues came initially into the Commonwealth coffers. Some of these revenues were then distributed to the states. Attempts were made to compensate the poorer states (at various times all the states except New South Wales and Victoria) with special grants and specific purpose payments. In 1974–5, for example, Western Australia received 39 per cent more than the average per capita grant, and Tasmania received 66 per cent more than the average (Holmes & Sharman 1977:162). State premiers and treasurers journey annually to Canberra to battle over the size of the grants to the states and the division of the spoils. Federal resistance to these disbursements produced the Fraser government's 'new federalism' in 1977—an attempt to make states impose their own additional income taxes. The Hawke government's fiscal restraint has often been won by reductions in the grants to the states.

However, even if we do follow political science's definition of regions as administrative units, our literature has focused on regions defined as states to the exclusion of regions defined by municipal government: councils and shires. The local authority is the first tier of political control and is a crucial point at which land use patterns are determined (hence both the former requirement that municipal voters be property owners, and the enthusiasm of real estate developers to be councillors). Some local councils have shifted their emphasis from 'roads, streets, bridges and drains' to meeting social needs, for example through the provision of welfare workers, community centres and local celebrations. These activities may help foster a local identity. Alan Wolfe (1977) argues that the increasing complexity and corruption of national governments has produced a sense of alienation, and it is only at the local level that vigorous political involvement and activity may be found, through residents' action groups, local history groups, and voluntary associations such as Apex and Lions.

Nevertheless there are factors which militate against the identification of regions with local government areas. Regions would hardly emerge or suddenly be swallowed up in response to the vagaries of state governments: creating local councils (often a haphazard process according to B. S. Marsden's (1972) study of Queensland); 'greater-izing' or combining municipal governments, as happened to Ipswich, Charters Towers, Maryborough, and elsewhere (Laverty 1980:121); or abolishing them for administrators when angry with the impertinence or malpractice of local councils, as has been done on the Gold Coast and in Sydney. Additionally, local governments are far less powerful than the federal or state governments. They are politically the creatures of state parliaments, created by state legislation. '[L]ocal government is exactly what State governments require it to be from time to time' (Virgo 1978:133). Local authorities control only 10 per cent of public budgets and tend to be small in population and space. The Brisbane City Council is the largest municipal authority in Australia, and the only one responsible for over half a million people; the Wiluna Shire in Western Australia covers 855 000 square kilometres. But these are the exceptions rather than the rule.

It is possibly because state governments are so powerful in relation to local governments and local governments often tend to be so small that regional planning has never gained much of a foothold in Australia. J. M. Powell (1988:169–94) outlines developments in regional and town planning theory between the 1920s and 1940s but concludes that the constraints of participation in a world economy defeated hopes to create partially autonomous communities. The Whitlam government's attempt to target areas larger than local councils and smaller than states with the Department of Urban and Regional Development and the Australian Assistance Plan were short-lived experiments. There were no regional political units to advocate or sustain such experiments. Administering Australia at the regional level may be as alien to Australian culture as thinking of Australia at this level (Auster 1987:35–6).

When we think of the term 'region' we most often think of an area that shares a similar geography, landscape and climate, which form the substructure for common economic pursuits. While there cannot be mining towns without minerals, or apple-growing without frosts, these are only constraints within which people have built their political and social worlds. It was not merely the climatic possibility of growing sugar that produced the Queensland sugar towns, but also a political decision to replace South-Sea Island labour with white labour and so shift from plantation farming to more labour-intensive small-scale farms. Logically, the mining town of Mount Isa should have found its port on the closer Gulf of Carpentaria, but it was cheaper to extend the existing railway line from Townsville. Proponents of the development of Townsville overcame the serious physical disadvantages of a muddy and shallow port to make it a significant regional town. As one of Townsville's promoters put it, Bowen was 'a good port far away' but he wanted 'a bad port close handy [sic]' (Lewis 1973:60).

Political economy: Chinese boxes

As discussed in chapter 4, national governments are not as sovereign as they often claim to be, especially in response to the movements of international capital. Political economists attempt to study the interaction between politics and economics in the development of regions, both in Australia and overseas. Frank Stilwell (1983) rhetorically asks 'Is there an Australian economy?'. He answers that there used to be, but the national economy is rapidly becoming fragmented. The post-Second World War boom was based on manufacturing development behind high tariff walls with subsidies and a protected home market for primary industries. The new international division of labour and the Pacific rim strategy (Crough & Wheelwright 1982) have led to the relocation of manufacturing in the cheap labour countries of Asia, while Australia is increasingly seen as a primary-producing (minerals and foodstuffs) nation.

Similar trends can be discerned in the United States, where the opposition of 'rustbelt' or 'frostbelt' to 'sunbelt' identifies the decline of the old manufacturing centres of the north and east and the growth of the south; in Canada, where the resource-rich provinces of Alberta, Saskatchewan and British Columbia are the focus of new economic activity; and in Britain, where the decline of the industrial north is in contrast to the growth of the south.

A. Markusen (1978) argues that in its pursuit of labour and commodity markets, capitalism destroys ethnic and cultural differences and produces more homogeneous regions. The uneven development of capitalism does have a spatial or regional dimension, but regions are now most clearly distinguished on the basis of economic growth or decay. Regions made poor by these international movements of capital often suddenly discover a local identity, but it is pitted against other regions rather than the processes of capitalist exploitation. Thus state governments in Australia seek infrastructure loans or the removal of tariff barriers if they are resource-based states; dying industrial cities in the United States seek the imposition of tariffs and the payment of subsidies.

The development in the 1970s of the resource-rich mining states, and more recently the growth of the service sector, along with the long-term decline of manufacturing (at least as an employer) in Australia, have produced three kinds of regional studies within the area of political economy. Some writers have taken the state as their unit of analysis. A group of analyses in this area asks why South Australia was able to develop a manufacturing base in the 1930s when other states, such as Queensland and Western Australia, failed to do so (O'Shaughnessy 1979; Mitchell 1962; Layman 1982; Bulbeck 1987).

Other writers have divided Australia into two regions—the core manufacturing states of New South Wales, Victoria and South Australia, and the peripheral resource-rich states of Western Australia and Queensland (and sometimes the Northern Territory)—and examined the ways in which different relations with international capital have moulded state politics (Harman & Head 1982; Head 1984). Patrick Mullins (1979;1984) has undertaken an international variant of this form of regional study, contrasting the 'sunbelt' states of the United States with Australia's sunbelt regions, for example the Moreton

Bay region. He argues that in Australia it is not the new high technology sunrise industries which sustain these regions but the consumption activities of leisure and tourism.

Others have undertaken studies of regional working-class manufacturing cities or suburbs in decline, and the newly built mining towns in boom, describing not only the life-styles and living conditions of the inhabitants as sociological community studies would, but how local events are connected to the movements of international capital (Williams 1981; Thompson 1981; Thompson & McKiernan 1980; Cribb 1983; Tsokhas 1985).

Queensland: a case study of regional analysis

Queensland may be taken as a case study of regional analysis in Australia. It is often seen as a uniquely different state, not only by Queenslanders but also the rest of Australia. Queensland was the last of the present states to become a separate colony; it was separated from New South Wales in 1859. Unlike the other mainland capitals, Brisbane's first university was not opened until well into the twentieth century. Another key aspect of Queensland's difference is that all mainland capital cities except Brisbane are central to their state's development. Only Brisbane has less than half of its state's population. Other states have a hub and spoke transportation network centred on the capital city. Along the Queensland coast each regional city has its own spur lines stretching into the hinterland; Brisbane lies at the end of the coastal line which connects these regional cities. The first railway in Queensland linked Ipswich and Granchester in 1865, and did not reach Brisbane for another decade (*Australian Financial Review*, 1 October 1963:37).

With the growth of manufacturing industry, at least in South Australia, New South Wales and Victoria, economic activity increasingly came to be centred on the capital city to the exclusion of the countryside and regional cities. Unlike Western Australia and the Northern Territory, Queensland was unique in its development of a labour-intensive rural activity, the sugar industry which, until the introduction of mechanized harvesting in the late 1950s, stemmed the flow of migrants to the capital. Terry O'Shaughnessy (1979) traces the emergence of a strong local capital in South Australia, based on an accommodation of pastoral and manufacturing interests (symbolized politically by the fusion of the two conservative parties as the Liberal–Country League). Local businessmen were thus well placed to enter joint ventures with overseas companies during the manufacturing boom. In contrast, Queensland's pastoral industry was dominated by southern capital and its mining industry is dominated by foreign capital.

As a result of decentralization and the focus on rural industry, Queensland politics has been described as populist anti-intellectual agrarianism (Lewis 1978:122-3) or authoritarianism (McQueen 1979:50). Queenslanders have been described as people who want 'public instruction rather than education, and free hospitals rather than more of either' (McQueen 1979:43). Patrick Mullins (1986) attempts to link the prevalence of populist politics from both ends of the political spectrum to the uncertainties produced by reliance on primary products sold at fluctuating prices on world markets. Populism is a form of politics which identifies the 'people' (often the 'common man' or the 'ordinary' people) in opposition to some presumed powerful enemy, for example the banks, Canberra politicians or communists.

Murphy (1978:82) opposes himself to writers such as Humphrey McQueen (1979) who argue that Queensland is a 'strange country which is different, while the rest of Australia is the same'. McQueen's article is one of a series published in *Meanjin* between 1978 and 1980 on 'The state of the states'. Most writers were able to identify factors that made their state different. Tasmania is an island built on suspicion (and jealousy) of the mainlanders (Robson 1978:226); South Australia is a 'place of rational and moderate dissent' (Lonie 1978:5,18); Victoria is a state that takes its politics, its business and even its pleasure seriously (Rickard 1978:280); Western Australia is 'a hard land to love, and yet they ended by loving it with a mad parochial passion, these secessionists' (Hewett 1979:241).

Only Peter Spearritt, who was to write for New South Wales, could not readily articulate the identity of that state. When his article finally appeared, Spearritt (1980:95) argued that New South Welshpeople (even the term was clumsy) have no notion of the separate existence of their state. Spearritt attributed this to two factors. First, New South Wales is often seen as Australia. The colony *was* Australia in the early years of settlement and was dismembered to create Victoria, Queensland and the Northern Territory. Secondly, as discussed above, Sydney has become the 'cultural capital' of Australia, the location for most national arts bodies, magazines, newspapers, monuments and television production.

Spearritt argues that New South Wales is also internally divided, into distinct regions with a greater diversity than in any other state. Some of the other writers made passing reference to this possibility that the state was not the appropriate unit of analysis, was not a significant identity that residents shared. L. L. Robson (1978:226) contends that the loyalties of Tasmanians to their regions, isolated by poor transport systems and the inability of telecommunications to penetrate the mountains, are perhaps greater than loyalties to the state or nation. However both John Rickard (1978:281) for Victoria and John

Lonie (1978:514) for South Australia saw the capital city as dominant over the state's hinterland. This supports the significance of the hub and spoke development in these states, as compared with the more regional development of Tasmania.

Conclusion: writing about regionalism from the periphery

What then is the meaning of 'region' and 'regionalism' in Australian studies? The key problems seem to concern autonomy and homogeneity. Regions are influenced by events beyond their borders, just as nations are. On the other hand, no empirical definition of region will yield a completely homogeneous geographic, cultural or economic area, all the characteristics of which are distinct from neighbouring regions. '[R]egional trends give way under closer examination to a vast and intricate mosaic' (Walker 1978:30). It would seem that the region cannot be defined by its size or independence from encompassing geographic units, except in a very rough and ready way.

Lewis Mumford wrote in 1925 that a region was 'any geographic area that possesses a certain unity of climate, soil, vegetation, industry and culture' (quoted in Auster 1987:33). This definition appears to capture many of the aspects of region discussed in this section. Mumford's region is a bounded space, it has a unity based on common economic pursuits and it is an 'imagined community' through its culture. Ralph Matthews, a Canadian sociologist, defines a region as follows:

> though it may be possible to identify numerous ways in which regions empirically differ in social organization, social behaviour, and culture, a distinctive region cannot be said to exist unless the residents of a region identify themselves as belonging to such a territory, and consequently modify their actions. One of the defining and necessary characteristics of any region is that its residents have a sense of *regionalism*. [Matthews 1983:16]

Even more so than Mumford's definition, Matthews focuses not on the territorial aspects of regionalism, but the social aspects, the sense of difference.

On the other hand Markusen (1978:43), the political economist, defines a region as 'a conceptual category that denotes a physically definable and contiguous geographic area with some political status'. He has identified as central the very factor that Mumford has omitted: the political variable. He chose this variable in the belief that the significant 'target of change is political structure and power'. He has ignored the cultural and social dimensions because the commercialization of culture and increased population mobility erode the cultural diversity between regions. Thus, as with much political economy, the emphasis is on the relationship between economics and politics to the exclusion of culture.

This comparison of three definitions would seem to confirm the claim that the 'definition of region . . . depends on the nature of the problem to be investigated' (McCarty 1978:90). Moreover, it also depends on the tools of analysis and concerns that guide the investigator. Community studies grew out of an opposition of community and association, literary criticism is hostile to the presumed parochialism of regional literature, regional histories often impose the dimensions of the contemporary region on a past which was characterized by different regions.

Malcolm McKinnon (1985:371), writing on New Zealand nationalism, suggests that New Zealand is on the edge of the world map. Local parlance confirms the rightness of this view; New Zealanders talk about being 'out here', out in New Zealand. While Australian nationalism may have gone a considerable way towards disrupting the notion that Australians live 'out' from the centre of Europe, or even the United States, perhaps that very nationalism and its geographical origins have produced in the peripheral areas of Australia—'out' from Sydney or Melbourne—the same sense of being on the edge of the map called Australia.

The other major theme developed in this chapter is that the study of regions and regionalism in Australia has been inhibited by the pursuit of national identity, national history, a nation state. This is not merely a reflection of the single language, the national capitalist economy, the federal government, the fact that there are significant commonalities in the Australian experience. It also reflects the concerns of academic writers. Academic disciplines are on the whole directed from the core metropolises of Melbourne and Sydney, where questions of regional diversity are less acute. Bruce Bennett, for example, suggests 'Australian has come to mean literature written within a day's drive of Sydney or Melbourne' (McKernan 1986:550–1). No other Australian city would presume to join the debate as to which capital city has pre-eminence that is explored in *The Sydney–Melbourne Book*.

Just as New South Wales, according to Spearritt (1980), is often identified with Australia, so academics can in the main presume to speak for and to Australia, whatever the regional or local content in their analyses. It is only when these versions of Australian studies reach the periphery that the disjunction between academic production and local experience may emerge. Regionalism is the voice of the 'periphery', the 'country', the 'town', asserting its difference from the 'metropolis', the 'city', the 'capital'. Because the periphery rarely presumes to speak for Australia, it is the site where regional studies are nourished.

CHAPTER SIX

NINETEENTH-CENTURY URBANIZATION

Gail Reekie

Chilla Bulbeck's discussion of regionalism in chapter 5 questions the vision of Australia as one nation. How we define Australia depends to a large extent on which part of it—which state, region or community—we investigate. There is, therefore, an important *spatial* dimension to Australian studies. Cities are significant spaces, or sites, of national identity. Not only do most of us live in cities or towns, but so have most Australians since the late nineteenth century. As a result, some historians have suggested that Australian history is essentially the history of cities and urbanization (Butlin 1964:6; Wells 1986:64).

This chapter examines some of the ways in which scholars have approached the history of cities and urbanization in Australia in the nineteenth century. By urbanization is meant quite simply the development of cities. Urbanization has been a feature of Australian history since white settlement and continues to be important in studies of contemporary Australia. However, the establishment of Australian cities and the formation of distinctively urban patterns of settlement were nineteenth-century phenomena. Cities and urban ways of life were an integral and inescapable part of the Australian environment, society and culture by the beginning of the twentieth century. The term 'urbanization' refers in this context specifically to the historical process of social and economic transformation in which cities came to dominate the local economy by concentrating labour, capital, technology, government, manufacturing and commerce within their boundaries. It is therefore crucial to understand the process of urbanization if we are to understand patterns of settlement and institutional dominance in Australia. We also need to know how Australians experienced urban life and urbanization, and to trace the relationship between urbanization and national culture.

This history of urbanization presents several problems. There is, first, the statistical problem of defining an urban centre of population (Ward 1978:173). When does a settlement become a city, and when can its inhabitants be assumed to hold urban rather than rural values? Urbanization is, moreover, a complex process—perhaps a combination of different processes—with multiple effects on Australian society and culture. Scholars in different disciplines tell us various things about the development of Australian cities. Geographers, for example, have their own approach to urbanization and identify different mechanisms of change than do social historians or political economists.

This chapter identifies two central questions for Australian studies which arise out of the history of Australian urbanization. First, we need to ask to what extent Australian urbanization followed a similar path to that of European and American cities, and whether it was distinctive in any way. What, in other words, is Australian about Australian cities? A second set of problems centres on the meaning of the city to Australians. What is a city? How has the meaning of the city varied for its inhabitants according to their class or sex? What role has the city and urban life played in the construction of national identity?

The history of Australia is the history of its cities

Returning to the first question regarding Australian distinctiveness, in at least one respect the Australian pattern of urban settlement appears to be unique. Whether they use the methods of geography, economics, history or sociology, writers on Australian urbanization agree that Australia was, by the late nineteenth century, one of the most highly urbanized countries in the world. By 1890 approximately two-thirds of Australians lived in areas classified as urban (Glynn 1970:3). Scholars also agree that Australia was remarkable for its degree of 'metropolitan dominance', that is, the extent to which the major cities or state capitals dominated their regions economically, demographically and politically. Australian cities are therefore unusual in the influence they have exerted over the nation's political development.

Australian cities also differ significantly from their older European counterparts in that they are relatively recent formations which were the result of commercial rather than industrial developments. In pre-industrial societies urbanization occurred as a direct consequence of the expansion of capitalist enterprises and the introduction of industrial methods of manufacture. Manufacturing employment attracted large numbers of migrants to the city—mostly agricultural labourers from depressed rural areas seeking waged labour. Their numbers swelled the city population and created a market for domestic goods and services. In Australia, however, the reverse process occurred. Because of its status as a settler capitalist society and the subsequent shortage of industrial capital and expertise, urbanization preceded industrialization. As Sean Glynn (1970:4) explains, Australian cities and towns 'developed *in advance* of both industrialization and rural settlement and played a vital role in channelling population movements and promoting these activities'. J. W. McCarty further distinguishes between 'traditional' pre-capitalistic cities such as London and 'commercial' cities which were pure products of the nineteenth-century expansion of commercial capitalism. He argues that because industrialization followed urbanization in Australia, its cities were of the commercial type (McCarty & Schedvin 1978:12).

Some writers note that comparatively high levels of urbanization were matched by an unusual degree of suburbanization. E. C. Fry (1978:32), for example, argues that as a consequence of comparatively high rates of home ownership and the abundance of urban space, the Australian city from its beginnings 'straggled out over the plentiful countryside, using the English country cottage as its model dwelling'. Donald Horne (1964:28-9) has suggested that Australia was perhaps the first suburban nation, even though Australians have been slow to accept its suburban character.

This reluctance, Horne argues, is due to the fact that many Australians prefer to see their national identity in terms of a rural rather than an urban ideal. Since settlement, but especially in the 1890s, Australians celebrated the values and traditions of bush life and constructed a national image around the mythical noble bushman. This preoccupation with rural life as the source of a distinctive Australian identity sat curiously beside its high level of urbanization. If Australia was one of the most extensively urbanized nations in the world by the 1890s, why then did Australians seek their identity in the bush? According to Glynn (1970:2) it is both ironic and significant that 'this overwhelmingly urban nation apparently prefers to present its image to the world very largely in terms of rural symbols' such as kangaroos, Aborigines and stockmen.

The image of Australia as an unusually urbanized society has, like the Australian bush legend, been constructed and maintained by a number of writers since the 1890s. Contemporary urban scholars frequently cite the observations of American urban sociologist Adna Weber who, in 1899, was one of the first to recognize Australia's distinctive pattern of urbanization. Weber observed in his comparative study of urban growth that 'the most remarkable concentration, or rather centralization, of population occurs in the newest product of civilization, Australia' (cited in Glynn 1970:3). His remarks were echoed by visitors to Australia and by T. A. Coghlan, the New South Wales statistician who, in 1901, referred to the unparalleled growth of Australian cities and the 'abnormal aggregation of the population into their capital cities' (cited in Spearritt 1987:132). The theme of the uniqueness of Australia's urban concentration was taken up by N. G. Butlin (1964), a particularly influential and much-quoted economic historian. In his study of Australian investment and economic development between 1860 and 1900, Butlin made the now familiar observation that by 1891 two-thirds of the population lived in cities and towns, adding that this was:

a fraction matched by the United States only by 1920 and by Canada not until 1950. Most of Australian capital equipment went into growing towns, most of the expanding workforce was employed in urban occupations and the greater part of gross product came from urban activity . . . The process of urbanization is the central feature of Australian history, overshadowing rural economic development and creating a fundamental contrast with the economic development of other 'new' countries. [Butlin 1964:6]

Perhaps more than any other book, Butlin's *Investment in Australian Economic Development 1861-1900* has been responsible for legitimizing the historical study of Australian urbanization (Berry 1983:8).

Urban history, long neglected in favour of more traditional historical concerns and an emphasis on the rural origins of Australian national character, began to attract researchers in the late 1960s with the foundation of the Urban Research Unit of the Australian National University. Glynn's *Urbanisation in Australian History 1788-1900* (1970) was one of the first book-length studies of the economic, geographical, demographic, political, social and cultural factors affecting Australian urban growth. Glynn's work was joined by more histories of urbanization in the 1970s, notably those of Max Neutze (1977), J. W. McCarty (1974), McCarty and Schedvin (1978), and E. C. Fry (1972; 1978). The growing interest in social history in the 1970s produced more detailed studies of particular cities at specific periods in the nineteenth century (Davison 1978; Bate 1978; Stannage 1979; Lawson 1973; Solomon 1976; Kelly 1978; Cannon 1975; Fitzgerald 1987; Davison, Dunstan & McConville 1985; Davidson 1986).

While these more recent urban histories provide important pieces of the jigsaw, we have very few historical overviews of the *process* of Australian urbanization. Glynn (1970) and, more recently, Michael Berry (1983) have pointed to this gap in Australian historiography. Berry argues that urbanization themes, or the 'spatial dimension to social life', have been neglected by Australian historians for four reasons: first, a preference for empiricist methodology which treated cities as simply 'bundles of facts'; second, the focus on a distinctive, and hence rural, Australian national character; third, a form of environmental determinism which clouded the class dynamics of history; and fourth, the preoccupation of historians writing before the

1970s with the dominant concerns of their time—war, nationalism, depression, federation.

Since the 1970s Australian historians have been writing in a social environment more sensitive to the effects of unregulated urban growth and to the need for town planning and city development policies that meet the needs of city dwellers (McCarty & Schedvin 1978:1, Fisher 1987:1–4). They have been influenced by what Berry (1983:7–8) calls the 'new urban sociology' of the late 1960s and after: sociologists, radical geographers, political economists and French urban Marxists who stress the need to develop a macro-sociological perspective with which to analyse social inequality and conflict. We can clearly see the influence of this urban sociology in Graeme Davison's introduction to his co-edited book on the 'outcasts' of Melbourne in which he draws on the work of the Chicago school of urban sociologists, radical urban sociologists such as Manuel Castells, and on structuralist historians such as Michel Foucault and Jacques Donzelot (Davison, Dunstan & McConville 1985).

Histories of Australian cities, to sum up, tell us something of the individual histories of particular cities, but little of the process of urbanization as a national phenomenon. Few historians have been interested in constructing models of urban development. Can we nevertheless detect *implicit* theories of urbanization? What factors or mechanisms of social change do urban scholars identify or give prominence to in their accounts of urban growth?

Theories of urban growth in nineteenth-century Australia

We are here interested in the distinctiveness of Australian urban growth. If a major question for investigation is the degree of 'fit' between Australian and non-Australian patterns of urban settlement, we should find out how geographers, historians and sociologists have *explained* the peculiar pattern of Australian urbanization or its degree of conformity with other western societies.

As we have already noted, the majority of urban histories treat the city as a collection of facts about people and institutions. Weston Bate (1974:111), for example, states that the history of each town or city is unique: towns are 'complex organisms' whose ethos 'varies according to the social, religious, and national composition of their inhabitants'. McCarty and Schedvin (1978:3–5) point out that this 'urban biography' approach, while useful, is eclectic and fails to relate specific studies to a central concept of urbanization and its consequences. Berry (1983:11) also criticizes the tendency to theorize the city as a convenient container in which to distil other historical essences such as developments in transport, public utilities and forms of popular culture. These histories describe, rather than explain, patterns of urban growth.

They also tell us what is different about Australian cities rather than what they hold in common.

Geographers, not surprisingly, tend to explain urbanization according to environmental and demographic factors. Neutze's *Urban Development in Australia* (1977) is a descriptive analysis which emphasizes the influence of physical features of sites and the importance of developments in transport and communication. Others stress the role of internal migration as a process of change and a mechanism of maintaining existing settlement patterns (Rowland 1979). City 'biographers' also often rely on environmental factors to explain patterns of urbanization, particularly when describing the initial choice of settlement site (Edwards 1978; Fry 1972; Turner 1978).

While geographical influences are undoubtedly important, they only become significant when acted upon by non-physical (and especially human) forces. As Glynn (1970:28) speculates, 'If the Chinese, instead of the British, had settled Australia, physical geography would have been the same but the degree and pattern of urbanisation might have been quite different'. Moreover, because cities all over the world are shaped by their geography, an emphasis on the influence of environmental factors is not particularly helpful in determining the distinctiveness of the Australian experience.

Accounts which stress the internal economic determinants of urban growth, on the other hand, provide a theory of urbanization that relates specifically to the Australian economy. McCarty (1974), Glynn (1970) and Fry (1972; 1978) are among those economic historians who draw attention to the primacy of economic factors in patterns of urban development. These accounts stress the importance of, for example, gaol services, sealing and whaling, the trading activities of the first settlers, the development of the wool industry and the location of commerce and administration in Sydney or Melbourne during the first half century of Australia's colonial history. McCarty and Schedvin (1978:5–6) suggest that the economic efficiency of the wool, wheat and sugar industries contributed to the pace of Australian urbanization, and conclude that the main cause of Australian urbanization as a nation-wide phenomenon was economic rather than social or political. Glynn (1970:13) cautions, however, that the process of urbanization is complex, hence 'any attempt to isolate single, or even basic or primary causes is a meaningless exercise'. Nevertheless, he suggests that economic factors were 'fundamental' in determining urban structures, whereas non-economic factors (for example, politics or geography) reinforced them.

Economic theories of urbanization rely heavily on the impersonal forces of the market to explain urban growth, just as environmentalist approaches imply that natural resources or technology are autonomous agents of social change. They largely ignore the role of human agency—the actions and motives of specific individuals or groups of politicians, merchants, administrators, manufacturers or workers—in the development of cities. Social historians can help to provide the crucial empirical evidence of the ways in which men and women acted upon the urban environment, the reasons they did so, and with what implications for the city. Michael Cannon (1975), Max Kelly (1986) and, for the twentieth century, Janet McCalman (1985) all suggest the ways in which local business or political élites actively shaped the cities in which they lived and over which they exerted considerable influence. Property ownership and the power it conferred on individual capitalists emerge as particularly significant determinants of urban development. According to Cannon (1975:17) Australian cities were shaped more than anything else by 'the basic policy decision to relinquish ownership of the land to a multitude of private freeholders'. Kelly (1986:41–3), in a detailed study of land ownership in early Sydney, found that the city was settled and shaped by the process of granting land to the city's wealthy elité.

While internal economic developments were clearly critical in determining patterns of urban growth, Australia was not unique as a region of recent settlement. McCarty (1974) states that Australia, the United States, Canada, Argentina and New Zealand had much the same economic histories due to the similarity of their natural resources and roles in the world economy as exporters of primary products. Cities in regions of recent settlement were all 'commercial' cities which linked their hinterlands to world markets (McCarty 1974:11). Commercial cities shared three major characteristics: they were established in advance of, and therefore shaped the development of the hinterland; they were unrivalled by cities of intermediate size; and they had similar patterns of geographical development as a result of changes in transport. The similarities between Australian cities and cities in other new societies of the nineteenth century, according to McCarty, were greater than their differences.

The value of this comparative approach, in which Australian cities are seen to develop along similar paths to their peers in regions of recent settlement, is that Australian urbanization is placed in the context of a capitalist world economy. Malcolm Alexander has shown in chapter 4 how Australia's economic history was determined by its dependence on British capital. Recent histories of urban growth also set Australia explicitly in this international economic and political framework. Andrew Wells (1986:65), for example, argues that because Sydney was financed by British capital and benefited from the British demand for wool it was 'the beachhead for British imperial expansion on the Australian continent'. Chris Maher (1987) finds that although in many respects Australia followed the same settlement pattern as other new societies it was distinguished among other things by the timing of its settlement.

Colonization was very much a function of the outward expansion of the European world economy, and the emergence of an integrated world industrial system. The absence of any permanent pre-industrial settlement meant that the pattern which emerged was unconstrained by any prior decisions, and thus was a direct response to the demands of the developing international economy. [Maher 1987:11]

In identifying the significance of historical periodization Maher is able to demonstrate the particular nature of Australian urbanization more successfully than McCarty.

Berry (1983) pursues the theme of dependent development within a global process of capitalist expansion in more detail. The problem of McCarty's comparative approach, he suggests, is that the city becomes an arena rather than a 'structuring element in the determination of social relations between real people'. In particular, he argues that we need to study urbanization—or the 'spatial dimension of social life'—as a product of class dynamics and the process of capital accumulation. Berry proposes a model of Australian urbanization which has four stages of capital accumulation, specified by the four long waves of expansion and decline (or crises) in the capitalist centre: colonial accumulation between 1788 and 1847; commercial accumulation between 1848 and 1893; industrial accumulation between 1894 and 1939; and corporate accumulation since 1939. Berry (1983:33) concludes that his model is an attempt to 'suggest a framework in which urbanisation in a capitalist world is analysed in terms of the forces or dynamic determining the movement of capital (and labour) over space and its (their) concentration and centralisation in space'.

Berry's model of urban growth in Australia has the advantage of incorporating both internal forces (class relations) and external forces deriving from Australia's dependence on the world economy. Berry (1983), Maher (1987) and Wells (1986), in locating Australian urban growth within the context of its imperial ties to Great Britain and the timing of its entry into the world capitalist system, also show the ways in which Australia both conformed to, and differed from, overseas patterns of urbanization.

Patrick Mullins (1988) analyses these similarities and differences in more detail in his article 'Is Australian urbanisation different?'. He defines urbanization as 'the spatial patterning of that mode of production called capitalism', and identifies the social forces affecting urbanization as social classes, the state, household and residential organization and social movements (Mullins 1988:518–21). Unlike Berry and other urban theorists who stress the significance of Australia's place within a capitalist world economy, Mullins (1988:528) argues that Australian urbanization in the period to 1940 was different from western patterns of urbanization because Australian capitalism was different. The distinctive nature of Australian capitalism created four major differences: the replacement of an industrial stage by an extended mercantile stage of urbanization; the greater role of the state in the period to 1920; the absence of occupational communities in which social bonds formed at work were reinforced in the residential area and vice versa; and relatively few urban social movements.

Mullins (1988) extends our understanding of Australian urbanization in several directions. While his 'mercantile' form of urbanization is similar to McCarty's 'commercial city', Mullins formulates a developmental model of urban growth—from mercantile to industrial to corporate forms—which is more dynamic and hence more sensitive to historical process than McCarty's classification of city types. Secondly, he directly and specifically addresses the question of Australian difference through a comparative analysis aimed at explanation rather than description. Mullins's third contribution to the study of nineteenth-century urbanization is his acknowledgement of the impact of household and residential organization created largely by women's unpaid labour.

Mullins's and Berry's analyses of urbanization reveal some of the strengths, and the limitations, of a predominantly sociological approach to Australian studies. Both theorists present a broad and schematic overview of urban development (in Mullins's case from the Middle Ages to the 1980s) in which there is necessarily little historical detail or precision. While their models of urbanization are of greater explanatory value than most conventional descriptive histories, some of their assertions require further research and empirical verification. Sociological accounts of historical processes also often tend to neaten the many loose ends and random events of history by placing data into fixed categories which become self-fulfilling. Thus Mullins specifies four causes of Australian difference, argues that these same four factors were the major social forces affecting western urbanization in general, and that therefore Australian urbanization differed from western urbanization. His four 'causes' of urbanization might also have been its effects. Despite its incorporation of the role of state intervention Mullins's model does not fully explain Australia's high degree of urbanization relative to other western societies (Mullins 1988:531). As with most of the central issues in Australian studies the puzzle clearly requires a multi-disciplinary approach.

The meanings of the city

The process of urbanization does not occur in a social vacuum. The growth of cities and their increasing prominence in the cultural life of the nation have significant effects on the people who live in them. Here we take up our second set of questions related to the meaning of the Australian city. If one purpose of Australian studies is to investigate the nature of Australian culture, then clearly we need to investigate the place of the city in our history, traditions and national myths.

The city is a social construct as much as it is a collection of shops, houses, warehouses, parks and streets. The city exists as an idea as well as a material reality. So when we ask 'What has the city meant to Australians?' we are really asking two related questions. First, we want to know how the city has influenced the experience of daily life for its inhabitants, and how the urban experience has affected different groups of people. We also want to find out how the city has been represented in various forms of national culture (literature, travellers' accounts, painting, popular periodicals, entertainment, and so on). The city in this representational form can be seen as an artefact, as a social construction that may or may not be related to the city as material reality.

Graeme Davison's *The Rise and Fall of Marvellous Melbourne* (1978) and the collection of essays *The Outcasts of Melbourne* (1985) suggest that late nineteenth-century Melbourne was seen as a metaphor of both material progress and urban decay, depending on the occupation and political viewpoint of the observer. The description 'Marvellous Melbourne' was used repeatedly by the boosters (city promoters) to draw attention to how rapidly and impressively Melbourne had grown into a world class metropolis comparable to London by the 1880s. Melbourne became a symbol of commercial expansion and urban sophistication, material and visible proof that Australia was about to join the ranks of the great industrial nations of the world.

Melbourne's critics—notably 'muckraking' journalists and slum reformers—drew unfavourable comparisons with the effects of urbanization in Europe. They pointed out that Melbourne, like London, had its underworld, its slums, its low life and its outcast inhabitants. The slum theory of poverty relied on notions of contagion and disease to explain the dangers of the back streets of Melbourne: it implied that vice, corruption, degradation and immorality would spread to the respectable classes and threaten the social order unless contained. For these fascinated observers of the underworld and its depraved inhabitants the city represented a source of obsession and titillation. For those who wanted to 'clean up' the city and intervene in potentially disruptive forms of working-class culture the city had overwhelmingly negative, even cataclysmic meaning. It stood for all that was bad, sad, repellant and frightening about urban industrial society.

Peter Bolger (1978) traces similar image changes related to the economic fortunes of Hobart. Initially portrayed in a negative light as little more than a home for convicts, by the 1850s descriptions of Hobart proudly provided abundant evidence of increasing prosperity. Its depression between 1857 and 1870, however, coincided with a more gloomy representation of a utopian but lethargic 'sleepy hollow'. We can also see from the enduring, and frequently bitter, rivalry between Sydney and Melbourne that images of the city served to cement intercolonial rivalries and provided city dwellers with a culturally significant sense of place and civic identity (Davidson 1986).

The work of social historians reveals the importance of class as a determinant of urban experience. Members of the city's wealthy and powerful elite saw the city as a source of profit and power. Industrial and commercial entrepreneurs located their businesses in the city because cities supplied labour, materials, financial services, transport, communication and markets. Australians aspiring towards a bourgeois life-style with a home of their own in the suburbs, or those who were fashioning a career for themselves in politics or public service, also saw the city as the locus of personal advancement. To many of the middle and upper classes the city represented prosperity and the potential for success.

However, as Shirley Fitzgerald points out in *Rising Damp* (1987)— a detailed study of Sydney's streets, factories, laundries, sweatshops and homes between 1870 and 1890—those who improved their social status during the years of rapid urbanization were comparatively few. The vast majority of ordinary Sydney inhabitants were adversely affected by untrammelled expansion, rampant property speculation, appalling working conditions, and the virtual absence of local government control over the city's chaotic development. The working class's experience of Sydney as a 'mercantile city' was marked by seasonal and itinerant employment and the slow development of residential infrastructure (Mullins 1988:531-3). Fitzgerald suggests that the quality of the urban environment did not deteriorate equally for all classes, but that the social divisions between good and bad suburbs hardened and increased, particularly as a result of public transport systems which favoured the wealthier districts. Fitzgerald argues that the disparity between reality and aspiration was greater for immigrant workers, who had come to Australia with dreams of the 'worker's paradise', than it was for the native-born. Many of Sydney's working class, whether new arrivals or established inhabitants, experienced what Stephen Garton describes in chapter 13 as 'poverty in paradise'.

Fitzgerald stresses the importance of gender as well as class differences in the experience of urbanization. The quality of public health, housing and the urban environment impinged directly on women because of their primary responsibility for home and family. If, as Mullins (1988:533) suggests, domestic labour was more extensive and intensive in mercantile cities than it was in industrial cities, Australian women could be expected to have had a doubly hard urban life. Infant and child mortality rates which, Fitzgerald points out, were significantly higher in Sydney than they were in London in the 1880s, would have profoundly affected women's responses to city life. Patricia Grimshaw (1986) also stresses the importance of urbanization to understanding colonial Australian women's experiences. Women had to cope with cramped houses, small backyards, lanes and alleys which were dirty and unsafe for children, and extreme difficulties in carrying out basic domestic chores such as cooking and laundering. Deteriorating living standards, moreover, forced many women to contribute to the family economy by, for example, taking in boarders or factory piecework.

Fitzgerald and Grimshaw suggest that the sexual division of labour became more rigidly defined, and the separation between workplaces and homes more significant, as urbanization and suburbanization increased in late nineteenth-century Australia. As a result, houseworkers and child-carers (mostly women) became increasingly separated from all other workers (mostly men) (Fitzgerald 1987:227). Judith Allen suggests in chapter 12 that women's lives were organized around marriage, motherhood and work. Most married working-class women in the city were confined to unpaid labour in the home, while male breadwinners worked for wages in the city and relied on women to provide their material needs and care for children (Grimshaw 1986:198). The meaning of the city, then, varied considerably for men and women, and for those who were married or single.

If the city represented different things to different groups of city dwellers according to sex, class, marital status, occupation or ethnicity, can we say then that there was a common perception of the place of the city, or of urban experience, in Australian culture? To return to Glynn's identification of the 'paradox' of Australian history, can we reconcile Australia's status as a highly urbanized society with the prevalence of bush images and rural mythologies? Glynn (1970:64-9) argues that the literary search for a distinctively national character extended to the urban milieu, and cites as an example the considerable attention paid by nineteenth-century writers to the city larrikin and his street gang or 'push'.

Glynn goes on to suggest that Australian nationalism was articulated through urban literary media in the early 1840s and in the 1890s, two periods of economic crisis which prompted the search for new values. Davison (1978) similarly proposes that the shattering of the dream of 'Marvellous Melbourne' in the 1890s led writers to turn from the city to the bush and pastoral values for national inspiration. The social and economic changes of the 1890s, the inescapable and undesirable effects of urbanization and the subsequent collapse of civic pride gave rise to 'rural fundamentalism and nationalism' (Glynn 1970:78). Glynn concludes that the similarities—in popular culture, technology, social structure and way of life—between Australian cities and their counterparts in the western world were far greater than their differences:

> Because of the nature and timing of its settlement, and the continuing importance of overseas connections, Australia—far from being a nation apart—was really one small part of an international urban, or suburban, culture, created by western civilisation. [Glynn 1970:79]

According to Glynn and many other scholars Australia's status as an urban nation casts serious doubt on any claims for its cultural distinctiveness.

Russel Ward, whose *Australian Legend* (1958) constitutes the primary target of many of these urban revisionists, has replied to his critics by reaffirming the significance of the bush experience. He argues that Australian society was not 'nearly as dominated by city ways and city numbers as the writers of urban history would have us believe' (Ward 1978:172). He provides three sets of evidence to support his position. First, he says that these writers deny or ignore the existence of bush values (drinking, primitive living conditions and the 'propensity for vulgarising the arts') among the working class of cities which remained raw frontier towns into the 1880s. Second, he asserts that throughout the nineteenth century most people lived in the bush—only 25 per cent of the population of New South Wales lived in Sydney in 1901, for example. Finally, he criticizes the 'urbanisers' for claiming as cities or urban centres every place with a population of more than 500 people: 'to imply as the work of Butlin, Glynn and others does, that the rustic denizens of Doodlakine, Boggabri and Camooweal share in the sophisticated life-style of Sydney slickers is to set up as producers in the theatre of the absurd' (Ward 1978:173). He points out, moreover, that the book never denied that Australians created and identified with outback values in response to increasing urbanization.

The debate between country and city continued into the twentieth century. Some of the common assumptions about the differences between city and country have not entirely disappeared even today. The paradox of a highly urbanized nation which adheres to a rural ethos is still largely unresolved, and the contribution of the city, urbanization and urban values to national culture remains to be fully investigated. As Mullins (1988:517) points out, what has been written about 'Australian urbanization' is in fact about 'western urbanization' or the urbanization process supposedly common to all western countries. A comparative approach which seeks sources of difference rather than similarity arguably provokes more questions and explanations, even if those theories are ultimately challenged or modified. As we saw earlier, the degree and, more importantly, the *process* of Australian urbanization in relation to its historically-specific interaction with the world economic system, appears to have been distinctive. What now needs to be explored are the ways in which that process was expressed in culturally significant forms.

References

4 Australia: A Settler Society in a Changing World

Arndt, H. W. 1965, 'Australia—developed, underdeveloped or midway?', *Economic Record*, September (repr. in H. W. Arndt 1968, *A Small Rich Industrial Country*, Cheshire, Melbourne).
Blainey, G. 1966, *The Tyranny of Distance*, Sun Books, Melbourne.
Blainey, G. 1985/86, 'Mr. Hawke's other Bicentennial scandal', *IPA Review*, vol. 39, no. 3.
Bolton, G. C. 1981, *Spoils and Spoilers: Australians Make Their Environment*, George Allen & Unwin, Sydney.
Butlin, N. G. 1986, *Bicentennial Perspective of Australian Economic Growth*, Economic History Society of Australia and New Zealand, Clayton, Vic.
Cannon, M. 1966, *The Land Boomers*, Nelson, Melbourne.
Castles, S., Kalantzis, M., Cope, B. & Morrissey, M. 1988, *Mistaken Identity: Multiculturalism and the Demise of Nationalism in Australia*, Pluto Press, Sydney.
Cochrane, P. 1980, *Industrialization and Dependence: Australia's Road to Economic Development 1870-1939*, University of Queensland Press, St Lucia, Qld.
Connell, R. W. & Irving, T. 1980, *Class Structure in Australian History: Documents, Narrative and Argument*, Longman Cheshire, Melbourne.
Davison, G. 1979, *The Rise and Fall of Marvellous Melbourne*, Melbourne University Press, Melbourne.
de Garis, B. K. 1974, '1890-1900', in F. Crowley (ed.), *A New History of Australia*, Heinemann, Melbourne.
Denoon, D. 1979, 'Understanding settler societies', *Historical Studies*, vol. 18, no. 73, pp. 511-27.
Denoon, D. 1983, *Settler Capitalism: The Dynamics of Dependent Development in the Southern Hemisphere*, Oxford University Press, New York.
Duncan T. & Fogarty, J. 1984, *Australia and Argentina: On Parallel Paths*, Melbourne University Press, Melbourne.
Ewer, P., Higgins, W. & Stephens, A. 1987, *Unions and the Future of Australian Manufacturing*, George Allen & Unwin, Sydney.
Fogarty, J. P. 1981, 'The comparative method and the nineteenth century regions of recent settlement', *Historical Studies*, vol. 19, no. 76, pp. 412-29.
Goodwin, Craufurd D. W. 1974, *The Image of Australia: British Perception of the Australian Economy from the Eighteenth to the Twentieth Century*, Duke University Press, Durham, NC.
Grant, B. 1988, *What Kind of Country?*, Penguin, Ringwood.
Gruen, F. H. 1985, How bad is Australia's economic performance and why?, The Australian National University Centre for Economic Policy Research, Discussion paper no. 127, Canberra, September.
Horne, D. (1964) 1977, *The Lucky Country*, 3rd rev. edn, Penguin, Ringwood.
Jackson, R. V. 1988, *The Population History of Australia*, McPhee Gribble/Penguin, Melbourne.
Jones, B. 1982, *Sleepers, Wake! Technology and the Future of Work*, Oxford University Press, Melbourne.
Macintyre, S. 1985, *Winners and Losers: The Pursuit of Social Justice in Australia*, George Allen & Unwin, Sydney.

Manning, I. 1988, 'Policy for restructuring: The boundaries of the debate', *National Economic Review*, no. 8, March, pp. 5–11.
Perkins, J. O. N. (ed.) 1972, *Macro-economic Policy: A Comparative Study: Australia Canada New Zealand South Africa*, George Allen & Unwin, London.
Perkins, J. O. N. 1987, *Australian Macroeconomic Policy, 1974–1985*, Melbourne University Press, Melbourne.
Reynolds, H. 1982, *The Other Side of the Frontier: Aboriginal Resistance to the European Invasion of Australia*, Penguin, Ringwood.
Robinson, R. 1972, 'Non-European foundations of European imperialism: Sketch for a theory of collaboration, in R. Owen & B. Sutcliffe (eds), *Studies in the Theory of Imperialism*, Longman, London.
Sawer, M. (ed.) 1982, *Australia and the New Right*, George Allen & Unwin, Sydney.
Schedvin, C. B. 1970, *Australia and the Great Depression: A Study of Economic Development and Policy in the 1920s and 1930s*, Sydney University Press, Sydney.
Schedvin, C. B. 1987, 'The Australian economy on the hinge of history', *The Australian Economic Review*, 1st quarter, no. 77.
Simms, M. 1982, *A Liberal Nation: The Liberal Party and Australian Politics*, Hale & Iremonger, Sydney.
Tregillis, S. 1988, 'The main game in town', *Australian Society*, May, pp. 34–6.
Vamplew, W. (ed.) 1987, *Australians: A Historical Library*, vol. x, *Australians: Historical Statistics*, Fairfax, Syme & Weldon, Sydney.
Ward, R. 1958, *The Australian Legend*, Oxford University Press, Melbourne.
White, R. 1981, *Inventing Australia: Images and Identity 1688–1980*, George Allen & Unwin, Sydney.

5 Regionalism

Alomes, S. 1988, *A Nation at Last? The Changing Character of Australian Nationalism 1880–1988*, Angus & Robertson, Sydney.
Anderson, B. 1983, *Imagined Communities: Reflections on the Origin and Spread of Nationalism*, Verso, London.
Astley, T. 1976, 'Being a Queenslander: A form of literary and geographical conceit', *Southerly*, no. 36, pp. 252–64.
Auster, M. 1987, 'Origins of the Australian regional and metropolitan planning movement, 1900–1940', *Journal of Australian Studies*, no. 21, November, pp. 29–39.
Australian and New Zealand Journal of Sociology, vol. 20, no. 3, 1984 (issue entitled 'Regional development in Australia and New Zealand').
Bryson, L. & Thompson, F. 1972, *An Australian Newtown: Life and Leadership in a Working-Class Suburb*, Kibble Books, Malmsbury, Vic.
Bulbeck, C. 1987, 'Colin Clark and the greening of Queensland: The influence of a senior public servant on Queensland economic development, 1938 to 1952', *Australian Journal of Politics and History*, vol. 33, no. 1, pp. 7–18.

References

Burnley, I. 1986, 'The postwar transformation of Sydney and Melbourne', in Jim Davidson (ed.), *The Sydney–Melbourne Book*, George Allen & Unwin, Sydney.

Buxton, G. L. 1967, *The Riverina 1861–1891*, Melbourne University Press, Melbourne.

Collins, J. 1988, *Migrant Hands in a Distant Land: Australia's Post-War Immigration*, Pluto Press, Sydney.

Connell, R. W. & Irving, T. H. 1980, *Class Structure in Australian History*, Longman Cheshire, Melbourne.

Cribb, M. B. 1983, 'Mount Isa strikes, 1961–1964', in D. J. Murphy (ed.), *The Big Strikes: Queensland 1889–1965*, University of Queensland Press, St Lucia, Qld, pp. 270–97.

Crough, G. & Wheelwright, T. 1982, *Australia: A Client State*, Penguin, Ringwood.

Davidson, J. 1978, 'Writing and the regional factor: Some notes', *Westerly*, vol. 23, no. 4, pp. 76–9.

Davidson, J. 1986, 'Introduction', in J. Davidson (ed.), *The Sydney–Melbourne Book*, George Allen & Unwin, Sydney.

French, M. & Waterson, D. 1982, *The Darling Downs: A Pictorial History 1850–1950*, Darling Downs Institute Press, Toowoomba, Qld.

Gans, H. 1962, *The Urban Villagers: Group and Class in the Life of Italian-Americans*, Free Press, New York.

Harman, E. J. & Head, B. W. (eds) 1982, *State, Capital and Resources in the North and West of Australia*, University of Western Australia Press, Nedlands, WA.

Head, B. 1984, 'Australian resource developments and the national fragmentation thesis', *Australia and New Zealand Journal of Sociology*, vol. 20, no. 3, pp. 306–31.

Head, B. (ed.) 1986, *The Politics of Development*, George Allen & Unwin, Sydney.

Hewett, D. 1979, 'States of the nation—Western Australia: No ratbag Eden', *Meanjin*, vol. 38, no. 2, pp. 234–45.

Higgins, B. 1981, 'Economic development and regional disparities: A comparative study of four federations', in R. L. Mathews (ed.), *Regional Disparities and Economic Development*, Centre for Research on Federal Financial Relations, Canberra.

Hirst, J. B. 1973, *Adelaide and the Country 1870–1917*, Melbourne University Press, Melbourne.

Holmes, H. & Sharman, C. 1977, *The Australian Federal System*, George Allen & Unwin, Sydney.

Kiddle, M. 1961, *Men of Yesterday: A Social History of the Western District of Victoria, 1834–1890*, Melbourne University Press, Melbourne.

Kramer, L. 1980, 'Islands of yesteryear: The growth of literary ideas', *Westerly*, no. 2, June, pp. 89–103.

Laverty, J. R. 1980, 'Greater Brisbane and local government', in D. J. Murphy et al. (eds), *Labor in Power: The Labor Party and Governments in Queensland*, University of Queensland Press, St Lucia, Qld.

Layman, L. 1982, 'Development ideology in Western Australia, 1933–1965', *Historical Studies*, vol. 20, no. 79, pp. 234–60.

Lewis, G. 1973, *A History of the Ports of Queensland*, University of Queensland Press, St Lucia, Qld.
Lewis, G. 1978, 'Queensland nationalism and Australian capitalism', in E. L. Wheelwright & K. Buckley (eds), *Essays in the Political Economy of Australian Capitalism*, vol. 2, Australia & New Zealand Book Co., Sydney.
Lonie, J. 1978, 'States of the nation: South Australia—A fading bourgeois utopia', *Meanjin*, vol. 37, no. 4, pp. 513–21.
McCarty, J. W. 1978, 'Australian regional history', *Historical Studies*, vol. 18, no. 70, pp. 88–105.
McDougall, R. 1985, 'On location: Regionalism in Australian and Canadian literature', *Island Magazine*, no. 24, pp. 3–11.
McKernan, S. 1986, 'Crossing the border: Regional writing in Australia', *Meanjin*, vol. 45, no. 4, pp. 547–60.
McKinnon, M. 1985, 'New Zealand nationalism', *Meanjin*, vol. 44, no. 3, pp. 364–74.
McQueen, H. 1979, 'Queensland: A state of mind', *Meanjin*, vol. 38, no. 1, pp. 41–51.
Markusen, A. R. 1978, 'Regionalism and the capitalist state: The case of the United States', *Kapitalistate*, no. 7, pp. 39–62.
Marsden, B. S. 1972, 'The whole colony was to become a municipality: The territorial foundation of local government in Queensland, *Urban Issues*, vol. 3, pp. 131–50.
Matthews, R. 1983, *The Creation of Regional Dependency*, University of Toronto Press, Toronto.
Mitchell, T. J. 1962, 'J. W. Wainwright: The industrialisation of South Australia, 1935–40', *Australian Journal of Politics and History*, vol. 8, no. 1, pp. 27–40.
Moran, A. 1988, 'Have Sydney and Australia become synonymous?', *Australian Society*, vol. 7, no. 1, pp. 38–40.
Mullins, P. 1979, 'Australia's sunbelt migration: The recent growth of Brisbane and the Moreton region', *Journal of Australian Political Economy*, no. 5, July, pp. 7–32.
Mullins, P. 1984, 'Hedonism and real estate: Resort tourism and Gold Coast development', in P. Williams (ed.), *Conflict and Development*, George Allen & Unwin, Sydney, pp. 31–50.
Mullins, P. 1986, 'Queensland: Populist politics and development', in B. Head (ed.), *The Politics of Development in Australia*, George Allen & Unwin, Sydney.
Murphy, D. 1978, 'Queensland's image and Australian nationalism', *Australian Quarterly*, no. 50, pp. 77–91.
O'Shaughnessy, T. 1979, 'Joh and Don: Capital and politics in two peripheral states', *Intervention*, no. 12, April, pp. 3–28.
Powell, J. M. 1988, *An Historical Geography of Modern Australia: The Restive Fringe*, Cambridge University Press, Cambridge.
The Review of Radical Political Economics, vol. 10, no. 3, 1978 (special issue on regional development).
Rickard, J. 1978, 'States of the nation: Victoria—the ideal state?', *Meanjin*, vol. 37, no. 3, pp. 275–312.
Robson, L. L. 1978, 'States of the nation: Tasmania—a personal reflection', *Meanjin*, vol. 37, no. 2, pp. 220–8.

Rowse, T. & Moran, A. 1984, ' "Peculiarly Australian"—the political construction of cultural identity', in S. Encel & L. Bryson (eds), *Australian Society*, 4th edn, Longman Cheshire, Melbourne.
Scott, R. (ed.) 1975, *Development Administration and Regional Projects*, Canberra College of Advanced Education, Canberra.
Shapcott, T. 1978, 'People placed in time, seminar postscript', *Westerly*, vol. 23, no. 4, pp. 66-70.
Spearritt, P. 1980, 'New South Wales: The non-existent state?', *Meanjin*, vol. 39, no. 2, pp. 139-49.
Stilwell, F. J. B. 1983, 'Is there an Australian economy?', in J. Aldred & J. Wilkes (eds), *A Fractured Federation: Australia in the 1980s*, George Allen & Unwin, Sydney, for the Australian Institute of Political Science.
Thompson, H. M. 1981, 'Normalization: Industrial relations and community control in the Pilbara', *Australian Quarterly*, vol. 53, no. 3.
Thompson, H. M. & McKiernan, J. P. 1980, 'A simple proposition: Buy a home and sell your soul', *Amalgamated Metal Workers and Shipwrights Union Monthly Journal*, March, p. 25.
Toënnies, F. 1957, *Community and Society*, Harper Torchbook, New York.
Tsokhas, K. 1985, 'The political economy of Mount Isa Mines', *Arena*, no. 70, pp. 133-59.
Virgo, G. 1978, 'State policies for local government', in R. Matthews (ed.), *Local Government in Transition: Responsibilities, Finances, Management*, Centre for Research in Federal Financial Relations, Australian National University, Canberra.
Walker, R. A. 1978, 'Two sources of uneven development under advanced capitalism: Spatial differentiation and capital mobility', *Review of Radical Political Economics*, vol. 10, no. 3, pp. 28-37.
Ward, P. 1978, 'What "sense of regionalism"?', *Westerly*, vol. 23, no. 4, pp. 70-2.
Ward, R. 1958, *The Australian Legend*, Oxford University Press, Melbourne.
Wells, A. 1986, 'Cities of capital', in J. Davidson (ed.), *The Sydney-Melbourne Book*, George Allen & Unwin, Sydney.
White, R. 1981, *Inventing Australia: Images and Identity 1688-1980*, George Allen & Unwin, Sydney.
Whitlock, G. 1984, 'Queensland—the state of the art in "the last frontier" ', *Westerly*, vol. 29, no. 2, pp. 85-90.
Wild, R. 1974, *Bradstow: A Study of Status, Class and Power in a Small Australian Town*, Angus & Robertson, Sydney.
Williams, C. 1981, *The Working Class in an Australian Mining Town*, George Allen & Unwin, Sydney.
Wolfe, A. 1977, *The Limits of Legitimacy: Political Contradictions of Contemporary Capitalism*, Free Press, New York.

6 Nineteenth-Century Urbanization

Bate, W. 1974, 'The urban sprinkle: Country towns and Australian regional history', in C. B. Schedvin & J. W. McCarty (eds), *Urbanization in Australia: The Nineteenth Century*, Sydney University Press, Sydney.
Bate, W. 1978, *Lucky City: The First Generation of Ballarat, 1851-1901*, Melbourne University Press, Melbourne.

Berry, M. 1983, 'The Australian city in history: Critique and renewal', in L. Sandercock & M. Berry (eds), *Urban Political Economy: The Australian Case*, George Allen & Unwin, Sydney.
Bolger, P. 1978, 'The changing image of Hobart', in J. W. McCarty & C. B. Schedvin (eds), *Australian Capital Cities: Historical Essays*, Sydney University Press, Sydney.
Burnley, I. H. (ed.) 1974, *Urbanization in Australia: The Post-War Experience*, Cambridge University Press, Cambridge.
Butlin, N. G. 1964, *Investment in Australian Economic Development 1861-1900*, Cambridge University Press, Cambridge.
Cannon, M. 1975, *Australia in the Victorian Age*, vol. 3, *Life in the Cities*, Nelson, Melbourne.
Davidson, J. (ed.) 1986, *The Sydney-Melbourne Book*, George Allen & Unwin, Sydney.
Davison, G. 1974, 'Public utilities and the expansion of Melbourne in the 1880s', in C. B. Schedvin & J. W. McCarty (eds), *Urbanization in Australia: The Nineteenth Century*, Sydney University Press, Sydney.
Davison, G. 1978, *The Rise and Fall of Marvellous Melbourne*, Melbourne University Press, Melbourne.
Davison, G., Dunstan, D. & McConville, C. (eds) 1985, *The Outcasts of Melbourne: Essays in Social History*, George Allen & Unwin, Sydney.
Edwards, N. 1978, 'The genesis of the Sydney central business district 1788-1856', in M. Kelly (ed.), *Nineteenth Century Sydney: Essays in Urban History*, Sydney University Press, Sydney, in association with the Sydney History Group.
Encel, S. 1971, *A Changing Australia, 1939-1971*, Australian Broadcasting Corporation, Sydney.
Fitzgerald, S. 1987, *Rising Damp: Sydney 1870-90*, Oxford University Press, Melbourne.
Fry, E. C. 1972, 'Growth of an Australian metropolis', in R. S. Parker & P. N. Troy (eds), *The Politics of Urban Growth*, Australian National University Press, Canberra.
Fry, E. C. 1978, 'The growth of Sydney', in C. B. Schedvin & J. W. McCarty (eds), *Urbanization in Australia: The Nineteenth Century*, Sydney University Press, Sydney.
Glynn, S. 1970, *Urbanisation in Australian History 1788-1900*, Nelson, Melbourne.
Glynn, S. 1974, 'Approaches to urban history: The case for caution', in C. B. Schedvin & J. W. McCarty (eds), *Urbanization in Australia: The Nineteenth Century*, Sydney University Press, Sydney.
Grimshaw, P. 1986, ' "Man's own country": Women in colonial Australian history', in N. Grieve & A. Burns (eds), *Australian Women: New Feminist Perspectives*, Oxford University Press, Melbourne.
Horne, D. 1964, *The Lucky Country*, Penguin, Ringwood.
Kelly, M. (ed.) 1978a, *Nineteenth-Century Sydney: Essays in Urban History*, Sydney University Press, Sydney, in association with the Sydney History Group.
Kelly, M. 1978b, 'Picturesque and pestilential: The Sydney slum observed 1860-1900', in M. Kelly (ed.), *Nineteenth-Century Sydney: Essays in Urban History*, Sydney University Press, Sydney, in association with the Sydney History Group.

Kelly, M. 1986, 'Nineteenth century Sydney: Beautiful certainly; not bountiful', in J. Davidson (ed.) *The Sydney-Melbourne Book*, George Allen & Unwin, Sydney.

Lawson, R. 1973, *Brisbane in the 1890s: A Study of an Australian Urban Society*, University of Queensland Press, St Lucia, Qld.

Lawson, R. 1978, 'Brisbane in the 1890s', in J. W. McCarty & C. B. Schedvin (eds), *Australian Capital Cities: Historical Essays*, Sydney University Press, Sydney.

McCalman, J. 1985, *Struggletown: Public and Private Life in Richmond 1900-1965*, Melbourne University Press, Melbourne.

McCarty, J. W. 1974, 'Australian capital cities in the nineteenth century', in C. B. Schedvin & J. W. McCarty (eds), *Urbanization in Australia: The Nineteenth Century*, Sydney University Press, Sydney.

McCarty, J. W. & C. B. Schedvin (eds) 1978, *Australian Capital Cities: Historical Essays*, Sydney University Press, Sydney.

Maher, C. 1987, 'The changing character of Australian urban growth', in S. Hamnett & R. Bunker (eds), *Urban Australia: Planning Issues and Policies*, Nelson Wadsworth, Melbourne.

Mullins, P. 1988, 'Is Australian urbanization different?', in J. Najman & J. Western (eds), *A Sociology of Australian Society: Introductory Readings*, University of Queensland Press, St Lucia, Qld.

Neutze, M. 1977, *Urban Development in Australia: A Descriptive Analysis*, George Allen & Unwin, Sydney.

Rickard, J. 1988, *Australia: A Cultural History*, Longman Cheshire, Melbourne.

Rowland, D. T. 1979, *Internal Migration in Australia*, Australian Bureau of Statistics, Canberra.

Sandercock, L. 1975, *Cities for Sale: Property, Politics and Urban Planning in Australia*, Melbourne University Press, Melbourne.

Schedvin, C. B. & McCarty, J. W. (eds) 1974, *Urbanization in Australia: The Nineteenth Century*, Sydney University Press, Sydney.

Solomon, R. J. 1976, *Urbanisation: The Evolution of an Australian Capital*, Angus & Robertson, Sydney.

Spearritt, P. 1978, *Sydney Since the Twenties*, Hale & Iremonger, Sydney.

Spearritt, P. 1987, 'City and region', in D. Borchardt & V. Crittenden (eds), *Australians: A Guide to Sources*, Fairfax, Syme & Weldon, Sydney.

Stannage, C. T. 1979, *The People of Perth: A Social History of Western Australia's Capital City*, Carolls, Perth, for Perth City Council.

Turner, I. 1978, 'The growth of Melbourne', in J. W. McCarty & C. B. Schedvin (eds), *Australian Capital Cities: Historical Essays*, Sydney University Press, Sydney.

Ward, R. 1978, 'The Australian legend revisited', *Historical Studies*, vol. 18, no. 71, pp. 171-90.

Wells, A. 1986, 'Cities of capital', in J. Davidson (ed.), *The Sydney-Melbourne Book*, George Allen & Unwin, Sydney.

White, R. 1981, *Inventing Australia: Images and Identity 1688-1980*, George Allen & Unwin, Sydney.

Williams, M. 1978, 'The making of Adelaide', in J. W. McCarty & C. B. Schedvin (eds), *Australian Capital Cities: Historical Essays*, Sydney University Press, Sydney.

PART III

SHAPING CULTURAL INSTITUTIONS

Introduction

The images through which the meanings of community life are conveyed are frequently thought to be produced by such cultural institutions as the press, literature, film and television. In what senses, however, can Australian literature or Australian film be talked about? Part III is centrally concerned with such issues.

7 INSTITUTIONS OF AUSTRALIAN LITERATURE

Chapter 7 discusses Australian literature from the perspective of the social and cultural institutions through which writing comes before readers (and comes before them as Australian literature). Through a case study of the early *Bulletin* magazine, plus comparisons with twentieth-century periodicals, the chapter examines the role of literary magazines and newspapers in the 'print economy' and the range of their functions for writers and readers. The literary periodical is seen as exemplary of the 'institutional' aspects of literary production.

8 NATIONALITY AND AUSTRALIAN LITERATURE

Discussion in chapter 8 takes its general orientation from a perceived need to work towards new ways of understanding the Australianness of Australian literature in the light of recent emphases in historiography and cultural studies on the construction of cultural meanings as a primary social process. Such new approaches will need to avoid both the essentialism of 'national character' criticism and the reductionism of many of the older critiques of literary nationalism. Building on the work of Richard White, Graeme Turner and others, the chapter defines and exemplifies a rhetorical approach to the phenomenon of nationality in several Australian texts, taking as its main focus the literary uses of 'epitomes of nationality' in these texts, selected from a range of historical periods.

9 AUSTRALIAN FILM AND TELEVISION

Chapter 9 looks at a variety of ways whereby Australian film and television might be defined. As a step towards developing a pluralistic and flexible definition it begins by distinguishing between films as texts and film as industry. It then develops a set of further distinctions around these two notions. However, an interest in the Australianness of locally produced film and television may have the effect of obscuring a series of other related issues. This chapter then discusses localism, class, gender and ethnicity in Australian film. Finally it examines *The Man From Snowy River* as a means of disentangling a number of definitional questions about a recent Australian film.

CHAPTER SEVEN

INSTITUTIONS OF AUSTRALIAN LITERATURE

David Carter with Gillian Whitlock

Introduction

As pointed out in the preface to this book, historical and literary works have led the debate about notions of Australianness. It is in these writings that we find some of the most persuasive and persistent versions of national identity. In the literary field, not only writers of poetry, prose and drama, but also literary critics, book reviewers, editors, teachers, even publishers and booksellers, have produced influential 'myths of Oz'.

Just as literature has played a major role in discussions of national identity, so too have questions of national identity played a key role in determining how people have read and discussed Australian literature. Literary texts have been read with such questions in mind as: How 'Australian' is this book? What does it tell us about the 'national character'? What does it tell us about the nation's growth towards cultural 'maturity'? Looking at literature this way, through the 'spectacles' of national identity, has given rise to a number of *totalizing* approaches to Australian literature and literary history. By totalizing we mean any approach which discusses the whole development of Australian literature in terms of a single theme (for example, the search for national identity or confrontation with the landscape); or any approach which takes the literature of a given period as representative of the whole period (in its various social, cultural and political aspects). Individual writers or texts are often seen to represent the spirit of their age, or are seen as stages in a cultural growth towards maturity. Such views tend to discuss the history of Australian literature, and culture generally, as if a literature were a single organism, growing, adapting, maturing (like a tree or a person). One such work, widely used in schools and universities, is Geoffrey Serle's *From Deserts* the *Prophets Come* (1973), later re-issued as *The Creative Spirit in Australia* (1987). This book contains many useful details about aspects of Australian culture in different periods, but its generalizations about the development of Australian culture often amount to tracing the rise and fall of some overall cultural growth to maturity. (For a critique of such approaches see Docker 1984:34–8.)

Other approaches within literary criticism have focused on individual texts and authors. *The Oxford History of Australian Literature* (Kramer 1981), in its chapters on Fiction and Poetry, provides a whole 'history' in these terms. Our approach, instead of studying Australian literature as if it were an organism or a simple aggregate of texts, is to see literature as an *institution* (or set of institutions). This approach means that instead of concentrating just on individual texts and individual authors, taken to represent the national culture, we will examine in some detail how writing comes before readers, how it comes before them as 'Australian literature', and how it is read in a given social context. Such an examination involves us on both a conceptual and a concrete level. We will want to know about possible literary and ideological influences such as contemporary notions of 'literature' and 'nationhood'; but also about contemporary technologies for publication and distribution, specific social groupings of writers and intellectuals, and the nature of the reading public for different kinds of writing. Australian culture is to be understood, not as a mysterious 'creative spirit' (Serle 1973), but as a network of social institutions and practices.

In this chapter we focus on the magazine or newspaper as exemplary of the institutional aspects of literary production. Through a case study of the *Bulletin*, plus comparisons with twentieth-century periodicals, the discussion centres on the role of such publications in the 'print economy' (see glossary at end of chapter) and the range of their functions for writers and readers. It is not the case that an author's work just 'appears' and is naturally or inevitably recognized as significant. Nor is there a single, nationally-constituted readership. We need to see authors and readers as only two elements in a much larger network which includes critics and reviewers; journalists, editors and publishers; academics and teachers; literary magazines and newspaper review pages; advertising and marketing practices; printing technologies; and curricula in universities and schools. Literary periodicals play a crucial part in this scenario—in publishing writing and criticism, defining areas of cultural debate, carrying advertisements, giving certain authors prominence, and giving literature a particular profile in the print economy.

Like American, Canadian and New Zealand literatures Australian literature is of fairly recent origin (see the discussion of settler societies in chapter 4). In all these countries literature has had a special place in debates about culture and nationality, and literary periodicals have been crucial in the development of a local literature and specific cultural milieux. As the *Bulletin* literary editor A. G. Stephens remarked, literature in the colonies was 'suckled at the breast of journalism' (Whitlock 1985:36). Nadel (1957) has shown that in the colonial period the presence of literature was identified with the general level of morality and civilization in a given society. According to this thinking, which might be identified with the colonial élite, literature in Australia was seen as the best way of civilizing a crude, uncultured and materialistic 'new' society. (The notion of a 'new' society is discussed in chapter 4 of White's *Inventing Australia* (1981).) At the same time, the development of a 'distinctive' literature was seen as evidence of a society's progress towards nationality. Literature was seen to be the product, not just of gifted individuals, but of the 'national mind' or 'national genius'. We can see the two views, literature as a civilizing influence and as a national expression, in the following quotation from 1837:

We consider . . . the diffusion and cultivation of literature to be one of the chief instruments of elevating and enlightening the minds of a people, and especially of a people formed under the peculiar circumstances of this colony . . . [A] taste must first be established for the literary offspring of others, before genius can be aroused to the desire of creating for itself. Until this, however, takes place, no national literature can be properly said to exist, for it is the expression of a nation's mind that constitutes literature. [Webby 1981:13]

The latter idea was still popular in 1878:

[S]urely as we are developing a national life and national types of characters, resembling, no doubt, but yet distinct from, that of the mother country, so surely shall we develop . . . a genuine literature of our own. For all literature is merely the artistic expression of national life and character. [Webby 1981:28]

Both quotations come from literary periodicals: from William a'Beckett in the Sydney *Literary News* and James Smith in the *Melbourne Review* respectively. Both ideas about literature still appear in the 1980s! Their recurrence might be explained by the colonial relationship to perceived metropolitan centres, a theme described in earlier chapters of this book. Each idea represents a way of negotiating the colonial dilemma, either by reinforcing the value of the known or encouraging the new. The *Bulletin* expressed both attitudes, seeing a local and a universal role for culture, but it vigorously rejected any hint of colonial inferiority. Newspapers and periodicals generally were crucial in mediating between local and 'imported' (and continue to be so).

The emergence of a 'new' literature demonstrates with particular clarity how many different kinds of intellectuals and different sites of intellectual activity are involved in what may seem at the outset to be a fairly simple or natural process in which an author's work is placed before a reader. When we think of 'literature' or 'Australian literature' it is probably certain individual texts and writers that first come to mind. But this picture is much too uncomplicated. The process whereby we recognize certain texts as 'literature' and 'Australian' is a complex one which involves social institutions, social groups and social practices.

We need to pay more attention to the social background of literature and how that social and institutional context affects the very nature of the literature itself—and what counts as literature—in a particular culture at a given moment. This means that literature is not to be understood as a fixed set of texts so much as a way or a number of different ways of *thinking about* texts. The boundary lines dividing the literary from the non-literary are not fixed, and have shifted quite clearly over time. It is important, then, to ask: (a) what concepts of the *literary* are operating for particular groups at particular times?; and (b) what are the *social institutions and practices* which produce and maintain such concepts of literature (Eagleton 1983:1–53)?

We chose the *Bulletin* of the 1880s and 1890s as our initial case study for a number of reasons. The *Bulletin* of those years already has a well-established (though contested) reputation in literary and historical studies, insofar as it has been seen as the birthplace of the so-called '*Bulletin* school of writers' and as the nursery of pre-federation nationalist politics. The magazine has been seen in social histories and in literary criticism as a watershed in the development of a truly indigenous national literature and a truly indigenous democratic political attitude. These have both been regarded as expressions of the national identity, and thus the *Bulletin* has been a conspicuous focus of totalizing approaches such as those referred to earlier, approaches in which the magazine is seen to reflect or express the spirit of the age, the nation, or the people (see Inglis Moore 1971; Palmer 1954). Further, as Sylvia Lawson (1983) argues, literary criticism has tended to isolate the 'literary' texts and authors from the magazine as a whole, thereby simplifying the way the *Bulletin* operated for both its readers and its writers. This in turn means a simplification of the magazine's social role and its place in cultural history.

The argument of this chapter is partly directed against these earlier versions of the *Bulletin*. Our discussion has been influenced throughout by Sylvia Lawson's work *The Archibald Paradox* (1983), which traces the life and journalistic career of the *Bulletin*'s most important editor, J. F. Archibald, and places the magazine in a richly elaborated context of newspaper and publishing history, social networks, and literary and political debates.

The *Bulletin* is widely available in libraries, at least on microfilm, and it is a very revealing exercise to look through the whole of one issue. This can begin to show how the literary contributions were situated in the paper and thus how the magazine operated for its readers and its writers. The examples used here are drawn from the *Bulletin* of 15 April 1893, though the points made apply generally. Details of the *Bulletin*'s publishing history can be filled in by consulting such texts as Lawson (1983) and Wilde *et al.* (1985).

As well as raising specific points about the *Bulletin*, we pose questions useful for understanding any literary periodical (and the role of literary journalism in any specific local culture). In line with the approach to literary studies outlined above, attention is directed to how the magazine acts as a mediator in bringing writing to readers and readers to writing. What kind of 'text' is a literary magazine? How does it influence the way writers write and readers read? How do magazines relate to other forms of publication in a given print economy? Who was writing, and for whom? Who was reading and how were they reading?

The print circus

What kind of text was the *Bulletin*? It is necessary to make clear that the *Bulletin* was a weekly news magazine rather than a literary periodical. This does not disqualify it for our purposes, but points up the variety of modes that literary publication outside book form can take.

We can first note the *Bulletin*'s characteristic tones and styles, its range of contents, and its diverse format. The editorials, generally addressing political issues, employ striking (and often irreverent) language: 'Even the minor *rascality* of the province might well *shudder* at the *deep damnation* of such a *national crime*, and join in the good work of politically *stoning to death* those by whom it is contemplated' (emphasis added). The editorial page and the columns which follow always cover an extraordinary range of topics, both local and overseas, and of tones, from moral outrage—'Flogging is a penalty enthusiastically approved by the capitalist class and extended only to men in the garb of workmen'—to smart jokiness: 'A Japanese merchant in Sydney states that he is being ruined by cheap and nasty Birmingham imitations of his wares'. The writers delight in exposing hypocrisy and privilege among the rich and powerful, identifying the reader's interest against vested interests.

A particular readership is addressed in various ways. The magazine advertises itself as 'The *National* Australian Newspaper', and as its motto has 'Australia for the Australians' (later 'Australia for the White Man'). It is announced to readers that:

The Editor will carefully read and acknowledge in the 'Correspondence' column all contributions submitted—whether in the form of Political, Social or Other Articles, Verse, Short Tales or Sketches (those dealing with Australian subjects, and not exceeding two columns in length, or say 3000 words, are specially acceptable), Paragraphs, Letters, or Newspaper-clippings.

This broad invitation is crucial in understanding how the *Bulletin* functioned for its writers and readers. The contributors were indeed acknowledged in the 'Correspondence' column, which sets up a highly entertaining public dialogue between editors, writers and readers: ' "Edward G. Madely": We dare not turn your thoughts loose on an unprepared world . . . "The Wirroo": Poetry on a yamstick. Better hire yourself out as a corroboree with a dingo accompaniment'!

Even the *Bulletin*'s advertisements are significant in range and contents. Those for such unlikely products as the Eureka Electric Belt for Nervous Men, for example, reflect contemporary concerns about masculinity (see Lake 1986). Generally the advertisements are from city-based small businesses—it was policy not to accept them from big firms—and they can be read as indicative of how the magazine conceived and managed its potential audience.

There are columns in each edition of the *Bulletin* on politics, business, culture and show business; a women's column ('My Dear Moorabinda'); numerous cartoons; and other assorted items (for example, an essay called 'Lovers Women Like: an Analysis of Woman's Weaknesses, By a Woman'). Then come the short stories or prose sketches, jammed in between gossip items, readers' contributions and more advertisements. We might leave this impression of the *Bulletin* pot-pourri (and give some of the flavour of 'the *Bulletin* legend') by quoting Henry Lawson. In a piece unpublished in his lifetime, written about 1900 and possibly addressed to an English audience (Kiernan 1976:345), Lawson wrote:

The *Bulletin* fills the place of an Australian Magazine and Review . . .; there is a page devoted to art and literature . . . cleverly written and edited by a literary editor . . . whom the old contributors love like an elder brother because he is trying to introduce what he calls 'culture' . . . and 'Art for Art's Sake'. There are the leader and the 'Plain English' pages. There are three full page cartoons . . . and two or three sketches on every page. There's the 'Wild Cat Column' for the comfort of Banks and mining and other companies and 'shindykits'. There are the 'Society' pages, 'A Woman's Letter' (written by the cleverest pen-woman in Australia), 'Personal Items' and 'Political Points'— all calculated to make the *Bulletin* well beloved by shaky politicians and Australia's scrubby aristocracy, and to make the irreverent Australian chuckle. There is the 'Sunday Shows' page and 'Poverty Point' for actors, and, of course, 'Sporting Notions', for Australia is the land of sport. And perhaps the most humorous, as well as pathetic, and, to some, the most tragic column of all is the 'Answers to Correspondents'. I know many *Bulletin* readers—not writers—who prefer that column. [Cronin 1984:879]

Sylvia Lawson (1983:150) describes the magazine in this era as 'a great print circus'. But we are not simply emphasizing diversity for its own sake; we need to think of the *Bulletin*'s range of tones, styles and materials, not just as individual or idiosyncratic qualities, but as a set of cultural meanings and effects (meanings and effects which are an important part of the social context for reading the literary contributions). What does the range of tones and material tell us? How might it affect our understanding of the literature printed in the magazine? Of the ways it was written and read?

To answer these questions we need to discuss the role of the magazine's distinctive format in setting it apart as different and new in the print economy of its period; its success in appealing to a mass audience, which was both geographically and socially widespread; and its role as a forum for a specific social group or cultural formation of writers and intellectuals.

'Nothing was too trivial' for the magazine, suggests Sylvia Lawson (1983:165) but the trivial details, the one-line jokes or the reader-contributed anecdotes and newspaper clippings, just as much as the editorials and short stories, worked in certain ways, produced certain effects and ways of reading. Here we can begin to see how the magazine distanced and distinguished itself from its contemporaries (and competitors), and thus how it appealed to a mass audience. Its styles and tones, its mix of materials, and indeed its very look, set it apart from the 'decorums' of the established press of its day (Lawson 1983:72–90). Unlike the established press, the *Bulletin* did not speak 'as' or from the position of the Establishment, the governors and ruling interests. It stressed entertainment, and it sought to appeal to a mass audience. It addressed an *implied audience* capable of appreciating a wide range of subject-matter—from the extended political analyses to the gossip, to the racist one-liners—and capable of entertaining a wide range of attitudes, from political outrage to cheeky irreverence.

Further, though the magazine never hesitated in expressing its editorial opinions, it did not speak for or to any single sectional interest whether ruling class or working class, bush or city, business or 'the family circle' (a popular target of other papers). Despite some similarity in policies, it was therefore very different from the *Worker* or the *Boomerang*, which defined their audiences more narrowly as 'labour' or 'worker'. The *Bulletin* defined its audience explicitly as 'national' and 'Australian'. It was not the only paper or periodical to do so, nor was its version of 'Australian' the only one, but certainly it was extraordinarily successful in reaching a diverse reading public, and crucial in this success was the audience implied in the magazine's pages.

The *Bulletin* did not emerge out of (or into) nothing. Here we return to an earlier point about the role of journalism in a 'new' literary culture and colonial print economy. Although there were very few locally produced and locally directed books (especially fiction) published in Australia until the late 1880s, the *Bulletin* was launched into a flourishing market of daily and weekly newspaper and magazine publications in regional towns as well as in cities. This is an important point because, as Ken Stewart has argued, with the high cost or sheer unavailability of local book publication, throughout the nineteenth century 'journalism remained in many respects the mainstay of colonial literary production . . . As a consequence, literary Australia was largely journalists' Australia' (Stewart 1988:180). The majority of poems, prose sketches, essays and stories which were published first appeared in, and indeed were written for, newspapers or magazines. This remained true in the last decades of the century, even though local book publication began to develop. The role of the country newspapers, and communication links between country and city, is also important in this period. As Stewart argues:

In the towns, displaced journalists ran some country newspapers which attained a 'literary-ness' and quality unimaginable today . . . From the 1860s onwards the literary weeklies, companions to the metropolitan dailies, were sent by coach and rail to thousands of country readers, some of whom in turn contributed to these journals. A high proportion of the most influential city journalists of the 1880s and thereafter . . . were previously editors or associates of country newspapers. This emphasis is not intended to idealise . . . the literary culture of rural areas . . . It may, however, help to explain the fact that the overwhelming majority of recognised colonial authors and journalists between 1860 and 1900 either were brought up in rural areas or spent a significant part of their writing careers there; and to place in a wider perspective the arguments of recent commentators who stress the extent to which images of the bush were created by city journalists in urban publications for suburban readers. [Stewart 1988:178]

Details of other papers and magazines are discussed in Green (1961), Walker (1976), Kinross Smith *et al.* (1978), Webby (1981), Gillen (1988). We need to note the range of journals which published fiction and verse. Lawson, for example, published in the *Worker*, *Truth*, and the *Town and Country Journal* as well as the *Bulletin*. Giles (1987) prints nineteenth-century women's fiction, including selections from the *Australian Ladies Journal*. Serialization of novels was also popular. Spender (1988) includes a novel by Ada Cambridge first published in the *Age* in 1881. Finally, in order not to isolate the *Bulletin* falsely, we quote the following discussion of the competing weekly papers: 'It is well to realize that the practical, respectable matter-of-fact [*Town and Country*] *Journal* and its cousin the *Sydney Mail* must have had a combined circulation far larger than the *Bulletin*; they reflected and satisfied the tastes, interests, values, aspirations of country folk better than the noisy, impertinent *Bulletin*' (Walker 1976:78).

This is the situation that the *Bulletin* grew out of and against which it defined itself. The wide range and mixture of seemingly incommensurable material in the *Bulletin* print circus was the expression of a new sense of the role of newspapers in entertaining a mass audience and appealing to a diverse set of local (which is not to say parochial) interests. The *Bulletin* also actively promoted itself as new. This set it apart from the established/Establishment press of the day, and its appeal to a wider audience also set it apart from the more narrowly defined sectional or political papers. (Neither was it a narrowly defined 'literary' paper for well-read ladies and gentlemen!) It conceived of its audience as nation-wide.

Rather than just addressing an audience that was ready and waiting, the *Bulletin* created an audience through its own textual mix and 'forms of address' to its readers; it 'constituted' a new audience, identified a new constituency, in a way no other paper had done. The distinctive mix of materials and tones is important in that it opens up a good deal of room to move for the reader so that the magazine could appeal to a wide audience—radicals and moderates, professionals and workers, town dwellers and bush people—including those readers who would not necessarily agree with its editorial line. We need to keep in mind that the appeal was broad, but that it was heterogeneous. It also had its limits: the implied audience was predominantly white and male. For attitudes to women and feminism in the *Bulletin* see Lawson (1983:194–204) and, more broadly, on the masculinist context, Lake (1986) and Schaffer (1988).

Writers and editors

The *Bulletin* came to be known as 'the bushman's Bible', a label its writers and editors cherished. But the centre of activity was definitely Sydney, especially inner-city Sydney—the *Bulletin* office, surrounding newspaper offices, some bookshops and publishers, and certain familiar cafés, pubs and boarding-houses (see map in Davison 1982). Most of the editors, managers and journalists associated with the *Bulletin*, from various parts of Australia and overseas, came to be centred in this inner-urban and cosmopolitan milieu, though we need to keep in mind the points about city/country influence raised earlier in the quotation from Stewart (1988).

The Oxford Companion to Australian Literature (Wilde et al. 1985) is a useful resource in coming to understand what kind of cultural formation the writers of the *Bulletin* comprised. (The term 'cultural formation' is used in a special sense derived from Williams (1981)—see glossary.) The careers of the writers and editors can be followed up in the *Oxford Companion* or in Cantrell (1977), which includes brief biographies of authors. It is revealing to look at birthplace/place of residence (city, town or country) and work or profession. A large percentage of writers were indeed journalists as Stewart (1988) suggests, and journalists before they were novelists or poets. On the other hand we meet someone like 'Scotty the Wrinkler', who has a short story published in the issue of the *Bulletin* that we selected. The *Oxford Companion* tells us that he was Philip Moubray, well known as a *Bulletin* short-story writer under his pseudonym. Moreover, he:

> adopted the name . . . after meeting . . . a Scottish shepherd who claimed to be an expert on wrinkles. Of Scots descent himself, Moubray seems to have been a British army officer who served in India and Abyssinia before travelling to America and Australia where . . . he was a miner, drover, tutor, cook and whaler . . . Henry Lawson wrote a poem, 'The Passing of Scotty', published in the *Bulletin*, to mark his death. [Wilde *et al.* 1985:496]

What does Scotty's biography tell us about writers of the *Bulletin*? Perhaps that they were not all city journalists, and neither were they all true native-born sons of the soil living in bark huts as the legend would have it. It also suggests a particular kind of interrelationship between outback, provincial town and city that the *Bulletin* was able to exploit or create; there were lines of communication through the magazine backwards and forwards between the metropolis and the regions that enabled someone like Scotty to be part of the same community as Henry Lawson (even if that community existed only in the pages of the magazine). Perhaps it also suggests links across the colonies, and the 'new' societies: the United States and Australia.

In 'Bohemians and the bush', chapter 6 of *Inventing Australia* (1981), White identifies as a distinct group the writers and artists who came to prominence in the 1880s and 1890s. He locates what he calls a 'cultural generation gap' between the new writers and artists and their predecessors, whom they saw as representing the cultural Establishment. Archibald, Stephens, Lawson and others were all in their twenties and thirties when the *Bulletin* began. This newer generation was more likely to be Australian-born, less likely to see 'culture' as something imported into the colonies as a civilizing influence. Many of them would have followed the path described above, moving from country to city (and possibly back again). The most important point in identifying this newly emergent group of writers and artists is that they represent a newly-professionalized intelligentsia. As White (1981:88) says, 'Science, art and literature were increasingly the province of full-time professionals rather than educated amateurs or men of letters with a private income'. Arguments concerning the function of local intelligentsias are discussed in chapter 1.

'Professionalism' here means a changed relationship between writer and market-place, writer and Establishment. One of the crucial points about the *Bulletin*, of course, was that it paid its contributors. There were careers to be pursued in journalism, literature and painting in ways that had not been widespread before. Not least among the contemporary developments enabling such professionalization was the growth of the popular press and popular literary forms, with the possibility of newspapers and books produced for mass consumption.

The career of a key figure such as Henry Lawson is exemplary, despite his dismal rendition of what might be involved in 'Pursuing Literature in Australia', the title of one of his essays (Cantrell 1977:4–12). Indeed this document is precisely the plaint of a professional writer. We could also examine the careers of J. F. Archibald and A. G. Stephens, or a contemporary such as the painter Tom Roberts, in these terms (for Roberts, see Clark & Whitelaw 1985).

One example of this professionalization among the intelligentsia is 'the discourse on journalism' in the *Bulletin*, its constant preoccupation with journalism itself (Lawson 1983:182–6). The *Bulletin* writers spoke of the 'new journalism'—meaning a mass-readership paper, critical of the Establishment and not self-interested, 'newsy' and not moralistic. This sense of their own newness and difference can be linked to the various journalistic and editorial practices in the magazine. Attention to the qualities of the magazine's writing overall might in turn affect how we understand its literary content. Archibald, Sylvia Lawson (1983:181) argues, did not have a narrow sense of literature: ' "literary" qualities lay everywhere to hand—and literary craft was no less present in the sharpening of a two-line comment than in the choice of Henry Lawson's better lines of balladry'. At least for the practising journalists, literature was not in another realm altogether from the realm of work (writing and editing) and this influenced the styles, subject-matter and presentation of writing. Lawson (1983:154–81) provides an important discussion of the relation between the *Bulletin*'s general editorial practice and its literary products.

The remarks above serve to demonstrate how simplifying it would be to attempt to understand the literature of the period just in terms of so many individual texts or individual authors. What was published and how it was read depended first on the sheer availability of papers like the *Bulletin*; the forms that writing would be liable to take, and the subject-matter it would consider, would then be influenced by the styles of the particular paper or magazine and the kinds of audience it sought to address. The magazine might help to define or create an audience for the literary writing, an audience that did not otherwise exist (so those who wrote for the *Bulletin* could address a much wider audience, conceived in different terms, than that addressed by more narrowly focused 'literary' journals). Further, a magazine might operate to forge a set of links between writers, to establish something like a 'school', and thus to encourage literary debate, literary self-consciousness, and group or local identifications.

We can analyse the writers and editors who congregated around the *Bulletin* in terms of Williams's notion of cultural formation. First, there were groups with more or less *formal membership* requirements, in particular the bohemian clubs like the Dawn and Dusk Club (White 1981:93–6). Though the *Bulletin* does not belong to any of these groups, they were certainly part of its milieu. Second, we might see the magazine in some respects as a *collective public manifestation*. Finally, we can identify a clear sense of *group identification* among these individuals, as professional, *Australian* writers and intellectuals. They were conscious of links between themselves rather than of links to any established group in society, a kind of self-conscious marginal status which, as White demonstrates, could take the form of urban bohemianism.

White's argument is part of an ongoing debate among historians and literary critics about the status and origins of the 'bush ethos', the celebration of certain values and attitudes, such as those of independence, anti-authoritarianism and mateship, associated with life in the bush. Most notably Ward in *The Australian Legend* (1958) has argued that this ethos arose among the nomadic workers in the bush but came to influence values and attitudes and the national image throughout society. In the 1880s and 1890s, Ward argues, the ethos finally emerged into expression in formal literature, in the works of Lawson, Paterson, and others associated with the *Bulletin*. Other writers, criticizing Ward, have reversed his picture and seen the bush ethos as a specifically urban product, the projection onto the bush of the values and attitudes—or the desires and anxieties—of urban intellectuals influenced by current literary and intellectual fashions and by the social effects of depression in the city (White 1981; Davison 1982). The *variety* of styles and themes in 1890s writing, beyond those dealing merely with the bush, has also been pointed out. The quotation given earlier from Stewart's article might suggest to us that we have a complex set of interrelations between country and city; between different intellectual and cultural traditions; and between individual experience and group identification. These complex interrelations suggest why we want to be as specific as possible about the role particular media played and about such questions as 'who was writing for whom'.

In sum, then, the writers of the *Bulletin* were drawn largely from a newly-professionalized local intelligentsia. Certain radical, bohemian, democratic, nationalist, or even simply professional attitudes drew them together into what can be described as a cultural formation. The cultural and political activities of this formation can be seen, in Williams's terms, as in some respects *alternative* (for example, offering alternative publishing outlets) and in other respects as *oppositional* (often republican and anti-imperialist in sentiment).

The readers

There was of course quite another layer of contributors to the *Bulletin*—not only those like Scotty the Wrinkler on the fringes of the professional writing world, but also the host of anonymous or near anonymous readers who responded to the *Bulletin*'s invitation and sent in newspaper clippings, anecdotes, yarns, verse sketches, bush recipes and so on. And, very importantly, these reader-contributors were acknowledged in the 'Correspondence' column (even if only to be rejected!). As Sylvia Lawson (1983:164-5) writes: 'They responded to the weekly invitation, were answered, and so turned, even if for only three lines worth of fame, from readers into writers—which was enough to get the paper sold to their cousins and neighbours'. This unique sort of audience participation created the illusion of dissolving the distance between readers and writers and was very important in the magazine's ability to sustain mass circulation and appeal to its audience as an Australian magazine. It printed bits and pieces from all over the nation but simply by publishing them together in the same pages presented them as if they shared something in addressing the common, local ('Australian') interests of the readership.

The booms of the 1880s created a new audience for books, painting, theatre and music. Education Acts were passed in the colonies from 1866 through to the 1880s (Clark 1978:271-92). Widespread public education meant mass literacy, creating by the 1890s a new, mass market for fiction and newspapers. Overseas, popular writers had sales as large as Lawson and Banjo Paterson; nevertheless their books did achieve the first mass sales of any locally-written, locally-produced books. It was this new, increasingly literate, popular audience—in city, town and bush, in workshop, home and office—that the *Bulletin* tapped and formed into a readership that was given some identity in the magazine as a continent-wide, Australian audience.

The *textual* means of addressing and creating an audience are what is important for our case study of the magazine in its 'institutional' function. We have already noted the way the magazine announced itself as a national Australian newspaper; from the very outset it addressed its readers as Australians. What this means for the *Bulletin*, at least in its editorial pages, can be seen by examining the specific language employed, its value system, and the oppositions through which it operates. The *Bulletin* characteristically addresses its readers' common Australian interests (to which it gives a populist and democratic meaning): 'This is not altogether Queenland's affair. It concerns, very intimately, the welfare of all Australia'. It can even appeal to these common Australian interests at a level beyond political factionalism: 'Labourer and Capitalist, Socialist and Single-taxer, Protectionist and Freetrader, Unionist and Non-Unionist, Prohibitionist and Publican—everybody, rich and poor, drunk or sober, not in the swim, should march to the ballot-box with an equal mind' (*Bulletin*, 15 April 1893:4).

Of course not all parts of the *Bulletin* address the reader in such a directly political manner. We might consider the 'Personal Items' column. It is very difficult to describe its contents—a mixture of titbits about people in the news, some political, some literary. There are curiosities:

Of the first eight names on the Melbourne Register of the Commercial Bank of Australia, five are those of clergymen.

Ibsen's latest psychological novel, 'The Master Builder', is advertised in a Melbourne daily as 'The Masher Builder'.

It is averred that Justice Boucaut, of Adelaide (S.A.), refused to take a K.C.M.G. when in England, because the Colonial Office would not forego the fees. His reverence for money is proved by the fact that, on Wednesday, April 5, he gave a man five years' gaol for stealing £2 6s.

LONDON, April 3. Colonel North's famous grey hound Fullerton, which was missing, has been found. The dog was wandering, footsore, at Oxtend, Surrey.
[*Bulletin*, 15 April 1893:8]

What can be said about this odd collection of items? The column clearly expects its readers to have a lively interest in public life, and an interest not marked by inferiority or deference towards the rich and famous. The tone established is probably just as important as any information conveyed. The column seems always on the lookout for signs of hypocrisy, philistinism, incongruity and pomposity. Its response is comic, knowing, potentially outraged, and readers are invited to join in the game. Wherever they may be, in Sydney or the bush, in pages like this one the magazine locates readers in the 'chattering promenade of the famous and notorious' (Lawson 1983:112). The items are collected from all over the colonies and from overseas—like the last-quoted, which might be seen to have a pointed appeal to 'colonials' or rather 'Australians' (this one, of course, reproduced in the *Bulletin* for its comic value but also carrying a political point). Again, the magazine is negotiating the relationship between colony and metropolis.

Even on the 'Personal Items' page, then, we can see the *Bulletin* working to create a community of readers, a readership defined in populist, democratic and nationalist terms (and crossing certain social and political boundaries). There has been a good deal of argument over the years about the politics involved here—How socialist was the *Bulletin*? Was it merely bourgeois liberal? (see Cantrell 1977:intro.; McQueen 1970; Lawson 1983:150-4). Without entering into this argument, perhaps we can say that, liberal or socialist, the *Bulletin*'s most significant social and cultural effects—its nationalism—lay in its relationship to its readership rather than in any explicit political platform it upheld. In establishing and sustaining a community of readers, a print community, the magazine for a certain period offered readers and writers the opportunity to participate in an imagined community, nationally conceived and frequently oppositional in its values (see Milner 1985 and discussion of Anderson 1983 in previous chapters). This was important for the literary writers because, however briefly, the magazine 'created the sense of a national literary club' (Stewart 1988:189).

We have to be careful not to become too folksy and reduce the magazine to a simple reflectionist or totalizing model (which might claim that the *Bulletin* expressed the spirit of the times or was the voice of the people). Again, it should be stressed that the implied audience was white, European and nearly always male. No doubt the actual audience was widely differentiated and there were specific audiences for particular parts of the magazine; some read it just for entertainment, some for political comment, some for gossip. The bohemians, the city lawyers, the shearers, the 'family circle', probably all read the paper very much in their own way. Though its wide range of materials did appeal to a wide range of readers we certainly should not imagine all, or even many, readers liking everything they saw in its pages. There were also Australians thoroughly offended by the *Bulletin*'s style and comment (and they were none the less Australian for rejecting the *Bulletin* polemic). It is worth keeping in mind too that part of the *Bulletin*'s success might have been due to its willingness to be controversial and to affront its audience.

The point is not that it was the voice of the people or the expression of the nation's spirit. What we have, rather, is a complex set of social and material circumstances involving, for example, an emergent group of journalists and writers; a newly formed mass readership; a political arena centred on arguments about the nation; new technologies enabling cheaper, better printing of newspapers; the absence of locally produced books; and changes in the dominant notions of literature all feeding into explanations of the *Bulletin*'s format, its attitudes and its successes.

To conclude, the *Bulletin* addressed a diverse and widespread audience. Not only was a new mass audience emerging, the magazine actively constituted its own (*implied*) audience in its styles of writing and address. Though broadly anti-Establishment and frequently polemical it did not see its audience in sectional terms but rather as the nation, the national interest, the people, categories which were nevertheless race and gender specific. The address to the readership occurred as much in the entertainment as in the political pages—indeed it might not always be easy to tell these apart. The *Bulletin* also drew into its pages material (and readers) from rural and provincial areas. It printed provincial matters side by side with reports of political and cultural events overseas. A community of readers existed at least in the pages of the magazine, a community defined locally and nationally, but not as parochial, exiled or colonial.

Journalism and realism

Our final task is to bring the various points raised so far to bear on our understanding of the literary writing in the *Bulletin*. H. M. Green

(1961:723) described the characteristic writing in the magazine as 'concise, pithy, "pointed", epigrammatic at times, self-conscious, rather artificial and full of mannerisms; disjointed but remarkably effective and entertaining'. This accords well with the examples we have examined. It is in the context of such writing, on a whole range of topics, that we can imagine the short stories, prose sketches and verse being read. This might lead us to expect stories and verse in relatively colloquial language, short rather than long, easy of access rather than highly formal or literary. We might also expect comic stories, possibly with a distinct local focus, and entertaining pieces directed towards a popular non-specialist audience. At the same time we would be looking for qualities which represent some of the shared values and attitudes of the professionals and intellectuals, for we also have writers here speaking to other writers. So together with the comedy and popular appeal we might expect to find in the writing a consciousness of doing something new, something local and Australian, something like the establishment of a national literature.

Of course not all of these qualities will be present everywhere, but they do provide a rough indication of the qualities of the stories and verse in the *Bulletin*. One exception is lyric poetry, which tended to be given an elevated role and was thus felt to be properly formal or sentimental. (Readers who enjoyed the irreverent editorials and vernacular tall stories could also, of course, feel properly sentimental or uplifted by lyric verse!)

We can identify two earlier critical approaches to the *Bulletin* writers which we might call, respectively, the nationalist and the universalist. The former, in ways suggested above, sees these writers as representing the first national school of Australian literature, and sees their writings as the first authentic expression of an Australian ethos or character, the first truly indigenous literary expression of Australia (see, for example, Inglis Moore 1971; Serle 1973; and discussion of radical nationalists in earlier chapters). We have suggested that the writers do need to be seen as constituting a school or cultural formation, though we would not define this in terms of their 'authentic Australianness'. The universalist approach, by contrast, stresses the writers' individual sensibilities and their treatment of universal themes. This approach is not particularly interested in literary schools, sociopolitical movements such as nationalism, or the material context of writing. It prefers to isolate literary texts and to analyse their 'literary' qualities, and it comes up with a quite different set of values for the appreciation of the writing (see, for example, Wilkes 1962; Heseltine 1962; and Docker 1984, who provides a polemical discussion of both critical tendencies). We have already suggested the limits of such an approach, focusing as it does just on individual authors and individual texts.

More recent approaches have stressed the influence on the *Bulletin* (and associated) writers of contemporary English, American and European artistic and political movements, and emphasized the writers' urban intellectual milieu (White 1981; Davison 1982; Jarvis 1981). These more recent writings have been very fruitful in establishing an intellectual and social context, though at times they have a rather dismissive tone, as if to identify an overseas or metropolitan influence were to discount the writing's local or national significance. Also they have not always given great attention to the details of the writing itself. However it will already be clear that we have drawn extensively on this work for our own purposes.

We can proceed directly by examining a *Bulletin* short story, an item from 15 April 1893: 'Blind Love' by E. D. (most likely Edward Dyson). The story as originally presented was squashed in between advertisements for blood purifier, hair tonic and corsets—not the sort of thing found on the literary pages of today's newspapers in their weekly arts supplements, where the advertisements are for books, art shows, operas and similar high cultural events.

What can we say about such a story, if we can even call it a 'story'? How do the points made so far about the *Bulletin*, its readers and its writers help us to read the story? We can probably begin by saying that if we were reading the story looking for evidence either of a national(ist) school of writers or of literary qualities we would not find a great deal to say at all! But there are significant things to be said about it, both to explain its particular form and how stories in the *Bulletin* worked for their readers.

We might first note that in the array of materials that the magazine printed, such a story does not stand out from other types of writing— there are similarities of tone, style, even subject-matter. The same sort of qualities are valued throughout, indeed the news items are often like tall stories, the stories often like yarns or documentaries. The clear distinctions between news and literature or between journalistic and literary writing, which we would expect in today's periodicals, are not so evident here—though of course there were still appropriate rhetorics for essay, fiction and verse writing respectively. We can recall earlier points about the predominance of journalists among the literary writers and Sylvia Lawson's remark about Archibald ('literary qualities lay everywhere to hand'). The sense of literature operating in the *Bulletin* was not the same as the narrower sense of the literary which has grown up for example in the institutions of academic literary criticism until recently; the *Penguin New Literary History of Australia* (Hergenhan 1988) shows a much broader approach.

Jarvis (1983) has examined the *Bulletin* in order to determine the magazine's taste in fiction. He sums up his findings by saying: 'The

Blind Love.

(For The Bulletin.)

Have you seen a man mutilated by a circular saw —seen a remorseless, shimmering steel cut its way into his writhing body, heard the one awful cry of its victim, and the horrible grinding of the teeth on quick bones? Heaven spare me such another experience.

Pescot was still living when we dragged him over the stained sawdust. We dared not lift him. The remains spoke. I can give that ghastly, mangled heap no other name. He rolled his eyes and seemed to select me from amongst the horror-stricken crowd, and I knelt by his side.

"What can I do, Dave?"

He touched me with a torn hand, and his voice was firmer than my own.

"My wife! This will break her heart. Let her down gently, won't you?"

I assured him I would do my best, and muttered vain words of hope and courage.

We made no attempt to help him. It was hopeless to endeavour to stem that crimson tide or to bind those terrible lacerations, and so we simply waited for the end, awed and silent, and watched the red circle extending in the saw-dust around him.

"Break it gently to her, old man."

His voice was still strong, but when he spoke again it had grown suddenly weak: "Do what you can for her!" he gasped.

Several times he repeated this plea before he died, and his last, faint, whispered words were just distinguishable, as I bent down to his lips:—

"My poor wife!"

Pescot had lived in a two-roomed log-hut, about a mile from the mill, at the cross-roads. I galloped on ahead of the boys with their sad burden to fulfil my painful trust.

Mrs. Pescot did not answer my knock. I pushed open the door and entered. A carelessly-folded note lay upon the table. It read:—

Dave Pescot,—This is to let you know I hav clered out with T.M. I got sick of this miserible live. Don't think you can catch us cause you can't.—Yours truly, Milly.

"Yours truly, Milly," was Mrs. Pescot. T.M. was the loafing, horse-thieving son of Milky Morgan, the publican.

Melb.   E. D.

Bulletin wanted a concise realistic tale, dramatically told and with an unexpected ending'. 'Blind Love' fits this formula very neatly. In a number of articles Jarvis has also traced the importance of contemporary European theories of realism in influencing the course of writing and its reception in Australia (Jarvis 1981; 1983). We can pick out a few points very briefly. First, realism was understood in opposition to other contemporary forms of writing, in particular popular forms of romance fiction (Giles 1988) and 'high culture' forms such as neo-classicism and Pre-Raphaelitism (Jarvis 1981). We might imagine the *Bulletin* writers taking up arms (or pens) against the types of writing advertised in another journal from the 1860s:

Historical romances and Legendary Narratives of the old country, will be mingled with Tales of Venture and Daring in the new; Nouvellettes, whose scenes will be laid in every nation, varied occasionally with Fairy Stories for the Young; and Parlour Pastimes for boys and girls. [Quoted in Webby 1981:22]

In contrast, realism was seen to be contemporary and local in its concerns. For these reasons it was also seen to be the appropriate art form for a new society—vigorous, egalitarian and actual. Thus realism could be associated with nationalist and democratic politics. Art, at least prose fiction, was to be socially useful and critical, and speak to the real conditions of ordinary people. We might note here the similarities between the role of journalism in the *Bulletin*, as described above, and the role of fiction. Both brought with them a sense of novelty, a new task and a new audience, and both the new journalism and realist fiction were liable to be accused of sensationalism. Of course, what looked realistic in art to readers of the nineteenth century might look quite otherwise to readers today, and the *Bulletin* stories are full of what now looks like the stock-in-trade of Victorian magazine fiction: melodrama, seduction of innocents, redemptions, and so on (Lawson 1983:178-81). Also, someone such as literary editor A. G. Stephens could bring to the *Bulletin* a more elevated sense of the mission of literature while recognizing the local importance, if not the high literary quality, of what he called 'the easy, detached, realistic sketch' (quoted in Lawson 1983:172).

What we most commonly find in the stories in the *Bulletin* is a form somewhere between the conventional magazine story, with an overt plot and a moral or sentimental resolution, and the journalistic sketch, a prose sketch of a typical incident or character. The form of the fictional sketch, or sketch-like story, became particularly attractive to those writers looking for local and popular effects and concerned with realism (see Kiernan 1980).

To bring these points to bear on 'Blind Love': the story is presented like an anecdote or sketch, though with some passages of identifiably literary effects ('to stem that crimson tide' for example). The story's very abruptness and brevity seem to say that this is not just a pretty made-up piece of fiction but a slice of real life. Of course it is very much a stage-managed piece of fiction, but here there is no pious moral to be grasped. The surprise ending makes the point that real life is not like the writers of romance fiction pretend it is! One aspect of the story's realism is precisely its internal critique of sentimental romance fiction. Perhaps the overtly literary language and sentimentality of the first part of the story just softens us up for the anti-romantic ending, where a different sort of colloquial language breaks through. While it might not be great literature according to anyone's definition, 'Blind Love' is not merely naive or primitive writing; it is calculated to achieve certain effects, it makes skilful use of a particular narrative voice and diction, and it knows its audience.

There is no overtly Australian view in the story. What is significant is that its local audience and Australian setting are simply assumed—'local colour' is not added just for the sake of it. The story might also be seen, in its last two paragraphs, to belong to a genre of humorous writing that is usually set in the bush or country town. Some of Lawson's and Steele Rudd's stories would be the best known examples. Perhaps 'Blind Love' works on two levels, for some readers predominantly in terms of the familiarity of its setting and character types, for others in terms of the familiarity of its kind of humour ('the loafing, horse-thieving son of Milky Morgan, the publican'). On one level the narrator of the story speaks not just about the ordinary workers but as one of them; the story implies a socially equal community of narrator, characters and readers. At the same time, on a somewhat different level, we can read the story as addressed to a 'knowing' audience, and it is not without a hint of irony at the expense of the innocent bushman. Perhaps it also contains just the type of misogynist joke to go down well among the predominantly male urban professionals. Certainly the story's anti-sentimentality, its style and tone, *and* its misogyny, fit well with writing going on elsewhere in the *Bulletin* of this era.

These points about 'Blind Love' could be tested by comparison with the other stories and sketches in this issue of the *Bulletin*. The variety of settings and subject-matter as well as the similarities should be noted; this issue includes one of Lawson's Mitchell sketches and a range of other short stories by such authors as Scotty the Wrinkler, Mulga Ned, and The Dipsomaniac. What, we might also ask, are the connotations of these pseudonyms?

This commentary on one particular issue of the *Bulletin* has addressed matters specific to that magazine, but at the same time a more general interest in literary periodical publication as one key aspect of the social institution of literature has been in play. By looking closely at one moment of the *Bulletin* we have seen how, in the nineteenth century, magazines and newspapers had a major part in the publication of local writing and the establishment of a locally directed literary culture. The diversity of the *Bulletin*, its writers and its readers, also provides a caution against totalizing historical approaches and literary criticism's isolation of individual texts and authors. The existence of the *Bulletin* as a newspaper, with a wide range of political, social and entertainment concerns, was crucial to its literary success. So was the apparent equality between editors, writers and readers (however much this was only a fiction acted out in the pages of the magazine). It allowed the publication of writing whose style and subject-matter had generally not been published in book form. Further, because of their context, the fiction and verse published in the *Bulletin* present themselves to readers as Australian writing (if not always as Australian literature).

Most important, this analysis of the *Bulletin* sets up not merely a description of diversity but a way of explaining and interpreting the complexity of literary production and circulation. To return to some of our earliest questions, we can see clearly that the magazine is not simply a neutral container for literary material. It plays specific roles for specific groups of writers and readers. No magazine can offer equal access to all writers and readers and each establishes its own implicit set of options and constraints. The very format of the magazine sets up relations between its various parts which influence how the literature is written and read.

Every magazine establishes a set of relations with an audience, both an actual readership and an implied readership, defined by its tones, styles, subject-matter, format, price and distribution. The readership of a magazine might be only half a dozen, but the implied readership might be something as encompassing as 'all thinking Australians' or 'all white (male) Australians'. The reader becomes a *Bulletin* reader, though he or she might just as well become a *Sydney Morning Herald* or a *Boomerang* reader at another time. In short, the literary magazine provides us with a good illustration of how reading as well as writing is a structured or mediated activity, dependent, in this case, on the function of the magazine in a given print economy, a print economy itself determined by its colonial situation.

Meanjin: a twentieth-century comparison

In the twentieth century magazines and periodicals have continued to play a major role in debates about national culture, and new forms of literary periodical publication have emerged. The 1920s and 1930s saw the rise of 'little magazines'. These publications were usually produced by and for a small group of intellectuals and artists, and they often carried a manifesto associated with a minority or oppositional aesthetic/political platform. Such details might indicate a further specialization or marginalization of the intellectual in society. The little magazines, which often only lasted for a few issues, carried such titles as *Vision, Stream, Masses, Strife* and, in the 1940s, *Angry Penguins*. No complete history of these journals has been written but further details can be found in Bennett (1981), Tregenza (1964), Wilde et al. (1985).

One of the most significant journals since the 1940s has been *Meanjin*, and we can use its history to illustrate further our remarks about literary periodicals in general. Our focus shifts, then, from a mass circulation, commercial, weekly news magazine which published some literary material, to a small circulation literary/cultural periodical. In some ways the early *Bulletin* bears closer comparison, as a weekly news magazine, with the present *Bulletin* or even, as popular entertainment, with a publication such as the *Australasian Post*, though neither comparison is especially helpful in explaining the magazine's cultural significance. Perhaps the point is that the early *Bulletin*'s diversity can no longer be found between one set of covers. We turn to *Meanjin* for our comparison because, as did the *Bulletin*, it represents important new developments in literary publication and in cultural debates. *Meanjin* also exemplifies the most familiar kind of post-war Australian literary periodical.

Meanjin began in Brisbane as a slim poetry magazine but rapidly became the most important vehicle for the expression of a liberal-humanist, 'cultural' nationalism, a position it held at least until the late 1960s (for further details see Docker 1974 and Strahan 1984). It also became one of the most important vehicles for the publication of Australian poetry and fiction, articles about Australian literature and culture, and discussions of overseas writing (discussions directed towards the local audience). The print economy no doubt operated rather differently in the 1940s from its operation in the 1880s and 1890s (Kiernan 1988; Nile & Walker 1988). A larger number of Australian writers, novelists in particular, were being published and distributed in Australia, and their works were often written with an Australian audience in mind. There were more books and more readers around, but there were still very few outlets for the periodical publication of poetry and fiction or for the reviewing and discussion of Australian writing apart from the weekly Red Page of the *Bulletin* (Bennett 1981:148–57). And there was very little Australian literature taught in the universities or schools. The newspapers reviewed a book or two at the weekends; non-literary magazines like the *Women's Weekly* published some stories (though the syndication of overseas material was seen to be a problem).

There was, then, an active enough commercial press (Walsh 1988); but this did not meet the needs of those we might call the 'literary intellectuals'. Writers and intellectuals had again taken up the task of putting names and texts together into what they saw as a tradition of

Australian literature, connecting past and present (Rowse 1978:176-84). *Southerly*, from the English Association of the University of Sydney, had commenced in 1939 with academic articles and reviews on Australian literature. But there was nothing like the American *Partisan Review* or the English 'higher journalism', dedicated to Australian writing and the national culture or concerned with entering overseas intellectual debates from an Australian perspective.

In such a context *Meanjin*'s cultural interests quickly became a cultural politics. It was not only dedicated to local writing and local writers, but saw this as an essential ingredient of a strong national culture. In this respect the magazine might be seen to share some of the aspirations of the early *Bulletin*. But just as the print economy had changed, so too (to return to our earlier agenda of questions) we find *Meanjin* to be a very different sort of 'text': a different conception of the literary can be perceived, and the literature published plays a different role in the magazine; the writers and editors comprise a different kind of cultural formation; and the magazine addresses or implies a different audience.

From its editorials to its poetry and reviews, and even its (few) advertisements, *Meanjin* covers a narrower range than did the early *Bulletin*. The magazine's style and tone is more decorous and more ordered. It operates almost wholly within the boundaries of the literary or the 'world of ideas'. Its contents are restricted to editorials on cultural and intellectual matters, poetry and short fiction (not as short as in the *Bulletin*), and articles and reviews related to Australian culture and history. There are also fairly firm lines separating the genres of writing in the magazine. Its non-fiction writing might be described as more journalistic than formal academic prose, but more academic than daily journalism. Its literary material is unmistakably 'literary' and is given prominence among the other contents, though the context the magazine establishes for its reading is not just that of the literary, in some universal sense, but that of Australian literature or the national culture. In short (though the point is not a simple one), *Meanjin* is a 'literary' magazine in a way that the *Bulletin* was not; a literary *quarterly* which suggests that we are to regard its contents rather differently. One further aspect of *Meanjin*'s role as a literary magazine is that its very format announces that, unlike the *Bulletin* and the newspapers, it is not a commercial enterprise.

Within the boundaries that it accepted, indeed claimed, *Meanjin* publishes a wide and diverse selection of material, as Lynne Strahan has shown. Founder and long-time editor C. B. Christesen (1951) repeatedly described the magazine as an 'open forum'. Of course this openness had its limits; in the editorial just mentioned Christesen also describes as his ideal a magazine whose 'natural political direction would be "democratic left of centre"', so the open forum had a certain leaning. What *Meanjin* describes is a distinct liberal intellectual sphere, defined above all by its discourse on culture. (For further discussion of the magazine's liberalism see Docker 1974; Rowse 1978; cf. Carter 1985.) And just as we argued that the *Bulletin* in part created its audience, so we can argue that *Meanjin* not only addressed this intellectual sphere but actively constituted it as a print community. A particular cultural sphere is defined not just by the magazine's explicit editorial statements, but by its overall selection and arrangement of contents, and by its implied audience.

Meanjin has never served as the platform for any sharply defined school of aesthetics or politics. This editorial openness is not just the result of a generous spirit but of the position from which the magazine speaks (at least until the 1970s); how it positioned itself *vis-à-vis* its competition in the contemporary print economy. *Meanjin* located itself in or as the mainstream of Australian culture, and was anti-sectarian in the interests of the perceived totality of this culture. Its pages do not merely present so many poems or so many stories in a neutral manner. Instead, in its selection and arrangement of material, the magazine is in effect working to define Australian literature. Our reading, then, is structured and mediated by its immediate context in the magazine, and less immediately by the magazine's reputation. The fiction and verse address themselves to readers as Australian literature in the fullest sense.

To turn to the question of the *writers*: though there are very few Australian writers from the 1940s to the 1960s who did not publish in *Meanjin*, it is nevertheless possible to identify a particular cultural formation most closely associated with the magazine. This formation comprises a group of liberal intellectuals, some journalists, some from the book trade, teachers, and some professional writers. There were also a significant number of academics, a development which suggests a shift in the nature (and sites) of intellectual professionalization since the 1890s. Some of the most important debates about the place of Australian literature in the universities appeared in *Meanjin* (see Hope et al. 1954). However the magazine was never much like a specialist academic journal, and this is largely because of the nature of its interest in Australian literature and culture. The academics and others would write in *Meanjin* more often as general readers or informed observers of Australian culture than in their disciplinary or specialist roles. What defines this cultural formation of liberal intellectuals, then, is their sense of responsibility to Australian culture, and this could absorb a relatively wide range of political and artistic opinion (see Buckridge 1988; and Milner 1988, who compares the radical intellectuals associated with the *Bulletin* and *Meanjin* respectively).

The implied *Meanjin* audience could be defined in a number of ways. The writing is usually addressed to the general reader, so specialist academic language is avoided. There might also be an appeal to some large imagined constituency such as 'every thinking Australian'. Clearly, however, the readership is conceived differently from the *Bulletin* audience described earlier. It is narrower (without negative connotations) and more specialized, requiring a relatively high level of what we might call literary competency. The magazine is addressed to a specialist audience after all; not as specialized as an academic discipline or an avant-garde, but nevertheless a delimited literary-competent and culturally-committed group. We make this point in part against the magazine's own sense of its role as cultural 'spokesperson', and place it more narrowly within a particular liberal intellectual sphere, as already suggested.

As case studies or areas of inquiry, both *Meanjin* and the *Bulletin* demonstrate how periodicals can generate a detailed sense of the functioning of the print economy at a given time. They can begin to tell us about relations between intellectuals and other sectors of society; about the formation of intellectual movements and cultural politics; about relations between literary and other discourses; and about the constitution of the reading public(s). The literary periodical is of particular importance in the context of a new literature. In Australia periodicals have acted as a crucial means of publication in the absence, until relatively recently, of a strong local publishing industry and a strong interest in Australian literature in, for example, secondary and tertiary education. The presence of these institutional developments in the late twentieth century will not necessarily mean the end of literary periodicals so much as changes in the way they present themselves; they might become more or less specialized, more or less literary. Some interesting recent examples are *Scripsi* (1982–) and the *Age Monthly Review* (1981–).

Literary periodicals, we have seen, do not merely act as neutral containers for the placement of literature. In their selections and arrangements of material, their favoured styles and characteristic tones, and in such things as their layout, price and distribution, they actively produce writing, not merely present it. Each periodical offers a set of options and a set of constraints to the writer, and to the reader. Each periodical in a sense invents its own readership (the implied audience) and its own cultural/intellectual sphere, though of course these will not all be equally effective or influential in a given period. The literary periodical, as one part of the larger literary institution comprising publishers, teachers, reviewers, critics, editors and so on, is one of the key sites of mediation between writer and reader. The effects of literary periodicals will be influencing our reading, more than likely, whether or not we read the periodicals themselves!

Note that we have not said much about the role of individual editors. The functions of selection, editing drafts and arranging contents are fairly obvious, and clearly an editor's personal biases will have a role to play. All this can be assumed. Our attention has been rather on the institutional aspects of periodicals, that is, not on individual roles but on the textual effects and social and cultural networks within which magazines function and which are in a sense beyond the 'control' of any single individual.

The print economy, of course, continues to change and so do periodicals. There are now numerous places where poetry and fiction might be published, and *Meanjin*'s role in this area is perhaps less significant in the overall market-place than it once was. Some mass commercial magazines, such as *Woman's Day*, continue to publish fiction, though none has a role comparable to the early *Bulletin*'s; they are generally not considered important in 'Australian literature' though they certainly have been in the past (Walsh 1988). *Meanjin* today might be compared with a journal such as *Scripsi*, which gives a greater prominence to the publication of poetry and fiction than to local cultural politics. The bulk of Australia's established literary magazines—*Southerly, Meanjin, Overland, Quadrant, Westerly, Island Magazine*—are still characterized by their degree of political identification with Australian culture. Though there are some marked differences in political alignment they occupy a similar arena of cultural debate. For *Scripsi*, however, many of the issues which drive the other magazines are relatively unimportant. Its editors are not in the habit of making overt statements of editorial intent or taking a political stance in relation to the national culture. The magazine prints Australian writing alongside English, American and European writing without any apparent sense of disjunction or 'importation'; its reviews also suggest a sense of the simultaneity of modern writing wherever it occurs. This is certainly not exclusive of a strong commitment to local writing, but it does suggest rather different ways of relating this writing to writing from elsewhere, a different sense of the responsibility of intellectuals to a national culture (if these terms are still appropriate) and, finally, a different kind of intervention in the contemporary print economy.

The literary periodical is only one of the ways in which writing comes before the reader, and in which we can see that both writing and reading are structured or mediated activities. To return to one of our initial remarks, a study of literature which concentrates merely on individual texts and individual authors will over-simplify the literature's social contexts and effects; its relations to other, political, aesthetic and intellectual, discourses; and the degree to which its very textual details are determined by the options and constraints offered by available forms of publication and dissemination. A study of literature in its institutional aspects, of the sort that we have been attempting to exemplify, will also prevent the totalizing and idealizing accounts of national culture and national character which we addressed in our introduction. We hope to have provided a useful set of approaches for the study of literary periodicals themselves, but this is only one possible area of enquiry. Other writers have begun to examine such areas as literary education, criticism as an institution, state patronage, and the book trade itself (see Buckridge 1988; Brett 1988; Gillen 1988). Our wider horizon has been to suggest ways of understanding literature as a distinct, but not privileged, form of social practice.

Glossary

Audience/implied audience A term to mean not so much the actual readers but the 'imagined', 'ideal' or *implied* reader in a text. We can ask: To whom is this addressed? What values or attitudes are assumed?

Cultural formation The term comes from Raymond Williams (1981). It refers to the variety of groups, schools or associations in which artists and intellectuals operate within society. Williams defines cultural formations according to their internal organization (formal membership, collective public manifestation, group identification) and external relations to existing institutions (as specialist, alternative or oppositional).

Print community/imagined community Terms that derive from Benedict Anderson (1983). Anderson defines 'the nation' as 'an imagined political community'. He argues that the establishment of such an 'imagined community' occurs significantly through print and through local rather than imported book and newspaper publication. Such material can create a 'print community' of readers and writers which produces national and regional identifications.

Print economy A term that can be used to define the broad and varied, but delimited, field of printed matter in the context of which literature is produced and consumed ('economy' is not used in a monetary sense).

CHAPTER EIGHT

NATIONALITY AND AUSTRALIAN LITERATURE

Patrick Buckridge

Chapter 7 has indicated some possibilities for studying Australian literature in 'institutional' terms. It is also important to develop appropriate styles of formal literary analysis, and it is the task of this chapter to provide some examples of these.

On the whole, but with some interesting exceptions, literary criticism in Australia has tended to be essentialist (see the glossary at the end of this chapter) in its assumptions about Australia, and about literature, treating both entities not as historical constructs, but as self-defining objects. Literary criticism of this kind is not generally very useful for our purposes, though of course the body of Australian criticism, historically considered, contains a great deal of information and insight that we would not want to be without. What are needed are ways of talking about Australian writing which are informed by an awareness of cultural construction as a primary process, even at the level of the individual text.

There have been some promising possibilities opened up in recent years. Richard White's book *Inventing Australia* (1981), with its emphasis on the construction of successive images of Australia, provides a more useful starting-point than traditional criticism, but the generality of his observations on Australian culture does not translate directly or easily into ways of dealing with individual texts. One book that does engage with them is Graeme Turner's *National Fictions* (1986), in which the theoretical perspectives of structuralism and semiotics are brought to bear upon a range of Australian literary and film narratives. The same approach, somewhat trimmed of its theoretical trappings, is used in his more recent study, with John Fiske and Bob Hodge, of some representative sites of Australian popular culture, *Myths of Oz* (1987).

The approach adopted in this chapter is a rhetorical approach, and it parallels the structuralist/semiotic approach of Turner and his collaborators in a number of ways: for example, it shares its major theoretical premise, concerning the constructed-ness of cultural meanings in general, and even some of its methods of applied textual analysis. It differs from it chiefly in its deliberate retention, even revival, of an older, more traditional technical vocabulary, and perhaps too in its greater emphasis on the persuasive functions of writing and other forms of cultural expression and communication.

The Marxist critic Terry Eagleton (1981) has argued that because of its inbuilt assumption that speech and writing are first and foremost persuasive activities, rhetorical criticism—originally the ancient study of oratory—provides an appropriate model for a politically aware mode of literary analysis, alert to the irreducible *politicality* of constructions such as 'the nation', 'Australia' and 'literature'. In its original form, rhetorical criticism aimed to show how a given text had used, combined, or modified conventional themes (topoi) and figures of speech (tropes) from a pre-existing inventory of such items. A contemporary rhetorical criticism might well adopt somewhat similar procedures, not using all the technical terms of the ancient rhetoricians of course, but recognizing and taking account of the ways in which writers constantly and deliberately make use of pre-existing models and examples.

Part of what we shall be looking at in our discussions of Australian writing will be the development, within and across particular historical moments, of a 'rhetoric of nationality', where 'rhetoric' refers both to strategies of persuasion and to an inventory of conventional tropes and topoi. A simple rhetorical method of analysis is illustrated by applying it to some literary texts chosen from a variety of forms and periods.

National culture in the 1890s

Since some attention was given to the writing of the 1890s in the preceding chapter, it may be useful to look first at some examples from that same crucial period in Australia's history, partly in order to demonstrate the compatibility of the proposed rhetorical approach to individual texts with the institutional approach to writing adopted there. There is another reason for doing so as well. This is that although John Docker has argued cogently against any over-unified conception of the 1890s—whether it be one of celebratory nationalism or gloomy nostalgia (Docker 1984:110–40)—there can be no doubt that nationality, in association with a variety of political interests and in various cultural forms, was a central preoccupation of the period. An interest in the national theme was by no means restricted to the radical republicans associated with the *Bulletin* and the *Worker* newspapers;

it was equally characteristic of more moderate political groupings (Blackton 1961), for whom nationality was more a matter of wattle, waratahs and lyre-bird motifs in cast-iron lace than of mateship, campfires and booze (White 1981:73-5). Moreover, it had been as actively pursued in other arts as it had in literature, especially in landscape painting—most notably the work of the Heidelberg school from the early 1880s—and also, more obscurely, in the musical compositions of Isaac Nathan and Henry Tate (White 1981:73; Covell 1967:68-9, 103-7).

How might a rhetorical approach to the writing of the 1890s work, and what might it contribute to our understanding of the period? We shall postpone the second part of the question until we have completed a couple of worked examples of rhetorical analysis to demonstrate an answer to the first.

What literary and other cultural texts of the period often seem to do is to epitomize Australia using certain carefully selected and highly condensed icons of Australianness and in doing so to suggest, demonstrate or assert the largely inexpressible virtue of the icon, and hence (by a metonymy which is often implicit) of 'Australia'.

A useful example is a poem called 'The Austral Light' by Harry Morant (better known as 'The Breaker'). It is reprinted in Leon Cantrell's anthology *Writing of the 1890s* (1977) but, as we shall be saying quite a lot about it, it will be convenient to quote it in full:

THE AUSTRAL LIGHT

We were standing by the fireside at the pub one wintry night
Drinking grog and 'pitching fairies' while the lengthening hours took flight,
And a stranger there was present, one who seemed quite city-bred—
There was little showed about him to denote him 'mulga-fed'.

For he wore a four-inch collar, tucked-up pants, and boots of tan—
You might take him for a new-chum, or a Sydney city man—
But in spite of cuff or collar, Lord! he gave himself away
When he cut and rubbed a pipeful and had filled his coloured clay:

For he never asked for matches—although in that boozing band
There was more than one man standing with a matchbox in his hand;
And I knew him for a bushman 'spite his tailor-made attire
As I saw him stoop and fossick for a fire-stick from the fire.

And that mode of weed-ignition to my memory brought back
Long nights when nags were hobbled on a far North-western track;
Recalled campfires in the timber, when the stars shone big and bright,
And we learned the matchless virtues of a glowing gidgee light.

And I thought of piney sand-ridges—and somehow I could swear
That this tailor-made young johnny had at one time been 'out there'.
And as he blew the white ash from the tapering, glowing coal,
Faith! my heart went out towards him for a kindred country soul.

[Morant in Cantrell 1977:142]

There are a number of things to notice about this rather engaging piece of nostalgia. The first is that the nostalgia itself is constructed, not simply evoked. The poem might be seen as an example of 'illocutionary' utterance, a term used in 'speech-act theory' to denote statements (like 'I now pronounce you husband and wife') which *do* what they say; in somewhat similar fashion, this poem both describes the arousal of the speaker's nostalgia for the bush (by means of the bushman's 'mode of weed-ignition') and offers to arouse the reader's nostalgia by the same means.

Whether or not Morant expected the bulk of his original readership to know what a 'gidgee light' was, the poem implies a collective male reader whose own bush culture enables him, like the speaker, to recognize a whole ethos in an isolated action which is supposed to signify nothing to the excluded majority, just as the stranger's 'light' conveys nothing to the rest of the 'boozing band' in the pub. Their slick, 'city-bred' slang ('pitching fairies', 'mulga-fed', 'tailor-made young johnny') contrasts with the laconic punning of 'matchless virtues' and the gentle self-mockery of 'mode of weed-ignition'. The crucial paradox, though, is that in suggesting qualitative differences between town and country, the poem also purports to reveal a close relationship between them. The stranger, after all, is to all appearances a townsman himself, apparently at his ease among the drinkers; and the speaker, too, is at home in that company, though he is able to detect the bush ethos and identify with it.

The poem, that is, constructs a relationship between the bush and the town which is only superficially one of polar opposition (cf. Williams 1973:289–98). At another level, the relationship is one of inward essence (the spirit or 'soul' of the outback) to outward existence (the 'body' of everyday life), as it might be found anywhere between Sydney and the bush. And just as the speaker discovers the bushman, well but not perfectly disguised in his city 'clobber', so the implied reader of this poem (and of many others like it) discovers the bush in a secret part of his own city-bred consciousness, and values it as the abiding reality of Australian society.

The rhetoric by which Morant's poem achieves these effects of fantasized identification is not, of course, something achieved by this poem alone. It can function as it does partly because other cultural texts were working in much the same way at about the same time. We need only think of Paterson's office-bound lawyer with his jealously guarded 'visions of Clancy' for a very similar instance (Cantrell 1977:140). Similarly, the whole carefully staged verse 'debate' in the *Bulletin* in the 1890s between (among others) Paterson and Lawson (Cantrell 1977:152–9) about the predominance of pleasure or suffering in the bush, repeats the pattern in a collective mode: the vehement disagreements about the quality of bush life, however sincerely felt on both sides, none the less function as a sort of cover for the deeper agreed truth about the bush, namely the quality of moral and spiritual character it breeds.

Read as an exercise in the 'rhetoric of epitome', Paterson's 'Clancy of the Overflow' is a somewhat subtler piece of writing than Morant's poem. The text actively makes Clancy into an epitome, not by reporting what he did or does, but by describing and framing him in a certain way. The first two stanzas will give some indication of the processes at work:

> I had written him a letter which I had, for want of better
> Knowledge, sent to where I knew him down the Lachlan, years ago,
> He was shearing when I knew him, so I sent the letter to him,
> Just 'on spec', addressed as follows, 'Clancy, of the Overflow'.
>
> And an answer came directed in a writing unexpected,
> (And I think the same was written with a thumb-nail dipped in tar)
> 'Twas his shearing mate who wrote it, and *verbatim* I will quote it:
> 'Clancy's gone to Queensland droving, and we don't know where he are.'
>
> [Paterson in Cantrell 1977:140]

Clancy's essential characteristic, from the poet's point of view, is his elusiveness, not only geographically but also epistemologically, that is, as an object of knowledge. At any given time his precise whereabouts are unknown, his exact occupation is uncertain. He exists for the poet (whose own phrases—'on spec', 'verbatim'—categorize him immediately as the city lawyer he is) in an ideal outback of nostalgic memory. The 'thumbnail dipped in tar' and the grammatical error ('where he are' is hardly bush slang) are both mildly comic *naivetes* rather than the stuff of legend; they are the incongruities that result from confusing everyday life with the ideal realm of myth and epitome. And their rhetorical function, arguably, is to act as a kind of decoy for the 'real-life' cynicism that would otherwise erode the credibility of the bush ideal Clancy embodies, and to enforce at least a temporary assent to its implicit claim to the representation of ultimate moral and social values.

As in 'The Austral Light', the idea of the bush is validated dialectically, by being presented as the synthesis of an opposition between the mixed realities of the bush and the city. In both poems, furthermore, the ideal is first 'objectified'—given a particular material representation in the external world—then 'subjectified'—made an integral part of the speaker's mental and imaginative equipment; and in this way even more thoroughly democratized as a resource potentially available to all, even while the poems affirm, on another level, its special and exclusive nature.

In both these examples, then, we can point to comparable rhetorical strategies for securing the value of an emergent cultural icon of Australia—that of the bushman. This is in itself an epitome of the nation, but the two poems take the epitomizing impulse a stage further, invoking ever more condensed synecdoches—the mode of weed-ignition, and the digital mode of bush writing—though, as suggested in the commentaries, the latter is more obliquely related to the central epitome of the bushman than the former, where the relation is quite direct, both rhetorically and logically. In general terms, however, the epitome is used in a strongly *celebratory* fashion in both poems, and of course in many others like them. Another set of examples will suggest somewhat different, more analytical functions for some of these same national epitomes.

In one of Lawson's best-known short stories, 'The Union Buries Its Dead', the Australian bush icons abound, but in a heavily ironic context:

> I left out the wattle—because it wasn't there. I also neglected to mention the heart-broken old mate with his grizzled head bowed and great pearly drops streaming down his rugged cheeks. He was absent—he was probably 'Out Back'. For similar reasons I omitted reference to the 'suspicious' moisture in the eyes of a bearded bush ruffian named Bill. Bill failed to turn up, and the only moisture was that which was induced by the heat. I left out the 'sad Australian sunset' because the sun was not going down at the time. The burial took place exactly at mid-day.
> [Lawson in Cantrell 1977:129-30]

Critical debate will no doubt continue as to the exact force and direction of Lawson's irony in this and similar stories, some of the debate revolving around the degree to which the narrator himself is taken to be an implicit target of irony. An awareness of contemporaneous Australian epitomes might suggest, for example, that the narrator's posture of anti-sentimental detachment in the passage just quoted (like the intemperate anti-clericalism he displays in the paragraph that precedes it) is itself a version of a then recognized national characteristic, in this case taciturnity and understatement. The story might even be taken, following Brian Matthews's (1976) argument on the 'radical uncertainty' in Lawson's fiction, as an exploration of the writer's problem of perceiving the limits of a given cultural frame, and being unable to speak outside it.

A different, perhaps less reflexive instance of the critical use of national epitomes is Barbara Baynton's story 'Squeaker's Mate' (Cantrell 1977:216-30) from her *Bush Studies* (1902). Here the epitome in question (very literally 'in question') is the one announced in the title, the 'mate'. The story describes the domestic aftermath of an accident in which a working woman, Mary, is crippled by a falling tree and loses her hold over her good-for-nothing sexual partner Squeaker, who takes advantage of her bedridden and paralysed state to recruit a younger partner or 'mate', whom he flaunts in the presence of the older woman. The story ends with the new mate barely escaping with her life, the silent fury of the old one, and with Squeaker being attacked (possibly killed) by the old mate's loyal dog. The term 'mate' has a key function in the story. On the one hand it points outside the text to the masculine code of mateship, one of the most popular epitomes of the national character; on the other it shifts around inside the text, providing what amounts to an implicit ethical commentary on the quality of human relationships so designated in the story, and in particular on the relative quality of people's relations with one another as compared with animals. The code of mateship, externally considered, is not directly or unambiguously attacked, but it is used as the iconic linchpin for a trenchant analysis of sexual and social relationships in the bush.

It is important to stress the range of social meanings being articulated around these national epitomes in the writing of the 1890s. It is equally important, though, to notice the relatively uniform rhetoric within which these differences are made evident. It might even be argued that in accommodating a diversity of meanings that rhetoric generates and regulates the diversity of meanings by focusing social and political debates on one or another of the currently popular national icons—mateship, the bush, unionism, laconic humour, language, realism—and weaving these into cultural discourses of very different tendencies.

Literature in the 1890s was conditioned by specific social and cultural factors, and there is no reason to doubt that the epitomizing rhetoric worked then in ways that were distinctive to the period. It is true none the less not only that certain particular icons of Australianness survived in literature and elsewhere long after the 1890s, but also that, more generally, an epitomizing rhetoric has continued to inform a great deal of Australian writing ever since. The main interest is not so much with the validity of this as a general proposition as with the analytical purchase it provides on a range of literary texts. However, it might be wise to mention some general qualifications to this thesis.

There is no reason to suppose either that the rhetoric of epitomes originated in the 1890s or that it was distinctive to Australian culture. Similar patterns may have developed in comparable national cultures. The concern is emphatically not with locating distinctive features or patterns in Australian culture but with examining how the *notion* of national distinctiveness has been deployed within it. None the less certain features of the 1890s context would have been especially conducive to an intensification of a rhetoric of just that epitomizing kind: for example, the popularity of the short-story form in this period, especially in the *Bulletin*, and the consequent drive towards thematic condensation and the kinds of literary device that facilitated it. In the decorative and plastic arts the vogue for what Richard White calls 'nativist fetishes'—furniture and fittings designed as wattle, lyre-birds and the like—is clearly congruent with a literary interest in national epitomes. The nativist vogue itself can probably be given a political dimension in that the very absence of a distinct political identity or of a revolutionary history created a patriotic focus on objects rather than events or broad principles as the national symbols readiest to hand. It may even be appropriate to invoke the residue of the convict culture to account for writers' and artists' interest in secret codes and barely accessible signs of community.

This discussion seems to lead towards the very old-fashioned conclusion that the writing of the 1890s formed a crucial foundation for the literary themes and practices of subsequent generations of writers; and at least as far as the theme of nationality in our literature is concerned, the conclusion may well be a sound one. It remains to be seen, though, how useful an approach by way of national epitomes will be for the literature of later periods.

Fiction and nationality: the 1930s and 1940s

In many novels of the 1930s and 1940s single icons of Australianness perform key functions in the narrative, often acting as points of thematic intersection or articulation, and also at times as points of ideological disturbance or contradiction. In Miles Franklin's prize-winning novel *All That Swagger* (1936), the image of 'swagger' functions in both these ways. The novel is a pioneering chronicle, following the fortunes of the Irish Delacy family through four generations of rural life in the Monaro district of New South Wales. Franklin draws frequent analogies between the family's history and the nation's, and it is clear that the novel's 'ideological project' includes an extended demonstration of the virtues of that pioneering society, virtues that needed to be revived in the period of cultural stagnation and political inertia in which she was writing (Modjeska 1981:178–9). 'Swagger' is used with significant frequency throughout the novel, primarily to denote the quality of masculine social and sexual irresponsibility which a mature nation can no longer afford to tolerate. As Drusilla Modjeska (1981:178) puts it, 'while the men swagger, it is the women who are the true progenitors of the legendary Australia and who lay the foundations, holding the pioneering society together'. But the social connotations of the term are more diverse and contradictory than her remark suggests.

The swagger, for example, also signifies the jaunty insolence of the rebellious Irish immigrants in their new relation to the English ruling class; it stands for the liberating process by which (thanks largely to horse-riding!) European 'bumpkins' could attain to the habits of the gentry, and the social rigidities of the Old World be rendered more flexible (Franklin [1936] 1947:99). And while it certainly typifies Robert, the carefree seducer of the second generation, and his wild companions ([1936] 1947:92, 102, 135, 147), it also expresses the aristocratic nonchalance of Mrs McHugh ([1936] 1947:134) and the fighting spirit of Della Delacy (1947:238). The upper-class swagger of the English gentleman is even placed on the same historical continuum as the spirit of Anzac:

> The Australian, whether clerk or yokel, had taken the English county gentleman as his pattern and lifted his wife out of the furrow for ever: and though using beasts in some places was an incredible feat, it was accomplished with the swagger brewed by such feats and grew into the psychology of a people to blossom later in daring exploits in South Africa or on Gallipoli. [Franklin (1936) 1947:240]

What emerges from this brief analysis is, on the one hand, the enormous task of rhetorical synthesis that this simple epitome is being called upon to perform and, on the other, the multiple ideological contradictions and uncertainties it exposes as it attempts to do so.

A much later example, neatly comparable with Franklin's hefty novel, is 'The Quality of Sprawl' by the contemporary poet Les Murray (1983:28–9). Like Franklin, he seeks to epitomize Australian nationality in the image of a (male) physical posture (McDougall 1987). There are many other examples of Australian literary texts in which particular physical gestures or mannerisms are invested with the same kinds of national meanings as Franklin's swagger or Murray's sprawl. Certainly there will be no difficulty in thinking of examples from Australian film and television, where the visual nature of the media puts a premium on signifiers of this kind. A moment's reflection will suggest how crucial the recognizably Australian gesture is to the popular appeal and commercial success, both here and overseas, of actors such as Paul Hogan and Bryan Brown.

One of the best-known instances of this in the literary field is the figure of the 'cultural cringe'. When the critic Arthur Phillips ([1950] 1958) first coined this phrase in an essay published in 1950, he clearly had a definite posture in mind, that of an obsequious member of the Anglophile middle class physically cringing in willing self-abasement before some personification of assumed British cultural superiority. The 'postural' image is only the starting point for a concise history of habits of reading and writing, in the course of which Phillips draws a distinction between the 'cringe direct' and the 'cringe inverted'. This blurs the original figure considerably, but the image of the cringe remains very much at the centre of Phillips's analysis and probably accounts for much of its rhetorical force and lasting influence. Like the more recent notion of the 'tall poppy syndrome', and like Franklin's 'swagger', it serves as a national epitome whose function seems to be not so much to unify national consciousness as to provoke or incite debate and discussion around the question of national identity.

But the figure of the cringe, striking innovation though it was, did not spring fully-formed from Phillips's brain in 1950. It has its own history, and not only as the always-implicit antithesis to the proudly upright stance of the bushmen and diggers of nationalist iconography, both republican and imperial (White 1981:63–84). It was also, arguably, a variation on the figure of the cringing convict, which some writers in the 1920s and 1930s regarded as an important key to understanding the so-called 'Australian psyche'. In our own day Robert Hughes has expressed a similar view in his narrative of Australia's convict past, *The Fatal Shore* (1987).

Novels and stories about the convict period have been a constant presence in Australian writing, from the convict narratives of the early years of the colony, through the classic mid-nineteenth-century epics of Marcus Clarke and James Tucker, the short stories of 'Price Warung' in the 1890s, the historical novels of Brian Penton and Eleanor Dark in the 1930s, to the recent fiction of Thomas Keneally and Jessica Anderson. The idea of the convict, however, has carried very different social and political meanings at different times. In the 1890s, for instance, Price Warung's tales of life under a brutally repressive system emphasized the inhumanity of the system itself, and were related to political struggles against what was seen, especially by the more anti-imperialist groups, as a system of colonial domination that was still oppressive to the true Australian spirit. In Brian Penton's novel *Landtakers* ([1934] 1972), by contrast, the psychology of the convict is a central concern. Through the characters Joe Gursey and Emma Surface, the 'convict mentality' emerges as an epitome of the contradictory structure of Australian radical consciousness, its smouldering resentment of authority and hierarchy continually undermined by a broken-spirited inability to act against them.

Hardly surprisingly, this diagnosis of Australia's problems in the 1930s did not meet with unanimous agreement, and Penton (a popular Sydney columnist at the time) was attacked by cultural nationalists such as P. R. Stephensen, Miles Franklin and Xavier Herbert, who saw 'convict literature' generally, and Penton's novel in particular, as being outside any true Australian literary tradition, and as accepting and perpetuating an essentially English attitude to Australia as a dumping-ground for its social refuse (Barnes 1969:232–6). There were also other positions taken on 'convictism' and national identity during this same period. In 1938, for example, the poet Rex Ingamells, best known for his leadership of the Jindyworobaks, a group of poets who devoted their energies to developing a genuinely 'native' Australian culture, wrote a manifesto for the group in which he argued (*pace* Stephensen, whom Ingamells greatly admired) that the convict tradition should be embraced, together with Aboriginal folklore and mythology, as a valuable part of Australia's cultural heritage. Both sources contained a record of that directly experienced contact between the individual and the physical environment that stood at the heart of the Jindyworobaks' cultural enterprise (Barnes 1969:260–2).

Since the previous decade the figure of the 'old lag' had functioned in another way as well, as a symbol of resistance to Establishment respectability. During the 1920s in particular, it became fashionable for bohemian artists and journalists in Sydney and Melbourne to boast of the 'convict stain' in their ancestry (Nelson 1984:498–9). In short, the image of the convict was functioning in very complex, even contradictory ways in Australian culture at this time: it became a focus, a point of intersection and intensification, for current debates about, for example, the British colonial connection (past and present), people's relationship to the land, Australia's much-discussed national character and the future of nationalist politics in Australia. In a novel like Penton's *Landtakers* ([1934] 1972), these various issues are articulated (not merely expressed, but linked together) by an image of the convict as an Australian epitome. This image performs a crucial narrative function within the novel itself: the 'convict mentality' emerges, gradually but inexorably, as the buried truth about colonial Australian society in general, its free settlers, politicians and bureaucrats as well as the real emancipists and escapees in the community.

Equally important, though, are the implications and effects— politically and culturally—which radiate out from the rhetorical claim this novel, and a few others like it, seemed to be making: the epitomizing claim that 'here, in the figure of the convict, is what Australia is like'. Stephensen, we saw, took up the claim in one way, Ingamells in another; for the culture generally it continued for some years to stand as a claim against which similar or rival syntheses and epitomes of the nation could define and test themselves.

All through the fiction of the 1930s and 1940s the search for national epitomes was pursued vigorously, in ways which are revealing both about the fiction itself and about the culture that was producing it. It has been generally agreed that the traumatic historical sequence of Depression and war engendered a revival of the radical nationalism of the 1890s, as an actively utopian response to the crisis of national self-confidence (White 1981:144–54). A valuable complement to this utopian emphasis is provided by Ian Reid's 1979 study of Australian and New Zealand fiction in the Great Depression, which stresses rather the analytical work done on the social and economic problems of the Depression in the fiction of Prichard, Stead, Davison, Vance Palmer and other Australian writers, and in the work of Sargeson and others in New Zealand. An initial focus on the use of epitomes in these writings (as well as providing a practically useful way in to the texts) has the advantage of bringing these two perspectives on the crisis together: epitomes in literature tend to be both utopian and analytical—perhaps because in the very act of epitomizing Australia in some traditional image the writer necessarily becomes aware of the ways in which the image no longer quite fits the facts. In the reflective context of the literary text the epitome's very explicitness and singularity of image raise doubts about its value as an epitome.

The familiar figure of the bushman appears in numerous poems, stories and short literary forms published in *Bulletin*, *Smith's Weekly* and other magazines and newspapers during this period. So too mateship, that old shibboleth which even in the 1890s, in stories such as 'The Union Buries Its Dead' and 'Squeaker's Mate', had been used to focus serious doubts and questions about contemporary national values, re-emerges in the 1930s and later as a key term in an ongoing critique of gender relations in Australian society. In the Hergenhan (1988) anthology, stories written thirty years apart, Gavin Casey's classic 'Short-Shift Saturday' (1942) and Thelma Forshaw's 'The Mateship Syndrome' (1967), both adopt the same epitome—mateship—from the national inventory, and use it to articulate different areas of social concern with the continuing, systematic oppression of working-class women in Australia. Casey's story, set in a small mining town, uses mateship to make precise and intricate connections between the slowly disintegrative effects of exploited labour on marital relations, and on male relations in and off the workplace. Interestingly, the mateship topos also allows a relieving glance at the parallel development of closer and more durable relations between married women: as individuals usually change rather than die under the pressure of oppressive working conditions and routines, so too their relationships change. New, unfamiliar and, from a patriarchal viewpoint, somewhat threatening forms of human intimacy begin to emerge.

Forshaw's story uses the mateship epitome in a similar fashion, as a way of articulating a range of social issues as themes: the male culture of booze and violence, men's emotional exploitation of women, male fear and contempt for 'intellectual' women, and the blocks to effective ambition-formation in the Australian workforce, both male and female. Most of these issues are fairly specific preoccupations of the late 1950s and early 1960s; they are central, for example, in the work of Elizabeth Harrower, especially her last novel, *The Watch Tower* ([1966] 1977), just as the uneasy apprehension about imminent transformations in the moral order detectable in Casey's story is very much a preoccupation of the 1930s (see, for example, the novels of Brian Penton, the early Christina Stead, and the stories of Vance Palmer). As time passes national agendas change, but the inventory of types, topoi, and epitomes which Australian writers have turned to as ways of addressing and interrelating the issues that arise on successive national agendas has not changed at anything like the same rate.

Other epitomes also work to focus, rather than evade, contentious issues in Australian life. Linguistic epitomes, for example, figure prominently in the work of many writers in this and other periods.

The fiction of Dal Stivens, especially his early short stories and his first novel *Jimmy Brockett* ([1951] 1983) show how Australian language idioms (including the Great Australian Adjective) can be actively complicit with that blurring of ethical boundaries which many other writers of the period also feared as the worst consequence of Depression and war (Stivens 1969). Stivens's work provides a particularly clear instance of the tendency for 'serious writers' to use traditional national epitomes as instruments with which to question rather than merely affirm, received national values.

In the work of several other novelists of the same period, however, national icons function similarly. Eleanor Dark and Marjorie Barnard both use the well-established image of 'sunshine' in the same problematizing way, and in their immensely popular *Come In, Spinner* ([1951] 1966), Dymphna Cusack and Florence James make gambling, the national pastime, into a complex emblem of Australia's historical experience and post-war prospects. The novels of Frank Hardy foreground the same 'national obsession' (Williams 1987); so, for that matter, does Peter Carey's prize-winning novel *Oscar and Lucinda* (1988). The national inventory, it might be suggested, has remained remarkably unaffected by the Bicentennial.

Realism and Australian literature: Patrick White

We have spoken thus far about various *images* and *practices* as epitomes of the nation; and because epitomes tend, almost by definition, to be simple and concrete things rather than complex abstractions, it is hardly surprising that the historical examples that come most readily to mind are of the former type. Mateship, by no means a simple notion, is perhaps the obvious exception here, but there is at least one other instance of an abstract and complex concept which has figured, no doubt within narrower, more intellectual contexts, as an Australian epitome in much the same way as those already discussed. This is the concept of 'realism'.

Like so many of the epitomizing ideas and images in Australian culture, this one too has its origins in the 1880s and 1890s, in the reading habits and writing practices associated with the *Bulletin*, as described in chapter 7. Australian realism in this period was clearly a crucial instance of nation-formation at the level of systematic literary practices; and yet, as with that other complex epitome, mateship, Australian realism seems to have been always already in dispute. If, as Jarvis contends, this writing shows a significant sharing of fictional subjects and methods, there is none the less ample evidence of equally significant disagreements, even among the *Bulletin* writers themselves, as to general principles and rationales for a national realism.

The fierce controversy over the work of Zola is an early example of the tendency for literary realism, as an idea, to provoke cultural and political debate (Jarvis 1983). A somewhat different and slightly later example is the famous 'bush debate', involving Paterson, Lawson and others in the *Bulletin* in the 1890s. The ostensible point at issue in this extended verse debate was simply whether 'modern poets' (Paterson *et al.*) who purported to describe the beauties of the bush were describing it 'realistically', that is, 'accurately' (Nesbitt 1971). Lawson denied it, but Paterson's response, to the effect that his ideal evocations captured the 'real essence' of the bush, effectively broached the larger question of what constitutes 'realistic' representation anyway—surface accuracy or deeper truth? That philosophical question bulks large in debates about the nature and effects of literary realism in Europe, the United States and Australia for most of the twentieth century.

The history of realism in Australian literature is yet to be written, a fact which is not altogether surprising despite the prominent place the concept always seems to have occupied on the national cultural agenda. For an adequate history would need to include, and to interrelate, accounts of the different forms of writing that have gone by the name of realism at various times as well as the changes both in the intellectual content of the term itself and of its sub-variants (social realism, socialist realism, psychological realism, critical realism), and in its shifting political (especially nationalist) alignments and ideological affiliations.

One of the most useful discussions of realism in literature is Raymond Williams's entry in *Keywords* (1976), in which he draws a distinction between realism as 'lifelike representation' and realism as a 'general attitude'. This distinction, which corresponds roughly to the two main meanings we assign to the word 'realistic' in ordinary speech, namely 'true to life' and 'practical', has often been ignored in recent discussions of realism in literature and film, which have restricted its meaning to the first of these, in effect equating realism with 'plausibility' (MacCabe 1974; Belsey 1980). The 'classic realist text', said to be characterized by narrative closure and a lack of interpretative ambiguity, is associated with conservative politics in these discussions, while the 'interrogative text' by contrast (usually modernist films or novels) is characterized by its challenging openness and ambiguity, and associated with progressive or revolutionary politics.

Literary–critical debates on Australian realism have been conducted largely around questions of *whose* realism or what *kind* of realism should be given the national imprimatur, rather than whether realism as such should be put to the question. The history of these debates has been touched on more fully elsewhere (Carter, 1985; Buckridge

1988), though no complete account of them yet exists. On the political left, especially, realism became closely identified with the Australian tradition in literature, the tradition of the 1890s and of the social realists of the 1930s and 1940s. Many of its main apologists—Katharine Susannah Prichard, Jean Devanny, Jack Beasley, Judah Waten, Jack Blake, Bernard Smith, for example—were Communist Party members themselves, and many of the writers they endorsed as both genuinely Australian and true realists were also on the political left. But realism, psychological rather than social, has also been invoked by critics from the political centre and on the right in support of certain writers and against others. Patrick White has been an interesting historical object of criticism in this respect, falling foul of leftist critics like Beasley and Prichard in the late 1950s and early 1960s for his sins against the canons of social realism (Buckridge 1988:206-8), and offending critics on the right, such as Leonie Kramer and Adrian Mitchell in the 1970s and 1980s, for his departure from the norms of psychological realism (Kramer 1973; 1981).

Of greater immediate interest than the critical debates, however, are the ways in which conceptions of literary realism, and of its close relation to the idea of the nation, have fed into and modified the literary practice of Australian writers, especially novelists. Patrick White, for example, in a well-known essay, 'The prodigal son', written for the journal *Australian Letters* in 1958, made it clear that the stylistic idiosyncrasies of *The Tree of Man* (1955) and *Voss* (1958) were in part a direct counter-practice to what White perceived as the dominant realist tradition in Australian fiction. His novels, with their heightened awareness of the textures and surfaces of language—'the rocks and sticks of words'—embody his determination, announced in 'The prodigal son', to change the course of the Australian novel tradition from one of 'dreary, dun-coloured . . . journalistic realism (White 1958). Equally clearly, the frequency with which freaks, perverts, eccentrics and other non-typical characters occupy central positions in his novels expresses his rejection of that 'celebration of the average' which he saw as implicit in Australian realism and in the national culture as a whole in the 1950s.

It is worth bearing in mind, though, that the outsiders that inhabit so much of White's fiction have a more positive general significance as well. Many of them evoke or directly represent the plight of the visionary artist in an uncomprehending and unappreciative society, and because of this they embody, to a degree, White's own early hopes for a critical, prophetic role in Australian society, one in which (as he put it in the 'Prodigal son' essay) he would be 'helping to people a barely inhabited country with a race possessed of understanding' (White 1958:158). Such sentiments tend to situate White squarely within the Australian realist tradition as defined by a general attitude of commitment to telling the truth about contemporary social life in Australia, and it was on this basis that some of the 'soft-line' leftist critics, like Mona Brand and Jack Blake, hailed White as a realist writer despite his stylistic and formal eccentricities (Buckridge 1988:207). It could be argued, for example, with reference to *Riders in the Chariot* (1961), that so long as the abstruse symbolism and the unflattering depictions of Australian workers could be seen as integral aspects of a wide-ranging critique of social relations and consciousness in Australia (and there is no doubt that they can be so seen) the novel could be defended as a work of realism, and hence assimilated to the Australian canon. It remains important, none the less, to remember the sense in which White's writing in the 1950s was written *against* Australian realism as he perceived it. In *Riders in the Chariot*, to stay with the same example, the natural, everyday perspective on ordinary realities is repeatedly disrupted and displaced by presenting them through the eyes and minds of a group of four extraordinary characters (and one fairly extraordinary narrator) whose perceptions and interpretations of reality are skewed away from the normal, largely by way of a 'wise-foolish' literal-mindedness about people and things. Characters like Mary Hare and Ruth Godbold and also, in more sophisticated ways, Alf Dubbo and Mordecai Himmelfarb, demonstrate the spiritually transcendent possibilities of ignoring, or consciously refusing, the ordinary duplicities and received hierarchies of everyday existence. This probing, destabilizing naïvety appears in a multitude of guises in the novel: thematically, in the implied comparisons between 'crimes' as incommensurable, in conventional moral terms, as Nazi genocide and Australian philistinism (Kiernan 1980:69–70); and stylistically, in the significant frequency with which the semi-comic figure of zeugma is used. At the same time, and as part of the same process, certain national shibboleths—notably mateship, sympathy for the underdog, and the 'fair go'—are exposed as fraudulent by placing them in juxtaposition with the much more *literal* instantiation of those ideals provided by the 'un-Australian' and/or 'un-male' quartet of visionary simpletons.

The general point is that Patrick White, like all of the writers looked at in part III of this book, uses established epitomes of Australia's national identity as fictional tools for a critical analysis of Australian society. In this sense, his practice differs less than he himself probably imagined at the time of 'The prodigal son', from the practice of many of the more critical novelists of the 1930s and 1940s—Penton, Dark and Barnard Eldershaw, for instance. Where he differs from most of them is perhaps in the degree of his disenchantment with the traditional Australian icons, and also in his early use of realism itself as a national icon requiring critical scrutiny and ironic distancing; and producing, in this way, a systematically 'anti-realist' set of writing practices within the broad tradition of Australian realism.

Recent fiction: present prospects

It has not been the purpose of this chapter to provide a history of the 'national theme' in Australian writing. The aim has been rather to exemplify, by selective illustration, a way of approaching the theme *rhetorically*, as something that is written into literary texts by way of a relatively constant inventory of tropes, formulas and epitomes, any one of which might serve to articulate the question of nationality with other political, social, philosophical or psychological themes. One or more of these articulated themes, rather than the national theme itself, will often be the main focus of interest in a given text, yet the marginal presence of the latter may inflect the whole in subtle but sometimes important ways.

The fiction of more recent years has shown no marked tendency to abandon the established inventory. There are large and important differences between Henry Lawson's 'The Drover's Wife' and Murray Bail's story of the same name, but the fact that their point of reference is the same is significant too. Contemporary writers such as David Ireland, Thea Astley, David Malouf, Roger MacDonald, Eric Rolls, Gerald Murnane and Peter Carey have also had frequent recourse to the established repository of national tropes and epitomes, sometimes (as in Ireland and Carey) as a source of satiric targets, and sometimes (as in Malouf and MacDonald on the First World War) as focal points of qualified affirmation.

There are also, however, some directions in contemporary writing which seem to be veering away from the traditional inventory. Not surprisingly, those in question here include ethnic and Aboriginal writers, whose command of different cultural mythologies makes the construction of alternative inventories for writing in Australia a feasible project; though even these writers find the traditional tropes useful for mapping the interface between their own minority cultures and that of the dominant Anglo-Australians.

Women's writing is a somewhat more ambiguous case. It is a moot point whether writers such as Helen Garner, Elizabeth Jolley, Kate Grenville and Jessica Anderson, for example, might best be described as engaging in the construction of a 'counter-inventory' to the heavily masculinist tropes and epitomes of the nation already in place (compiling, in effect, a register of figures, voices and values more consistently relevant to women's interest in, and experience of, Australian society and history); or as continuing to draw on the resources of the established inventory for figures with which to conduct new critiques and different valorizations of the national culture (Walker 1983; Schaffer 1988). There are elements of both strategies in the field of contemporary women's writing in Australia, and to the extent that the implied alternative represents a dilemma in the cultural politics of gender, it is perhaps worth seeing it as a variant of recent debates in the international women's movement around concepts like the 'mother tongue' and 'women's language' (Whitlock 1985).

Writing which is strongly regional in orientation also shows signs of an attempt to extend and modify, if not abandon, the national inventory. David Malouf and Thea Astley are both interesting cases in point here. Both have described themselves as 'Queensland writers' rather than Australian writers (Astley 1976; Davidson 1983); but more importantly their fiction provides evidence not just of a preoccupation with distinctive Queensland settings and social types, but also—this is especially true of Malouf (Buckridge 1986)—of a sustained and systematic compilation of motifs, tropes and epitomes of 'Queenslandish-ness'! In story collections like Astley's *Hunting the Wild Pineapple* (1979) and Malouf's *Antipodes* (1985), the inventory of regional epitomes—mangoes, flying foxes, pineapples, 'oddballs', timelessness—is functioning not merely as a list of imputed Queensland characteristics, but as a source of rhetorical figures with which to explore and articulate a range of moral and psychological themes, not entirely displacing the master-inventory of Australian epitomes in this function, but operating as an important supplement to it.

A conclusion

The argument pursued with some relentlessness throughout this chapter is that much Australian writing since the 1890s has dealt with the theme of nationality, often critically, by means of an allusive rhetoric of Australian epitomes. Since no comparisons with other national literatures have been drawn, no assumptions can safely be made about the distinctiveness or otherwise of this process, though some speculative suggestions were offered as to why the epitomizing habit became popular with writers in the 1890s. There is thus no sound basis here for arguing that Australian literature, as a historical institution, has been more conservative than other national literatures in the particular sense of remaining closely connected (whether by affirmation, negation, or simply recognition) to a relatively stable core of postulates concerning the national character. It does seem possible, however, that further investigation, including some rigorous cross-national comparisons, might show that to be the case.

In any event, it is questionable whether the term 'conservative' is appropriate, since an essential part of the argument proposed here is that by conceptualizing 'national reference' in literature in terms of multiple epitomes rather than a single mythic narrative (Turner 1986:19, 50–1), the possibility, indeed the actuality, of writers radically questioning and resisting the politics and ideologies of nationalism from within the system of national reference is explicitly recognized. The national inventory, in other words, would seem on the whole to have functioned rhetorically more than ideologically, though to the degree that it has functioned not just as a rhetoric but also as an agenda, its ideological effect cannot be entirely discounted, and recent moves to displace or modify it may be well-founded. It remains true, none the less, that it has sponsored an exceptionally wide variety of literary forms, styles and themes in the course of the last hundred years—from Katharine Susannah Prichard to Patrick White, from 'Breaker' Morant to A. D. Hope—so that to say that Australian writers seem to have been extremely interested in what it means to be Australian is not to detract from the value and variety of what they have written.

Glossary

Articulation Not a rhetorical term, but one that is useful for rhetorical criticism because it defines the kinds of literary strategies for constructing meaning that such criticism envisages, namely, strategies which involve working mainly within existing inventories of terms and themes, achieving innovation not by inspiration out of nowhere, but by making new connections. It is to be understood in its two senses of 'expression' and 'connection', with some leaning towards the latter as the means by which expression is achieved.

Epitome A highly condensed, abridged, or miniaturized representation of a subject.

Essentialist A term frequently used in cultural studies, and elsewhere, to denote the kinds of thinking which assume that certain conceptual categories and oppositions reflect the 'essential' properties of things to which they refer. 'Essentialist' can be contrasted with 'constructivist' and 'historicist' kinds of thinking, both of which emphasize the making or constructing of those categories and oppositions (hence their 'constructed-ness') within specific cultural contexts.

Icon An image or figure, usually with some symbolic significance, originally religious.

Inventory A common term for a complete list or set of items. In the rhetorical context it refers to the finite range of topoi and tropes which are current at a particular historical moment.

Metonymy A figure of speech which substitutes one term by another with which it is closely associated in time or space (as distinct from a term which is analogous with the other, which defines *metaphor*).

Structuralist, semiotic Both terms refer to a range of approaches to the analysis of culture in which culture is conceived as a system of signs. The meaning of any given sign is determined by its relation to other signs within the same system, not to objects outside it.

Synecdoche A figure of speech closely related to metonymy, but characterized by a part-to-whole relationship between the two terms.

Topos (pl. topoi) A conventional or traditional theme or idea recurrently associated with a particular subject.

Trope A conventional or traditional figure of speech (e.g. a particular metaphor or simile) recurrently used in association with a given subject.

Zeugma The syntactic pairing of semantically incongruous words. The effect is usually intentionally or inadvertently comic, as in the standard example: 'He heaved a sigh and a brick'.

CHAPTER NINE

AUSTRALIAN FILM AND TELEVISION
Albert Moran

Industry and text

This chapter concerns Australian film and television. It asks the questions: What might the terms Australian film and television mean? How have they been used? In other words, the chapter looks at applications to specific cultural industries of the sorts of general questions suggested in chapter 2 (see p. 16). In what follows I suggest some answers to these questions and conclude with a case study of one particular film as a way of illustrating how a film or television programme might be examined in the light of these issues.

As a first step, we might focus on the objects of enquiry—film and television. Film and television are modern culture industries and as such they have a double nature. On the one hand they are, like the car or food industries, characterized by mass production and distribution. Like the car and food industries, the film and television industries are economic ventures involving different kinds of capital equipment to produce objects designed to yield a profit. As such, they are subject to the constraints any Australian product faces on the world market and to competition within Australia from imported products. The problems presented to any Australian industry by the world economic order are discussed in chapter 4; the particular nature of these problems for film and television will be canvassed here.

As industries, film and television have three stages or moments: production, distribution and exhibition. However the analogy with the car or food industry can only be taken so far. A film is not like a car or a tin of food. It is, for example, more durable; it can be consumed repeatedly by a mass of people. Moreover, as film-goers we do not purchase a film but rather purchase access to a viewing of the film.

Films are cultural texts. They carry deliberately encoded meanings of a kind not found in other manufactured objects. As a first step, it is useful to remind ourselves that we might be talking about two different but related objects: on the one hand the film and television industries and, on the other, a text or set of texts. If we concentrate on the Australian film and television industries and ask in what ways they are Australian, certain paradoxes emerge. In the area of film, the interests of Australian film distributors and exhibitors have historically been different from those of film producers. The latter have always looked to local distributors and theatre owners for the exhibition of their films. Exhibitors, on the other hand, have been primarily interested in ensuring a ready supply of films. In the earliest stages of Australian cinema, between 1896 and 1915, this was an international supply coming from sources as diverse as Italy and Sweden (Shirley & Adams 1983:22–3). Around 1915, however, this situation changed. The First World War disrupted the supply of European films to countries such as Australia, and American film companies seized the opportunity to become the major film suppliers to Australia. This takeover had the effect of forcing out of the market not only films from other countries but also those made by Australian film-makers.

At the Royal Commission into the Moving Picture Industry of 1927, (Bertrand & Collins 1982:45–52) several local film producers, notably Raymond Longford, complained about not being able to gain local theatrical release for their films. It was not that the Australian film exhibition circuit had been taken over by American companies; the two major exhibition chains, Hoyts and Greater Union, then as now, were Australian companies. Rather, it was a particular market practice of American film distributors, block booking, that squeezed out Australian producers from easy theatrical release for their films. (Block booking is a practice whereby an exhibitor agrees to take a block or a package of films rather than a single film from a distributor.) Although the situation has eased somewhat since the early 1970s, with Australian film producers gaining more access not only to Australian cinemas but to international cinemas, historically Australian film producers have had a very marginal place on Australian screens. The case of film director Cecil Holmes is relevant here. Holmes was born in New Zealand, worked briefly at the New Zealand Film Unit and came to Australia in the late 1940s. He directed two interesting feature films in the 1950s—*Captain Thunderbolt* (1951) and *Three in One* (1956) (Shirley & Adams 1983:187–91). Both films had poor distribution and thereafter Holmes worked in documentary film. There is no doubt that had better distribution been available for these films Holmes could have continued in feature film production. Instead, although the exhibition chains were owned by Australians, Australian cinemas were in effect part of the global exhibition circuit of the American cinema.

Much the same situation has existed historically in Australian television but some qualifications are in order. The bulk of programmes shown on Australian commercial television since the service began in 1956 has been imported from the United States while the national service, the Australian Broadcasting Corporation, has shown much British material. Thus Australian television is an important exhibition arm of American and British television production industries. However Australian television does screen a sizeable amount of locally-originated material in such areas as news and current affairs, documentary, variety, drama, sport, outside broadcasts, and children's programmes. While some of these programmes (notably drama, current affairs and variety) are produced for the networks by independent packages using network equipment, personnel and other resources, for most Australian television stations, whether in the capital cities or in the country, much programming material is produced in-house. In other words the Australian television industry shows a higher degree of vertical integration between production, distribution and exhibition than does the Australian film industry. We can therefore say that Australian television has been more Australian than Australian cinema has been or is.

Australian film as chameleon

There is less need to develop distinctions around the notion of film and television as texts, in part because these emerge later in this discussion. Instead we can turn to the central focus of this chapter— the particular meaning of the term 'Australian' film or television. We can note the force of the phrase 'Australian film and television' as we can a series of other national screens (British film and television, Canadian film and television, New Zealand film and television) whereas there is much less temptation to speak about American film. With the latter we are more inclined to use other terms such as 'Hollywood' or, more simply, 'the movies'. In the former cases, however, the combination of film and nation seems irresistible.

Australian film is far less recognizable than Hollywood film. For one thing, we are talking of far fewer films. In the case of cinema features, we are speaking of only several hundred films as against the tens of thousands of films that Hollywood has produced in nearly eighty years. Neither is Australian television comparable in output to American television. Australian television has produced about 5000 hours of programmes whereas the Hollywood television industry's output has to be measured in tens of thousands of hours. Moreover, the history of Australian film production has been very varied in output. Production dropped sharply in the 1920s, steadied somewhat in the 1930s, revived briefly in the 1940s but faded into nothing by the early 1960s, revived with government assistance in the 1970s, dropped sharply in the early 1980s, only to boom again for about six years. By 1987 the production industry was again in crisis. The pattern has aptly been described as boom and bust. Nor is this production pattern unique to Australia. It can be found in the film production history of many other countries. Compared with this, Hollywood has had a much steadier production history. Even though there have been increases and decreases in output, they have usually been fairly controlled and there are few of the endemic crises of Australian film production.

Australian film has been much more chameleon-like in character than its Hollywood counterpart. From 1910 onwards, international audiences came to recognize Hollywood films, whether westerns, crime stories, melodramas, comedies or whatever, as a distinct kind of cinema; a stable, dependable product, marked by stories with strong, causal chains and neat endings, good-looking stars and clear, attractive settings (Thompson 1985:1-20). These qualities have persisted down to the present as hallmarks of the Hollywood film. By contrast, the Australian film evokes no consistent image or impression. It is always a matter of qualification: which Australian film, at which time, by which Australian film-maker, in which genre? Thus although *The Sentimental Bloke* (1919) and *Picnic At Hanging Rock* (1976) are Australian films, it is hard to see anything they have in common apart from the geographical accident of having been made in Australia. Do they have anything else in common? Wherein might lie their Australianness? How might we locate it? These are by no means academic questions.

Since the early 1970s the Australian government has subsidized the film production industry out of taxpayers' money. It is thus an urgent and practical policy issue to define Australian film in such a way that film assessors, bureaucrats and others can decide whether this or that film project is Australian and whether it qualifies for support. It is not my intention here to quote from the various and changing pieces of legislation, policy statements and guidelines that have attempted to define Australian film—useful discussions of these are available elsewhere (Dermody & Jacka 1987; Harrison 1980). Some of the practical effects of these definitions as they have affected film production in the past twenty years have also been canvassed (Dermody & Jacka 1987; O'Regan 1982a; Moran & O'Regan 1985; O'Regan 1985). More important for my purpose here is to notice that state support has been a central feature of the recent Australian film production industry. Australian cinema shares this feature with many other cinemas, including Britain, Canada and New Zealand. State support has made it necessary to develop a set of explicit definitions of what the national cinema is or might be. The American cinema, by contrast, has been and continues to be a cinema of the free market, operating without subsidy or other forms of economic support from the American government. American film has therefore been able to remain blissfully unconcerned with defining itself, a luxury denied many other national cinemas including that of Australia.

A plurality of definitions

If recent thinking about Australian films has carried a high degree of self-consciousness, this is merely part and parcel of recent thinking about Australia itself. As other writers in this book have shown, earlier writings on the subject of Australia have imagined their subject as constituted by some persistent core or essence. By contrast, recent writers have suggested that this search for an essence is a search for an illusory object, a modern form of myth-making. What is possible is to talk about Australia by talking about the different ways that others have talked about Australia. I accept this point of view here, arguing that there is no single answer to the question: What is an Australian film? Rather there are a variety of answers, depending on which elements we take as defining that object.

Australian films might, as a minimum, be defined as those films made in Australia. Such a definition is a generous one and would cover a wide range of films. But it also conjures up difficulties around other films—made in Australia but by visiting production personnel. Such a list includes a series of Ealing films—*The Overlanders* (1946), *Eureka Stockade* (1949), *Bitter Springs* (1950), *The Shiralee* (1957) and *The Siege of Pinchgut* (1959); Twentieth-Century Fox's *Kangaroo* (1952); the CSI television series 'Whiplash' (1961); Stanley Kramer's *On The Beach* (1959); and, more recently, Werner Herzog's *Where The Green Ants Dream* (1983). These films are not all of the same kind. But nevertheless they might be seen as fitting into two different national film traditions—one Australian, the other British, American or German. They are part of film projects conceived elsewhere. The Ealing films, for example, are part of an Ealing world view in which Australia had an important if peripheral place (Barr 1974). In the Ealing films of the 1940s and 1950s the metropolitan centres of Britain mostly form the settings of serious, realistic drama (*It Always Rains on Sunday, Mandy, The Man in the White Suit*). Surrounding this is a comic periphery. Sometimes this is England (*Passport to Pimlico, The Titfield Thunderbolt*), but more usually the outlying regions of the British isles form the setting for social comedy about the winsome ways of the Scots (*Whiskey Galore, The Maggie*), and the Welsh (*A Run for Your Money*).

In turn there is an outer rim, constituted by Australia and South Africa, which form a frontier—the setting for male action and adventure films—a kind of Empire western (Australian Ealing films *The Overlanders, Eureka Stockade, Bitter Springs, The Shiralee, Where No Eagles Fly, West of Zanzibar*). The Australian Ealing films are then part of British film tradition. They also belong to an Australian archive. Andrew Pike and Ross Cooper (1980) in their definitive list of Australian feature films made between 1901 and 1977 have no trouble treating *The Overlanders* and several of the other films mentioned here as Australian. Pike and Cooper's strategy in including a film such as *The Overlanders* is an opportunistic one. In defining a canon of Australian film they are implicitly using a flexible notion of how a film might be Australian. In the case of *The Overlanders*, although the film's director Harry Walt was Scottish, Ralph Smart was British, as was the production company; the subject setting, cast and technicians were all Australian. Thus Pike and Cooper include the film in their Australian canon. A contemporary film critic took the matter of the place of origin of the film one interesting step further in an argument about the film's Australianness. Lee Robinson (1949), in an article about the filmic possibilities of the Northern Territory (the location and setting for much of the film) argued that because the film was made on location rather than in a studio, and because the Northern Territory is the most Australian place on the continent, this spirit of place has seeped into the film in such a way as to make this film a truly Australian film.

Metaphysical arguments of this kind are finally unverifiable and there is little evidence that such an argument finds ready acceptance. If there are many instances where films made in Australia but originated elsewhere have been accepted as Australian, there have also been occasions where this has been contested.

At the moment we lack any study of films from elsewhere, studies that offer the kind of understanding that, for example, Pierre Berton (1977) has offered of Hollywood's image of Canada, and Luke Gibbons and John Hill (1987) have more recently offered of British and American cinemas' account of Ireland. Were such a study undertaken on that group of films indicated above it would not tell us whether such films were truly Australian. Rather it would offer us a systematic opportunity to note what such films did and did not say about Australia, their emphases as well as their omissions.

A second line of approach might be to think of Australian films as those made for an Australian audience. Several historians have noted that many early Australian films, such as *The Sentimental Bloke* and *The Kids Stakes*, were made for a local audience (Lawson 1965; Tulloch 1981), and that they spoke in a direct, unmediated way to that audience. Nor is this a thing of the past. The ocker film cycle of the early to mid-1970s that included such films as *The Adventures of Barry McKenzie, Alvin Purple* and *Don's Party* were made on budgets designed to enable them to clear their costs and go into profit in the Australian market. It has been suggested that such films could then deal with crude and monstrous forms of behaviour familiar to Australians but not necessarily to others (O'Regan 1989). Elsewhere too I have noted that the Crawford police series made between 1964 and 1975 ('Homicide', 'Division 4', 'Matlock Police') had a density of local reference and situation that was facilitated by being implicitly addressed to a local audience (Moran 1982).

Such instances are instructive. On the basis of these examples it could be argued that these films often have a density of reference, even idiosyncrasy of idiom, that make them less accessible to audiences elsewhere. They are marked too by a lack of self-consciousness about their origin. They are not as explicitly Australian as some other genres and films that will be discussed shortly. However this does not make them any more authentic than films that are self-consciously Australian. Rather we might note some of the ways that certain market considerations often affect textual features of a particular film or group of films.

We can contrast these examples with films and television programmes made for international sales and an international audience. A good example of the latter, made at the same time that Crawford Productions was producing its cycle of police series, was the Fauna Production series 'Skippy'. The thinking that led to this series developed out of the involvement of several of its principals in the British–Australian co-production *They're a Weird Mob* (1966), arguably a forerunner to the ocker cycle of films of the early 1970s:

> Three of us who had been together in the making of *They're a Weird Mob*, Bob Austen, Lee Robinson and I, put our heads together and decided to make a series of half hour films for television. At first we thought we'd follow up the success of *Weird Mob* with a spin-off comedy based on the film. But then we realised that this would be too Australian and insular a subject for world sales which we had to aim at if we were to make films for international release. [McCallum 1979:232]

Instead they settled on a staple of the genre of American children's television, the animal-centred half-hour series ('Lassie', 'Rin Tin Tin', 'Flipper' and so on), varying the formula by making the animal a kangaroo and the setting Australian bush and waterways (usually unidentified). Moreover, although it would be nearly ten years before Australian television converted to colour, Fauna decided to take on the added expense of producing the series in colour so that the series might sell into markets, including American and British television, which had already switched to colour. 'Skippy' is the most successful television series ever made in Australia and has sold in over 120 countries across the world.

A less problematic way to define Australian films, one that I have already touched on, is to assume that a film made by Australians will *ipso facto* be Australian. This definition usually forms part if not all of the basis for deciding whether a film project will gain a subsidy or tax exemption from film assessors and bureaucrats. However not all production positions are equal. In practice the definition differentiates key production roles such as director, writer, actors and, perhaps, producers and cinematographers. In recent years bitter disputes have been engendered around acting roles being given to overseas rather than to local actors. For example, were American stars Stacy Keach and Jamie Lee Curtis necessary for the central roles in *Roadgames* (1981), Sigourney Weaver for *The Year of Living Dangerously* (1982) and Meryl Streep for *Evil Angels* (1988)? Producers invariably claim that such stars are necessary for the correct artistic interpretation of the roles they play, that they are vital to the definition of particular characters. Actors' Equity, the union of Australian actors, has claimed that the decisions to cast these and other foreign stars is economic rather than artistic. The presence of a recognizable international (usually American) star is designed to persuade overseas distributors and exhibitors to handle the films.

If the presence of international stars constitutes one conundrum for film assessors and bureaucrats as well as cultural critics, another exists around the phenomenon of the Australian film-maker working abroad. Are the resultant texts Australian? We claim film director Peter Weir's *Picnic At Hanging Rock* (1975) as Australian but do we claim his film *Witness* (1985)? We cite director Gillian Armstrong's film *My Brilliant Career* (1981) but should we also consider her *Mrs Sofel* (1985)? We acknowledge Fred Schepisi's *The Chant of Jimmie Blacksmith* (1978) but what of his *Barbarossa* (1982)? And if *Evil Angels* represents a return of the native, is this film Australian? These puzzles may seem like needless hair-splitting but they have a capacity to take on very real, practical dimensions. The case of the film *The Return of Captain Invincible* is relevant here.

The Return of Captain Invincible was produced by an Australian distributor, Andrew Gaty, written by Gaty and an American scriptwriter, Stephen de Souza, and directed by Phillipe Moras, an Australian expatriate. The film had two overseas leads, American star Alan Arkin and British star Christopher Lee. It had a budget of $A7 million, very high by Australian standards, and was funded locally under the 10BA tax provisions. The film has an American theme and super-hero as its central character. Some of the film's action is set in Australia although most occurs in the United States. The supporting cast was almost all Australian although they played Americans in the American sequences. The crew was Australian and most of the film was shot locally. The film obtained provisional 10BA certification so that its investors could claim 150 per cent of their investment as a tax deduction (as well as 50 per cent of the film's profits). The film was completed in June 1982.

To qualify for the exemptions a film had to be certified by the Minister for Home Affairs as an Australian film. Relevant factors included subject-matter, locations, nationality of personnel, share owners in the production company and sources of finance but no formal guidelines or definitions existed. To gain American distribution, Gaty recut the film but this version was then denied certification as an Australian film by the minister in late 1982, both on the grounds of its recutting at the behest of a foreign distributor and because the script had not been written in Australia. Gaty took legal action against the minister's decision. In May 1984 a judge overturned the decision, arguing that despite the admitted American origins of the script 'there is no property in an idea'.

The case is an interesting example of the way that attempts to define and insist on Australianness in local film and television may run counter to other interests, in this case property rights and natural justice. In addition it shows the way in which different groups, institutions and agencies may see the matter of a film's Australianness in quite different, even conflicting ways. And finally, the case of *The Return of Captain Invincible* demonstrates a set of ways in which a film might or might not be Australian and the relative importance or unimportance that might be placed on these elements. Susan Dermody and Elizabeth Jacka (1987:146–9) discuss the film in their book *The Screening of Australia*.

Australian subjects

Probably the most vexed but also the most interesting category of Australian film are those films that might be said to be about Australia. Again there are many ways in which films might be about Australia, that is, have Australia as their subject-matter. I have already mentioned a category of film whose budget has been set on the basis of clearing its costs in the Australian market. Such films have been made for the local market and are not usually concerned to foreground their Australianness. To those already mentioned above we can add various other groups and cycles of feature films, including those low-budget social realist films of the late 1970s and 1980s that have been dubbed 'poor cinema' (Ricketson 1979) or that might also be seen as Australian art cinema (Bordwell 1985), films such as *Mouth to Mouth* (1978), *Monkey Grip* (1982) and *Kostas* (1979). The category of films that are tacitly or implicitly about Australia, made by Australian film-makers for Australian audiences, is much wider than this. For example, much of the independent avant-garde film-making of the past fifteen or twenty years might be said to be Australian according to these criteria (Herd 1983; Martin 1989).

When we turn to films as texts we can use three approaches in pondering the questions of whether Australian film might constitute a genre. These are narrative, the imagery or look of the film in question and, finally, the kinds of themes and issues at play in a film—its discourses (Neale 1980). To what extent might Australian films be expected to have found their own principles for organizing subject-matter—narrative schemes, genres and so on? This is a novel question and one hardly ever comes across it. As far as I am aware only one local critic has raised it. John Flaus has maintained that Australian film-makers could legitimately be interrogated about whether they have developed their own narrative schemes or merely adapted those developed elsewhere. However, this seems far-fetched. On this criteria almost no film made locally would be Australian. We need not have doubts about organizational schemes originating elsewhere. Australian films have much in common with films produced elsewhere. The *Mad Max* films, for example, are fine reworkings of action narratives typically found in such Hollowood genres as the Western and the crime film, while the period films of the late 1970s and early 1980s rework some of the narrative structures of the European art film. Australian television soap operas have much in common with soap operas elsewhere. Even many avant-garde films belong in an international context. To note all this is not to deny these films the name Australian. It is, rather, to recognize that in order to speak film-makers here have frequently had to resort to tropes and figures received from elsewhere. This does not undermine the Australian nature of their projects. To assert otherwise would be equivalent to denying that Australian poetry written in English is Australian.

The second approach to Australian films as texts is to consider the kinds of imagery that Australian films do or might offer. One kind of imagery that comes easily, perhaps too easily, to mind are images of the bush and the outback, and here there is a consistent recurring pattern running from *The Kelly Gang* (1906), *The Back of Beyond* (1952), through to the use of such imagery in the period film cycle of the late 1970s and 1980s. *We of the Never Never* (1985) is one of the latest films in this long line. However, Australian society since at least the 1920s has been an urban society and these bush outback settings do not mean as much to the majority of Australians as other filmic settings. We can find more meaningful imagery in Australian television drama series of the 1960s and early 1970s, for instance the interaction of narrative and physical setting in such programmes as 'Homicide', 'Division 4', 'Matlock Police', 'Bellbird', 'My Name's McGooley, What's Yours?' and 'You Can't See Around Corners'. The references to place are both contemporary and specific in those programmes, whether it be particular areas of Melbourne in 'Homicide' and 'Division 4', Victorian country towns in 'Matlock' and 'Bellbird', or the Sydney suburbs of Balmain in 'McGooley' and Newtown in 'You Can't See Around Corners'. In some ways place is the central subject of these programmes. Certainly the programmes imply an indigenous audience, for they conjure up a set of geographic images that were either known directly or indirectly by their Australian viewers. As one critic so aptly put it at the time:

> Anything but outright fantasy has to anchor itself solidly to a recognisable and concretely presented environment. For *Homicide* and *Division 4* the dramatic regularities of character, action and ethic are embedded in the world we know. The sub-industrial landscape of narrow-gutted South Melbourne timber cottages, Carlton back streets and lanes, the Victoria docks and the Dynon Road railway yards. The Australian series are proletarian through and through. Knitted, sleeveless pullovers don't raise a second glance. Kev Dwyer plays Saturday arvo football. Vickers has a sporting trophy in his office and Frank Banner is known in every pub from City Road to Fitzroy Street. The world we see in the gritty photographed, sharply edited exteriors is a topography of TAB's, Ampol service stations, used car yards and cluttered verandah-fronted shopping centres. [Murray 1973:18]

Again, I am not suggesting that this kind of film imagery invalidates images of the bush and the outback. Rather, it indicates that there are several ways of constructing an Australian setting; Australia is, after all, a geographically varied place.

The third approach to Australian films as texts is to consider the kinds of discourse they employ. It is by no means the case that films made in Australia by Australians will necessarily entail discourses about Australia and Australianness. 'Homicide', for example, as befitted a crime series, posed questions about law, social order and the nature of crime. It consistently did this without raising issues about the nature of Australia, its people and what it was to be Australian. Discourses about Australia are confined to a small number of particular films, cycles and genres made locally. We can notice two types of films in which this kind of disclosure is very often present: historical–period films and comedy.

In the period film and the historical mini-series there is a consistent linking of history and nationhood. By locating themselves in the past, many of the films and the television series are implicitly offering to explain how Australia's present stage of development has been reached. There are a variety of formative stages and experiences. Those have sometimes been recorded in the history books: *Gallipoli* (the Australians in the First World War), *The Last Outlaw* (the Kelly outbreak), *The Dismissal* (the sacking of the Whitlam government) and *The Last Bastion* (Australia at war in 1942–43). Sometimes we are in the margin of historical record: *Shout* (the advent of rock-and-roll in Australia), *Newsfront* (newsreel film-making in Australia) and

Vietnam (how one particular family is affected by the Vietnam war). Finally there are other films in which the events are more private and domestic (for example, *My Brilliant Career, The Irishman* and *All The Rivers Run* but which are none the less part of this process of dramatizing an Australian past. A further element running through these films is the strategy of contrasting Australians with other national types as a way of suggesting various features in the Australian character (for example, *Breaker Morant, The Light Horsemen* and *A Town Like Alice*).

Comedy very often turns on sharp contrasts and clashes in different kinds of social behaviour. Frequently these differences can be given a national basis. Comic clashes of manners between Australians and others, that call into question what it is to be Australian, have been a recurring element in feature film comedies as diverse as *It Isn't Done* (1937), *They're a Weird Mob* (1966), *The Adventures of Barry McKenzie* (1972) and *Crocodile Dundee* (1986). In Australian television comedy it has been a recurring note in series as diverse as 'McGooley' (1966), 'The Last of the Australians' (1975) and 'Home Sweet Home' (1980).

Having designated those films and television series in which discourses about Australia are engendered, it is worth reiterating that these discourses are not found in very many Australian films nor does that invalidate those films that are not explicitly about Australia. Equally, there is no reason to decide in favour of period films and historical mini-series at the expense of social comedy films on the basis that the former are more serious in their pursuit of national questions. To do so would be to allow narrative strategies to cloud our thinking.

A diverse Australian film

I have to this point examined various ways in which films might and might not be Australian. However this stress on the Australianness of local films can mask or hide other questions that we might ponder. Some European researchers in mass communications have recently pointed out that a stress on the flow of communication messages between nations will have the effect of implying that a nation state is more unified than it necessarily is (Nordenstreng & Varis 1973). There are often crucial differences of class, gender and ethnicity inside the nation. There may also be differences based on such factors as region, geography, language and religion. In other words, by focusing on Australia as I have to this point in the discussion, I have been working with a concept of the nation as unified and homogeneous. This is not necessarily the case. In 1974 Australia was declared a multicultural nation. This proclamation implied that Australia was more diverse and heterogeneous than had often been recognized. To what extent have Australian films articulated this diversity? I will discuss four elements in film that tend to undermine the notion of the unified, homogeneous nation: localism, class, gender and ethnicity. While none of these has been a very persistent or dominant factor in locally-produced film, collectively they do fruitfully complicate and qualify the notion of the unified nation.

Of the four concepts, locality is certainly the most elastic in that it is difficult to decide where locality begins and even if it is a very useful term to employ. For example, the Act of parliament that established the South Australian Film Corporation (SAFC) was cultural as well as commercial: 'to establish a viable film industry within this state and to reflect our way of life with truth and artistry, showing South Australians to Australians and the world' (*South Australian Film Corporation Act 1972*:1-2). However if one examines the feature films made by SAFC, from *Sunday Too Far Away* (1975) to *Playing Beattie Bow* (1986), one is very hard put to say in what ways they might show South Australia and South Australianness. Despite the conceptual difficulties that surround the notion of localism there have been some interesting instances in Australian film and, especially, television. Here we can mention not only the cycle of locally produced drama of the 1960s and 1970s already discussed above, programmes such as 'Homicide' and 'You Can't See Round Corners' that were always about specific places, but also the live programmes of the first phase of Australian television between 1956 and 1965.

As I have discussed elsewhere (Moran 1982), in the years up to 1965 television stations, both national and commercial in state capitals other than Sydney and Melbourne, originated some of their own programmes. The commercials concentrated on variety/tonight shows, while the ABC produced a surprisingly large number of plays. For example, by the mid-1960s in Brisbane one of the commercial stations ran a tonight show, 'In Brisbane Tonight', two evenings a week; 'Theatre Royale' ran on one of the opposition stations one evening a week; while the other had 'The Club Show'. The ABC had a variety show. In addition, in 1965-66 the ABC produced three plays in its Brisbane studios which were transmitted nationally. This kind of localism was important both for station identity and local employment. However the introduction of better production recording facilities in the mid-1960s and satellite broadcasting in the mid-1980s has seen the erosion of most of this localism in favour of national television networking after the American style. Much of the production that now occurs in Australian television in areas such as news, current affairs, children's programmes, sport and advertising is based in Sydney. In other words a great deal of Australian television and film might more legitimately be described as Sydney television and film.

Few recent Australian films have focused on questions of class, as for example the films of the Waterside Workers Film Unit did in the 1950s with *Pensions for Veterans* (1953); *The Hungry Miles* (1955);

November Victory (1956). Some recent films such as the ocker cycle (including *Crocodile Dundee* have succeeded in gathering a mass audience in ways that both the recent period and art cinema cycles have not. The working class have attended those former films but have stayed away from the latter. We cannot, though, conclude that these in any way form an Australian working-class cinema. We might also note the extent to which the television drama cycle of the 1960s and early 1970s ('Homicide', 'The Battlers', 'McGooley', and so on) gravitated to working-class milieux. These were partly inspired by a cycle of working-class drama series on British television that produced programmes such as 'Coronation Street' and 'Z Cars'. But although the cycle created interesting and credible settings, it was not concerned with questions of social inequality.

In the field of institutional documentary there have been some interesting although isolated images of working-class life. For example, a 1973 episode of the ABC television series 'Chequerboard' parallels an upper-class and a working-class marriage. Yet the programme is apolitical, suggesting that marriage transcends and unites classes. In the field of recent independent documentaries there have been some films that offer a more conflictual account of Australian society, emphasizing working-class struggle. The most notable are those of Tom Zurbricki, especially *Waterloo*, *Friends and Enemies*, and *Diary of a Strike: Kemmira*. Yet we can also extend our interest in class to other Australian films, for it is not the case that the working class is exclusively male and white. Gender and ethnicity are other important areas of power relations. Thus the feminist film *For Love or Money* (1983) on women's work is important for understanding class as well as gender relations. The 1970s and 1980s in Australia have witnessed a large number of women's films, ranging from mainstream features such as *The Getting of Wisdom*, *Caddie* and *My Brilliant Career*, documentaries through to more avant-garde films such as *We Aim To Please* (1977) and *Serious Undertakings* (1983). Yet as has been noted, few women's films have been concerned to connect gender with class (Blonski & Freiberg 1989). For example in *Caddie* (1977) the heroine's downfall is entirely at the hands of men. Although she moves from middle to working class, neither she nor the film recognizes that class and gender subjugation has occurred.

Despite these shortcomings, these films, like those that foreground locality and class, do belie the sense of a monocultural Australia in favour of a more pluralistic society. Much the same can be said about recent films that suggest ethnic diversity in the nation. This diversity includes not just non-Anglo-Australian minorities such as the Greek and Vietnamese communities but also Aborigines, whether in remote or urban situations and communities. Non-Anglo-Australians and Aborigines were a shadowy presence in Australian film before the late

1960s. *They're a Weird Mob* (1966) was the first feature film to feature a non-Anglo-Australian (an Italian migrant) in a central role. The book of the same title, which appeared in 1958, was much more assimilationist in spirit than the film. Although it ends with the Italian marrying an Irish-Australian, therefore gesturing towards social and cultural assimilation, the film at other points suggests that there is a noticeable Italian community in Sydney.

More recent films have taken this further, indicating not only ethnic diversity in Australian society but also linguistic diversity. For example the two soap operas *The Girl from Steel City* (1986) and *City West* (1987), both commissioned and put to air on the multicultural television network the Special Broadcasting Service (SBS) are located in places with a high migrant presence—Wollongong and the western suburbs of Sydney. Many of the non-Anglo-Australians speak in languages other than English, these conversations being translated into English subtitles. Equally there have recently been an increasing number of films concerned with conflict and tensions in black–white relations: films such as *The Chant of Jimmie Blacksmith* (1978), *Where the Green Ants Dream* (1983), *Backroads* (1977) and others. Many of these have been produced by a troubled white liberal conscience and they tend to see racism as phenomenal and inexplicable rather than being linked to power relations such as class and gender. Nevertheless there are some exceptions. One noticeable one was the television mini-series 'Women of the Sun' (1982), which focused on four representative Aboriginal women across the period of white settlement. The series implicitly suggested that Australia was and is a diverse nation, marked by a series of differences including those of gender, ethnicity, language and religion and characterized by inequitable power relations.

Case study: *The Man From Snowy River*

I have to this point been concerned to offer a series of possible definitions of Australian film to suggest that there are many ways in which a film might be Australian. I have touched on a large number of films and television programmes but have not examined any at length. The following case study of the film *The Man From Snowy River* (1982) is offered partly as a means of making concrete some of the issues explored to this point and partly as a particular test case. The film was chosen not because it is a good film, aesthetically worthy of consideration (I believe it is but many would disagree) but because material on the film is easily available. Some of the analysis is textual. Though I am interested in aspects of the production, circulation and consumption of the film, I am, above all, interested in the ways that it might and might not be said to be Australian.

The Man From Snowy River was filmed around Mansfield in Victoria in early to mid-1981 with a budget that some reports put at $A3 million and others at $A5 or $A6 million. The film was privately financed by a consortium of 285 investors, the theatrical entrepreneur Michael Edgley heading the consortium and acting as producer and marketing company for the film. There was no investment from the Australian Film Commission, the government film body which from the mid-1970s until well into the 1980s had been a strong promoter of the quality period film. By contrast *The Man From Snowy River*, although set in the past, did not fall into this cycle.

The film was suggested by the Banjo Paterson poem of the same name, a classic of Australian literature. However as Geoff Burrows, the producer, and George Miller, the film's director, explained in an interview (Tosi 1982), the poem is only five minutes long. It provided a strong ending for the film (Jim wins the tussle with the wild horses and recaptures the colt from Old Regret) but they had to develop an equally strong beginning and middle for this story. They thereby avoided what they saw as a depressing tendency in recent Australian films. Some critics have also noticed this trend in Australian film and literary fiction: the passive, reactive hero as symptomatic of a malaise in Australian society and culture (Ryan 1980; Turner 1986). By contrast, the kind of story structure that Burrows and Miller developed has been seen as characteristic of Hollywood films. Although the action in the poem is set in the Australian Alps, the film-makers chose the southern location of Mansfield. The mountains around Mansfield were more beautiful but also 'Kosciusko does not look like a mountain, just a feature on a high plateau' (Tosi 1982).

Putting these elements together, we can notice two different aspects of the production. On the one hand there was the inclusion of authentic elements such as the poem and the bush setting. But on the other hand there was the operation of poetic licence in the screenplay and the preference for Mansfield over Kosciusko. This extended to various other parts of the production, including the casting. Jack Thompson brought a certain authenticity to his role as Clancy. He had learned to ride in the Northern Territory and worked on a sheep station for six years. He said yes to the role 'provided he could work with the horses and in the mountains for real, to get the right feel. Thompson is very real in the saddle cracking a stockwhip' (Hawley 1981). The casting of the Hollywood actor Kirk Douglas was more contentious:

To the nationalist Australians within the film industry it smacked of a rip-off. The Americans move in to take what they could while the Australians were ripe for the picking . . . Already there are fears by many that the Australian cinema is in danger of going the way of the Canadian industry, with a loss of national identity, in opting for the considered marquee value of American leads. [Whitburn 1981:46–7]

The article that notes these worries about the casting also produces a justification for the casting of American star Kirk Douglas:

> A few nights before his accident, Thompson, still in his Clancy outfit, refutes any criticism aimed at Douglas over a beer at the pub. Thompson explains there were a lot of Americans around at that time. They went to California after gold and many, who didn't find it, moved on to Australia seeking their fortunes. He's been a strong lobbyist for the open door policy in Actors Equity's moves to block the influx of foreign talent into Australian movies. He is empathetic in his belief that Australian films need names familiar to world audiences to ensure survival. [Whitburn 1981:47]

This is a richly mythological moment. Although it was Burrows and Miller who cast Douglas and although Thompson had nothing to do with that decision, it is the actor who is chosen here to justify it. His credentials as authentic Australian are relevant here (but these are strengthened by other touches of authenticity—witness his bush experience and his abilities with horse and whip, the Clancy outfit, pub, beer). His generous justification of the American actor is a mark of Thompson's mateship. Moreover, although a member of Actors' Equity (solidarity with his union and his mates), he is independent, not a mindless follower of the Equity line on imported actors. He is also a nationalist, putting the survival of the Australian film industry above the narrower, more short-term interests of a union.

The film was released in Australia in mid-1982 with strong publicity and promotion (the journalistic pieces I have drawn on were part of this publicity). The film was also backed by an extensive marketing campaign organized by the Edgley group. By the end of 1982, after twenty-two weeks, the film had grossed more than $A12 million in the Australian market. It went on to become the highest-grossing film ever released in Australia to that time. The marketing campaign produced an extensive range of merchandise that was promoted in and around the film. This included not only a book, records and posters, but also a range of bush gear such as clothing (hats, boots, coats, shirts, jeans and pants), saddles, whips, and so on. This merchandizing was reportedly worth $A20 million in Australia. On the basis of the film's success in the Australian market, the American major Twentieth Century-Fox paid US$2 million and a percentage of the profit to distribute the film in the United States and internationally.

Was the film Australian? My argument in this chapter has been to suggest that there are many ways in which a film might or might not be Australian. In the case of *The Man From Snowy River* there is available a series of different responses to the film that have a large bearing on this kind of question. To Burrows and Miller the film was 'a love letter to the mountains . . . to Australia' (Tosi 1982). They also cited the reaction of an Adelaide audience that clapped at the end when the hero Jim brought the horses back:

Because the film is intrinsically Australian, it is socially and culturally specific to Australia, when Jim wins, Australia wins . . . . What turns an audience on is the feeling we want to generate in the audience when Jim beat those horses and alone and unassisted brought them back was similar to a team winning the Grand Final [sic]. When Carlton wins a Grand Final, 20 players don't win it. Hundreds of thousands of people win it. When Jim beats the horses everybody in the audience wins. [Tosi 1982:31]

If this response entailed elements of male identification, some girls at the Perth *première* reported that the film had made them proud to be Australian and this they ascribed to an honesty in the character Jim and in the script. For example when Jim thanks Spur for a horse, 'you obviously felt he meant it, he was not a smarty arse' (Tosi 1982). Other audiences focused on other features of the film. A *New York Times* review began: 'There are not so many big Westerns around that one can easily dismiss the Australian *The Man From Snowy River* . . . To appreciate it fully though one must have a completely uncritical fondness for Kirk Douglas as he acts his heart off in two roles' (Canby 1983). One of the most interesting articles on the film, written by Tom O'Regan (1982b) also began by noting that the film was a Western. Whereas the *New York Times* saw it as a Kirk Douglas (and therefore by implication a Hollywood) Western, O'Regan saw it as a Kangaroo or Australian Western, belonging with such films as *The Overlanders*, *The Kangaroo Kid* and *The Phantom Stockman*. O'Regan went on to tell two stories about the film's audience in the Queensland city of Rockhampton. A young police constable drove 110 kilometres to take his girlfriend to see the film at a drive-in—his fourth viewing of the film, her first. They left before the second film so that his experience of the film was not cluttered by another film. In the meantime a local radio station was advising would-be patrons of the drive-in to book so as to avoid the disappointment of those who had been turned away on the previous weekend. Rockhampton is an industrial port and this led O'Regan to speculate on why the film might appeal to such an audience. He concluded that many of the concerns of the film, such as feminism, animal liberation, ecology and country mobility, had a contemporary resonance. He also saw the film as meaningful in an Australian context, albeit in no way unique to Australia:

The emergence within metropolitan and provincial cities the length and breadth of Australia of Country and Western [music] in the last few years has been staggering. There are Country and Western stations in all the major state capitals that consistently get large audiences. The marketing and push for Western gear has coincided with this development. R. M. Williams opening up shops in Sydney and Melbourne is symptomatic. A range of Western gear shops is prominent in new suburban shopping complexes across Australia. On the outskirts of every metropolitan and provincial city area are numerous riding schools and, of course, the ubiquitous hobby farms. Horses are a reason for having a hobby farm. Many do not have gardens but you can bet your life that they have a couple of horses and cows. Concomitant with this industrial urban explosion has been the development and success of the rodeo circuit, a success used to sell the Castlemaine-Tooheys Four X beer in Queensland, to provide numerous specials on television Australia wide, and sell, construct and package *The Man From Snowy River*. [O'Regan 1982b:246-7]

O'Regan's point, although hypothetical, is an interesting and sophisticated one. He sees the film as being inside popular, commercial culture. To the extent that that culture had its beginnings elsewhere, that culture is not Australian, but to the extent that it has been adapted and transmuted it is Australian. Seen in this context *The Man From Snowy River* is authentically Australian.

References

7 Institutions of Australian Literature

Anderson, B. 1983, *Imagined Communities: Reflections on the Origin and Spread of Nationalism*, Verso, London.
Bennett, B. (ed.) 1981, *Cross Currents: Magazines and Newspapers in Australian Literature*, Longman Cheshire, Melbourne.
Brett, J. 1988, 'Publishing, censorship and writers' incomes, 1965-1988', in L. Hergenhan (ed.), *The Penguin New Literary History of Australia*, Penguin, Ringwood.
Buckridge, P. 1988, 'Intellectual authority and critical traditions in Australian literature 1945-1975', in B. Head & J. Walter (eds), *Intellectual Movements and Australian Society*, Oxford University Press, Melbourne.
Cantrell, L. (ed.) 1977, *Writing of the 1890s: Short Stories, Verse and Essays*, University of Queensland Press, St Lucia, Qld.
Carter, D. 1985, 'Coming home after the party: *Overland*'s first decade', *Meanjin*, vol. 44, no. 4, pp. 462-76.
Christesen, C. B. 1951, 'The uneasy chair: The wound as the bow', *Meanjin*, vol. 10, no. 1, pp. 4, 83-91.
Clark, C. M. H. 1978, *A History of Australia*, vol. IV, *The Earth Abideth For Ever*, Melbourne University Press, Melbourne.
Clark, J. & Whitelaw, B. 1985, *Golden Summers: Heidelberg and Beyond*, International Cultural Corporation of Australia, Melbourne.
Cronin, L. 1984, *A Campfire Yarn: Henry Lawson Complete Works 1885-1900*, Lansdowne, Sydney.
Davison, G. 1982, 'Sydney and the bush: An urban context for the Australian legend', in J. Carroll (ed.), *Intruders in the Bush: The Australian Quest for Identity*, Oxford University Press, Melbourne.
Docker, J. 1974, *Australian Cultural Elites: Intellectual Traditions in Sydney and Melbourne*, Angus & Robertson, Sydney.
Docker J. 1984, *In a Critical Condition: Reading Australian Literature*, Penguin, Ringwood.
Eagleton, T. 1983, *Literary Theory: An Introduction*, Blackwell, Oxford.
Eagleton, T. 1984, *The Function of Criticism: From the Spectator to Post-Structuralism*, Verso, London.
Giles, F. (ed.) 1987, *From the Verandah: Stories of Love and Landscape by Nineteenth Century Australian Women*, McPhee Gribble, Fitzroy.
Giles, F. 1988, 'Romance: An embarrassing subject', in L. Hergenhan (ed.), *The Penguin New Literary History of Australia*, Penguin, Ringwood.
Gillen, P. 1988, 'Mightier than the sword?', in V. Burgmann & J. Lee (eds), *Constructing a Culture*, McPhee Gribble/Penguin, Melbourne.
Green, H. M. 1961, *A History of Australian Literature*. vol. I, *1789-1923*, Angus & Robertson, Sydney.
Hergenhan, L. (ed.) 1988, *The Penguin New Literary History of Australia*, Penguin, Ringwood.
Heseltine, H. P. 1962, 'The literary heritage', *Meanjin*, vol. 21, no. 1, pp. 35-49.
Hope, A. D. *et al.* 1954, 'Australian literature and the universities', *Meanjin*, vol. 13, nos 2-4, pp. 165-9, 429-36, 591-6.

Inglis Moore, T. 1971, *Social Patterns in Australian Literature*, Angus & Robertson, Sydney.
Jarvis, D. 1981, 'The development of an egalitarian poetics in the *Bulletin*, 1880-1890', *Australian Literary Studies*, vol. 10, no. 1, pp. 22-34.
Jarvis, D. 1983a, 'Lawson, the *Bulletin* and the short story', *Australian Literary Studies*, vol. 11, no. 1, pp. 58-66.
Jarvis, D. 1983b, 'Morality and literary realism: A debate of the 1880s', *Southerly*, vol. 43, no. 4, pp. 404-20.
Kiernan, B. (ed.) 1976, *Henry Lawson*, University of Queensland Press, St Lucia, Qld.
Kiernan, B. 1980, 'Ways of seeing: Henry Lawson's "Going Blind" ', *Australian Literary Studies*, vol. 9, no. 3, pp. 298-308.
Kiernan, B. 1988, 'Perceptions of Australia, 1915-1965', in L. Hergenhan (ed.), *The Penguin New Literary History of Australia*, Penguin, Ringwood.
Kinross Smith, G. et al. 1978, *The Australian City: Australian Writers and the City*, Deakin University, Waurn Ponds, Vic.
Kramer, L. (ed.) 1981, *The Oxford History of Australian Literature*, Oxford University Press, Melbourne.
Lake, M. 1986, 'The politics of respectability: Identifying the masculinist context', *Historical Studies*, vol. 22, no. 86, pp. 116-31.
Lawson, H. 1976, 'The Sydney *Bulletin*', in B. Kiernan (ed.), *Henry Lawson*, University of Queensland Press, St Lucia, Qld.
Lawson, S. 1983, *The Archibald Paradox: A Strange Case of Authorship*, Allen Lane/Penguin, Ringwood.
McQueen, H. 1970, *A New Britannia*, Penguin, Harmondsworth.
Milner, A. 1985, 'The "English" ideology: Literary criticism in England and Australia', *Thesis Eleven*, no. 12, pp. 110-29.
Milner, A. 1988, 'Radical intellectuals: An unacknowledged legislature?', in V. Burgmann & J. Lee (eds), *Constructing a Culture*, McPhee Gribble/Penguin, Melbourne.
Nadel, G. 1957, *Australia's Colonial Culture: Ideas, Men and Institutions in Mid-Nineteenth Century Eastern Australia*, Cheshire, Melbourne.
Nile, R. & Walker, D. 1988, 'Marketing the literary imagination: The production of Australian literature, 1915-1965', in L. Hergenhan (ed.), *The Penguin New Literary History of Australia*, Penguin, Ringwood.
Palmer, V. 1954, *The Legend of the Nineties*, Melbourne University Press, Melbourne.
Rowse, T. 1978, *Australian Liberalism and National Character*, Kibble Books, Malmsbury, Vic.
Schaffer, K. 1988, *Women and the Bush: Forces of Desire in the Australian Cultural Tradition*, Cambridge University Press, Melbourne.
Serle, G. 1973, *From Deserts the Prophets Come: The Creative Spirit in Australia 1788-1972*, Heinemann, Melbourne (republished in 1987 as *The Creative Spirit in Australia*).
Serle, G. 1987, *The Creative Spirit in Australia: A Cultural History*, Heinemann, Melbourne.
Spender, D. (ed.) 1988, *The Penguin Anthology of Australian Women's Writing*, Penguin, Ringwood.
Stewart, K. 1988, 'Journalism and the world of the writer: The production of Australian literature, 1855-1915', in L. Hergenhan (ed.), *The Penguin New Literary History of Australia*, Penguin, Ringwood.

Strahan, L. 1984, *Just City and the Mirrors: Meanjin Quarterly and the Intellectual Front, 1940-1965*, Oxford University Press, Melbourne.
Tregenza, J. 1964, *Australian Little Magazines 1923-1954*, Libraries Board of South Australia, Adelaide.
Walker, R. B. 1976, *The Newspaper Press in New South Wales, 1803-1920*, Sydney University Press, Sydney.
Walsh, R. 1988, 'Periodicals', in Australian Geographic Society, *The Australian Encyclopaedia*, Terrey Hills, NSW, pp. 2262-8.
Ward, R. 1958, *The Australian Legend*, Oxford University Press, Melbourne.
Webby, E. 1981, 'Before the *Bulletin*: Nineteenth century literary journalism', in B. Bennett (ed.), *Cross Currents: Magazines and Newspapers in Australian Literature*, Longman Cheshire, Melbourne.
Webby, E. 1988, 'Writers, printers, readers: The production of Australian literature before 1855', in L. Hergenhan (ed.), *The Penguin New Literary History of Australia*, Penguin, Ringwood.
White, R. 1981, *Inventing Australia: Images and Identity 1688-1980*, George Allen & Unwin, Sydney.
Whitlock, G. 1985, 'The bush, the stock-yard and the clearing: "Colonial realism" in the short stories and sketches of Susanna Moodie, C. L. R. James and Henry Lawson', *Journal of Commonwealth Literature*, vol. 20, no. 1, pp. 36-48.
Wilde, W. H. et al. 1985, *The Oxford Companion to Australian Literature*, Oxford University Press, Melbourne.
Wilkes, G. A. 1962, 'The eighteen nineties', in G. Johnston (ed.), *Australian Literary Criticism*, Oxford University Press, Melbourne.
Williams, R. 1981, *Culture*, Fontana, London.

8 Nationality and Australian Literature

Astley, T. 1976, 'Being a Queenslander: A form of literary and geographical conceit', *Southerly*, vol. 36, no. 3, pp. 252-64.
Astley, T. 1979, *Hunting the Wild Pineapple*, Nelson, Melbourne.
Barnes, J. (ed.) 1969, *The Writer in Australia, 1856-1964*, Oxford University Press, Melbourne.
Belsey, C. 1980, *Critical Practice*, Methuen, London.
Bennett, T. 1979, *Formalism and Marxism*, Methuen, London.
Blackton, C. 1961, 'Australian nationalism and nationality, 1850-1900', *Historical Studies*, vol. 9, no. 36.
Buckridge, P. 1986, 'Colonial strategies in the writing of David Malouf', *Kunapipi*, vol. 8, no. 3, pp. 48-58.
Buckridge, P. 1988, Intellectual authority and critical traditions in Australian literature, 1940-1975', in B. Head & J. Walter (eds), *Intellectual Movements and Australian Society*, Oxford University Press, Melbourne.
Cantrell, L. (ed.) 1977, *Writing of the 1890s: Short Stories, Verse and Essays*, University of Queensland Press, St Lucia, Qld.
Carey, P. 1988, *Oscar and Lucinda*, University of Queensland Press, St Lucia, Qld.
Carter, D. 1985, 'Re-viewing communism: *Communist Review* (Sydney) 1934-1966: A checklist of literary material', *Australian Literary Studies*, vol. 12, no. 1, pp. 93-105.
Covell, R. 1967, *Australia's Music: Themes of a New Society*, Sun Books, Melbourne.

Cusack, D. & James, F. (1951) 1966, *Come in Spinner*, Pacific Books, Sydney.
Davidson, J. 1983, Interview with David Malouf, in *Sideways from the Page*, Fontana, Melbourne (first published in *Meanjin*, vol. 39, 1980).
Docker, J. 1984, *In a Critical Condition*, Penguin, Ringwood.
Eagleton, T. 1976, *Criticism and Ideology*, New Left Books, London.
Eagleton, T. 1981, *Walter Benjamin: Towards a Revolutionary Criticism*, New Left Books, London.
Ferrier, C. 1983, 'Is an "images of women" methodology adequate for reading Elizabeth Harrower's *The Watch Tower?*', in S. Walker, *Who Is She? Images of Women in Australian Fiction*, University of Queensland Press, St Lucia, Qld.
Fiske, J., Hodge, R. & Turner, G. 1987, *Myths of Oz: Reading Australian Popular Culture*, George Allen & Unwin, Sydney.
Franklin, M. (1936) 1947, *All That Swagger*, Angus & Robertson, Sydney.
Harrower, E. (1966) 1977, *The Watch Tower*, Angus & Robertson, Sydney.
Head, B. & Walter J. (eds) 1988, *Intellectual Movements and Australian Society*, Oxford University Press, Melbourne.
Hergenhan, L. (ed.) 1986, *The Australian Short Story: An Anthology from the 1880s to the 1980s*, University of Queensland Press, St Lucia, Qld.
Hergenhan, L. 1988, *The Penguin New Literary History of Australia*, Penguin, Ringwood.
Hughes, R. 1987, *The Fatal Shore*, Collins Harvill, London.
Ingamells, R. (1938) 1969, 'Conditional culture', in J. Barnes (ed.), *The Writer in Australia, 1956-1964*, Oxford University Press, Melbourne.
Jarvis, D. 1983, 'Morality and literary realism: A debate of the 1880s', *Southerly*, vol. 43, no. 4, pp. 404-20.
Kiernan, B. 1980, *Patrick White*, Macmillan, London.
Kramer, L. 1973, 'Patrick White's Götterdämmerung', *Quadrant*, no. 83, vol. 17, no. 3, pp. 8-19.
Kramer, L. (ed.), 1981, *The Oxford History of Australian Literature*, Oxford University Press, Melbourne.
MacCabe, C. 1974, 'Realism and the cinema: Notes on some Brechtian thesis', *Screen*, vol. 15, no. 1, pp. 4-10.
McDougall, R. 1987, 'Sprawl and the vertical', in R. McDougall & G. Whitlock (eds), *Australian/Canadian Literatures in English: Comparative Perspectives*, Methuen Australia, Melbourne, pp. 205-37.
McInherny, F. 1983, ' "Deep into the destructive core": Elizabeth Harrower's "The Watch Tower" ', *Hecate*, vol. 9, nos 1, 2, pp. 123-34.
Malouf, D. 1985, *Antipodes*, Chatto & Windus, London.
Matthews, B. 1976, 'Henry Lawson's fictional world', in L. Cantrell (ed.), *Bards, Bohemians and Bookmen: Essays in Australian Literature*, University of Queensland Press, St Lucia, Qld.
Milner, A. 1985, 'The "English ideology": Literary criticism in England and Australia', *Thesis Eleven*, no. 12, pp. 110-29.
Modjeska, D. 1981, *Exiles at Home: Australian Women Writers, 1925-1945*, Angus & Robertson, Sydney.
Murray, L. 1983, *The People's Otherworld*, Angus & Robertson, Sydney.
Nelson, P. 1984, 'Adam McCay and Sydney's literary bohemia, 1911-1947', *Australian Literary Studies*, vol. 11, no. 4, pp. 495-502.
Nesbitt, B. 1971, 'Literary nationalism and the 1890s', *Australian Literary Studies*, vol. 5, no. 1, pp. 3-17.

Penton, B. (1934) 1972, *Landtakers*, Angus & Robertson, Sydney.
Phillips, A. (1950) 1958, 'The cultural cringe', in *The Australian Tradition: Studies in a Colonial Culture*, Longman Cheshire, Melbourne.
Reid, I. 1979, *Fiction and the Great Depression: Australia and New Zealand, 1930-1950*, Edward Arnold, Melbourne.
Rowse, T. 1978, *Australian Liberalism and National Character*, Kibble Books, Malmsbury, Vic.
Schaffer, K. 1988, *Women and the Bush*, Cambridge University Press, Cambridge.
Serle, G. 1987, *The Creative Spirit in Australia: A Cultural History*, Heinemann, Melbourne.
Stephensen, P. R. (1935) 1969, 'The foundations of culture in Australia', in J. Barnes (ed.), *The Writer in Australia, 1856-1964*, Oxford University Press, Melbourne.
Stivens, D. (1951) 1983, *Jimmy Brockett: Portrait of a Notable Australian*, Penguin, Ringwood.
Stivens, D. 1969, *Selected Stories 1936-1968*, Angus & Robertson, Sydney.
Turner, G. 1986, *National Fictions: Literature, Film and the Construction of Australian Narrative*, George Allen & Unwin, Sydney.
Walker, S. 1983, *Who Is She? Images of Women in Australian Fiction*, University of Queensland Press, St Lucia, Qld.
White, P. 1958, 'The prodigal son', *Australian Letters*, vol. 1, no. 3, pp. 156-8.
White, R. 1981, *Inventing Australia: Images and Identity, 1688-1980*, George Allen & Unwin, Sydney.
Whitlock, G. 1985, *Gender and Writing*, School of Humanities, Griffith University, Qld (course HP 13b, part-time BA programme).
Wilde, W., Hooton, J. & Andrews, B. (eds) 1986, *The Oxford Companion to Australian Literature*, Oxford University Press, Melbourne.
Williams, P. 1987, 'Gambling with socialism: A hardy obsession', *Southern Review*, vol. 20, no. 1, pp. 69-87.
Williams, R. 1973, *The Country and the City*, Chatto & Windus, London.
Williams, R. 1976, *Keywords: A Vocabulary of Culture and Society*, Fontana, London.

9 Australian Film and Television

Barr, C. 1974, 'Projecting Britain and the British character: Ealing Studios Part 1', *Screen*, vol. 15, no. 1.
Berton, P. 1977, *Hollywood's Canada*, Take One, Montreal.
Bertrand, I. & Collins, D. 1982, *Government and Film in Australia*, Currency Press, Sydney.
Blonski, A. & Freiberg, F. 1989, 'Double trouble: Women's films', in A. Moran & T. O'Regan (eds), *The Australian Screen*, Penguin, Ringwood.
Bordwell, D. 1985, *Narration in the Cinema*, University of Wisconsin, Madison.
Canby, V. 1983, 'The screen—"Man From Snowy River"', *New York Times*, 21 January, p. 132.
Dermody, S. & Jacka, E. 1987, *The Screening of Australia*, vol. 1, Currency Press, Sydney.
Flaus, J. 1987, Interview, ABC Radio National, 25 November.

Harrison, K. 1980, *The Points System for Australian Television Content*, Royal Institute of Public Administration, Brisbane.
Hawley, J. 1981, 'The making of Snowy River', *Age*, 18 April.
Herd, N. 1983, *Independent Film-making in Australia 1960-1980*, Australian Film and Television School, Sydney.
Lawson, S. 1965, 'Not for the likes of us', *Quadrant*, May/June (repr. in A. Moran & T. O'Regan (eds) 1985, *An Australian Film Reader*, Currency Press, Sydney).
McCallum, J. 1979, *My Life With Googie*, Heinemann, London.
Martin, A. 1989, 'Indefinite objects: Independent film and video', in A. Moran & T. O'Regan (eds), *The Australian Screen*, Penguin, Ringwood.
Moran, A. 1982, 'Localism in Australian television', in S. Dermody, J. Docker & D. Modjeska (eds), *Nellie Melba, Ginger Meggs and All That*, Kibble Books, Malmsbury, Vic.
Moran, A. & O'Regan, T. (eds) 1985, *An Australian Film Reader*, Currency Press, Sydney.
Murray, J. C. 1973, 'Defending the defenders', *Lumiere*, April.
Neale, S. 1980, *Genre*, British Film Institute, London.
Nordenstreng, K. & Varis, T. 1973, 'The non homogeneity of the national state and the international flow of television', in G. Gerbner, L. Gross & W. Melody (eds), *Communications, Technology and Social Control*, John Wiley, New York.
O'Regan, T. 1982a, 'Australian film: Its public circulation', in A. Hutton (ed.), *The First Australian History and Film Conference Papers*, Australian Film and Television School, Sydney.
O'Regan, T. 1982b, 'The Man From Snowy River and Australian popular culture', *Filmnews*, vol. 12, no. 9 (repr. in A. Moran & T. O'Regan (eds) 1985, *An Australian Film Reader*, Currency Press, Sydney).
O'Regan, T. 1985, The politics of representation: An analysis of the Australian film revival, PhD thesis, Division of Humanities, Griffith University, Qld.
O'Regan, T. 1989, 'Cinema oz: The ocker films', in A. Moran & T. O'Regan (eds), *The Australian Screen*, Penguin, Ringwood.
Pike, A. & Cooper, R. 1980, *Australian Film 1900-1977: A Guide to Feature Film Production*, Oxford University Press in association with the Australian Film Institute, Melbourne.
Ricketson, J. 1979, 'Poor movie, rich movie', *Filmnews*, January (repr. in A. Moran & T. O'Regan (eds) 1985, *An Australian Film Reader*, Currency Press, Sydney).
Robinson, L. 1949, 'Photogenic frontiers', *Film Monthly*, August.
Rockett, K., Gibbons, L. & Hill, J. 1987, *Cinema and Ireland*, Croom Helm, London.
Ryan, T. 1980, 'History in film', in P. Beilby & S. Murray (eds), *The New Australian Cinema*, Nelson/Cinema Papers, Melbourne.
Shirley, G. & Adams, B. 1983, *Australian Cinema: The First Eighty Years*, Angus & Robertson/Currency Press, Sydney.
South Australian Film Corporation Act 1972, South Australian Government Printer, Adelaide.
Thompson, K. 1985, *Exporting Entertainment: America in the World Film Market 1907-34*, British Film Institute, London.

Tosi, G. 1982, 'Geoff Burrows and George Miller: Two men behind Snowy River', *Cinema Papers*, no. 38, June, pp. 206–12, 283.
Tulloch, J. 1981, *Legends on the Screen*, Currency Press, Sydney.
Turner, G. 1986, *National Fictions*, George Allen & Unwin, Sydney.
Whitburn, D. 1981, 'The bushmen love hard riding—but some actually don't', *Bulletin*, 19 May.

PART IV

ORDER AND CONFLICT

Introduction

At first glance the title 'order and conflict' sits uncomfortably with popular views of Australia as a peaceful, egalitarian society mercifully free of the political upheavals that have characterized other countries in the last few hundred years. Australia, as a new and prosperous colony of white settlement (particularly after the gold-rushes), provided great opportunities for economic gain and social mobility and was free of the social conflicts that troubled the Old World. Supporters of this view point to the high standard of living enjoyed by Australian workers, the lack of city slums and, more importantly, the absence of the social revolutions, foreign invasions and civil wars that have marked the histories of other western nations (Jackson 1977:1-27). By these criteria a favourable comparison can also be made with other 'new' societies, notably the United States. Australia, as the eminent historian Douglas Pike wrote in 1962, is 'the quiet continent'.

Not everyone has agreed with this view. The radical historian Brian Fitzpatrick (1968:62) believed that Australia's history was one of conflict between 'the organised rich and the organised poor'. This is not a view which has captured the popular imagination but it has influenced many radical, labour and socialist historians in Australia. They have pointed to the serious struggles between capital and labour—the 1890s strikes, the general strike of 1917, the 1949 coal strike and the 1973 Broadmeadows strike, to name but a few—as evidence of the importance of conflict in Australian society (Connell & Irving 1980). Few deny that such conflicts have been significant in Australia's history, but are they temporary disruptions to an otherwise peaceful society or manifestations of more fundamental conflicts in capitalist society? It is the latter view which distinguishes socialist and Marxist accounts of Australian society; these accounts argue that class struggle is the fundamental characteristic of Australian capitalist society.

Other areas of serious conflict in Australian society have been highlighted in recent research. In Aboriginal studies abundant evidence has been assembled to state that Australia was invaded by white settlers. They took the land of the original inhabitants, often by violent means, in what amounted to a war which accounted for the deaths of perhaps 20 000 Aborigines. Moreover, Aborigines resisted this invasion, utilizing guerrilla warfare tactics, killing as many as 3000 settlers (Reynolds 1987:30,53). By the criterion of armed conflict, the forging of the Australian nation was far from bloodless.

Women's studies have pointed to other dimensions of conflict in Australian society. Feminists have described the marked inequalities of women in relation to men, measured in lower wages, fewer educational opportunities, restrictive sex stereotyping and poor levels of funding for services for women (Summers 1975). For some, these disadvantages are the product of sexist attitudes which require legal and cultural redress. Other feminists focus on more fundamental levels of sex conflict evident in violence against women—rape, sexual assault, domestic violence and pornography. In this focus feminists have argued that sexist attitudes are merely the representation of a deeper structure of conflict, namely patriarchy or the rule of women by men (Eisenstein 1984).

Class, race and sex conflict are now well established as important structures in Australian society. These are not the only forms of conflict. Others include the contest over the preservation of the environment, sectarianism, struggles between inmates and warders in institutions and conflicts between migrants and Anglo-Australians. From these conflicts come significant features of Australian society: inequality, poverty, industrial unrest, political protest and violence. The analysis of these conflicts and their associated characteristics has come from a number of disciplines and fields of study—history, sociology, social policy, anthropology, political economy, Marxism, women's studies and Aboriginal studies to name some of the most important. Each of these disciplines and fields of study contributes important dimensions to the analysis of the problem of conflict. None the less there are debates about the causes and character of these conflicts (Western 1982). Are these conflicts embedded in the very structure of Australian society? In what ways have these conflicts determined the course of events in Australia and the daily experiences of Australians?

Answering these questions involves the consideration of a second problem—order. If the popular conception of Australia is one of relative stability and consensus, how then have the effects of conflicts been contained and social order maintained? The problem of order focuses attention on the role of the state in Australia. The aim of the state—parliament, bureaucracy, military, police, prisons, hospitals and schools—is often argued to be the maintenance and protection of the existing social order. Force is one means to maintain order. The police and military have been used to quell violent conflicts and protests against government policies. The more usual way to achieve order is through the provision and maintenance of particular institutions—schools, families and the media—which produce and reproduce the general culture in which people live. Another means is by the provision of direct benefits to particular social groups. The development of the welfare state is one example. But, just as there are debates about the causes and character of conflict, so there are debates about the role and purpose of the state in maintaining social order. Is the state an arbiter between different social groups aiming to achieve some agreed social contract or does it serve the interests of particular social groups to the detriment of others? Does the state rigidly enforce order or is

Introduction 187

it a set of conflicting institutions which provide opportunities for particular groups to press for social change (Sydney Labour History Group 1982:7–12)?

These questions have a particular pertinence for debates in Australian studies, for problems of social order and the management of conflict were central to the European occupation and settlement of Australia. Throughout the colonial period and into the twentieth century the constantly expanding population required or demanded new institutional solutions to problems of subsistence, housing, rural settlement, segregation of resistant or unwanted groups and so on. The forms of British government and administration were sometimes suited to resolving such demands; at other times they were not. The histories of state measures and instrumentalities—such as immigration programmes, incentives for reproduction, arbitration of wages and industrial conflict, the dispersal, segregation or protection of Aboriginal peoples—require analysis in terms of the specific conditions of European settlement in Australia. Debates about the peculiarity of Australian solutions to these conditions or their grounding in more general processes common to modern societies, capitalist or not, are important for understanding modern Australian society.

Our aim here is not to resolve these debates but to introduce the problems of order and conflict in Australia and the debates that are associated with the analysis of these problems. This is done by examining four themes of order and conflict. The first three focus on areas of study which analyse conflicts in Australia: Aboriginal history, class and women's history. The final theme focuses on a product of conflict and inequality and the attempts to solve this problem: poverty and social welfare. Some areas of conflict have not been included, notably the environment and sectarianism. Some, however, are covered in other chapters in this book, including aspects of the conflict between capital and labour, migration and ethnic conflicts, conflict between political parties and cultural conflict.

The four themes in part IV serve to demonstrate a variety of conflicts in Australia and the means for maintaining order. Each chapter introduces some of the major debates and questions in the area, drawing on contributions from a number of disciplines and fields of study. The associated reference lists, although not comprehensive, represent some of the important works in each field and are useful guides to further reading.

10 ABORIGINAL HISTORY

Chapter 10 explores the making of particular histories of Aborigines in the light of relations between blacks and whites in Australia. It examines the changing concerns of historians, the contexts which produce new questions and interpretations and the methodological problems involved in writing histories of Aborigines. It examines recent critiques by Aborigines of the preoccupations of Aboriginal history.

11   LABOUR, CLASS AND CULTURE

Themes in the writing of labour history are examined in chapter 11. The development of labour history in Australia was closely tied to the political project of radical nationalism. The tendency in earlier work to concentrate on the history of the labour movement has been replaced in more recent studies by attention to class structures, to the problems posed by the sexual division of labour and to the relation between class formation, aspects of national culture and state intervention. These developments are surveyed through discussion of some key texts in labour history, women's work and the nature of state arbitration.

12   FROM WOMEN'S HISTORY TO A HISTORY OF THE SEXES

Chapter 12 investigates the use of women as 'order' in penal and colonial Australia, the ordering of women's lives around marriage, motherhood and various forms of paid and unpaid work throughout the nineteenth and twentieth centuries, and the manifestations of conflict and resistance to their situation that can be identified in different categories of women during these two centuries. Important themes of the chapter are demographic, social, sexual and cultural options facing the sexes in Australia. The argument is advanced that more work is needed on the history of *men* as a sex, framed with the benefit of the insights gained from two decades of Australian women's history.

13   POVERTY IN PARADISE

Debates about the nature and extent of poverty in Australia are examined in chapter 13. What are the causes of poverty? What methods of analysis have allowed us to uncover evidence of poverty in a nation that was meant to be a 'workingman's paradise'? In addition this chapter explores the history of welfare provision for the poor, focusing particularly on debates about the purpose and effectiveness of Australian welfare systems.

CHAPTER TEN

ABORIGINAL HISTORY

Stephen Garton

In 1788 Arthur Phillip claimed the continent of Australia as a British possession. In making this declaration he was implementing the principle of *terra nullius* (literally 'no person's land'). This meant that the British government had declared Australia to be uninhabited and hence available for annexation as a new territory, free of the obligation of negotiating treaties with an existing population (Frost 1981:513-23). Of course the continent of Australia was not uninhabited. Most authorities have estimated the Aboriginal population at the time of the First Fleet to be about 300 000. More recently N. G. Butlin (1983) has argued that the total population was possibly as high as a million, declining rapidly in the first years of white settlement because of smallpox epidemics. More cautious estimates now put the first contact Aboriginal population at 750 000 (Mulvaney & White 1987:115-17). In addition, it has been estimated that Aborigines had been in continuous occupation of the land for at least 50 000 years (Broome 1982:9-10).

The colonization of Australia was part of a broader European imperative. The European exploitation of the resources of other cultures fuelled the rapid pace of economic development known as the Industrial Revolution. Land was seen as Australia's greatest resource and Australia became one of a distinct group of European colonies—a colony of white settlement. Settlement and economic exploitation of available resources required the dispossession of the original Aboriginal inhabitants. This process of dispossession occurred in the south-east corner of the continent in the first half of the nineteenth century. In the second half of the nineteenth century the frontier extended into Queensland, northern and western Australia. By 1920 this process was largely complete and Australian governments were left with the decision of how to deal with those Aborigines who had survived their dispossession. But what was the nature of this dispossession? Was it an orderly settlement fulfilling the need for Europe to expand its frontiers and extend the benefits of economic growth? Or was it an invasion, an illegitimate conquest of the original Aboriginal inhabitants? The answers to these questions stand to tell us much about the character of European colonization. They are also inextricably linked to political conflicts over land rights for Aboriginal peoples. History has been seen as the arena for settling these questions.

Although the formal and legal dispossession of the Aborigines was unproblematic for British authorities, the realization of settlement and conquest proved to be protracted. A central element in this struggle was Aboriginal resistance to invasion, and this history of black–white conflict has been the context for the production of histories of the relations between white settlers and the Aborigines. The process of writing, and rewriting, this history of black–white relations is currently a major area of historical research and debate. But what have been the dominant representations of Aborigines and white settlement within this historiography? In what ways have Eurocentric and racist assumptions constructed these representations? These questions are important for understanding the ways in which knowledges are produced and the interrelations between knowledges and wider social and political structures. But these questions are also relevant to the broader political issue of the nature of European colonization and the contemporary Aboriginal struggle for self-determination.

Benevolent settlement?

Although W. K. Hancock titled the first chapter of his famous *Australia* (1930) 'The invasion of Australia', this was a metaphor for the conquest of the natural environment, not for another culture. Few historians before the 1960s considered white settlement to be anything other than natural and inevitable. But had colonization benefited the original inhabitants? The answer to this question stood to reveal much about the nature of colonization and could serve as a guide to future policy. Most early historians of Australia preferred to ignore these issues. Australia was usually seen as a land ripe for settlement and much colonial policy focused precisely on the issue of the best methods of settlement. Nineteenth-century histories of Australia perpetuated this view. Their concern was with charting the exploration and later settlement of the land. It was a story of hardship, the overcoming of harsh conditions, the throwing off of the convict past and the emergence of Australia as a prosperous 'workingman's paradise' free of the dilemmas of the Old World. In this context the Aborigines were rarely accorded a mention, except as guides or obstacles to exploration or, more significantly in the earliest accounts of colonization, as curiosities far removed from civilized 'man'. Only a few considered the larger moral issues raised by the treatment of Aborigines in colonial Australia.

The relegation of Aborigines to the margins of historical concern is perhaps not surprising. It reflected prevailing conceptions of Aborigines as close to brutes in 'the great chain of being' and from the late 1860s, when social Darwinist ideas became popular, as a dying race doomed to extinction by natural selection (Reynolds 1987:109-23). Many settlers believed that the sooner Aborigines were eradicated the better (Reynolds 1987:58-62). But there were alternative colonial opinions. A small group of humanitarian officials and clergy, particularly active in the 1830s, were concerned to protect the Aborigines from the ravages of settlement (Reynolds 1987:83-8).

In the first half of the nineteenth century men such as Governor Macquarie, G. A. Robinson and the Reverend L. E. Threlkeld believed that Aborigines could be civilized and converted to Christianity. They established schools and missions to facilitate this process. These were not happy experiments. Of the 200 Aborigines taken to Flinders Island by G. A. Robinson only fifty survived to 1847. Macquarie's Natives Institution closed after a few years and Threlkeld's Lake Macquarie Mission limped along in the 1840s suffering from declining numbers and the resistance of some Aborigines to the conversion process. Some began to doubt that the Aborigines were capable of being civilized. The 'natives' were seen as irretrievably 'savage'. From the 1870s these failures reinforced the new social-Darwinist beliefs that the Aborigines were an unfit race, incapable of improvement, and doomed to extinction. In this new climate of opinion many missionaries began to see conversion not as the first step in civilizing the Aborigines but as the means for giving the dying race a decent Christian burial. Only a few remained convinced that the Aborigines could become Christian citizens (Curthoys 1982:37-49).

It was in this context that James Bonwick ([1870] 1970), an evangelical lay preacher and schoolmaster, published his history of the Tasmanian Aborigines. Writing in the 1860s, he concluded that the 'civilizing' process had failed, but disputed the accepted reasons for that failure; it was not the innate inability of Aborigines to reform that was the problem, but drink. Alcohol, argued Bonwick, had a bad effect on many people, but on 'savages' doubly so, since they lacked a moral conscience. The force of this argument was that the Aborigines were not irredeemable. They were 'savages' because they had not benefited from 'civilization' but they were not incapable of improvement. This conclusion challenged the pessimistic views of the period. Bonwick believed that the civilizing programme was the correct one but was undermined by other factors. In this story George Augustus Robinson is represented as a hero and the Aborigines as the romantic victims of a tragedy and destroyed by forces beyond their control.

The existence of frontier conflict has been, and continues to be, a historiographical problem. Decisions about how to represent the nature and extent of racial violence have been seen as interconnected with assessments about the legitimacy of British colonization and the course of government policy. Evidence of unprovoked and extensive violence against Aborigines challenges the representation of colonization as a beneficial and progressive set of developments rooted in 'natural laws' of economic expansion. Such a view was at the heart of British beliefs in the legitimacy of colonization.

In the nineteenth century few historians addressed themselves directly to the issue of frontier conflict as the measure of colonial policy. One important exception was G. W. Rusden, who dealt with the question of Aboriginal policy at length in his three-volume *History of Australia*, published in 1883. Rusden was unequivocal in his condemnation of the history of white reactions to Aborigines. In his view the violent clashes on the frontier were almost solely the fault of the settlers, who indiscriminately destroyed the blacks. The police forces, particularly the Native Police, were among the worst offenders. The crimes of the settlers went unpunished. The only persons making a positive contribution to the welfare of the Aborigines were missionaries and members of the Aborigines Protection Association. Rusden was not reticent about his purpose: he hoped to arouse public support for more 'humane' policies towards the Aborigines.

Few subsequent histories of Australia accepted Rusden's conclusions. Major works, such as F. Jenks's *A History of the Australasian Colonies* (1895), H. G. Turner's *A History of the Colony of Victoria* (1904), E. Scott's *A Short History of Australia* (1916), and S. H. Roberts's *History of Australian Land Settlement* (1924), all dealt with the Aborigines and frontier conflict in a few pages. In doing so they implicitly justified the movement for the expansion of settlement, and dismissed Aboriginal resistance as either non-existent or sporadic lawlessness. They ignored the 'moral' issues raised in Rusden's account and represented the squatters' view of the Aborigines as marauding bandits to be an accurate account (Biskup 1982:13–14). Evidence of violence was minimized, seen as inevitable or placed against accounts of Aboriginal atrocities.

The general absence of Aborigines from historical accounts continued until the 1930s and 1940s when two important histories of native policy were published. E. J. B. Foxcroft's *Australian Native Policy* (1941) and P. M. C. Hasluck's *Black Australians* ([1942] 1970) were the first substantial studies of black–white relations since Rusden and Bonwick. The gap reflected beliefs in 'the dying race' but the resurgence of historical interest in native policy grew out of new developments in the treatment of Aborigines.

In the second half of the nineteenth century, despite the 'doomed race' theory and strong racist antipathy to blacks, Aborigines were becoming an important source of labour in some industries—notably the pastoral industry in northern Australia. Although racist ideas justified lower wage rates, it was important for employers to maintain the supply of Aboriginal labour. Employers supported some initiatives to isolate Aborigines on government reserves and church missions but opposed those reserves and missions, notably Coranderrk and Maloga, where Aborigines were achieving a measure of self-sufficiency. By resuming the prime reserve land, settlers were able to make reserve Aborigines a dependent social group needing to work on local stations in order to survive (Broome 1982:69–87).

Officials at the turn of the century confronted another problem. The Aborigines had not died out. On the contrary the birth rate seemed to be increasing and many of the children were of mixed descent, often referred to as 'half-castes' (Rowley 1972a:138–9). This fact became apparent at the height of popularity of eugenics, a theory which argued that western civilization was being undermined because the unfit (the poor, drunks, lunatics and lower races) were breeding at a faster rate than the fit. In this context new protection policies were developed to deal with the Aboriginal and half-caste problem. Government reserves became places for 'full-blood' Aborigines, where they could be separated from the wider population to prevent inter-breeding. Half-caste children (at least the fair-skinned) were removed from their parents on the reserves, sent to institutions for training and then apprenticed out to prevent further mixing of the races (Read 1982:2–15).

In the 1920s and 1930s the protection policies seemed to be assuming a different character. Prominent anthropologists such as A. P. Elkin (1951;1974) pointed to the complexity and richness of Aboriginal culture. Elkin was instrumental in challenging many of the simplistic evolutionary assumptions that underpinned prevailing attitudes towards Aborigines. But he believed that the 'true' Aboriginal culture had been largely eroded by the impact of white settlement, pastoralism and the growth of a half-caste population. In his view the remaining full-bloods had to be segregated in an attempt to protect the remnants of the original culture but half-castes had to be assimilated into the larger white society. This did little to alter the policy of protection and the removal of children but it placed the rhetoric of assimilation into the forefront of 'native policy' debates. This rhetoric was reaffirmed at the 1937 Commonwealth and State Government Conference on Aborigines (Rowley 1972a:305–40). It was in this context that Foxcroft (1941) and Hasluck ([1942] 1970) reviewed the history of Aboriginal policy.

Foxcroft based his reassessment of 'native policy' on an application of modern anthropological theories to the understanding of the failures of past policies. He was particularly influenced by the work of Elkin, and other writers such as Daisy Bates. His argument on the issue of Aboriginal culture was clear:

> Today we are familiar enough with the notion that the social organisation and mode of life of the natives . . . are neither bestial nor unintelligent. The view, however, that their social scheme is complex, yet not irrational, that within this scheme their ethical conduct is high, that their language is good . . . and that altogether their kind of life is a remarkably intelligent adaptation to the environment is less popularly known. [Foxcroft 1941:11].

Such a view was central to Foxcroft's interpretation of the history of Aboriginal policy but Foxcroft's focus on policy led him to minimize the extent of frontier conflict in black–white relations. He believed this was only sporadic and marginal in comparison to disease and bad policies. Where Bonwick and other early historians believed that 'civilization' policies had not been pursued adequately, Foxcroft argued that they were inevitably doomed to failure because they took no account of the nature of Aboriginal culture.

These assumptions formed the basis of Foxcroft's conclusions about the course of 'native policy' in the 1930s and in the future. He came down in favour of segregation as the only way to protect the remaining 'tribal' Aborigines. However, he concurred with the influential views of Elkin: the ultimate aim of native policy should be assimilation. Effort therefore had to be directed towards education, the payment of decent wages, the provision of sufficient food and medical services, the granting of full citizenship rights and the extension of a measure of self-government on reserves. Although assimilation was the ultimate goal, segregation was the immediate policy. Reserves would provide sanctuaries of a temporary nature until the best means of facilitating assimilation could be worked out.

Hasluck, like Foxcroft, believed that western colonization was the extension of a 'natural law' of social contact between different social groups. If it was a natural tendency, an almost inescapable driving force of any society, then no blame could really be attached to the colonizers—they were merely implementing long-standing social needs. Hasluck was also insistent that reports of violence should not be exaggerated or sensationalized. In arguing thus he argued for the legitimacy of white settlement in Australia. If settlement had been both inevitable and legitimate, the question remained: Had it been responsible? His conclusion was not a favourable one. Despite early attempts to achieve important principles in native administration these attempts were, on the whole, failures. None the less Hasluck was quick to point out that this failure was the result of circumstances rather than bad intentions.

Although his story was similar to Foxcroft's, Hasluck differed in his assessment of the reforms of the twentieth century. He argued that the policy of segregation was merely an expedient; it was a 'salvage operation' that was a convenient way of getting out of a number of difficulties (Hasluck [1942] 1970:205-6). For Hasluck it was also an unrealistic policy. He stated that there were very few tribalized Aborigines left and they could only be kept on reserves in the unwanted parts of Australia. Segregation was a policy which avoided the central responsibility of the colonizer; it did not provide Aborigines with the full fruits of citizenship and substituted a welfare system for a proper programme of education. For Hasluck full assimilation was the answer.

The works of Hasluck and Foxcroft are important examples of liberal-inspired paternalism. In this framework the Aborigines were the students or children while white reformers were the guardians or fathers who would educate the Aborigines and facilitate their assimilation into the wider society. Their work represented and legitimated the viewpoint of reformers who favoured assimilation. While the assimilationist position was humanitarian, it denied Aborigines self-determination. These histories also accepted that white settlement had been a natural and largely peaceful process. In Foxcroft and Hasluck's histories good intentions had been undermined by ignorance, and the decline of the Aboriginal race was due to disease not violence. Colonization was thus seen as a process of settlement, not invasion. This remained the accepted view of the course of Aboriginal-white contact until the 1960s.

Frontier conflict

In the 1950s and 1960s assimilation became the accepted government policy in relation to Aborigines. But at the same time as Australian governments sought to improve the position of Aborigines, developments overseas challenged the paternalism that underpinned these policies. In the post-1945 years indigenous nationalist movements throughout Africa, Asia and South America struggled to remove colonial powers such as Britain, France, Portugal and the Netherlands from their lands. Violent confrontations often resulted. Nationalists claimed that these European nations were imperialist and colonialist powers that had taken and destroyed the original political structures of the Third World in the pursuit of profit and dominance. They challenged the colonial ideas which created an image of European powers bringing civilization to primitive peoples.

In the United States another form of struggle developed with the emergence of the black rights movement. Fundamental to the growth of these movements was the debate about racism. Blacks began to analyse the nature and extent of racism, and its central place in imperialism, colonialism and slavery. It was argued that racism had been a central ideology in the period of colonial expansion and continued to be a major factor in the domination of 'coloured' peoples (Van Den Berghe 1967).

These developments had their effect in Australia. The Menzies, Holt, Gorton and McMahon governments professed support for United Nations resolutions critical of racism. Also, these governments were ostensibly more receptive to proposals for the reform of Aboriginal policy. In this context they established such institutions as the Institute for Aboriginal Studies in 1962 and initiated forums such as the 1965 Aboriginal Welfare Conference. Nevertheless, the harvest of policies from these debates was meagre. Although the 1967 referendum granted Aborigines citizenship rights few reforms were initiated, although much discussion was given to the problems involved. In part, the failure to implement significant reforms in the late 1960s and early 1970s stemmed from the strong resistance to reform, particularly from state governments, notably Queensland and Western Australia, and from mining companies and large sections of the white rural population (Broome 1982:171-94).

Despite this opposition the Aboriginal rights movement continued to grow in Australia. Although there had been a significant black movement since the 1920s, largely organized by blacks, it had been systematically ignored by governments and the media. In the late 1960s the involvement of whites drew greater media attention to the movement for reform. Aborigines and university students were prominent in the campaign. In 1965 'freedom rides' were organized by well-known black activist Charles Perkins; students used hired buses to tour rural townships and protest over the living conditions of blacks. There they confronted violent resistance from locals and the resultant publicity highlighted the extent of racism and discrimination in rural areas. Central to these campaigns was the assertion of the right of Aborigines to self-determination—to the establishment of conditions which allowed Aborigines to make their own decisions, free of the influence of white missionaries, reserve managers, bosses or politicians. Out of this movement land rights became the key to achieving self-determination (Broome 1982:175-83). In this context a number of historians began to reassess the history of black–white contact in Australia. One of the first and most influential was C. D. Rowley, whose three-volume *Aboriginal Policy and Practice* (1972b) became a standard work in Aboriginal historiography.

Rowley concentrated on Aboriginal policy and surveyed familiar themes and events, such as the early attempts to 'civilize' the Aborigines, the efforts of George Augustus Robinson on Flinders Island, the Port Phillip Protectorate, the establishment of the Native Police Force, the reserves movement, the 1929 Bleakley Report and the 1937 Commonwealth–States Conference. In doing so he was not greatly extending the range of 'facts' that could have been ascertained from such sources as Bonwick, Rusden, Foxcroft or Hasluck. Instead, Rowley was reinterpreting these facts, reconstructing their significance and meaning and providing a different political context for their production. By juxtaposing evidence of frontier conflict, particularly white massacres of Aborigines, Rowley (1972a:26) constructed a picture of a harsh, violent society where paternalist Christian reforms were simply another aspect of racist assumptions about the nature of Aboriginal society. In this construction the history of black–white relations was one of a 'long drawn out process of conquest and of hopeless but stubborn resistance'.

Rowley's arguments represented an important shift of emphasis in the reading of 'the facts of settlement'. In earlier constructions settlement was an inevitable, even necessary and legitimate, process of expanding white 'civilization'. Frontier conflict was an unfortunate series of isolated incidents largely perpetrated by frustrated settlers. Similarly, the 'tragedy' of 'native policy' was the failure of well-intentioned reform and the inability of Aborigines to adapt to white society. In Rowley's version settlement was a process of conquest which inevitably entailed systematic frontier conflict to facilitate the expansion of the pastoral economy. Attempts to civilize the Aborigines were founded on racist assumptions that white society was superior and enforced principles of 'moral' coercion characteristic of prisons, asylums and other supposedly reformative institutions. This was not to suggest that all white settlers, particularly missionaries, were consciously racist or deliberately cruel. On the contrary, many reforms were well-intentioned, but the very founding principles of these policies embodied racist assumptions about the nature of Aborigines. In Rowley's view the growth and development of Australian society was founded on racist assumptions and the implementation racist policies towards Aborigines.

There were other implications in Rowley's focus on frontier violence and racism. Underpinning his concerns was a powerful plea for land rights. The Aborigines had been forcibly dispossessed of the most important element of their culture—land. If this was so, then land rights needed to be granted to give back what had been wrongfully taken. In the 1970s a number of other historians, notably Markus (1974), Evans, Saunders & Cronin (1975), Reynolds (1978) and Ryan (1981), took frontier violence as the central theme in the history of black–white relations in Australia.

Some historians stressed other aspects of frontier conflict. The impact of feminism, and theoretical developments in the relations between racism and sexism, was apparent in work which examined the distinct experiences of Aboriginal women on the frontier. Raymond

Evans (1982) presented an uncompromising picture of black–white relations. On the frontier there was a marked sex imbalance in the white population: men far outnumbered women. In this situation black women were particularly vulnerable to sexual aggression from male settlers. In his view inter-racial sexual relations occurred 'within a context of unfreedom, exploitation and terror'. While there was some initial *rapprochement* between black males and settlers over Aboriginal women, where the women were used as exchange objects to construct traditional ties of reciprocity, this fell foul of white ignorance of Aboriginal traditions. White males consequently developed the view that Aboriginal women were particularly degraded and were to be used in any way they saw fit.

The most comprehensive study of white racism and violence has been Henry Reynolds's *Frontier* (1987). Reynolds has charted the complexity of white responses to Aborigines, from the humanitarian to those who advocated the extermination of the race. Underpinning each, however, were racist or paternalist ideas which denied the Aborigines the right to self-determination. Reynolds also pointed to many of the unrecorded battlefields in Australia, mapping the numerous instances where settlers killed Aborigines. Most importantly, he argued that the Aborigines fought back, killing a number of settlers and delaying the progress of settlement in outlying regions by many years. The Aborigines did not passively submit to white settlement but resisted the dispossession of their land. Similar arguments are presented in Lyndall Ryan's study *The Aboriginal Tasmanians* (1981). Ryan's important study shows the processes of dispossession and resistance and dispels the myth that the Tasmanian Aborigines became extinct in the 1870s. But the greatest concern of Rowley, Markus, Reynolds, Ryan and others was the actions of whites towards Aborigines. Only Reynolds and Ryan pointed to black responses to invasion. It is this issue that has been a major concern of historians in the 1970s: what was it like on the other side, the black side, of the frontier?

The other side of the frontier

In the late 1970s Henry Reynolds began to publish the fruits of his research into black resistance to invasion. This culminated in the publication of his book *The Other Side of the Frontier* (1982). Reynolds's work represented a challenge to established views and historiographical traditions. In his view the dominant characterizations of Aborigines in Australian history underestimated the variety and complexity of Aboriginal responses to invasion. The notion of a static, 'primitive' society incapable of adapting, or the passive Aboriginal victim of white violence failed to deal with resistance and innovation by blacks. In arguing for a new characterization Reynolds was well aware of its political implications. A complex rationalization of the legitimacy of white settlement was founded upon the view of Aborigines as passive and primitive. A challenge to that orthodoxy, Reynolds argued, undermined many of the comfortable beliefs in the inevitability and justice of white settlement.

Reynolds used oral evidence and a critical re-reading of documentary sources to provide evidence to construct a history of the black experience. Far from being the passive victims of white cultural domination, Aboriginal culture retained many of its traditions and social relations despite the white onslaught. Reynolds argued that Aboriginal culture was not static or incapable of adapting to new circumstances but, on the contrary, was particularly innovative. Aborigines had an existing cultural framework with which to accommodate outsiders (it was not their fault that settlers refused to accept the Aboriginal overtures) and proved receptive to the arrival of European goods such as axes and flour. Aboriginal culture was inventive enough to acknowledge the technical superiority of such goods and flexible enough to assimilate their use without disrupting traditional social relations. But white principles of individualism and personal gain were in sharp conflict with Aboriginal principles of reciprocity. The result was that settlers continually transgressed traditional cultural values. When this was added to the taking of land and the killing of tribal members, Aborigines reacted to the white assault. In Reynolds's view the variety of Aboriginal responses to invasion reflected a people anxious to retain their traditions in the face of an attack by a race whose war technology and numbers were superior. In fighting a war of guerilla resistance they considerably hindered the process of settlement.

In the early 1980s other works which concentrated on black resistance to invasion were also published. Two prominent examples were N. Loos's *Invasion and Resistance* (1982), and R. Broome's *Aboriginal Australians* (1982). This story of black resistance was, in part, a plea for a more sympathetic response to black struggles for autonomy in modern Australia. Reynolds, Loos and Broome hoped to prove that, despite marked cultural differences between blacks and whites, the Aboriginal response to invasion was logical in its context. Unless Aborigines received due recognition for their struggle by the dominant white society they would never be adequately accepted into Australian culture and white Australians would perpetuate the racist practices of their forebears.

The study of Aboriginal responses to settlement have mainly concentrated on violent resistance. Reynolds, however, pointed to other dimensions to the Aboriginal response, most importantly the ways in which Aborigines accommodated themselves to the dominant white culture. Some of these themes have been developed in other studies, notably Ann McGrath's *Born in the Cattle* (1987). McGrath examined the important role of Aboriginal labour in the pastoral industry in northern Australia. Aborigines were the only source of labour and, despite racist slurs about 'lazy blacks', they proved to be extremely skilled as drovers and labourers. Women were an active part of this labour force—nearly half the drovers were Aboriginal women. In this way Aborigines became a vital part of the economy and incorporated western work habits into their own cultural traditions.

The focus of this new critical approach was contact history. It was an attempt to provide the black view of the struggle that had been well documented from the white point of view. In the 1970s, however, there was another focus of history concerned with black culture. Some historians began to examine the history of black culture before the arrival of the Europeans.

Pre-contact history

In the 1960s and 1970s research by archaeologists and physical anthropologists into the history of Aborigines was flourishing. Research covered such areas as the arrival of Aborigines in Australia, the spread of Aboriginal culture over the continent, the material life of the Aborigines, the structure of the Aboriginal population, adaptation to the environment and contact with other cultures, particularly the Macassan traders from Indonesia, before the arrival of European settlement.

The findings of this research challenged some of the long-standing anthropological characterizations of Aboriginal culture, which in turn had influenced popular perceptions of the Aborigines. These old views had presented a picture of Aboriginal culture as economically primitive: it was a stone-age culture, based on a hunter–gatherer economy, living in a harsh climate on the edge of starvation, and in a set of social and economic relations that had remained unchanged for thousands of years. The new archaeological and anthropological research provided evidence to dispute this picture (Mulvaney 1969). The importance of the new work was recognized in *The Australians* Bicentennial history project, the first volume of which was almost entirely devoted to the history of the Aborigines before the arrival of white settlers (Mulvaney & White 1987).

Archaeological research has now established that Aborigines have inhabited the continent for at least 50 000 years. Thus they have had to adapt to dramatic climatic changes; the warming of the planet after the last Ice Age created large areas of desert where previously there had been a tropical environment. Although the environment was not as abundant, Aborigines adapted successfully to changed conditions.

They had intimate knowledge of inland water systems, plants and game that allowed them to survive comfortably in an environment in which later European explorers would perish. Far from being a static, unchanging society, Aboriginal culture had proved to be remarkably innovative and adaptive to new conditions (Broome 1982:10-14).

The other major revision in conceptualizations of Aboriginal culture concerned the view that Aborigines were a stone-age hunter-gatherer society. Research into the material culture and environmental practices of Aborigines tended to qualify that picture. For instance, it was found that Aborigines worked mines to obtain useful minerals. Perhaps most significant was evidence that Aborigines had not simply lived off the land; on the contrary, they had changed the environment in an attempt to increase their food supplies. The most important technique was burning-off. By setting fire to large tracts of land they were able to turn bush into grassland. The grassland encouraged the feeding and growth in population of such game as kangaroos and wallabies. In other words, Aborigines had not simply been hunters and gatherers; rather, hunting and gathering was part of a wider system of astute environmental management (Mulvaney & White 1987:11-22).

New archaeological research led Geoffrey Blainey in his *Triumph of the Nomads* (1975) to characterize the Aborigines as 'the prosperous nomads'. Blainey drew some interesting comparisons between Aborigines and typical Europeans living in 1800. In his view the Aborigines had as high if not a higher standard of living. Freedom from famine and ample leisure pointed to the advantages Aborigines had over many Europeans. This comparison served an important function in Blainey's argument. The Aborigines were triumphant in their economic adaptation to the environment. The implications of such an argument, in the context of the 1970s, is clear: Aboriginal culture had not been a hopelessly primitive one, justifiably swept aside by a superior culture. At the time of settlement the European standard of living was in many respects not as advanced as that of the Aborigines.

The logic of Blainey's argument, however, also led in other directions. One implication of his argument was that although the two cultures, European and Aboriginal, were comparable in 1800, the material advance of Europe during the Industrial Revolution led to significant improvements in the western standard of living. The problem is that Blainey's argument relies exclusively on Eurocentric criteria of economic management. The focus on economic criteria, at the expense of cultural factors, is vulnerable to arguments that within a few years of settlement European economic supremacy was established and hence legitimate. Despite his favourable representation of pre-contact Aboriginal culture Blainey implicitly endorsed the legitimacy of colonization, and this placed him in a historiographical tradition different from that of historians such as Reynolds, Markus, Ryan and Broome.

In the 1970s and 1980s, however, some Aboriginal historians began to criticize the Eurocentric bias of most of the histories of Aborigines that had been written, be they studies of invasion or resistance. They argued that they were histories for white readers and failed to address the needs and interests of Aborigines. In contrast they stressed the importance of oral history, and a few pointed to more radical conceptions of what Aboriginal history should be.

Aboriginal histories

Biographies of Aborigines have been a common genre in Aboriginal history since the Second World War but have usually been written or rewritten by white authors for a largely white audience. The result was the loss of a distinctively Aboriginal way of telling the story. In the 1970s and 1980s researchers became more concerned to provide an authentic record of Aboriginal history as Aborigines would tell it, retaining the unique style of Aboriginal oral memory.

Oral testimony has served the purpose of pointing to unknown massacres, strategies of resistance, and black perspectives on the dominant white culture. Some historians, notably Reynolds, have used such evidence for their larger project. A second approach has been to leave Aboriginal oral evidence relatively untouched to provide an intimate understanding of the concerns of Aborigines and their culture. Noteworthy in this field is Bruce Shaw, who has published accounts of the lives of a number of Western Australian and Northern Territory Aborigines (Shaw & McDonald 1978; Shaw & Sullivan 1979). Shaw, however, did attempt to relate these accounts to the wider contexts of dispossession, resistance and Aboriginal experiences in the pastoral industry.

The use of oral history entails particular methodological problems, more so when interviewer and informant are from different cultures. Cultural differences harbour the possibility of unrecognized misinterpretation of statements. Similarly, informants aware of the ritual significance of certain types of information will withhold it from the interviewer. Interviewers find it more difficult to verify the statements made when there are few written records of the culture. The nature of Aboriginal speech and its concern with particular sentence rhythms also poses a problem for historians wishing to publish this material. They are inscribed within a larger structure of publishers and readerships whose agents and constituency are largely white. The dilemma is whether to present the material verbatim, with the possibility that a white readership will not follow it, or to edit it for a white audience. These are familiar methodological problems in the use of most types of oral evidence. Many historians therefore have counselled caution in the use of oral evidence, despite the fact that it is often crucial to the reconstruction of particular social histories. Phillip Pepper's *You Are What You Make Yourself to Be* (1980) is one example of an Aboriginal oral history that retains the concerns and language of Aborigines with minimal editorial interference. It has a number of distinct features. Most important is the structure, rhythm and focus of the narrative. Like many stories constructed from memory it has a disjointed quality, jumping from point to point. What distinguished this account was its relative lack of concern with dates, or relation to a wider set of events, as might be expected of similar white narratives which often situate themselves in terms of world wars, depressions, prime ministers or kings and queens. Some of the story focused on resistance but, more importantly, its concern was the relationships between the Aborigines in the area; it was a history of family and kin.

Some academic historians, however, expressed doubts about the usefulness of this approach. Their criticisms amounted to a plea for greater 'professional' use of the material. It was a primary source that should have been used by a trained historian and incorporated into a wider social history of 'native policy' and black response. Diane Barwick (1981), a noted anthropologist, criticized the academic reaction to Pepper's book. She pointed to the culturally-loaded assumptions of these criticisms and argued for the validity of a black 'world-view' which did not have to be assimilated into professional contexts to be worth while.

Implicit in Barwick's critique was the argument that history as a discipline was developed in Europe in the nineteenth century as a response to nationalist political struggles of the period. The point here was that the techniques developed in this context were unlikely to be adequate to express the experience of people from a very different culture. Far from being a universal method applicable to any time, place or culture, the history discipline was a particular set of practices and procedures through which European cultures constructed a concept of the past and the means of representing that concept. It expressed a distinctively western set of cultural values.

This argument has been developed more fully by a working party of Aboriginal historians. In 1977 and 1978 a group of Australian historians, led by Professor Ken Inglis of the Australian National University, began to discuss the role of historians in the Australian Bicentennial celebrations in 1988. It was decided that a large-scale cooperative history project would be published to coincide with the celebrations. For Aborigines, however, celebrations of white settlement were not events to rejoice in. While the celebrations were meant to be a commemoration of national unity and achievement, for Aborigines they symbolized the invasion, conquest and dispossession of their land. A commemorative history project threatened to perpetuate a white view of settlement and white perceptions of the Aborigines. The bicentennial history project therefore became an arena for political intervention by Aboriginal historians.

The venue for this intervention was the 1981 Bicentennial History Conference held at the Australian National University. A working party of Aboriginal historians was invited to speak at the conference. What followed was a short but comprehensive critique of white history (Working Party of Aboriginal Historians 1981:21–5). The working party argued a case in support of cultural difference. The nature of Aboriginal culture, perception and communication was argued to be different from that of the dominant white culture. The consequence of this was the view that no matter how well-intentioned, liberal or sympathetic, white historians could not write Aboriginal history. White historians could not understand the rhythms of Aboriginal narrative, the spiral rather than linear chronology, or the nuances of non-verbal communication. As a result they often misinterpreted the intentions of Aborigines or represented them as poor, defeated, helpless, displaced persons. They missed the continual cultural subversion of the dominant society.

Some Aboriginal historians claimed the right to write history for their own people. This was a vital tool in the attempt to maintain their traditions in the face of cultural theft. Historians had usually appropriated information from Aborigines and used it to construct representations of Aboriginal experience alien to the Aborigines. Aboriginal history, as conceived by the working party, would be a means of passing on the cultural heritage and re-educating those who had lost access to that heritage.

Significant in these arguments was the critique of many fundamental historical methods. Aboriginal historians argued that they had different sources, different means of establishing their veracity, different chronologies and different narrative structures. This was a challenge to western history. Most white historians had assumed that the philosophical tradition of rationalism and realism, with its procedures for establishing evidence, facts and truth, was a universally applicable system. The rest was superstition, faith or belief. In contrast, Aboriginal historians argued that this was a culturally specific system. What white culture called faith, myth or legend, Aboriginal historians saw as the foundation of their system of truth and the cornerstone of their world-view.

These arguments also challenged common perceptions of temporality. In western cultures a few thousand years is a long period of time. Western notions of time as a day-to-day succession of events oriented the chronological focus of the discipline of history. Historians studied short periods of time—months, years, decades, centuries, occasionally a few centuries. In the Aboriginal world-view such temporal frameworks were mere specks in an oral culture which ranged over periods of 50 000 years or longer. In this system the succession of events and change over time was a foreign set of concerns. The spiral chronology served to establish kinship relations, and legend in Aboriginal history bypassed chronology.

The arguments of the Working Party of Aboriginal Historians raise important issues about how history can be culturally specific in its concerns. They also suggest that the histories of contact, frontier violence, accommodation and black resistance written by white historians are histories *of* Aborigines—observations of a different culture—and not Aboriginal history (a history written by Aborigines in terms relevant to their own culture). But this does not invalidate the histories of contact and violence. They illuminate aspects of the black experience and chart important dimensions of racism and paternalism in Australia, the contours of native policy, the nature of settlement, patterns of work and the growth of the Aboriginal rights movement. Without an adequate understanding of these issues Australian society may perpetuate the racist errors of the past. In this sense the historiography of Aborigines furthers debate on appropriate policies and may provide the conditions for racial tolerance in white Australian society. But Aboriginal history, written by Aborigines, creates the means for Aborigines to maintain their own culture. The two are both important but different projects.

CHAPTER ELEVEN

LABOUR, CLASS AND CULTURE
Mark Finnane

Founding labour history

In the study of conflict in Australian historiography labour history has had a privileged place. Although its academic form is largely a post-war development, there was a body of earlier works which addressed matters of keen interest in the rise and fall of the labour movement's fortunes. Reviewing this longer tradition, John Merritt (1982) has pointed to the work of Labor intellectuals such as Vere Gordon Childe ([1923] 1964) and H. V. Evatt ([1940] 1979), both concerned with the problem of the labour movement in government. Earlier, union organizer and founder of what became the Australian Workers' Union, W. G. Spence, had published *Australia's Awakening* (1909), the first major account of the rise of labour, linking this theme, as its title suggests, to the future of the nation. Against the tendency to cast the national history as prosperous and conflict-free, the earlier works of labour history presented a less comforting story, even if not always complimentary to the leadership or achievements of the labour movement itself. For French visitor Albert Métin ([1901] 1977:51) had already noted the distinctively pragmatic politics that characterized labour in Australia: 'In appearance they constitute what we [French] know as a class party leading the struggle against the bourgeoisie: in practice they accept private ownership and the wages system, seeking simply to ensure good working conditions in the world as it is'. If labour history was the major point of conflict in the country then there was from the beginning a doubt about the degree of that conflict.

Nevertheless the study of conflict in Australian society has frequently originated in the study of the labour movement and of the conditions which gave rise to it. In this context the key referent has been the concept of class. But just as Métin had talked of the *appearance* of class politics in the forms of labour organization in Australia, so in historiography the appearance of class as a concept was infrequently matched by elaboration of its fundamental bases. Consideration of the treatment of class in labour historiography will illustrate some of the insights and limits to the suggestion that class conflict has been of fundamental importance in Australian history.

The major context for the study of labour history as a subject of specialized academic enquiry was the post-war influence of radical nationalism. The history of the labour movement, said the radical nationalists, was central to the maintenance of a radical tradition in Australia. It seemed, wrote Ian Turner in 1959, that:

aggressive militant democracy was not only a function of the international labour movement, but was deep-rooted in Australian popular history; that fraternity existed not only in the popular front but in the Australian tradition; that 'comrade' had much in common with 'mate'. [Turner 1982:9-10]

As the terms of this quasi-manifesto suggested, the project of labour history was the history of the male working class. The great priority, however, was the reconstruction of radical political struggles, for which a developed concept of class was not seen as central.

Consequently, the major works of this founding period of labour historiography are not marked by an explicit treatment of class. Limited attention is paid in these works to the particular forms of the capital–labour relation in Australia, but rather more to the cultural and political correlates of the major economic shifts of the period from the gold-rushes to the First World War. For writers such as Gollan ([1960] 1967) and Ward (1958) an important theme was the peculiar advantage of the worker in Australian contexts. The artisans who dominated the early formation of the trade unions achieved conditions such as the eight-hour day as much because of the 'weak bargaining position of the employers as the manly independence of the artisans' (Gollan [1960] 1967:72). Later in the colonial period, however, the phenomenon of 'new unionism' suggests the pertinence for Gollan of a Marxist understanding of the formation of class consciousness. By the 1880s, suggests Gollan ([1960] 1967:104), the working class in Australia 'was becoming conscious as a class'. This working class was becoming conscious not only through common experience, as did the shearers who 'worked and lived together', but through the diffusion of socialist thought through the union movement and its media.

While Gollan eschewed the necessity of a definition of class at the outset of his book, it appears that a strong cultural and political notion of class as a collectivity underlies the work. This was less developed, however, than in the later publication of Ian Turner's *Industrial Labour and Politics* ([1965] 1979). This was the most avowedly Marxist of the Old Left labour histories. Its articulation of the class politics of the post-federation period remains influential. A brief comment on its project and method suggests some of the limits as well as appeal of the argument.

Where Gollan and Ward had emphasized the conditions of formation of a radical nationalism and democratic institutions in the nineteenth century, Turner portrays a labour movement that had a more ambiguous relation to the state and the prevailing social order. In examining what he calls the 'dynamics of the labour movement' in eastern Australia between 1900 and 1921, Turner seeks to show that movement as a 'unique social institution'. In the institutions (party, union, strike) of the labour movement in this period, Turner sees 'the means by which working men were challenging the right of *elites* to determine their fate, and for these institutions it could legitimately be claimed that they were, however laboriously and imperfectly, "forming the structure of the new society within the shell of the old" ' (Turner [1965] 1979:235). These words, evoking a socialist transformation, nevertheless do not blind Turner to the limitations placed on the labour movement during these decades, not least from within the movement itself. For Turner demonstrates powerfully in the course of the book the depth of division which had arisen between the two wings of the movement: the industrial (union-based) and the political (party and government-based).

Unlike Gollan, Turner started with a definition of what he meant by 'working class'. For him it was 'an objective social category: the class of men and women who work for wages, as distinct from the employers of labour and the self-employed' (Turner [1965] 1979:xiv). Although wage labour was therefore the criterion of inclusion in this class, it was a static definition which gave no place to the sense in which the English labour historian E. P. Thompson ([1963] 1968), for example, contemporaneously posited class as a 'relationship'. Although class in this definition threatened to be a somewhat static category, Turner did point to the historical problems which had to be addressed in an account of the working class. Thus, for example, the use of the word implied that there were 'class interests' which could divide employers and workers, but not all members of a working class were 'always conscious of these interests'. Further, the working class was not homogeneous: there were divisions by industry, skill and culture.

The implication of Turner's analysis is that the organization and consciousness of the working class can be read from an account of the economic and industrial distribution of the workforce. Thus 'unskilled workers tend to be more militant' and 'the social [Turner seems to refer here to the range of skills] composition of the railway unions led them towards industrial action' (Turner [1965] 1979:6). In this account, then, class relations and class consciousness are largely given. The emphasis is on the relation between class position and political and industrial organization. In the preface to the 1979 edition of the book Turner himself admitted the influence of a 'mechanistic Marxism' in such passages.

Yet while Turner's analysis took for granted the nature of class relations or consciousness, it did provide the basis for understanding conflict and division in the labour movement. The understanding of class may have been mechanistic but the analysis of the labour movement was centred on a more historical view of its institutions and politics. For Turner the direction of the labour movement was to be understood as the product of a complex historical analysis of the contest and negotiation between labour leaders and the 'rank and file'; between the parliamentary Labor Party and its socialist critics (themselves organized in a number of parties); between unions and state institutions; and between competing programmes of union organization and their relation to political and social change. This analysis was developed above all through Turner's portrait of the growing strength of 'industrial labour' (the militant unions) and 'political labour' (the Labor parties in government at both Commonwealth and state levels).

This brief review of the earlier work on the formation of working-class politics suggests the priorities of labour history in the service of radical nationalism. From a later point of view, informed by the impact of New Left critiques and the rise of new social movements focusing attention on the histories of women or of racial minorities, the work of Turner, Gollan and Ward appeared overly preoccupied with the history of the politically active, male working class. From the late 1960s much of the debate on class in Australian history was taken up in the form of critiques of earlier work.

Class, race, sex

What were the grounds of critique and how did they influence the interpretation of class as a factor in social order and conflict? An important influence was the work of English labour historian E. P. Thompson. His postulate, in *The Making of the English Working Class* ([1963] 1968) that class was a relationship, was frequently appealed to by New Left historians in Australia dissatisfied with the static categories they discerned in earlier labour history. The effect of Thompson's work, however, was refracted through other priorities and concerns, some theoretical, others political and rhetorical. The first substantial and influential challenge was that of Humphrey McQueen in *A New Britannia* (1970). In place of the combative and class-conscious working class of the radical nationalist historians, McQueen posited a racist, ultimately docile working class and a labour movement which was dominated by a party which had been formed and dominated by petty bourgeois functionaries. Leftist anxieties about the drift of Labor from its socialist origins were fundamentally misplaced. What they failed to understand, suggested McQueen, was the history of 'Laborism'.

A New Britannia was an account of the formation of Laborism (indicating those tendencies in the labour movement emphasizing parliamentary strategies and accommodation with capital). Through an analysis of Australian radicalism and nationalism in the nineteenth century it was argued that the Australian Labor Party (ALP) was antisocialist from the very start. Hence any political strategy in the 1970s to get the ALP back to its supposed socialist origins was misconceived (McQueen 1970a:11). In pursuit of the origins of Laborism McQueen's book outlined those themes in Australian history which pointed to what he regarded as the petty bourgeois, imperialist and racist nature of the Australian labour movement in the nineteenth century. It was a classic of the revisionist, myth-breaking genre, and its fiercest attacks (besides those on Laborites who had betrayed the workers) were reserved for the radical nationalists of the Old Left.

The essence of McQueen's argument concerning the ALP was that it had been founded by those who were not of the working class but of a class which he close to call the petty bourgeoisie. But this was not the most iconoclastic of McQueen's thrusts against radical nationalist myths. In attempting to describe the material basis of the party's formation he argued that indeed there was *no* working class in Australia in the nineteenth century, only a formation which could be described as a petty bourgeoisie. In this book and other writings, however, McQueen failed to develop the substance of this thesis. Although at some points he suggested that indeed the economic position of Australian labourers constituted them as a class in a capitalist society, it was at no point clear why a particular type of experience would produce a consciousness which was inherently working-class, defined in terms of a commitment to overthrow capitalism (Macintyre 1978:235–8). The concentration on 'consciousness', which McQueen read directly from selective examples of the aspirations of particular organizations, led him to postulate a petty bourgeoisie which spawned the Labor parties. For McQueen Labor was an anachronism produced by nineteenth-century conditions and irrelevant to the interests of twentieth-century workers, which were to be resolved in revolution.

The postulation of a petty bourgeoisie as a class and the failure to provide an account of the concrete social conditions of existence of the working class were identified as major problems in McQueen's analysis (see Macintyre 1978; Ward 1978). Other features of the analysis were better received; the attack on the racism of Australian workers and their organizations was the beginning of a series of studies of this problem by younger historians. And McQueen's emphasis on the dependency of Australia, suggested by the title *A New Britannia*, stressed the importance of taking account of a larger than national view of Australia's historical development, one which highlighted Australia's imperialist connections.

One consequence of New Left critiques of which McQueen's was but one was a move away from a concern solely with the fate and fortunes of the labour movement towards a history of class relations in Australia. In attempting to explain the post-war quiescence of the labour movement, historians critical of the Old Left tradition began to ask questions about the society which had spawned such a phenomenon (see Irving & Berzins 1970). The most substantial product of the new direction was the combined effort of R. W. Connell and T. H. Irving in their *Class Structure in Australian History* (1980). A wide-ranging and eclectic introduction set out their theoretical dispositions, drawing in part on the historical work of Thompson to emphasize the importance of class as a relationship which was made historically; but also drawing out the implications of recent work in Marxist theory. From Gramsci especially they developed their interpretation of the idea of hegemony, the process by which class domination is secured in obtaining consent of the working classes through the operation of cultural and ideological institutions.

Connell and Irving's work represented the most substantial development of the New Left critique in Australia. Their project departed significantly from the exclusive concern with the history of the organized working class which had dominated labour history. They sought to focus on the mechanisms of class rule through attention to the processes of class mobilization of various factions of the bourgeoisie and of the working class. Though hampered by the scope of the project, which rested substantially on already published sources, the book drew attention to the ways in which cultural, educational, familial as well as work relations were articulated to reproduce class society in Australia. In spite of this achievement the faults were also obvious: the superficial attention to social groups who did not fit the largely two-class model of the book; the indifference to the wider international contexts which decisively influenced the shape and fortunes of the Australian economy (Gollan, McQueen & Rickard 1981).

Class Structure in Australian History was published at a time when the traditional concerns of labour history were under review from a variety of quarters. The New Left critique of the founding texts of labour history included attacks especially on the racism of the Australian labour movement during its formation and rise to power. McQueen in particular had highlighted this neglected feature of previous historical work and new students of working-class and labour history followed him, though not always in agreement. A variety of positions on the question of racism was spelt out in the collection *Who Are Our Enemies?* (Curthoys & Markus 1978). For some, racism was functional for the reproduction of capitalism in the nineteenth century; for others it required analysis of racist ideologies and their influence on popular mentality in the nineteenth century. Whatever the explanation of working-class racism, the volume of work on the subject from about 1970 represented a decisive break with the view that the labour movement in Australia had a noble and meritorious past. New questions preoccupied labour history, with their effects particularly noticeable in the concerns of *A People's History of Australia* (Burgmann & Lee 1988), a product of many of the new labour historians. Under what conditions was the working class in Australia formed to allow the generation and dissemination of racist ideas and policies? What were the factors shaping the Australian economy which made the question of race such a central tenet of labour ideology? The prominence of such questions in the work of labour historians had an additional manifestation in their role as historiographical critics of Geoffrey Blainey's resuscitation of the fear of immigration in 1985 (see Markus & Ricklefs 1985).

A different kind of challenge to labour history was offered by feminist theoretical and historical work from the early 1970s. The consequences of this work for understanding the history of the sexes are reviewed in chapter 12. The way in which such histories affected the assumptions and directions of labour history require some further comment here. An early concern of feminist history was the problem of what constituted women's work. *Gentle Invaders: Australian Women at Work, 1788–1974* by Edna Ryan and Anne Conlon (1975) was a history primarily of women's wages. It stressed the disadvantaged position of women in a sex-segregated workforce and the institutional barriers which were still inhibiting the achievement of equal pay.

More complex questions were posed by the dual roles of women in Australia, whether as paid workers or as unpaid domestic labourers. Beverley Kingston's *My Wife, My Daughter and Poor Mary Ann* (1976) was a short history of the theme foreshadowed in its sub-title, *Women and Work in Australia*. The book had begun as part of a broader search to find out 'where women had fitted into the past in Australia'. It concentrated on the social and economic conditions which informed and constrained women's choices. The historical analysis was necessarily sketchy since, as Kingston noted, there was in Australia an 'absence of any of the basic social historical research' which would permit anything more definitive. What the book did was set in place some of the key issues of a feminist history—the social organization and consequences of women's reproductive role, the implications for women's status and experience of the institution of the family, the relation between paid and unpaid work, the significance of women's sexuality for their work options, for example in relation to prostitution.

Kingston's discussion brought out the ambivalent results for women of crucial changes in the organization of work attendant on the growth of industry and the production of an ever greater range of commodities. Domestic servants, for instance, offered middle-class women a sphere of freedom which disappeared with the introduction of labour-saving devices (washing machines, vacuum cleaners). On the other hand, the decline of domestic service itself was more to be explained by the growth of factory employment for women in Australian cities. In Kingston's argument, women chose the factory against the isolation and subjugation implicit in the role of domestic servant.

The effects of this choice on the structure of the workforce were considerable. It was not just that a greater percentage of women were employed in factories but that an increasing proportion of the total industrial workforce (one in three in New South Wales in 1907) was female. At the same time Kingston's analysis suggested the great complexity posed for a history of women at work by women's manifold position in Australian society. Women were not only workers; they were also the essential component of the family and responsible for reproduction of the population. Because of these other roles their participation in the workforce was a source of conflict in ways that were quite different from those of male workers. Women's position in the workforce provided competition for male workers, and in conjunction with a widespread concern about declining population their factory labour became a contentious issue for governments and pro-natalist political forces.

As Kingston indicated, a major problem in writing the history of women and work was the paucity of Australian research on the workplace and urbanization. The second of these two areas has received much attention in Australia in recent years (see part II). But the former has been less well served, at least in historical work. The bulk of Australian labour history concentrated on the labour movement, unions and parties. The emphasis on labour politics and industrial organization disguised the lack of attention among labour historians to the specific histories of the formation of the labour market, its change over time, and the nature of the capital–labour relation, not in politics, but in the workplace. One of feminism's major contributions to Australian labour historiography has been its increasing attention to the conditions of labour. This has been a result of two factors: first, the importance to feminism of an adequate theoretical understanding of women's work; secondly, the very extent of women's absence from the organized labour movement in Australia required a history that would address the particular conditions of women's economic position and the barriers to organization of women workers. These issues have been addressed in numerous publications and conferences since 1975, especially in the Women and Labour conferences (Curthoys, Eade & Spearritt 1975; Windshuttle 1980;

Bevege et al. 1982; Women and Labour Publications Collective 1984; Bulbeck 1986; Francis 1986; Reekie 1987).

The new historical work on the impact of race and sex or gender differences in Australia had important consequences for understanding the history of class. Principally, such work implied at the very least that the history of the labour movement had in many respects been far from progressive. The burden that the working class had carried in earlier histories—of being the main bearers of progressive thought and social action—was shaken by evidence of its complicity in the construction and maintenance of White Australia; the mounting evidence of the indifference to or outright hostility against women workers and equal pay added to the strength of the revisionist case mounted by the New Left some years before. But in the history of class in Australia the consequences were more far-reaching than this straightforward political point would suggest. The history of women's work in particular raised serious doubts about the mono-causal assumptions underlying much of labour history's conventional preoccupation with the history of labour movement institutions and the most active sectors of that movement in particular. For much of women's work was either not paid or poorly paid in relation to the male working class. And where progressive labour forces had achieved acclaimed victories in the areas of wages or work conditions the consequences for women's work were often ambiguous to say the least. The effect of arbitration has been an example, though itself subject to historical debate, as we will see below.

A further consequence of this work was a growing sense of the importance of the role of the labour movement in a particular type of social order in Australia. Connell and Irving (1980) followed Turner in seeing the federation period and its aftermath leading up to the First World War as the acme of working-class mobilization. But this prominence could cut both ways: arguably out of the indispensability of the working-class vote came the setting in concrete of the White Australia Policy; out of male labour's political and economic strength came a state-sanctioned sexual division of labour. The new labour history was more inclined to cast a sceptical eye over the claims of an earlier generation that the 'new unionism', for example, reflected an important advance in class consciousness in Australia. Revisions of the founding decades of the labour movement by historians such as Markey (1985) sought to identify the limits to radicalism of the labour movement in Australia wrought by the social and economic differentials affecting its formation and composition.

Although the understanding of labour history has been substantially altered by the attention to sex and race differentials in working-class experience, there have been other strands of work developing out of new political and theoretical issues. Prominent among these has been an increased interest in the role of the state in the history of the labour movement and the organization of work. An important historical example, illustrating the dual role of the state in relation to questions of both social order and the resolution or management of conflict, is the development of arbitration.

Arbitration and state intervention

Research into the role of the state has become a priority for so many areas of historical and social science investigation in recent years that its bearing on labour history must follow almost as a matter of course. Apart from the renewed theoretical interest in the subject, however, there have been important grounds for seeing the history of the labour movement in Australia as intimately tied to changing forms of state regulation and intervention in social relations. An area of notable interest in this respect is the history of arbitration. As a form of state intervention in the labour market and workplace, arbitration can be seen as illuminating the study of the relations between forms of economic conflict in Australia and the construction or reproduction of dominant forms of social order. At one level, that is, arbitration can be seen as a specific institution for the resolution of conflict, a conflict which had been particularly intense in the years prior to its adoption. At another level, however, arbitration becomes an agent in the historical process, its legal and regulatory framework stimulating the formation of labour, and, much more tardily, employer organizations, but also playing a key role in the maintenance of economic divisions, including the sexual division of labour.

Debates about the history of arbitration can be examined for what they contribute to our larger understanding of the forms of social conflict and order in Australia. The discussion which follows addresses two questions. First, what factors influenced the establishment of arbitration around the time of federation? Second, how far can the institution of arbitration be seen as responsible for the maintenance of particular forms of social relations, such as the sexual division of labour?

From its inception in the 1890s to New Right attacks on it in the 1980s (H. R. Nicholls Society 1986) arbitration has been seen as a peculiarly Australian instance of 'state socialism'. Undoubtedly its ready adoption in the colonies and the new Commonwealth owed much to the prominent organizing role of the state in Australia (Connell & Irving 1980; Sydney Labour History Group 1982; Head 1984). But what were the particular contexts which encouraged the introduction of state arbitration? Like many other aspects of labour history the years of the early 1890s emerge as the crucible for this institution. The economic disruption and social conflict engendered in the course of maritime and shearers' strikes helped to place arbitration on the political agenda (Rickard 1976). The context of the strikes suggests one dimension of the institution's adoption. But the idea of a prominent state role in determining or overseeing outcomes in the labour market had other stimuli. In particular the Victorian preoccupation with conditions in 'sweated industries' in the 1880s had prompted the formation of wages boards in that colony which were intended to combat sweating (Lee 1987).

Two important factors, then, influenced the increasing attention paid to the state's role in the labour market through particular institutional interventions. And each of them operated in rather different contexts to produce forms of intervention that mirrored their formative period: arbitration, linked to the function of conflict resolution in New South Wales and Queensland; wages boards, linked to the protection of the industrial workforce in Victoria (Macintyre 1985). What was common of course was the idea of the state's guiding hand, even if that hand was more directive in the case of the arbitration commissions than the wages boards.

Some writers have attached a more general significance to the political culture which nurtured the adoption of arbitration. Hence Rickard has stressed the labour movement's ready acceptance of compulsory arbitration after the 1890s in contrast with continuing suspicion of it by British labour leaders. 'Bourgeois standards of respectability' among the Australian labour leaders contributed, he suggests, to their faith in the justice of legal forms and an expectation that judicial institutions would give their case a fair hearing. In Australian political culture more generally Rickard (1976) saw a variety of predisposing factors for the ready adoption of arbitration: the well-established predilection for state action; a tendency to political pragmatism (evident in the incremental development of arbitration through gradual adjustments to the original acts); and an inclination to defuse conflict by shifting the arena of the latter away from the political or economic towards the judicial.

By contrast, critics from the left have stressed arbitration's emergence in a period of intense conflict as signifying its intelligibility above all in terms of the history of class struggle in Australia (Connell & Irving 1980:213–19). Rickard's approach, suggested McQueen (1984) polemically, treated 'class struggle as an optional extra'. Regardless of the particular origins of this institution, it is important to remember that these cannot explain the distinctive role that arbitration came to play in the economy and social order, nor of the continuing focus on it in political discourse. For far from being simply a rubber stamp of decisions made elsewhere, arbitration commissions at state and federal levels (the Commonwealth court was established in 1904) came to have a crucial productive role in their own right.

This was as true for the institutions of the labour movement itself (arbitration encouraged union registration) as it was for national economic policy and for the division of labour. The nature of this productive role, however, continues to be a matter of debate. We can examine it briefly through surveying some of the implications of the wage-fixing power which came to be central to arbitration's role.

While arbitration had judicial form its scope of action and responsibility was from the beginning a matter of debate and uncertainty. Hence the influence of the Commonwealth Arbitration Court's second president, H. B. Higgins, was crucial. Higgins's role was that of an activist, both in advancing the commission's standing and in seeing it as an important actor in the national economic process by protecting standards of justice in the social order. This activist role, described and justified in his later lectures on 'a new province for law and order' (Higgins 1922), found an early outlet in his determination of a 'living wage' in the 1907 *Harvester Case*. Here he developed principles for the calculation of a 'fair and reasonable' wage for the male worker with a spouse and three dependent children. Although the principles themselves have been the subject of academic debate, what is now clear is that this wage was determined at just that level which had been regarded as a norm prior to the 1890s depression (Macarthy 1969; Macintyre 1985). Economically, an important consequence of Higgins's adoption of this standard, however, was his insistence that 'the profits (or lack of them) made by an individual employer were not a relevant consideration' in the determination of the basic wage (Rickard 1984:175). This was a crucial intervention in the debates over the labour market and the possibility of its regulation. While there are grounds for considering that the Harvester wage judgement had a minimal immediate impact on living standards (for example in its slow adoption as a minimum standard: Forster 1985) it is also clear that Higgin's intervention stood in a line of actions which had been oriented to the creation of a social order characterized by labour movement desires for a white and predominantly male workforce and liberal, particularly Deakinite, desires for a nation made healthy by 'New Protection' (Rickard 1984; Macintyre 1985). In this context the institution of arbitration was a state intervention of a highly productive kind. In coming decades it was occasionally to be seen as so central to the organization of the labour market and to the strength of the labour movement that it might have to be abandoned to allow new economic and social relations to be put in place (Radi 1974; McGuinness 1985).

The Harvester judgement restored the wage norm to that existing before 1890, or so it has been argued (Macarthy 1969). In doing so, however, it legitimized another aspect of the social order which was of nineteenth-century origin. The idea of the individual wage-earner's desire and responsibility to maintain a wife and family had become entrenched in the British and Australian labour movements from at least mid-century (Secombe 1986; Benenson 1984; Lake 1986). Campaigns against sweated or underpaid labour had often been informed by an ideology which stressed the unmanning effects of the wage labour system. Hence the declaration of Justice Higgins that a fair and reasonable wage should be defined as the family maintenance responsibilities of the male wage-earner was a victory for such labour traditions. More importantly, it might produce significant changes in the labour market and the social economy.

Specifically, it has been an intense point of debate in recent years whether or not the Harvester judgement may be credited with setting in concrete the marked differentials in wages between female and male workers. Here, it is suggested, is a further instance of the role of arbitration in producing particular characteristics of social order in Australia. Critics of Higgins have pointed to the development of the basis of Harvester of a succession of arbitration decisions which limited the wages of most female workers to a little over half to two-thirds of the male wage. Hence Ryan and Conlon (1975) argued that the concept of the 'living wage' was institutionalized by the Harvester judgement, having an 'extraordinary impact on working women'. In this view the arbitration court was seen as having power of a substantial kind in determining wage differentials and the labour market segmentation of which they were an expression.

Our understanding of the role of state intervention is limited, however, if we overlook the substantial forces existing outside state institutions which the latter organize, respond to or seek to limit. An example is provided by a more recent critique of the emphasis on Higgins and the Harvester judgement in determining the characteristic patterns of the sexual division of labour in Australia. Thus Bennett (1984) has argued that Ryan and Conlon were too inclined to explain the operations and effects of the arbitration court's decisions by reference to the influence of sexist ideologies and the paternalism of the judges. Bennett insisted instead on understanding the arbitration system within the parameters set by the circumstances of Australia as a liberal capitalist society with a labour market which is characterized by the sexual division of labour, quite outside the effects of the arbitration court. Where Ryan and Conlon emphasized the importance of action in the arbitration arena to improve women's remuneration and workforce participation, Bennett's analysis suggested that improvements in women's position in the labour market would necessarily be determined by social change of a much more substantial kind. This debate shows the necessity of addressing those larger social historical contexts affecting women's and men's differing positions, as discussed further in chapter 12.

Labour history, originally a project of commitment to the reconstruction of a radical politics in Australia, has been profoundly influenced by shifting political and theoretical concerns. In place of the narrative emphasis on the emergence, tribulations and triumphs of the labour movement we now read of the structural conflicts and social divisions that have limited that movement's achievements. Far from being one of the measures of Australian progress and enlightenment, the labour movement is now viewed as an active participant in the construction of a social order that has been marked by sexual and racial divisions. Important institutions such as arbitration, which have been integral to the history of the labour movement, have also been interpreted in a new light. Far from being a peculiarly Australian resolution of the problem of social conflict, such a form of state intervention may now be seen as itself an agent in the construction of social order. In the transition from its position as the intellectual arm of the labour movement, labour history has become more closely related to a history of social relations and the conditions of their maintenance.

CHAPTER TWELVE

FROM WOMEN'S HISTORY TO A HISTORY OF THE SEXES

Judith Allen

Introduction: why a focus on women?

Research on the distinct situation of Australian women gained unprecedented momentum in the 1970s. While notable work was published in the fields of literature, the arts and social sciences, *historical* interrogations of women—and by extension men and sexuality—published in the past two decades have been particularly relevant to the dual theme of part IV of this book, 'order and conflict'. Historians have argued that a special relationship was drawn between women and social order in Australian colonial culture and politics. This argument has generated interesting, if unresolved, debates as to the 'ordering' of women's life options since 1788 and the degree to which the ordering of gender relations has unleashed conflict and resistances. Some of these debates are explored here because the history of women and of the relations of the sexes have considerable significance for the inclusion of the discipline of history in Australian studies.

Arguments concerning the particularity of Australian culture, politics, economy and social organization cannot be complete unless they admit the category of sex. Too many generalizations within Australian history upon which Australian studies draws, for instance about national identity, radical politics, living conditions or race relations, are 'sex blind'. That is to say, such generalizations fail to recognize that men and women typically have had different experiences in the areas at issue. Consequently, considerable modification of 'mainstream' Australian history writing can be expected as the outcome of a full interrogation of the category of sex. Since such questioning has begun only relatively recently it remains uncertain how unique to Australia the findings will be. More comparative historical research will be needed before useful generalizations already offered by historians of women and identity can be secured.

Before examining some of the key debates in Australian women's history it may be useful to consider the context for the emergence of women's history. Why did historians begin to focus on women as a historical and social group? What are the implications of this focus? Several explanations for the focus on women since the 1970s can be explored. Scholars argue that this focus was the direct and simple effect of the Women's Liberation Movement of the period. One of the earliest demands of that movement was an end to the exclusion of women from the making of knowledges, to be achieved in part by the establishment of women's studies programmes (Morgan 1970:513). Moreover, women's history was furthered in alliance with the so-called 'new social history', a form of history concerned with the everyday and life course history of entire populations, especially of population groups usually obscured from historical gaze (Grimshaw 1985:38). Unlike earlier understandings of social history as 'history with the politics left out', the new social history gave analytic priority to the investigation of relations of power and resistance, deploying a broad notion of politics to investigate groups such as peasants, children, colonized races, ethnic minorities, prisoners, patients, slum residents, multicultural communities and women.

A third and more local factor in the development of Australian women's history is 'demographic'. *Women* historians have tended to be the ones who have asked probing questions about the invisibility of women within Australian history. Yet until the 1960s there were *no* women with research expertise in the area of Australian history in permanent academic posts in history departments in many Australian universities, while those few departments with any women in the area had only one or two (Grimshaw 1985:42). Although there are still no women who are full professors in the field of Australian history, women now hold almost a fifth of tenured Australian history positions. Of course, by no means all of these women have worked and published in the field of women's history. None the less, the presence of even this small number acting as teachers, researchers and dissertation supervisors has been a decisive pre-condition for the development of Australian women's history.

Within this context the immediate impetus for women's history from 1970 was the recognition that women—half the population—were either substantially invisible or questionably represented in the mainstream historical canon. While some historians of women set about investigating women's historical experience solely to 'set the record straight' (sometimes to 'add women and stir' to an unquestioned discipline), others were concerned to ask searching questions about

Australian history. As Daniels (1977:vii) contended, it was not as if women had somehow accidentally slipped out between the grids of historical analysis. It was rather that Australian history was forged with criteria of significance, assumptions and methods of reading evidence that marginalized the female half of the population. This marginality was of a profound and different order from that of other groups marginalized by mainstream history. For, as Grimshaw remarked, women are half of the working class, half of the Aborigines, half of the children, half of the ethnic and religious minorities. They are also half of the ruling classes, half of the colonizing race and half of any dominant culture and of any subordinate culture (Grimshaw 1985:35–6).

Yet whatever positions women have occupied in the organizing categories of class, race, age, ethnicity or religion, it was the men of these groupings that were investigated as historical subjects, as if their experience simply could be generalized for both sexes. Women, despite all of these categories marking differences between them, appeared united in the sense that *as a sex* they were marginal to the concerns of Australian history. Daniels concluded that the inclusion of women's experiences—the demarginalization of women—could not be accomplished without grave disruption to the conventional grids of Australian historical analysis. It would be a history fundamentally altered by the inclusion of women (Daniels 1977:vi–vii).

By including women in Australian history major areas of both order and conflict can be identified: ones that were always right under mainstream historians' noses as it were. Work published in women's history since 1970 discloses the impossibility of ending 'sex blindness' with regard to one sex, women, without also seeking to end it as regards the other sex, men. Much of the history of order and conflict in women's past is equally the history of conflict and order in the past of men as a sex. New questions and problems need to be posed for the full implications of the history of the sexes for Australian studies to be explored.

Women *as* 'order'?

During the first decades of the British invasion of Aboriginal lands in Australia white women were outnumbered by white men at times as much as six to one. Caldwell (1987:23–4) notes that in 1800 men constituted nearly 80 per cent of the population aged over twelve years. By 1861 there was a 38 per cent surplus of males over females, persisting to some degree until the Second World War, only to return temporarily under the impact of male-dominated post-war immigration. This unbalanced sex ratio evoked official anxiety and corrective plans throughout the penal and colonial periods. The lack of women posed a threat to social order, or so successive governors, commissioners, officers, clergy and pastoralists said. What was implied by this claim? What was the nature of this threat? On what reading of penal and colonial Australia's demographic trends did this claim rely? And how were women supposed to allay this threat?

To understand this alarm about the white sex ratio and the impact that discourses about it may have had on women's and men's lives, some discussion of early population trends is in order. The principal cause of the sex imbalance was that convictism (the main source of population growth) was overwhelmingly a masculine institution which persisted in New South Wales until 1840, in Van Diemen's Land until 1853, and in Western Australia until 1867 (Shaw 1966:275, 351, 358). Sex parity for Australia overall was not achieved until around the turn of the twentieth century, but the imbalance remained extreme in frontier states with substantially rural economies. Furthermore, the sex imbalance was exacerbated by the uneven inter-colonial and regional distribution of penal and colonial white Australians by sex and marital status. With a primary produce economy dominated by whaling and fishing, farming and grazing, mining and public works such as road-building, work opportunities were designated masculine and many lay outside the main cities and towns. Employers favoured single men as employees. The consequence was that women of all marital statuses and age groups tended to be concentrated in urban areas, while rural areas were populated, sometimes entirely, by mainly single men. While men had a choice of the full range of available work, historians argue that paid work options for women were scarce and unreliable. Alford (1984:29) demonstrates that in general women had only three viable options for their livelihood: domestic service, prostitution or marriage.

What was the outcome of these demographic conditions for women? Some historians have argued that Australian women faced with this paucity of choices married more universally, married on average at earlier ages and thus gave birth to more children than British women in the same period (Alford 1984:30; Anderson 1983:91–3). The British sex ratio of women outnumbering men in marriageable age groups permitted the flourishing of a nineteenth-century culture of spinsterhood unavailable to equivalent women in Australia (Faderman 1981: 178–203). By contrast fewer Australian men were married than their British counterparts—43 per cent compared with 58 per cent of male adults in 1851 (Alford 1984:26). Anderson's study of Western Australia highlights the regional extremities of this trend. In the 1881 census of women in the 45–49-year age group only 3 per cent had never married, but of men of the same age 44 per cent were bachelors (Anderson 1983:89). To demonstrate the urban/rural distinction she reports that in Perth and Fremantle there were 68 marriageable women to every 100 marriageable men, but in the hinterland only 34 to 100 (Anderson 1983:89).

Other historians have disputed or modified this generalization about women's typical life course on the basis of regional studies. Grimshaw and Fahey (1985:93-6) found that women in the Victorian town of Castlemaine from the mid-nineteenth century married at ages comparable with English women. From her study of late-nineteenth-century Sydney marriage registers Fitzgerald (1987) too is sceptical about the claim that colonial women married earlier than English women. At most, she contends, there was approximately a one-year difference, while in the 1880s and 1890s the trend moved towards later marriages, with New South Wales statistician Coghlan in 1891 reporting a medium marrying age for women of twenty-five years. Her account stresses the importance of regional variation, for, despite the shortage of women prevailing throughout the nineteenth century, women of marriageable age outnumbered men in Sydney, creating what was known in England as the 'spinster problem'. And if, overall, the male population had much higher rates of those 'never married', men who did marry could do so in their thirties and forties, pushing the male average age at marriage upwards. By contrast, women over thirty married more rarely, highlighting the role of male desire and prescriptions as to youthfulness which affected women's but not men's access to marriage (Fitzgerald 1987:183-4).

Age may even have worked in men's interests to some extent. The legacy of convictism was not only high demographic masculinity but also a skewed age structure, with more men in older age groups compared with England. In rural areas the ages and sex gaps were most accentuated, and Kingston (1988) notes the partriarchal dynamic in marriages between 'younger unconfident, colonial bred wives' and older, immigrant men. Conversely, more equity could exist for women in marriages to men closer to their own age—most likely in areas of more even sex ratios, especially urban areas. So for Kingston, numerical scarcity alone did not produce a favourable marriage market for women. The expectation that 'theirs was a seller's market' was undermined by the typical age gap between spouses which reinforced the authority of the husband with age and experience, especially if he was English-born (Kingston 1988:119). Marriage could be imbued with a father–daughter dynamic (Kingston 1986:37). In general then, Kingston criticizes the tendency to concentrate on the simple imbalance of the sexes in historians' assessments of (especially native-born) women's position as regards marriage, to the neglect of the issues of age and birthplace of husbands.

The questions of age and ethnicity could be crucial in a context such as late-nineteenth-century Queensland 'which had a large male immigrant population' and 'one of the largest average differences in marriage ages' (Kingston 1986:35-7). Although scarcity could endow a young woman with a certain power 'to play the field', once a woman married she lost that power and significance (Kingston 1988:119). Indeed, misogyny and deep resentment towards women can be detected in the popular culture of the 1860–1900 period. Kingston emphasizes that its context was a population with, on the one hand, an excess of girls and very young women and, on the other, an excess of ageing immigrant males who did not manage to marry. Such a context of structural asymmetry in the organization of relations between men and women could only render sexuality an area of tension. Whereas women could expect to marry, 'men feared they may not' and were 'frequently forced to lower their expectations' (Kingston 1988:119). This did not bode well for women's experience of married life.

Yet married life or forms of cohabitation with men have provided the livelihoods of most white women of the British invasion of Australia and their descendants. Varied readings of this 'fact' of women's history have been advanced by historians. Some regard marriage as women's trade as being perfectly acceptable. Perrott (1983) represents the penal colony of New South Wales as a land of 'economic opportunities' for women, primarily through marriage:

there were greater opportunities to gain some status and position in colonial society and to become wealthy because of the shortage of women . . . Marriage was the greatest economic opportunity available to convict and ex-convict women of New South Wales—it provided security and protection in a society where the males outnumbered the females. [Perrott 1983:43,99]

Robinson (1979:10) too contends that marriage provided opportunities for social mobility for industrious women. This 'scarcity permitting women's social mobility' thesis is disputed by both Anderson and Fitzgerald whose mid- and late-nineteenth-century regional studies document the typical trend of women marrying either into the same class or into a lower class (Anderson 1983:89–90; Fitzgerald 1987:174–7). Alternatively, Kingston's (1986:33) argument seems to support the possibility of some material social mobility. Unlike Perrott and Robinson, however, her assessment is tempered by a nuanced consideration of the younger, inexperienced and possibly despised colonial wife's experience of marriage to a man conscious of having lowered his expectations (Kingston 1986:38).

The same 'fact' of nearly universal marriage as women's livelihood is read completely differently by historians of women who reject the dual idea that marriage should be the livelihood of women and that the biological potential to reproduce should organize or confine their life options. For historians such as Summers (1975), Dixson (1976) and Alford (1984) women's 'choice' of marriage may well have been their best livelihood option when the other options were domestic service or prostitution (in many penal contexts indistinguishable). But to read this as colonial women's sensible recognition of 'economic opportunities' is for them an unacceptable distortion. They argue that the situation women faced, as a sex, was coercive. One way or another they were forced to exchange sexual and domestic services in return for board, lodgings and 'keep'. Insofar as the only choice women generally had was whether to 'live off' one, several, or many men, Summers (1975:270) describes women as subjected to a state of 'enforced whoredom'. In this formulation she draws attention to the connections and continuities between women's options and experiences whether wife, spinster or whore. And whatever their formal classification, white Australian women lived in a community dominated by single men. This was not a situation likely to breed sexual egalitarianism, nor even minimal respect for women.

Even historians advancing the favourable marriage market and social mobility theses concede that life as a colonial spinster was dangerous and that the power of the husband was strengthened by women's lack of safe alternative living arrangements (not that marriage was always free of dangers). Grimshaw and Fahey (1983:93–6) argue that despite the hazards of patriarchal husbands 'the nature of the economic organization and cultural beliefs, the hazards both material and cultural of being single and female in that society appeared greater'. Since we are concerned here with order and conflict in the history of the sexes in Australia since 1788, it is worth asking from what hazards women needed 'protection' in the form of the marriage contract? The threat would seem to be from historical forms of men's sexual practices— from rape through to street and workplace sexual harassment and appraisal of women and girls. If women needed to marry for safety, so as to have a publicly recognized male protector, then to call marriage 'economic opportunity' may be to make a virtue of necessity. The prevalence of bachelorhood was allowed to operate as a threat to spinsters. Paradoxically, the threat did not end for wives, because arguably the cultural visibility of bachelors inflected the formation of colonial masculinities. Husbands did not behave as if they had won a rare prize. They moved in a wifeless male work-world in which their situation could be represented as unusual and constraining. The itinerant nature of much male work was conducive to wife desertion, infidelity, the use of prostitutes and casual cohabitations.

'Hydraulic' notions of male sexuality formed the basis of official anxiety about the uneven sex ratio. Men were represented as afflicted with an instinctive, irrepressible, 'natural' need for sexual release, conveyed in the language of 'floods' and 'spurts' and 'dams' and 'torrents'. Women, mercifully, did not share this affliction, making them, potentially at least, the modest, moral sex capable of restraint. Military and naval experience showed that settled groups of womanless men became dangerously frustrated, difficult to control even with strict discipline, and prone to brutish expression of their thwarted lusts. Ensuring men's sexual access to women, whether as wives, servants or prostitutes, became a tacit aspect of the penal authorities' brief. As Daniels observes in her study of prostitution in penal and colonial Tasmania, anxiety regarding sexual relationships between men became so intense in the 1840s that 'heterosexual behaviour of any kind, however far from the ideal of marriage, seemed to the authorities to serve a useful purpose' (Daniels 1984:41). The evidence, in her view, warrants the inference that state agents acted as procurers, managers, extortionists and clients of prostitutes, while rapists of women 'of doubtful character' were shown leniency in recognition of men's 'use of these women as sexual commodities' (Daniels 1984:43).

In the light of this evidence Daniels argues that it is both futile and discreditable of subsequent historians to focus on quantifying prostitutes—the 'bad' women of the colonizing settlement—and to place them and the official involvement in the regulation of their services in a kind of conceptual quarantine, marginal to the analysis of the penal and colonial social order and thereby outside historical understandings. The sexual use of women as commodities for the social ordering of men is, rather, integral to any understanding of the political dynamics of the invading culture established in the penal and colonial periods. If this has been unnoticed by mainstream historians it is because almost to a man, they have shared the contemporary commitment to notions of hydraulic, 'natural' male sexual needs, accompanied almost automatically by the assumption that widespread prostitution of women therefore would be inevitable in the context (Alford 1984:44).

'Natural' phenomena tend to be of only passing concern to historians, who have tended to place nature in a dichotomy with culture, society and politics, the more central concerns of the discipline. To declare an area of practice 'natural' often is to locate it beyond social, political and historical enquiry as the province of the biological sciences. For feminist historians of colonial Australia this is an unacceptable intellectual closure; a closure originating from the experiences and interests of men as a sex; a closure that is 'masculinist' (Lake 1986a:123–5). Instead, the sexual use of women, whether as prostitutes, servants or wives, is completely amenable to historical enquiry. Its analytical neglect constitutes a 'fatal flaw' in purportedly general historical accounts of penal and colonial Australia.

Miriam Dixson (1976) argues that the sexual abuse of women in a Christian culture that stigmatized and scapegoated prostitutes, bequeathed for women, as a group, a historical legacy of poor self-identity and degradation. She contends that the enduring consequence of the use of women as order was a uniquely misogynist Australian culture, a culture that was male dominated and hostile to women's participation in civil and social existence. Windschuttle disagrees, arguing that the conditions and problems faced by colonial and subsequent generations of Australian women were entirely comparable with those of women in other western, industrializing and urbanizing cultures of the same period (Windschuttle 1980:29). Which of these arguments has the greatest validity? A discussion of the forces ordering the lives of the majority of colonial and twentieth-century Australian women can provide some basis for evaluating these conflicting claims.

The 'ordering' of women?

Which forces have ordered women's lives in Australia since 1788 and with what effects? Any assessments are made on the basis of quantitative and qualitative evidence. They could apply, however, only to white women in Australia, since Aborigines were not included in censuses and statistical returns until after 1967 (reducing the sources of quantitative evidence), while Aboriginal women's provision of qualitative evidence of their experiences of colonization to their colonizers has been understandably sparse. What inferences about the ordering of their lives does remaining evidence about primarily white women permit? Did the patterns of their lives disclose Dixson's peculiar 'degradation' or did they resemble those of women in new settlements the world over? How much agency did women have in the patterning of their life options? In what ways was their situation distinct from that of the men of their families, classes, races and communities?

Historians of women have investigated the ordering of women's lives at a number of levels. Some have focused on the distinct bodily experiences of women in Australia, exploring sexuality, women's domestic labour, reproduction, child-rearing, economic activities, domestic and sexual violence. Others have probed the economic, civil, legal and cultural ordering of women's lives, arguing that these realms have been subject to immense change since the colonial period. A further area of historical speculation has been the psychical aspects of women's lives consonant with these other areas of ordering.

Marriage has been central to all these realms of ordering women's lives. Official pressure to marry, combined with high (if regionally and age varied) demographic possibilities of marriage, dictated the nature of most women's livelihoods and sexual experience as 'heterosexual, monogamous, legal . . . ' (Matthews 1984b:111–12). In the absence of viable choices, Matthews contends that marriage was uniquely compulsory for women in Australia. Unlike for men, it was both women's work and their total sexuality. In this context the only imaginable alternative *work* options—domestic service and prostitution—were onerous, dangerous and stigmatized, while the possible *sexual* alternatives of celibacy or lesbianism were peculiarly reviled (Matthews 1984b:115).

Historians of women have shown the extent to which colonial wives were fully engaged with back-breaking domestic work, child-bearing, lactation and child-rearing. While domestic service remained the single largest area of paid employment for women until the Second World War, no more than 20 per cent of households employed servants throughout the period. Most domestic work was performed by wives, and, if they were fortunate, by the daughters sent by Providence. Labour-saving devices, pre-packaged foods, and cleaning materials were available unevenly only from the inter-war and post-war periods. Thus most household work was performed by hand using mainly unprocessed goods and tools (Kingston 1975:24, 34–44; Matthews 1984a:69–70). Without gas, electricity, hot water or, often, accessible running water, nineteenth- and early-twentieth-century women cooked, washed, ironed, cleaned, sewed clothes and manchester, tended vegetables, raised poultry and, in many areas, did dairy and agricultural work. It is probably reasonable to infer that the notion of 'leisure' was inapplicable to them or even less visible in their lives than in the lives of women in Britain in the same period (Bailey 1986:18).

While Australian women's colonial demographic history remains far from exhaustively studied, it seems that wives carried out this heavy domestic workload in the context of rising fertility rates. Rural birth rates generally were higher than urban. Alford found that average births per marriage in New South Wales in 1845 were 4.64, higher than the British average; by 1870 the New South Wales average had become 7.69 (Alford 1984:56; Allen 1982a:111). There is some evidence that middle-class families were the first to grow to the stereotypically large Victorian scale, suggesting the possible connection between improved nutrition and more frequent ovulation—hence potential fertility. In rural Western Australia Anderson found a higher fertility rate than that for women in mid-nineteenth-century New South Wales. Of a sample of 100 women married between 1850 and 1853 the average completed family was nine children. These babies arrived at an average of 25-month intervals, spreading child-bearing, lactation and early childhood care across women's fertile life span between marriage and menopause at about age forty-five. Women born in 1850 could expect to live until the age of fifty-five (Matthews 1984b:32). Therefore Anderson (1983:93) concludes that reproduction and its consequences almost entirely dominated Australian colonial women's adult lives.

In addition, most women would experience infant deaths within a year of birth, still-births, miscarriages and the fear of their own death in childbirth. Australian maternal mortality rates were higher than British rates until the 1940s, when penicillin revolutionized the treatment of post-natal complications. Lack of access to professional medical or midwifery services made rural women more vulnerable than urban, particularly with their birthrates significantly higher than those of their city sisters. And, although nowhere statistically registered, many women suffered all their lives from the after-effects of poor midwifery (Anderson 1983:96).

Nineteenth-century cultural discourses readily represented 'womanhood' and 'home' synonymously. Married, cohabiting women were rarely recorded as paid workers in Australian colonial censuses and statistical returns. Deacon (1985:46) demonstrates the extent to which the designation of wives as 'dependents' obscures the extent of paid work done by them. Her critic F. L. Jones (1987:64), while disputing her argument regarding the masculinist motives of Australian statisticians, concedes that there can be little doubt that prevailing social conventions about married women's roles meant that their economic contributions were understated in the official statistics. High rates of bachelorhood alone provided demand for services beyond prostitution. Wives took in laundry, did mending, sewed clothes, cleaned lodgings, minded children, made jams, cakes, bread, confectionery, meals and drinks, and often sold them as well as eggs, fruit, vegetables and flowers, from the front room of the family home (Matthews 1984a). They also worked in the fields and in dairy work in some rural areas, despite claims to the contrary by contemporary observers and the burdens of large numbers of children—cited by F. L. Jones (1987:71) against Deacon's argument for the prevalence of unrecorded non-domestic work by wives. In the ill-fated soldier settlement schemes of the inter-war period, for instance, the availability of the wife's labour on the farm was assumed by authorities in the calculation of costs and entitlements for ex-servicemen. Women's exhaustion, ill-health or termination of the marriage were major factors in the failure of the scheme throughout the 1920s and 1930s (Lake 1987:177–94).

Moreover, from the beginnings of secondary industry in Australian cities and towns, wives took in outwork paid at piece rates. It is the definition of work as executed outside the home for fixed, daylight hours that has obscured from mainstream economic historians' consideration women's extensive economic activities additional to 'home duties'—another masculinist closure based on *men's* experience of work (Matthews 1984b:55). Such work performed by wives could mean the difference between survival and destitution in many working-class families, especially in the event of widowhood, desertion by the husband, or his unemployment.

Such paid work notwithstanding, however, women's fertility and domestic labour responsibilities kept their social identities relatively isolated within home and family. On the one hand, 'the home' was exhorted to be women's 'natural' sphere. On the other hand (as late-nineteenth-century feminists were fond of observing), extraordinary effects were made to close all alternatives—efforts that surely were redundant if women's desire for 'house arrest' (Lake 1988:163) was so 'natural'? Rigid sex segmentation of paid work has characterized all stages of economic and industrial development in Australia from the penal period until the present day. Customary rates of pay for women's jobs averaged at approximately half the average rates paid for men's jobs across the second half of the nineteenth century, only to be formalized by the early twentieth century arbitration system, both by specific pronouncement and by the establishment of the family wage paid to male breadwinners (Ryan & Conlon 1975:89–91). At best women were defined, as Edna Ryan's title signals, as *Two Thirds of A Man* (1984). Women's wages, then, did not allow a fully independent existence for single women, let alone those with dependents. If challenges to workforce sex segmentation and unequal job opportunities and average earnings have been made more recently, the situation remains today almost as stark as its history: women in the workforce earn only two-thirds of men's average earnings and are substantially confined to eighteen unskilled or low-status occupations of the sixty-four main ones classified in the census.

If these forces have ordered women's workforce positions to be marginal or secondary, the trade union movement, far from offering conflict and resistance, has substantially colluded, both actively and by neglect, in this sexual ordering of paid work. Lake identifies the trade unions, the labour movement and the socialists of the early twentieth century as 'the men's movement', informed by misogynist, masculinist politics and a strong view of women's place as being in the home (Lake 1986b:61–2; 1988:155). Thus labour historian Frances (1988:123) concludes that even with the slightly expanded work options taken by single women in the inter-war years, marriage rather than unionism appeared to be 'the solution to their poor pay and conditions'.

Marriage was an 'order' that shaped the options and livelihoods of all women, married or not. Women's legal position was made consonant with their economic and demographic position. In general, the presumption that women were or would be wives was used to authorize the subsuming of women's legal identities into those of their husbands or fathers. While adult men were enfranchised and bestowed related citizen rights in 1859, women were not. It was reasoned that the men of their families adequately represented them in the public sphere. By the same logic, women became legally *femme covert* upon marriage, relinquishing their 'maiden name' in favour of their husband's surname. Any property, income, real estate, goods and chattels hitherto theirs became his, and they could no longer make contracts, sue, sell, buy or otherwise dispose of property and money in their own right (Mackinolty 1979:73). The wife was to be domiciled at the place of her husband's choice. Any children of the marriage remained under the sole guardianship of the father, reverting to the mother upon his death only if he had not made other custody arrangements (Radi 1979:121-2). And while one act of adultery by wives was sufficient legal grounds for husbands to petition for divorce, wives could only petition if they could prove repeated adultery compounded by other marital offences, such as cruelty, habitual drunkenness or desertion and non-support (Golder 1979:42-3).

While late-nineteenth-century feminists challenged aspects of women's legal position, and saw certain reforms secured in advance of Britain and other western countries by the early twentieth century (notably enfranchisement and extension of grounds for divorce), reforms in other areas—including access to the professions, public office, jury service, guardianship of children, credit and property ownership, nationality and citizenship, and many relevant aspects of criminal and welfare law—lagged behind Britain (Jones 1986:164-5, 221; Radi 1979:129; Allen 1979:116). Since many aspects of women's legal position came under state rather than federal jurisdiction, anomalies from state to state persisted well into the twentieth century. Each state maintained a different age of consent, different grounds for divorce, different penalties for crimes involving women and different regulations governing the employment of women and girls.

If masculinist forms of legal regulation of women provided one dimension of the ordering of women, the other side of this could be the non-regulation of men's criminal behaviour towards women. Daniels (1984:23) observes that 'the state recognised . . . the sexual rights of husband over wife inside marriage by its non-intervention in many aspects of domestic life'. The use of non-fatal violence to secure men's 'conjugal rights' or to discipline wives for perceived insubordination was prevalent and, at least among men, tacitly condoned (Saunders 1984:72-3; Allen 1982a:10). Lake (1988:158) quotes French-Canadian exile Francois-Maurice Lepailleur, resident of Parramatta, New South Wales: 'We hear more women crying in the night here, than birds singing in the woods during the day'.

Should domestic violence tempt wives to flee the marital home, representations of the world outside could make them think again: sensational publicity, for instance, attended a series of violent gang rapes in Sydney, some of which ended with the serious injury and deaths of women aged between their mid-thirties and fifties, estranged from husbands and working as prostitutes (Allen, forthcoming). Historians have noted the controversies surrounding rape and its outcomes in the criminal justice system in the late nineteenth century (Walker 1986:28-9; Summers 1980; Reekie 1983:33-4). Women's alarm and anxiety about their safety in public places was heightened by the international publicity surrounding the Whitechapel slayings of several older women in 1889-90, later called the 'Jack the Ripper' murders. The spectres of male fiendishness and women's vulnerability were always highlighted (Walkowitz 1982:551).

Feminist theorist Marilyn Frye (1983:33-4) contends that violence is an inefficient and clumsy tool of social order if it is required constantly to negotiate everyday transactions, especially compared with methods that obtain the voluntary co-operation of those 'moulded' by a particular social order. Several historians of the ordering of women's lives in modern Australian history have pointed to the significance of new social managers or 'experts'—doctors, social workers, architects, nurses, industrialists, philanthropists, psychologists, publishers, editors, journalists, advertisers—intervening to order women's position as wife and mother in the home. From the late nineteenth century Reiger (1985:69-70) identifies the increasing influence of these experts on women's management of domestic work, pregnancy, childbirth, child-care and socialization, family planning and sexual behaviour. The mission of these experts, she argues, was to achieve efficiency, rational management, discipline, thrift, planning and hygiene.

The intensive ordering of women's lives does not preclude the possibility that many or even most women in Australian history have lived in contentment if not 'happiness', with no articulated ambition to move into different forms of livelihood and identity. The status of the study of 'happiness' in Australian women's history has generated debate (Daniels 1982:40). Some have argued that women's history should privilege a focus on the 'happy' or 'typical' or representative woman of the past. Others have contended that the experience of the deviant, marginalized or rebellious woman will be more revealing of the basic processes and underlying norms organizing past Australian culture and politics (Daniels 1982:49). If this debate remains unresolved it seems that with the forces ordering women's lives since 1778, from religion to violence, from babies to 'experts', it may be wondered what have been the moments of conflict and possibilities for women's resistance to the masculinist Australian social order. In view of these forces for order, the wonder may be not that there was so little resistance by women but, rather, that there was so much.

Women's conflicts and resistances

Women have been in conflict about aspects of their situation throughout white Australian history. Most of the forms of resistance they have taken have been invisible to historians of Australian politics because of narrow definitions: of the kinds of activities and processes that count as 'political'; of who are likely to be political actors; and of what can be considered as 'political' effects or outcomes. What have been the main aspects of women's situations to generate conflict and forms of political resistance? How have women sought to challenge the forces ordering their lives? In which areas have women succeeded in changing their conditions and options? Which areas of women's lives have been most resistant to change? Women's conflicts and resistances are usefully examined in a number of different arenas. Their involvement in political movements of various kinds is one obvious area. The issue of fertility control is another, and one with great consequences for women for the historical formation of alternatives to monogamous marriage. Women's participation in the paid workforce is a third area that repays scrutiny in the assessment of conflicts and resistances in Australian women's history. Finally, a brief examination of aspects of women's challenges to their legal and cultural representations, and their resort to crime and instances of individual rebellions against prescribed femininity, complete this discussion of conflict and resistances.

Not surprisingly, marriage has been a principal focus of conflicts and women's attempts to resist and alter established patterns. Historians of women identify marriage and its consequences as central to women's individual and collective political activisms, especially to moments of organized feminism. Kingston (1975:136) argues that marriage created the most significant divisions of experience and interest between late-nineteenth and early-twentieth-century women, as significant as those 'between labour and capital'. The 'house arrest' of the majority of married women has, to a marked extent, left the more formal realms of political struggles for legislative and policy changes to the spinsters or child-free wives or widows—the like of Rose Scott, Vida Goldstein, Annie and Belle Golding, Bessie Rischbieth, Catherine Helen Spence, Muriel Heagney and Jessie Street (Allen 1988a; Mulraney 1988; Brownfoot 1983; Kingston 1983; White 1982; Margarey 1985; Wright 1975). Dinners to be cooked, children to be fed, washed, supervised, clothes to be washed, shopping to be done have severely curtailed married women's time for political, civic or cultural activities of any kind. For much of the period, church-going and related events were wives' only 'outside' contacts.

Yet it was in the contexts of wives' church work that the largest conventional political mobilization of women in Australian history took place—the women's temperance movement (Hyslop 1976:29–42). In moving to demand the regulation of the sale of alcohol and seeking 'to persuade the public that [it] was . . . a destructive drug', Grimshaw (1988:73) argues that temperance women were feminist in motive: 'they saw men as holding an unfair and often oppressive power over women and they fought publicly to remove women's disabilities'. It was these women and their children who bore the brunt of the cultural inseparability of masculinity and drinking, and the frequent outcome of violence and poverty. In addition to the drink issue, temperance women often supported and worked in the campaigns of feminists around issues such as women's suffrage and citizenship, the age of consent, prostitution and illegitimacy (Lake 1986a:124–7). The popularity of temperance among women was symptomatic of sex antagonism and sex conflict that could be built into women's situation in their chief industrial workplace—the home. Hence the temperance activism undertaken by dependent wives in the 1890–1910 period was entirely comparable with the men's movements of industrial unionism of the same period. Moreover, women's temperance protest was a decisive assertion of a dissident cultural politics in the context of the drunken, bohemian, libertarian radical-nationalist celebrations of Australian manhood of the period (Lake 1986a:127). It was disloyal to 'civilisation' (Woolf [1938] 1977:125); and it would seem that it still is, judging from recent attempts to reject characterization of this culture as 'masculinist' (McConville 1987:433).

Women's conflicts and resistances have not been confined to collective political movements. Possibly the most momentous area of resistance to their situation has been demographic. From the 1850s, after transportation and mass immigration had largely ceased, the most important element of population growth in underpopulated Australia became 'natural increase' (Jackson 1987:11). The period since the 1880s has been called 'the demographic transition' in the disembodied language of demography. In fact, *women* reduced their fertility both dramatically and rapidly. Between 1836 and 1882, Australia-wide, most married women produced six or more children. Suddenly, from 1887 until 1911, the majority of married women had only three or four children. By the late 1930s the all-time average low of two children per married woman was reached. With temporary variations the trend has continued to the present average of between one and two children. Like all averages these declines signal large proportions of women having no children or having only one child. Thus Australia has reached zero (natural) population growth.

How did women achieve this dramatic reduction, refusing to perform their 'natural' function prior to birth control clinics (established from the 1930s and later to popularize the diaphragm and spermicide), and decades before the pill and the intra-uterine device (IUD)? Historians of women contend that they achieved this by as far as possible securing men's co-operation in methods of natural and artificial contraception (coitus interruptus, abstinence, the condom, vaginal pessaries, douching and other contraceptive sexual practices) and by abortion. With the currency of faulty theories of ovulation connecting fertility and menstruation, which were not refuted until 1928 (Weeks 1981:148), it is likely that, despite the use of preventive strategies, abortion ultimately was a decisive guarantor of reduced fertility in Australia as elsewhere (Allen 1982b:120; Knight 1977:79; McLaren 1978:249; Petchesky 1985:106).

Hicks found in his study of the New South Wales Royal Commission into the Decline in the Birthrate (1903) that while doctors provided conflicting estimates of the incidence of abortion by social class, most believed that it had greatest acceptance 'among the least well to do'—the largest social class in the community (Hicks 1978:46). His analysis tends to stress artificial contraception due to evidence of its availability. Yet he concedes that such contraception was used in the context of the faulty theory of ovulation which designated mid-cycle the 'safe period' (Hicks 1978:38).

Major problems of evidence attend claims that any single factor *caused* the decline in the birth rate, since actual and effective use of any method is undemonstrable and can be discussed only by inference and deduction. To conclude that a combination of strategies caused the decline may then seem reasonable. Some historians, however, are dissatisfied with such a combination formula. Kingston and Smith believe that celibacy is underestimated in prevailing accounts—a flaw that for Kingston is the consequence of libertarian and post-Keynesian sexual assumptions being imposed anachronistically on late Victorian colonial culture (Kingston 1988:144–5; Smith 1979:118–20). Alternatively, McLaren (1978:245) contends that artificial contraception is over-estimated as *the* cause of fertility decline in the light of evidence that nineteenth-century working-class men often regarded the 'sheath' as a check on their manhood, seeing 'prevention' as the woman's problem. Hence he views abortion as causally central in any account of fertility decline and comments further that its neglect by historians in favour of artificial contraception (in which male agency and co-operation was required) reflects patriarchal bias. For abortion was undertaken by women without any necessary male involvement at all. Its analytical neglect by historians, despite extensive evidence of its significance, displays their reluctance to consider that women would play an active part in determining family size (McLaren 1978:250).

Considering the incomparable difference between nine children and two children for the material and psychical conditions of married women's lives, this staggering reduction over only two generations may usefully be read as a profound form of political and industrial resistance to prevailing expectations of womanhood. Historians have demonstrated that the experience of motherhood became simultaneously more prescriptively invested and policed (Reiger 1985:214–15) and that domestic life even with only a couple of small children was still restrictive (Grimshaw 1988:78). None the less, reduced fertility contracted the period of adult women's lives spent in full-time child-rearing. By the post-war period most women had completed their child-bearing by their early thirties. Matthews (1984b:33) observes that a consequence of decreasing fertility has been an increasing longevity in generations of women whose health was not weakened by the stresses of excessive child-bearing and poor obstetrics. From an average age of death of 55 for women in 1901, the average age is currently 80 (compared with 72 for men). Women completing their child-bearing in their thirties have nearly half a century of life ahead of them.

Not only has reduced fertility enhanced the quality of women's lives, it has allowed women to re-enter the paid workforce on a part- or full-time basis. The formal participation of married women in paid work grew slowly during the first half of the twentieth century, but rapidly since 1960 (Matthews 1984b:51–5). Lack of free or even tax deductible child-care has been one major brake on married women laying claim to a part non-familial identity after completing their child-bearing. Husbands, families, communities and mass media too have often been less than enthusiastic about married women working. In times of depression or recession working women have fought to keep their jobs against the tide of criticism that male breadwinners with dependants should have priority. Married women's increased participation in the paid workforce has also brought them into sharp conflict with husbands over domestic authority, housework and 'parenting'. The prospect of women leaving violent and unsatisfactory relationships and being able to support themselves has been hard for Australian men to accept. They have often retaliated with violence (Allen 1982a:5). From the time divorce became available in the 1870s Australian women have generally outnumbered men as petitioners, often markedly so (Golder 1985:151).

When the combination of reducing women's economic dependence on husbands and reducing fertility can so rapidly destabilize the historical order of near universal marriage, historians are prompted to ask critical questions about that 'orderly' past and its social foundations. The Institute of Family Studies estimated in 1983 that 40 per cent of Australian marriages would end in divorce, and that the then current average duration of marriage was between ten and fifteen years. Moreover, 50 per cent of husbands surveyed had had extra-marital affairs, compared with 25 per cent of wives. One in every three men involved in heterosexual cohabitations was estimated to become violent towards his partner at some stage in the duration of the partnership, while sexual abuse is estimated to be the experience of one in four Australian daughters (Connell 1987:14; Scutt 1983:68, 97–8). While these latter estimates may be shocking, their existence and public discussion may well signal a serious decline in the general tolerance of men's power to abuse their dependants. We will never know the rates of such abuse in the past, but the current estimates may be lower than past reality.

It is clear then that for the area of Australian studies concerned with order and conflict, the histories of marriage, reproduction and women's paid work provide apt demonstration of Michel Foucault's truism that where there is power there is resistance. Since the 1970s feminist activism has been effective against entrenched opposition to women's right and capacity to combine parenthood and paid work as men do, and against the patriarchal edifice of law, custom and policy. Engagement with the state has generated the distinctly Australian identity of the 'femocrat' and considerable international interest in her (Eisenstein 1985:114; Watson, forthcoming).

In addition to further resistances on the demographic, economic, interpersonal and legal fronts, cultural production and criticism have been other areas where Australian women have been in conflict with the dominant national culture and its meanings. Despite their substantial exclusion from cultural production, Australian women's interventions into domains such as fiction writing, journalism, literary criticism, visual art, film-making, religion and social policy have shown decided 'disloyality to civilization' as defined by two centuries of masculinist national culture (Modjeska 1981; Sheridan 1988; Burke 1981; Roe 1986, 1987). As cultural producers, critics and commentators women have constantly, if somewhat wearily, made the point that there is nothing 'national' about the culture and its rituals as produced primarily by the men of Australia. Rather, Australian national identity has been constituted by particular kinds of white male patriotism adorned with men's preoccupations of different historical moments—sometimes republican, sometimes populist, sometimes bohemian, sometimes conservative—but always masculinist. Against this, women as cultural critics and producers have often attempted to articulate different preoccupations, experimenting with forms and modes appropriate to specifying women's experience in Australia.

Such criticism of Australian cultural meanings and rituals has not been confined to 'high art'. In the early 1970s women marched into the public bars of Australian city hotels demanding to be served and in some cases chaining themselves to the bar. Their protest was against both the misogynist exclusion of women (who in Australian hotels were consigned to a separate ladies lounge where they were charged more for their drinks than men were in the public bar) and the way in which the pub, as a male-dominated place where men got drunk, contributed to the endangering of women in the surrounding communities, inhibiting women's free movement in the environs and opening them to the threat of harassment. And in the early 1980s, on Anzac Day (the holiday created to celebrate the forging of Australian nationhood in blood and sand at the 1915 battle of Gallipolli), silent processions of women dressed in black marched under the banner 'In memory of all women, of all countries, raped in all wars'. This was an exercise in cultural politics, disrupting the meaning of a national ritual by advancing a competing one relevant to women (Pringle 1983:31-5). The marches generated fierce and violent resistance on the part of ex-servicemen and women, police and the media. In Sydney in 1983, for instance, 159 women were arrested in George Street and charged with 'causing serious alarm and affront to the citizens of Sydney'.

Beyond such organized challenges to Australian culture and politics, women have throughout the period since 1788 committed isolated rebellions against authority, often by flouting expected codes of femininity. Summers and Daniels and Murnane document some spectacular riots undertaken by women at the female factories and prisons in the various Australian colonies (Daniels & Murnane 1980:19-20). Women convicts would outrage prospective husbands and masters by turning their backs when assembled in muster, bending over, lifting their skirts (underwear was not the custom) and emitting obscene sounds and 'slapping their posteriors with a loud report' (Summers 1975:284). To evade sexually harassing employers, convict and identured servants practised insubordination, indolence or domestic incompetence, so enraging the lady of the house that they could be sure of a sacking (Daniels 1984:31-8). Merritt (1982:81-7) found many cases of deliberate sabotaging of tasks to ensure termination of employment contracts.

Historians have shown interest in women's individual resistance to difficult or impossible domestic situations through nervous breakdown and psychiatric incarceration. Garton has shown that a stay in the late-nineteenth- or early-twentieth-century asylum could be a respite for battered wives or women simply overburdened with children, husbands and unrelenting manual work. Moreover, in the language of women's 'insanity'—the fears or angers they expressed—protest against their position was manifest. Women's tendency to suffer from depressions, in which hostilities towards others were for a time turned upon themselves, still drew the attention of family and friends to their unhappiness (Garton 1988:146).

Rebellion was not confined to poor and burdened wives. The best-known woman rebel in inter-war and post-war Sydney was Bea Miles. Against the expectations of her brutal father, a wealthy businessman, she 'lived in sin' and refused to marry, refused to have children, and refused to make a home at a fixed address. She spent her middle and old age riding Sydney's public transport and refusing to pay fares. She made money by making bets with other passengers and by reciting Shakespeare's sonnets, despite a constant round of summary convictions which brought her to public notice (Allen 1988b:217-18).

Perhaps the most enigmatic form of conflict and individual resistance was offered by the small handful of women in modern Australian history who resolved conflicts over domestic power by murdering their spouses. Arsenic and strychnine were the principal methods used by colonial and early-twentieth-century women (Allen, forthcoming). More recently, perhaps with restrictions on poisons, women homicide offenders shot or stabbed their sleeping husbands. In general these offenders had experienced habitual violence from their husbands over a prolonged period, and they had faced police refusal to intervene. The plight of such women was dramatized when a public campaign began in 1980 for the release of Violet Roberts, a New South Wales woman sentenced to life imprisonment for the fatal shooting of her husband in 1975. Premier Neville Wran ordered Roberts's release from custody late in 1980 and soon after established a task force to enquire into domestic violence. The activist group organizing the Roberts campaign was called Women Behind Bars—apposite for a culture whose colonizing settlement was built in part on the ordering of women into the kind of house arrest that permitted the private, prolonged abuse of women such as Violet Roberts.

Conclusion

Women have made their own history in Australia but not under conditions of their own choosing. The moulding of their existences *as a sex* in the interests of a social order in which women of all classes and races rendered service unto men of their own (and sometimes other) classes and races, in which men did not serve women as women served men (Frye 1983:10), has initially appeared to have been smooth and orderly during the period since British invasion of Aboriginal lands. The forces deployed in this moulding have been considerable and, like most habitual mouldings, whether of individual bodies or entire populations, the outcome appears 'natural', 'inevitable', and the one desired by all protagonists. Yet the evidence suggests that women individually attempted to organize key aspects of their existence in directions at variance with a social order that located them as subordinates. Enough individual women negotiating different modes of life on a large scale effected marked social changes, such as contraction of national population, extension of female longevity, expanded demand for married women's workforce participation, increased rates of divorce and related marital breakdown, and significant challenges to attributes of Australian social and public policy, legal culture, national culture and popular rituals.

While enquiry into women as a sex has disclosed a rich Australian history of both order and conflict, that history has as its as yet shadowy companion a corresponding history of men as a sex. Many questions and problems remain to be posed and solved. Prostitution is one obvious area. What is the history of men's use of prostitutes at different times in Australian history? How might the social profile of men most likely to be the clients of prostitutes have undergone change? What proportion of their incomes were clients of prostitutes prepared to commit to purchasing sexual services? What did they most often want to buy, and under what circumstances has the nature of client demand changed?

Marriage is another key area. How important has marriage been in ordering men's lives in Australian history? Have men perceived their position in relations with economically dependent wives and children as one of power? How frequently have husbands and fathers negotiated with family relations through physical violence? What about verbal violence? Has the frequency of men's family violence changed and, if so, in what direction and why? How adequately have men seen marriage as fulfilling their personal needs? What has been the place of alcohol in men's domestic lives? On what basis have husbands apportioned a share of wages to dependent wives for housekeeping? What proportion of husbands' wages has been retained for their personal/recreational use? What has been the extent of men's extra-marital sexual relationships and what factors could lead to changes? How much domestic maintenance work have men done throughout Australian history? How negotiable has a domestic sexual division of labour been? How might the nature of men's relationships with their children be characterized, and has this varied by the sex and age of the children involved? And finally, how have the variables of class, race, ethnicity and region modified possible answers to all such questions?

Many other areas of men's historical experience as a sex raise pressing questions whose answers stand to re-inflect the writing of Australian history. If Daniels is correct in saying that the inclusion of women's experience in mainstream history would cause a radical transformation of that history, the same surely would be true of the inclusion of men, interrogated as a sex. The order and conflict of women's experiences in Australia since 1788, then, can point to ways that a history of the sexes might be imagined and written.

CHAPTER THIRTEEN

POVERTY IN PARADISE

Stephen Garton

The 'workingman's paradise' has been one of the dominant and most persistent national images of Australia. In the late nineteenth century visitors to the colonies, among them the novelist Anthony Trollope and essayist J. A. Froude, marvelled at cities where 'everyone has enough to live on'. Colonists echoed these views. The journalist Richard Twopeny declared at the end of his travels in 1883 that there was 'no poor class in the colonies' (White 1981:29–46). These views were echoed again after the publication of Donald Horne's *The Lucky Country* in 1964. This was an ironic and critical look at post-war Australia, but many ignored the irony in the book, and instead used the 'lucky country' image to reinforce a belief that Australia was an egalitarian new society, free of the extremes of wealth and poverty that characterized the Old World of Britain and Europe. In this scenario the serious depressions of the 1890s and 1930s were temporary interruptions to the general prosperity of Australians; prosperity that could be measured by the higher wages and better standards of living for Australian workers and their families in comparison with their counterparts overseas.

The investigations of economic historians have supported the workingman's paradise image. T. A. Coghlan's pioneering study *Labour and Industry in Australia* (1918) argued that Australian workers earned higher wages and suffered less unemployment than British workers in the boom years before the 1890s collapse. The more recent investigations of N. G. Butlin and others have established that the late-nineteenth-century colonial economy was characterized by significant economic growth and a high standard of living for workers (Jackson 1977:1–27). Other economic historians, notably W. A. Sinclair (1976), have suggested a more complex picture. Sinclair argues that after 1880 prosperity began to decline and that some Australians did not enjoy the full benefits of economic growth. After these qualifications, however, he concludes that the majority of Australians in the late nineteenth century were well off by world standards (Sinclair 1976:76–117). The post-Second World War years have also been seen as prosperous—Australia's second long boom. High rates of home ownership, rising wage rates and low unemployment rates were the indicators of Australia's prosperity. Again historians such as Sinclair (1976:247–57) have suggested that not everyone shared in this wealth but that this story is marginal to the larger theme of economic growth.

In the 1960s a few dissident voices began to suggest that the fruits of this prosperity were not distributed as evenly as many Australians believed. Social welfare advocates argued that half a million Australians (5 per cent of the population)—mainly the aged, widows, single parent families, low income families and the unemployed—were living in chronic poverty (Stubbs 1966:1–3). A few years later C. D. Rowley (1972b:305–79) added the Aborigines to the list of groups excluded from sharing the benefits of economic growth. The Henderson Poverty Inquiry (1972–75) confirmed these earlier findings; in a favourable economic climate almost 10 per cent of the population lived below an austere poverty line and almost that number again hovered close to that level of poverty. This conclusion cast doubt upon cherished beliefs in the egalitarianism of Australian society and the adequacy of our social security system.

In the 1970s and 1980s conditions worsened. The downturn in the international economy revealed the vulnerability of the Australian economy. By the mid-1980s Australia was being seen as a Third World economy with a first world standard of living, a contradiction that required immediate address if we were not to become a 'banana republic'. Detailed investigations revealed increasing numbers of poor Australians (over 2 million by 1984), as unemployment rose and social security payments lagged behind inflation rates (Browne 1987:34–5). At the same time some large businesses were making record profits, a conjunction that suggested that serious inequalities existed in Australian society. In this context a number of people began to investigate the roots of these inequalities, an enterprise in which histories of social welfare and poverty have become important. Understanding the relationships in which poverty is produced stands to tell us much about Australian society.

A crisis for all?

Economic recessions causing high unemployment have had an important role in producing poverty. The plight of Australians during times of economic crisis has been well documented. Images of chronic unemployment during the 1930s Depression—long food queues, evictions, tent cities and men tramping around the country on sustenance (the 'susso')—are still vivid in Australian popular culture. Equally calamitous were the major depressions of the 1840s and 1890s. At these times chronic poverty became the lot of a significant proportion of Australia's population. Comprehensive statistics on unemployment are not available but partial estimates for the 1890s and 1930s show that a third of all trade unionists were unemployed during these depressions. In the 1930s this was one of the highest rates in the western world. But not everyone was a trade unionist and it is likely that these figures underestimate the extent of unemployment in the rest of the workforce (Macintyre 1985a:25-7). There is much evidence to suggest that Australia, as a primary product export economy, was particularly vulnerable to international economic downturn and that the effects were felt by many Australians (Sinclair 1976:193-201). But were they felt by all?

Many general histories of the depressions in Australia have described them as periods of national crisis where everyone to more or less degree suffered the ill effects of the economic downturn (Robertson in Crowley 1974:418). But was this the case? Studies of unemployment, eviction and bankruptcy point to the dimensions of economic crisis in the major depressions but examinations of individual companies show that some weathered the storms well, and even prospered, by buying cheaper land and equipment, forcing down wages and capitalizing on these advantages in the form of economies of scale, monopolization and profit (Connell & Irving 1980:270-87). Other studies of the social life of the wealthy classes in the major cities suggest that the depressions did little to dent the routine of parties, balls and society weddings, nor to reduce the employment of domestic servants by the social élite (Cottle 1979; Wheatley 1988). The depressions hardly seem to have affected the daily lives of many of the social élite.

The depressions were also periods of heightened social conflict. At these times many feared social revolution, and the state, particularly the police force, was important in containing conflict. The strikes of the early 1890s in the maritime, shearing and mining industries are justly famous. Police were used to smash picket-lines, enforce lock-outs, break up demonstrations and arrest prominent trade unionists. The role of the state in destroying labour movement mobilization in this decade has been a major focus of Australian labour history (Gollan 1960:129-35; Rickard 1976:7-37). Less attention has been given to the role of the police in attempting to control movements outside of the trade union movement. But in the 1890s and 1930s depressions there were significant demonstrations by the unemployed, local protests at evictions and riots at food distribution stations. Again police played a significant role in suppressing these demonstrations (Wheatley 1981; Fox & Scates 1988).

Other measures were also developed to discipline the unemployed. Governments and philanthropists made the provision of relief dependent on men passing a work test. In the 1890s labour camps were established and unemployed men had to travel to distant camps or work on public works gangs for sustenance wages. This forced men to leave the cities where they were thought to be a threat. In the 1930s Depression men were put on relief work in country districts, or required to move from district to district registering with local police each time to qualify for sustenance relief. This ensured that the unemployed never stayed in any one place long enough to stir up trouble. It did, however, create local resentments; unemployed families resisted the arrival of unemployed men who received scarce supplies and undermined work opportunities for locals. There were local protests against the newly arrived unemployed, notably in Wollongong, which sometimes resulted in violent clashes (Richardson 1984:75–101). Here we can see the effectiveness of the strategies for dispersing the unemployed but also the desire of the unemployed to be reintegrated into the workforce. Few questioned the wider economic structures which precipitated these periodic crises. The question for some historians has been: Why did the widespread distress not lead to more organized forms of protest and revolt (Macintyre 1985a:26–7)?

The long boom?

It is understandable that widespread distress existed in times of economic crisis but how was it possible for poverty to exist in times of economic prosperity? Many influential economic historians have denied that widespread poverty existed, particularly during Australia's great economic boom from 1860 to 1890 (Jackson 1977:22). But this conclusion has been challenged in recent years. Sinclair (1976:76–117) has argued that the indicators of economic prosperity are illusory. From 1880 the economy was expanding but productivity declined, leading to a fall in individual fortunes well before the onset of the 1890s depression. Sinclair also notes the existence of poverty, slums and poor standards of public health which undermined the living standards of some Australians. Another important analysis has been that offered by Lee and Fahey (1986). They argue that the benefits of economic growth were reaped primarily by skilled workers whose scarcity gave them an effective position to bargain for higher wages. Skilled workers were also members of well-established craft unions which further strengthened their bargaining position. Unskilled workers, especially labourers in rural areas, on the wharves and in the building trades, were often employed on a casual or seasonal basis. In this situation workers might earn good wages for two or three days a week or six or seven months a year but were unable to get work at other times.

Many only just made a living wage and others struggled to survive during off periods. Similar arguments have been offered in Fitzgerald's (1987:103-68) insightful study of late-nineteenth-century Sydney, O'Brien's (1988:65-78) detailed investigation of poverty in late-nineteenth- and early-twentieth-century New South Wales, and Buckley and Wheelwright's (1988:140-63) economic history of nineteenth-century Australia.

Economic relations intersected with other social relationships to produce poverty even in times of growth and prosperity. The sexual division of labour meant that women were particularly vulnerable to poverty. Their role has traditionally been seen to be in the home but recent histories—notably those of Sinclair (1981), Lynzaat (1979), Francis (1986), O'Brien (1988) and Kingston (1975)—have demonstrated that a high proportion of women had work outside the domestic sphere: single women worked as domestic servants and factory operatives; married women often worked as launderers, domestics, tailors and milliners to supplement an inadequate labourer's wage; while those married to farmers often helped on the farm. Usually this work was in addition to their chores at home. Because their role was seen as primarily domestic, women's work was considered to be less skilled and of less value than men's, resulting in consistently lower wages for women workers. In the late nineteenth and early twentieth centuries a growing number of women found work as factory workers and out-workers in the clothing trades. In the factories women were often employed on piece-rates which forced them to work long hours to earn an adequate income. Out-workers likewise had to work long hours at home for small reward (Francis 1986; Fry 1956). One justification for lower wages for women was that they did not have families to support, but this was not always the case; single women sometimes had to support ageing parents, and widowed and deserted mothers had children to support. The lower wages for women placed a great financial strain on those women who were breadwinners, making them particularly vulnerable to poverty.

Old age and family breakdown also played significant roles in the production of poverty. Historians, notably Dickey (1986, 1987a) and O'Brien (1988), using the wealth of available charity records, have been able to reconstruct the dimensions of poverty among groups denied access to the colonial labour market. Old age, illness and infirmity were particularly important factors in Australia where the high proportion of immigrants in the colonies meant that many of the aged and infirm had no families or relatives to support them. O'Brien (1988:51-60) estimates that 29 per cent of all people aged over 60 years in late-nineteenth-century New South Wales had no means of support. Over 90 per cent of people admitted to aged asylums were immigrants and two-thirds of these had no relatives. Deserted, widowed and single mothers and their dependent children or families where the father was seriously ill were also particularly vulnerable to poverty. O'Brien (1988:13) found that these families were half of all the cases assisted by the Benevolent Society in New South Wales. Hazardous work conditions, overcrowding and poor health facilities could rob families of their breadwinner. Equally, the structure of the colonial labour market made it easy for men to leave their families or pregnant girlfriends; they could follow the shearing work up country, travel to other colonies or leave in search of gold. Charities found that there was a sharp increase in applications for assistance from deserted mothers during the gold-rushes (Dickey 1986:23). These opportunities made it very difficult for mothers to place maintenance orders on deserting fathers. The poorer work opportunities for women compounded their problem and many placed their children in charitable or state orphanages (O'Brien 1988:91).

Economic and social inequalities had other ramifications. Unskilled and casual workers were more vulnerable than their skilled counterparts to impoverishment from illness and injury. Skilled workers afforded themselves some protection against expensive medical fees and loss of income by contributing to friendly societies or other mutual aid funds (Green & Cromwell 1984). These contributions guaranteed them assistance in times of crisis. Unskilled workers, however, often had insufficient income or only casual employment, which prevented them from making regular contributions to these societies. They faced certain unemployment and destitution if afflicted with serious illness or injury. Many friendly societies excluded women from membership, thus exacerbating women breadwinners' vulnerability to poverty.

Historians of health such as Lewis and Macleod (1987) have pointed to a central contradiction in the 'workingman's paradise' historiography. If there were no slums and little poverty in colonial Australia why did the colonial cities have mortality rates comparable with, and even exceeding, those of London and other major European cities? They use this question as the starting point for an analysis of urban poverty and the inadequacy of colonial health and sanitation provisions. Other historians have charted the high incidence of epidemic diseases—particularly typhoid, dysentery and at times plague—among slum dwellers, as well as high rates of infant mortality. Poor hygiene and ignorance have been blamed but Fisher (1982), Clark (1978), Mayne (1982) and Lack (1985) have pointed to other factors in this story. Attempts to improve sanitation, water supplies, the quality of food and standards of hygiene were frequently thwarted by local council corruption, toothless legislation, inefficiency and, more fundamentally, a commitment by authorities to promote business interests at the expense of poorer sections of the community.

Rural poverty is another focus of attention. The seasonal cycle of drought and flood always played an important part in rural fortunes but government policies also played a role. The plight of late-nineteenth-century selectors is one of the tragedies of Australia's past; lured by the prospect of independence as yeoman-farmers they were often out-manoeuvred by unscrupulous squatters and forced to select poorer tracts of land. Many lacked sufficient capital and expertise and struggled to survive in harsh and unfamiliar environments. Rural labourers faced the challenge of technological change in late-nineteenth-century Australia. New harvesting machines made many labourers redundant; while there were shortages of labour in some industries, in others there was an oversupply of workers, forcing some into unemployment or to accept lower wages (Kingston 1988:16–28; Markey 1988:57–67). Oral histories such as Carter's *Nothing to Spare* (1981) and autobiographies, particularly Facey's *A Fortunate Life* (1978), have done much to illuminate the arduousness and difficulties of rural life at the turn of the century. They provide an important human dimension missing from many of the general histories of rural life.

Most historians of the Selection Acts and the failure of the yeoman ideal have concentrated on the plight of the selector and his family as a unified social group. But Marilyn Lake (1981; 1987) has raised a different question. She argues that the experiences of pioneer women have to be seen as distinct from those of the male breadwinner. Pioneer women had particular problems: they worked long hours combining farm chores with their traditional domestic tasks and child-rearing. The arduous hours of work took their toll on women's health. Rural families and more particularly women were the hidden poor.

People struggling to earn a living sought shelter in the cheaper areas of towns and cities, and the resulting poverty in colonial cities has become an important area of study in recent years. Urban historians such as Kelly (1978), Fitzgerald (1987:13–49) and Davison (1985:1–28) have countered long-standing beliefs that colonial cities did not have slums. They have documented the existence of back-slums, rookeries and seedy boarding-houses in nineteenth-century cities, especially Sydney and Melbourne, comparable to some of the worst conditions in Britain and Europe. In these slums lived a thriving sub-culture of unskilled workers and their families, itinerant labourers, sailors, waifs, petty criminals, prostitutes, beggars, hawkers, barrow-men and Chinese traders. They lived in cramped tin sheds and huts, decaying cottages, Chinese opium dens, pubs and common lodging houses. The consequences of economic and social inequalities in the 'workingman's paradise' were most apparent in the colonial slums.

In the early decades of the twentieth century many of the conditions which had produced colonial poverty persisted. Unskilled workers, especially those employed in seasonal and casual work, were vulnerable to poverty, as were the aged, ill, fatherless families and women breadwinners employed as 'sweated' out-workers and piece-workers. In the 1920s returned soldiers who settled on the land under government settlement schemes faced the same problems as colonial selectors—poor land and insufficient capital—which forced many to leave after years of work, destitution and indebtedness. Some soldier settlers were broken in health by their labours, while their wives suffered equally from ill-health in coping with the double tasks of housewife and farm-hand (Lake 1987:101-91).

None the less there were attempts to improve the prospects of workers through the introduction of pensions, workers' compensation, arbitration and factory and shop legislation. Pensions for the aged and invalid were an important means of assisting some of Australia's poorest citizens. But they were not generous pensions and many of the aged continued to seek charitable assistance despite these new welfare benefits (O'Brien 1988:223-7). Other social experiments of the period helped to entrench social relationships that produced poverty. The establishment of the family wage principle of 'frugal comfort' by Justice Higgins of the Conciliation and Arbitration Court in 1907 provided a basis for trade unions to press for adequate wages. These have been seen as significant achievements won by the labour movement against the entrenched interests of employers (Gollan 1960:151-69). Historians of women's work, such as Ryan and Conlon (1975:10-70) and Francis (1986) have argued that these reforms did not benefit all workers. They actually exacerbated problems of poverty among women. To the continued detriment of female breadwinners the Harvester judgement helped to institutionalize the principle that women should be paid less than men. Factory and shop legislation, by policing the exploitation of female labour, removed the incentive for employers to hire cheap female labour, thus denying some women their only opportunity to earn a living.

Slum clearance programmes likewise did not always work to the benefit of the poor. In the 1920s and 1930s major clearance programmes were introduced, often by Labor governments. But they broke up communities which had offered crucial forms of support to poor families in times of crisis and forced some to pay higher rents they could little afford (Spearritt 1974). Government housing schemes helped workers rather than impoverished families. In effect many of the reforms in the areas of wages, conditions and housing that have been praised by labour historians as measures of special justice were of greater benefit to workers in regular employment than to the unemployed, underemployed and destitute (Castles 1985:102-9). If this is so then it points to significant divisions in the working class; divisions maintained by workers in trade unions who saw themselves as respectable and thus different from unskilled, casual and itinerant labourers and their families.

The post-Second World War period has been seen as Australia's second 'long boom'. The growth of manufacturing industry, fuelled by the large migrant intake, provided the conditions for significant economic prosperity, rising wages and a very low unemployment rate. Prominent politicians in the 1950s and 1960s asserted that Australia had the least poverty of any country in the world (Stubbs 1966:1-17). But in 1966 John Stubbs published his influential study *The Hidden People* in which he claimed that half a million Australians lived in a state of chronic poverty. He drew upon such important works as Hutchinson's *Old People in a Modern Australian Community* (1954), Aitken-Swan's *Widows in Australia* (1962) and Martin's *High Rents and Low Incomes* (1964) which had done much to reveal the structures of inequality in modern Australia. Stubbs's claims led to a public outcry and the 'rediscovery of poverty' in the media. Subsequent studies pinpointed the specific groups vulnerable to poverty: the aged, Aborigines, the unemployed, workers with large families and single-parent families. More significantly, they demonstrated that the social welfare system had done little to redress the plight of these groups and showed that even in the most prosperous economy poverty could still exist (Masterman 1969; Henderson 1970; Hollingworth 1972).

The dimensions of poverty in the 1970s and 1980s have been well charted. The Henderson Poverty Inquiry (1972-75) provided comprehensive documentation of the diverse social, economic and legal factors that contributed to poverty. In addition to the groups traditionally vulnerable to destitution new problems emerged in this period. A severe rural crisis revealed that small farmers and their families were one of the most indebted and impoverished groups in modern Australia. Worsening economic conditions and a rising unemployment rate significantly increased the number of people living below the poverty line (Browne 1987:34-5). Government policies also played an unintended part. The stricter policing of welfare recipients revealed some cheats but made it harder for those in genuine need to receive assistance (Windschuttle 1979:180-220). Other government policies have exacerbated the problems of some groups. The important policy of releasing mental patients back into the community has not always been accompanied by adequate community support services, resulting in widespread distress and homelessness among ex-patients (Garton 1987).

The worsening economic conditions in the 1970s and 1980s have caused more extensive poverty and a decline in the living standards of many working- and middle-class Australians, leading some commentators to argue that there is an increasing polarization of rich and poor in Australian society. Reading journals such as *Australian Society* and the *Australian Journal of Social Issues* provides important insights into the extent of modern poverty and the conflicts over the development of social policies to combat the growing problem. The post-war consensus over the necessity for a social security system is now under challenge from 'new right' thinkers who advocate the dismantling of the welfare state, work for dole schemes and the return of many welfare functions to the family (Graycar 1983:1–12).

Studies of poverty throughout the period of white settlement reveal important structures of power and wealth in Australian society. Even in prosperous times there were significant numbers of Australians living in poverty. Marked inequalities of class, race and sex have been held responsible for much of this poverty. But if such inequalities have existed why have major conflicts not occurred over the distribution of wealth and power? In other chapters of part IV it is argued that such conflicts have occurred but have been contained in various ways. One of the major containment mechanisms has been the welfare state (Connell & Irving 1980:211). In what ways have welfare, charity and other forms of assistance to the poor undermined protest? What has been the purpose of these forms of assistance?

Welfare or social control?

The measures pursued by philanthropists, charities and governments to alleviate poverty have been a central focus of analysis, and welfare history is now a flourishing field of study. Although the twentieth century has received greater attention than the nineteenth, some general trends are clear. Nineteenth-century colonial philanthropists and reformers believed that poor relief should be the province of private charities and these views helped shape the provision of relief in Australia. Unlike Britain and the United States, the Australian colonies did not adopt a Poor Law—a system of local parish provision for those in need. In the 1830s critics believed that the Poor Law encouraged people to seek assistance rather than work, and that making access to relief more difficult would discourage idleness.

These ideas influenced colonial authorities to reject a Poor Law system in preference to private charity. Charity was based on the principle that assistance was not a right but an act of benevolence bestowed on the genuinely needy. According to this view poverty was often the result of moral depravity and refusal to work; poor people were to be rejected and only the 'deserving poor' (the aged, ill, infirm, widowed and deserted mothers) were to receive assistance in the form of food, medicine or accommodation. In addition some charities sought to combat idleness by operating reformatories and schools for the education, training and moral reform of the children of the poor (Dickey 1987a:21–47).

The proliferation of private charities in colonial Australia enshrined private benevolence as an important means of poor relief. But the real picture is more complex. The colonial middle classes were small and their contributions to charities insufficient to maintain these organizations and as a consequence many relied on government subsidies to continue their operations. In addition, governments provided institutions for some groups neglected by charities: the infirm aged, the insane and delinquent children. Sometimes colonial governments assumed responsibility for the poor as private funds and facilities were insufficient to meet the need for poor relief, particularly after the rapid influx of population due to the gold-rushes. Governments, however, often appointed philanthropists to the boards of public institutions. Clearly there was considerable interaction between public and private authorities in the provision of poor relief. The nature of the mix varied from colony to colony. In Victoria there were numerous private charities, while in New South Wales the heavily government-subsidized Benevolent Society was a major provider of poor relief, with the government and churches providing the bulk of the institutions for paupers. In South Australia however, the government, through the auspices of the Government Destitute Board, was the dominant provider of poor relief (Dickey 1986). Nineteenth-century poor relief, then, was partly a system of private action supported by the public purse; in other areas colonial governments, in the absence of suitable private ventures, acted directly to assist the deserving poor and the socially outcast (Dickey 1987a:21–47). But what was the purpose of charitable action?

A number of historians (Windschuttle 1980:53–7; Evans 1976:93–5) argue that the aim of colonial philanthropists was to control the working class. This argument is forcefully developed in Richard Kennedy's 1985 study of the Melbourne Charity Organisation Society. Kennedy points to the niggardly assistance provided by colonial charities; there was no attempt by philanthropists to alleviate poverty, only a concern to make the poor docile workers. In support of this argument he focuses on the procedures of assistance. Philanthropists interviewed and investigated all applicants for relief and rewarded only those thought to be deserving. But the assistance to these groups was meagre in the hope that this would be a spur to self-help. Large numbers of people from the working classes were classified as undeserving, particularly if they were capable of working, drank, sought to offset the meagreness of the charitable benefit by going to more than one charity, or showed any signs of insolence. If deemed undeserving the applicant was denied assistance. These interview and classification procedures were designed as a deterrent to force the poor to rely on their own resources rather than seek help, and to adopt middle-class ideals of thrift and frugality. The aged, infirm and insane were locked away in large institutions. Children were sent to reformatories to be reformed and made into docile workers. In Kennedy's (1985:231–42) view humane and Christian sentiments expressed by philanthropists were a mask for a sustained attempt to force workers to submit to capitalism without protest. This social control interpretation is disputed by other historians, notably Brown (1972:170–2) and Dickey (1987a:xvii). Brian Dickey (1987b) has discussed the dimensions of this dispute. He accepts many of the points made by the social control historians: charitable help was meagre, selective and moralistic, and institutions were overcrowded and more like prisons than places of assistance or reform. But in Dickey's view these problems did not reflect an intention by philanthropists to control the working class. On the contrary philanthropists were motivated by high Christian ideals and a genuine desire to help the poor but their efforts were undermined by inadequate financial support, poor facilities, the enormity of the pauper problem, ignorance of the causes of disease and the regrettable but understandable blinkers of evangelical ideas of moral reform. Dickey highlights aspects of colonial philanthropy absent from the social control account. Some charities gave more generously than the ideal of meagre assistance and some philanthropists ignored the problem of the undeserving or turned a blind eye to infractions of the rules, providing assistance to many who under a rigorous system would have been struck off the books. Christian sympathy for the poor, in Dickey's view, often overcame the harsh moralism of evangelicalism. Charity was a flawed but humane system that provided essential assistance without which the poor would have starved.

The major involvement of women in philanthropic work has also become an important area of debate. Windschuttle (1980) and Godden (1982) argue that middle-class women were freed by domestic servants and increased leisure time to pursue charitable work. They advanced the ideal of women as sympathetic and nurturing, the inhabitants of the domestic sphere, but took these ideas further, arguing that women had qualities that made them useful and important in distributing relief to the poor. Middle-class women were able to expand their sphere of influence and construct meaningful public roles. None the less, in working as philanthropists women acted in the interests of their class, disciplining and controlling the working-class recipients of assistance. Women philanthropists defended middle-class morality and used this morality to determine who was deserving of relief. In contrast Marilyn Lake (1986) has argued that the condemnation of women philanthropists and temperance advocates as 'wowsers' by journals such as the *Bulletin* points to the widespread sex conflict that characterized many aspects of colonial politics. Middle-class women recognized that the source of much distress among working-class women was men and struggled to protect women and improve their lot. Men resisted attempts to restrict male privilege. In Lake's view, to concentrate solely on class conflict to explain the nature of philanthropy and social reform is to miss the central role of sex conflict and the opposed politics of feminism and masculinism in the history of these problems.

The significant development in twentieth-century welfare was the shift from charity to the creation of a welfare state or, in the formulation of Brian Dickey (1987a:72-5), the shift from selective to universal criteria for relief. Although private charities continued to provide important services it was the establishment of social security payments and government services that was the hallmark of the new welfare state. The emergence of this welfare state has been traced back to the late nineteenth and early twentieth centuries. At this time Australia earned a reputation as the 'social laboratory of the world'. The enactment of female suffrage, factory and shop legislation, old age and invalid pensions and conciliation and arbitration schemes—all before the First World War—placed Australia in the forefront of modern social experimentation (Roe 1976:3-20). What were the reasons for Australia's advance in these fields?

The usual explanation for the significant social reforms of the period has been that liberals were increasingly persuaded that state action for the collective good would not undermine individual initiative. This new liberalism combined with an emerging nationalism to place Australia in the vanguard of social legislation (Kewley 1973:3-7). This notion of progressive idealism has been challenged by historians who have placed these reforms in a broader historical context. Dickey (1987a:72-5) argues that the emergence of a powerful labour movement was the crucial factor. The rising labour movement, the 1890s depression and the serious conflicts between capital and labour during the 1890s raised the spectre of class conflict. Liberals alarmed by this conflict sought to smooth the relations between capital and labour by offering new welfare benefits to the labour movement. Following the work of Connell and Irving (1980), Dickey represents the social experiments of the period as a strategy of containment to diffuse working-class radicalism. Castles (1985:11-21) has refined these arguments further. He points to the important role of liberals in acceding to labour reforms but suggests that the focus of reform under the influence of labour was improving the lot of trade unionists. The thrust of the reforms was to improve the lot of male workers, not to establish a welfare state to assist the poor.

If Australia 'led the world' before 1914, it was left behind in the 1920s and 1930s. In these years there was a massive investment in soldier settlement and war pension schemes but virtually no new social security services for other Australians (Roe 1976:103-10). The welfare state became bogged down in conflict over the future direction of welfare services. Conservative forces attempted to shift Australia's welfare benefits to an insurance system similar to that of Britain and Europe, while the Labor Party remained committed to a policy of financing welfare from general revenue, ensuring that those on higher incomes contributed their fair share to assisting the poor. The consequent deadlock meant that Australia lacked a comprehensive scheme to deal with unemployment, illness and poverty (Jones 1983:31–45).

Some historians argue that the foundation of Australia's welfare state was laid in the 1940s not the 1900s (Watts 1987:x–xiv). The Curtin and Chifley Labor governments of the 1940s finally introduced the elements of a comprehensive social security system—unemployment benefits, child endowment, widows pensions, sickness and pharmaceutical benefits. These new benefits, however, were financed from consolidated revenue, not from insurance, and because doctors refused to participate in a government-controlled service the system did not contain a health service. More importantly, Watts (1987:125–8) has argued that the new welfare state was a liberal reform that did not address the basic social inequalities in Australia. Far from being a Labor Party triumph and a significant gain for the working class the welfare state left existing social inequalities intact.

What were the forces that determined the shape of the welfare state in Australia? An older tradition, exemplified by Mendelsohn (1979:35–41) and Kewley (1973:550–2), focused on the struggle by enlightened liberals to improve social justice in Australia. These reformers confronted major obstacles, from bureaucratic inertia and conservative opposition to financial constraints, and the resulting policies, born of compromise, often fell far short of the ideals of equity. This is a story of good intentions hampered by economic and political realities, but although progress was slow the history of the welfare state demonstrates a gradual improvement in the services provided for the disadvantaged in the community.

Critics have provided a different interpretation. Connell and Irving (1980:211) argue that the welfare state is essentially a strategy of containment designed to defuse working-class radicalism. They point to the introduction of new welfare measures at times of social and political crisis. In the years before 1914 the increasing strength of the labour movement, widespread strikes and the influence of socialist agitators alarmed liberals and conservatives. In this context governments were receptive to industrial and welfare reforms which improved the position of some workers. Castles (1985:82–8) focuses on the strength of the trade union movement as a central factor in the emergence of the welfare state. A strong movement was able to win concessions from conservative parliaments but these concessions benefited trade unionists not other disadvantaged groups. Higgins

(1982) also accepts that sections of the working class won limited benefits from the state. But in his view the concessions were minor and the working class, by accepting limited benefits, became locked into the status quo, fearful of losing hard-won benefits and reluctant to push for genuine reforms which would change the nature of those social relationships which produced oppression. The welfare state promises much, delivers little and debilitates movements for genuine social reform. Thus the structure of capitalist power remains unchanged.

Liberal and socialist analysts of the welfare state agree that the system falls far short of needs. It is a system that is residual—helping people in times of crisis—with little emphasis on preventive social policy or access to welfare as a right. It is also a system designed for favourable economic times. The economic downturn of the 1970s and 1980s has revealed the fragility of the welfare net (Watts 1987:x–xiv). A sharply rising unemployment rate taxed the resources of governments and led to a climate of opinion where the unemployed and other welfare recipients were stigmatized as 'bludgers' (Windschuttle, K. 1979:155–79). Much energy was expended on the problem of welfare cheats at the cost of the hardships of the majority of genuine poor created by worsening economic conditions. Governments—Liberal, National and Labor—sought ways to cut rising welfare costs, leading some critics to claim that the poor were being sacrificed in a 'retreat from the welfare state' (Graycar 1983:1–12).

This supposed 'retreat' raises questions about the adequacy of theories which explain the welfare state as being a response to social and political crisis. If this were true then one would suppose that welfare measures would grow, not shrink, in times of extended hardship. That this has not been the case points to further dimensions of the welfare state debate (Macintyre 1985b:138–46). In times of economic crisis working-class organizations might agree to limit their demands upon the state in order to keep the economy going, and hence employment for workers, in return for controls on prices, negotiated wage rises and industry safeguards. In this instance those groups not represented by trade union organizations—mainly women, the unemployed, the aged, some migrants, children—bear the brunt of welfare cutbacks. The state itself might limit working-class demands by pointing to the 'fiscal crisis' it faces: ever-increasing demands for services but limited financial resources and strong opposition to broadening the tax net. In this context the state in Australia has set particular agendas for winding back government intervention and returning responsibility for welfare services to families and private organizations. This strategy has not been welcomed by all. New policies of de-institutionalization for the mentally ill and juvenile delinquents have been condemned by some doctors, welfare workers and families as measures to cut costs at the expense of the welfare of patients, inmates, families and the community (Garton 1987). These issues are at the forefront of current debates about the welfare state. New questions about women and welfare have also been raised in the last twenty years. Feminists have documented the increasing feminization of poverty since 1945. Women, especially single, deserted, divorced and widowed mothers, have always been a significant proportion of the poor, but rising rates of divorce and family breakdown since the war have placed a considerable burden on increasing numbers of women (Baldock & Cass 1983). Feminists have also pointed to the limitations of a cash payment security system, arguing that an adequate welfare system needs child-care services, equal employment opportunities, refuges, measures to deal with domestic violence and effective maintenance provisions to fully grapple with the sources of women's poverty (O'Donnell & Craney 1982; Brennan & O'Donnell 1986). These issues point to the inadequacies of those theories which focus exclusively on the class dimensions of the modern welfare state.

Debates over the nature and effects of the welfare state raise important issues about inequality, social justice and the state in Australia. A number of competing interests—governments, business, trade unions, women's groups, community groups, welfare lobby organizations—are central participants in these debates. Underpinning these debates, however, is the obvious point that despite improved welfare services and the growth of capitalist enterprise significant inequalities persist and are responsible for the production of much poverty and distress in modern Australia.

References

Introduction

Connell, R. W. & Irving, T. H. 1980, *Class Structure in Australian History*, Longman Cheshire, Melbourne.
Eisenstein, H. 1984, *Contemporary Feminist Thought*, George Allen & Unwin, Sydney.
Fitzpatrick, B. 1968, *A Short History of the Australian Labor Movement*, 2nd edn, Macmillan, Melbourne.
Jackson, R. V. 1977, *Australian Economic Development in the Nineteenth Century*, Australian National University Press, Canberra.
Reynolds, H. 1987, *Frontier: Aborigines, Settlers and Land*, George Allen & Unwin, Sydney.
Summers, A. 1975, *Damned Whores and God's Police: The Colonisation of Women in Australia*, Penguin, Ringwood.
Sydney Labour History Group (ed.) 1982, *What Rough Beast? The State and Social Order in Australian History*, George Allen & Unwin, Sydney.
Western, J. 1982, *Social Inequality in Australia*, Macmillan, Melbourne.

10 Aboriginal History

Barwick, D. E. 1981, 'Writing Aboriginal history: Comments on a book and its reviewers', *Canberra Anthropology*, vol. 14, no. 2, pp. 74–86.
Bell, D. 1983, *Daughters of the Dreaming*, McPhee Gribble/George Allen & Unwin, Sydney.
Berndt, R. M. & Berndt, C. M. 1951, *From Black to White in South Australia*, Cheshire, Melbourne.
Biskup, P. 1973, *Not Slaves, Not Citizens: The Aboriginal Problem in Western Australia, 1898–1954*, University of Queensland Press, St Lucia, Qld.
Biskup, P. 1982, 'Aboriginal history', in G. Osborne & W. F. Mandle, *New History: Studying Australia Today*, George Allen & Unwin, Sydney.
Blainey, G. 1975, *Triumph of the Nomads: A History of Ancient Australia*, Sun Books, Melbourne.
Bonwick, J. (1870) 1970, *The Last of the Tasmanians; or the Black War of Van Diemen's Land*, Johnson Reprint Corp., New York.
Broome, R. 1982, *Aboriginal Australians: Black Response to White Dominance, 1788–1980*, George Allen & Unwin, Sydney.
Butlin, N. G. 1983, *Our Original Aggression: Aboriginal Populations of Southeastern Australia 1788–1850*, George Allen & Unwin, Sydney.
Corris, P. 1968, *Aborigines and Europeans in Western Victoria*, Australian Institute of Aboriginal Studies, Canberra.
Curthoys, A. 1982, 'Good Christians and useful workers', in Sydney Labour History Group (ed.), *What Rough Beast? The State and Social Order in Australian History*, George Allen & Unwin, Sydney, pp. 31–56.
Elkin, A. P. 1951, 'Reaction and interaction: A food gathering people and European settlement in Australia', *American Anthropologist*, vol. 53.
Elkin, A. P. 1974, *The Australian Aborigines*, 4th edn, Angus & Robertson, Sydney.
Evans, R. 1982, ' "Don't you remember Black Alice, Sam Holt?" Aboriginal Women in Queensland History', *Hecate*, vol. 8, no. 2, pp. 7–21.

Evans, R., Saunders, K. & Cronin, K. 1975, *Exclusion, Exploitation and Extermination: Race Relations in Colonial Queensland*, Australia & New Zealand Book Publishing Co., Sydney.
Farrell, F. 1980, 'Aboriginal history', *Teaching History*, vol. 14, October.
Foxcroft, E. J. B. 1941, *Australian Native Policy: Its History Especially in Victoria*, Melbourne University Press, Melbourne.
Frost, A. 1981, 'New South Wales as terra nullius: The British denial of Aboriginal land rights', *Historical Studies*, vol. 19, no. 77.
Gilbert, K. 1973, *Because a White Man'll Never Do It*, Angus & Robertson, Sydney.
Gilbert K. 1977, *Living Black: Blacks Talk to Kevin Gilbert*, Penguin, Ringwood.
Goddall, H. 1982, An intelligent parasite: A. P. Elkin and white perceptions of the history of Aboriginal people in New South Wales, Paper delivered at History '82 Conference, University of New South Wales, Kensington, NSW, 26–28 August.
Hancock, W. K. 1930, *Australia*, Ernest Benn, London.
Hartwig, M. 1972, 'Aborigines and racism: An historical perspective', in F. S. Stevens, *Racism: The Australian Experience*, vol. 2, Australia & New Zealand Book Publishing Co., Sydney.
Hasluck, P. M. C. (1942) 1970, *Black Australians: A Survey of Native Policy in Western Australia, 1829–1897*, Melbourne University Press, Melbourne.
Horner, J. 1974, *Vote Ferguson for Aboriginal Freedom*, Australia & New Zealand Book Publishing Co., Sydney.
Kiddle, M. 1961, *Men of Yesterday: A Social History of the Western District of Victoria, 1834–1890*, Melbourne University Press, Melbourne.
Lippmann, L. 1981, *Generations of Resistance: The Aboriginal Struggle for Justice*, Longman, Melbourne.
Loos, N. 1982, *Invasion and Resistance: Aboriginal-European Relations on the North Queensland Frontier, 1861–1897*, Australian National University Press, Canberra.
McGrath, A. 1978, 'Aboriginal women workers in the Northern Territory, 1911–1939', *Hecate*, vol. 4, no. 2.
McGrath, A. 1987, *Born in the Cattle*, George Allen & Unwin, Sydney.
Markus, A. 1974, *From the Barrel of a Gun: The Oppression of Aborigines, 1860–1900*, Victorian Historical Association, Melbourne.
Markus, A. 1977, 'Through a glass darkly: Aspects of contact history', *Aboriginal History*, vol. 1, no. 2.
Mulvaney, D. J. 1958, 'The Australian Aborigines, 1606–1929: Opinion and fieldwork', *Historical Studies*, vol. 8, no. 30, and vol. 8, no. 31.
Mulvaney, D. J. 1969, *The Prehistory of Australia*, Penguin, Ringwood.
Mulvaney, D. J. & White, J. P. (eds) 1987, *Australians to 1788*, Fairfax, Syme & Weldon Associates, Sydney.
Pepper, P. 1980, *You Are What You Make Yourself to Be*, Hyland House, Melbourne.
Perkins, C. 1975, *A Bastard Like Me*, Ure Smith, Sydney.
Read, P. 1982, *The Stolen Generations: The Removal of Aboriginal Children in NSW 1883 to 1969*, Government Printer, Sydney.
Reece, R. H. W. 1974, *Aborigines and Colonists: Aborigines and Colonial Society in New South Wales in the 1830s and 1840s*, Sydney University Press, Sydney.

Reece, R. H. W. 1979, 'The Aborigines in Australian historiography', in J. A. Moses (ed.), *Historical Disciplines and Culture in Australasia*, University of Queensland Press, St Lucia, Qld.
Reynolds, H. 1972, *Aborigines and Settlers*, Cassell, Melbourne.
Reynolds, H. (ed.) 1978, *Race Relations in North Queensland*, James Cook University, Townsville, Qld.
Reynolds, H. 1982, *The Other Side of the Frontier: Aboriginal Resistance to the European Invasion of Australia*, Penguin, Ringwood.
Reynolds, H. 1987, *Frontier: Aborigines, Settlers and Land*, George Allen & Unwin, Sydney.
Rowley, C. D. 1972a, *The Destruction of Aboriginal Society*, Penguin, Ringwood.
Rowley, C. D. 1972b, *Aboriginal Policy and Practice*, Penguin, Ringwood.
Rusden, G. W. 1883, *History of Australia*, vol. 3, Chapman & Hall, London.
Ryan, L. 1981, *The Aboriginal Tasmanians*, University of Queensland Press, St Lucia, Qld.
Shaw, B. & McDonald, S. 1978, 'They did it themselves: Reminiscences of seventy years', *Aboriginal History*, vol. 2, pt 1.
Shaw, B. & Sullivan, J. 1979, ' "They same as you and me": Encounters with the Gadia in the East Kimberley', *Aboriginal History*, vol. 3, no. 2, pp. 97–108.
Stanner, W. E. H. 1968, *After the Dreaming: Black and White Australians—An Anthropologist's View*, Australian Broadcasting Commission, Sydney.
Stevens, F. 1980, *The Politics of Prejudice*, Alternative Publishing Co-operative Ltd, Sydney.
Turnbull, C. 1974, *Black War: The Extermination of the Tasmanian Aborigines*, Sun Books, Melbourne.
Van Den Berghe, P. 1967, *Race and Racism: A Comparative Perspective*, Wiley, New York.
Watson, L. 1976, ' "From the very depths . . ." A black view of racism', in H. Mayer & H. Nelson (eds), *Australian Politics*, Cheshire, Melbourne.
Woolmington, J. 1973, *Aborigines in Colonial Society: 1788–1850*, Cassell, Melbourne.
Working Party of Aboriginal Historians 1981, 'Aboriginal history and the bicentennial volumes: Australia 1939–1988', *Bicentennial History Bulletin*, vol. 3, May, pp. 21–5.

11 Labour, Class and Culture

Benenson, H. 1984, 'Victorian sexual ideology and Marx's theory of the working class', *International Working Class History*, no. 25, pp. 1–23.
Bennett, L. 1984, 'Legal intervention and the female workforce: The Australian Conciliation and Arbitration Court 1907–1921', *International Journal of the Sociology of Law*, vol. 12, no. 1, pp. 23–36.
Bevege, M., James, M. & Shute, C. (eds) 1982, *Worth Her Own Salt: Women at Work in Australia*, Hale & Iremonger, Sydney.
Bulbeck, C. 1986, 'Manning the machines: Women in the furniture industry, 1920–1960', *Labour History*, no. 51, pp. 24–32.

Burgmann, V. 1978, 'Capital and labour', in A. Curthoys & A. Markus (eds), *Who Are Our Enemies?*, Hale & Iremonger, Sydney.
Burgmann, V. 1984, 'Racism, socialism and the labour movement, 1887–1917', *Labour History*, no. 47, November, pp. 39–54.
Burgmann, V. & Lee, J. (eds) 1988, *A People's History of Australia*, 4 vols, McPhee Gribble/Penguin, Melbourne.
Childe, V. G. (1923) 1964, *How Labour Governs*, Melbourne University Press, Melbourne.
Connell, R. W. & Irving, T. H. 1980, *Class Structure in Australian History*, Longman Cheshire, Melbourne.
Curthoys, A., Eade, S. & Spearritt, P. (eds) 1975, *Women at Work*, Australian Society for the Study of Labour History, Canberra.
Curthoys, A. & Markus, A. (eds) 1978, *Who Are Our Enemies?*, Hale & Iremonger, Sydney.
Daniels, K. 1977, 'Women's work in the nineteenth century', in K. Daniels et al. (eds), *Women in Australia*, vol. 1, Australian Government Publishing Service, Canberra.
Daniels, K. (ed.) 1984, *So Much Hard Work: Women and Prostitution in Australian History*, Fontana/Collins, Sydney.
Evatt, H. V. (1940) 1979, *William Holman: Australian Labour Leader*, Angus & Robertson, Sydney.
Farrell, F. 1981, *International Socialism and Australian Labour*, Hale & Iremonger, Sydney.
Forster, C. 1985, 'An economic consequence of Mr Justice Higgins', *Australian Economic History Review*, no. 2, pp. 95–111.
Francis, R. 1986, 'No more Amazons: Gender and work process in the Victorian clothing trades, 1890–1939', *Labour History*, no. 50, pp. 95–112.
Gollan, R. (1960) 1967, *Radical and Working Class Politics: A Study of Eastern Australia 1850–1910*, Melbourne University Press, Melbourne.
Gollan, R., McQueen, H. & Rickard, J. 1981, 'Class structure in Australian history', *Historical Studies*, no. 76, pp. 440–53.
Head, B. (ed.) 1984, *State and Economy in Australia*, Oxford University Press, Melbourne.
Higgins, H. B. 1922, *A New Province for Law and Order*, Workers' Educational Association (NSW), Sydney.
H. R. Nicholls Society (ed.) 1986, *Arbitration in Contempt: The Proceedings of the Inaugural Seminar*, H. R. Nicholls Society, Melbourne.
Hunt, D. 1978, 'Exclusivism and unionism', in A. Curthoys & A. Markus (eds), *Who Are Our Enemies?*, Hale & Iremonger, Sydney.
Irving, T. & Berzins, B. 1970, 'History and the new left: Beyond radicalism', in R. Gordon (ed.), *The Australian New Left: Critical Essays and Strategy*, Heinemann, Melbourne, pp. 66–94.
Kingston, B. 1976, *My Wife, My Daughter and Poor Mary Ann*, Nelson, Melbourne.
Lake, M. 1986, 'Socialism and manhood: The case of William Lane', *Labour History*, no. 50, pp. 54–62.
Lee, J. 1987, 'A redivision of labour: Victoria's Wages Boards in action, 1896–1903', *Historical Studies*, no. 88, pp. 352–72.
McCarthy, P. G. 1969, 'Justice Higgins and the Harvester judgement', *Australian Economic History Review*, vol. 9, pp. 30–5.

McCarthy, P. G. 1970, 'The living wage in Australia: The role of government', *Labour History*, no. 18, May, pp. 3–18.
McGuinness, P. P. 1985, *The Case Against the Arbitration Commission*, Centre for Independent Studies, Sydney.
Macintyre, S. 1978, 'The making of the Australian working class', *Historical Studies*, no. 71, pp. 233–53.
Macintyre, S. 1983, 'Labour, capital and arbitration 1890–1920', in B. W. Head (ed.), *State and Economy in Australia*, Oxford University Press, Melbourne, pp. 98–114.
Macintyre, S. 1985, *Winners and Losers: The Pursuit of Social Justice in Australian History*, George Allen & Unwin, Sydney.
McQueen, H. 1970a, *A New Britannia*, Penguin, Ringwood.
McQueen, H. 1970b, 'Laborism and socialism', in R. Gordon (ed.), *The Australian New Left*, Heinemann, Melbourne.
McQueen, H. 1983, 'Higgins and arbitration', in E. L. Wheelwright & K. Buckley (eds), *Essays in the Political Economy of Australian Capitalism*, vol. 5, Australia & New Zealand Book Co., Sydney, pp. 145–63.
McQueen, H. 1984, *Gallipoli to Petrov*, George Allen & Unwin, Sydney.
Markey, R. 1985, 'New unionism in Australia, 1880–1900', *Labour History*, no. 48, pp. 15–28.
Markus, A. & Ricklefs, M. (eds) 1985, *Surrender Australia*, George Allen & Unwin, Sydney.
Merritt, J. 1982, 'Labour history', in G. Osborne & W. F. Mandle (eds), *New History*, George Allen & Unwin, Sydney.
Métin, A. (1901) 1977, *Socialism Without Doctrine*, tr. R. Ward, Alternative Publishing Co-operative Ltd, Sydney.
Radi, H. 1974, '1920–29', in F. K. Crowley (ed.), *A New History of Australia*, Heinemann, Melbourne.
Reekie, G. 1987, ' "Humanising industry": Paternalism, welfarism and labour control in Sydney's big stores, 1890–1930', *Labour History*, no. 53, pp. 1–19.
Rickard, J. 1976, *Class and Politics: New South Wales, Victoria and the Early Commonwealth, 1890–1910*, Australian National University Press, Canberra.
Rickard, J. 1984, *H. B. Higgins: The Rebel as Judge*, George Allen & Unwin, Sydney.
Ryan, E. & Conlon, A. 1975, *Gentle Invaders: Australian Women at Work, 1788–1974*, Nelson, Melbourne.
Ryan, P. & Rowse, T. 1975, 'Women, arbitration and the family', in A. Curthoys, S. Eade & P. Spearritt (eds), *Women at Work*, Australian Society for the Study of Labour History, Canberra, pp. 15–30.
Secombe, W. 1986, 'Patriarchy stabilized: The evolution of the male breadwinner wage norm in nineteenth-century Britain', *Social History*, vol. 11, no. 1, pp. 53–76.
Spence, W. G. 1909, *Australia's Awakening*, The Worker Trustees, Sydney.
Sydney Labour History Group 1982, *What Rough Beast? The State and Social Order in Australian History*, George Allen & Unwin, Sydney.
Thompson, E. P. (1963) 1968, *The Making of the English Working Class*, Penguin, Harmondsworth.
Turner, I. (1965) 1979, *Industrial Labour and Politics*, Hale & Iremonger, Sydney.

Turner, I. 1982, *Room for Manoeuvre*, Drummond, Melbourne.
Ward, R. 1958, *The Australian Legend*, Oxford University Press, Melbourne.
Ward, R. 1978, 'The Australian Legend re-visited', *Historical Studies*, no. 71, pp. 171-90.
Windshuttle, E. (ed.) 1980, *Women, Class and History*, Fontana/Collins, Melbourne.
Women and Labour Publications Collective 1984, *All Her Labours*, Hale & Iremonger, Sydney.

12 From Women's History to a History of the Sexes

Alford, K. 1984, *Production or Reproduction: An Economic History of Women in Australia*, Oxford University Press, Melbourne.
Allen, J. 1979, 'Breaking into the public sphere: The struggle for women's citizenship in NSW 1890-1920', in J. Mackinolty & H. Radi (eds), *In Pursuit of Justice: Australian Women and the Law 1788-1979*, Hale & Iremonger, Sydney.
Allen, J. A. 1982a, 'The invention of the pathological family: An historical study of family violence in New South Wales, 1880-1939', in C. O'Donnell & J. Craney (eds), *Family Violence in Australia*, Longman Cheshire, Melbourne, pp. 1-27.
Allen, J. A. 1982b, 'Octavius Beale reconsidered: Infanticide, baby-farming and abortion in New South Wales, 1880-1939', in Sydney Labour History Group (ed.), *What Rough Beast? The State and Social Order in Australian History*, George Allen & Unwin, Sydney, pp. 111-29.
Allen, J. A. 1988a, ' "Our deeply degraded sex" and "The animal in man": Rose Scott, feminism and sexuality, 1880-1925', *Australian Feminist Studies*, nos 7, 8, Summer, pp. 65-94.
Allen, J. A. 1988b, 'Beatrice Miles', in H. Radi (ed.), *200 Australian Women*, Hale & Iremonger, Sydney, pp. 217-18.
Allen, J. A. forthcoming, *Sex and Secrets: Crimes Involving Australian Women Since 1880*, Oxford University Press, Melbourne.
Anderson, M. 1983, 'Women in mid-nineteenth century Western Australia', in P. Crawford (ed.), *Exploring Women's History*, Sisters, Carlton, Vic., pp. 87-128.
Bailey, P. 1986, *Leisure and Class in Victorian England: Rational Recreation and the Contest for Control 1830-1865*, Methuen, London.
Brownfoot, J. 1983, 'Vida Goldstein', in B. Nairn & G. Serle (eds), *Australian Dictionary of Biography* vol. 9, *1891-1939, Gil-Las*, Melbourne University Press, Melbourne, pp. 43-5.
Burke, J. 1981, *Australian Women Artists 1840-1940*, Greenhouse Publications, Collingwood, Vic.
Caldwell, J. C. 1987, 'Population', in W. Vamplew (ed.), *Australians: Historical Statistics*, Fairfax, Syme & Weldon Associates, Sydney, pp. 23-41.
Connell, R. W. 1987, *Gender and Power*, George Allen & Unwin, Sydney.
Daniels, K. 1977, 'Introduction', in K. Daniels, M. Murnane & A. Picot, *Women in Australia: An Annotated Guide to the Records*, vol. I, Australian Government Publishing Service, Canberra, pp. v-xix.
Daniels, K. 1982, 'Women's history', in G. Osbourne & W. F. Mandle (eds), *New History: Studying Australia Today*, George Allen & Unwin, Sydney, pp. 32-50.

Daniels, K. 1984, 'Prostitution in Tasmania from penal settlement to civilised society', in K. Daniels (ed.), *So Much Hard Work: Women and Prostitution in Australian History*, Fontana, Melbourne, pp. 15-86.
Daniels, K. & Murnane, M. (eds) 1980, *Uphill All the Way: A Documentary History of Women in Australia*, University of Queensland Press, St Lucia, Qld.
Deacon, D. 1985, 'Political arithmetic: The nineteenth century census and the construction of the dependent woman', *Signs*, vol. 11, no. 1, pp. 27-47.
Dixson, M. 1976, *The Real Matilda: Women and Identity in Australia, 1788-1975*, Penguin, Ringwood.
Eisenstein, H. 1985, 'The gender of bureaucracy', in J. Goodnow & C. Pateman (eds), *Women, Social Science and Public Policy*, George Allen & Unwin, Sydney, pp. 104-15.
Faderman, L. 1981, *Surpassing the Love of Men*, William Morrow & Co., New York.
Fitzgerald, S. 1987, *Rising Damp: Sydney 1870-90*, Oxford University Press, Melbourne.
Frances, R. 1988, 'Never done but always done down', in V. Burgmann & J. Lee (eds), *Making a Life*, McPhee Gribble/Penguin, Melbourne, pp. 117-32.
Frye, M. 1983, *The Politics of Reality: Essays in Feminist Theory*, The Crossing Press, Trumansburg, NY.
Garton, S. 1988, *Medicine and Madness: A Social History of Insanity in New South Wales 1880-1940*, University of New South Wales Press, Kensington, NSW.
Golder, H. 1979, 'An exercise in unnecessary chivalry: The NSW Matrimonial Causes Act Amendment Act of 1881', in J. Mackinolty & H. Radi (eds), *In Pursuit of Justice: Australian Women and the Law 1788-1979*, Hale & Iremonger, Sydney, pp. 42-55.
Golder, H. 1985, *Divorce in Nineteenth Century New South Wales*, University of New South Wales Press, Kensington, NSW.
Grimshaw, P. 1985, 'Women in history', in J. Goodnow & C. Pateman (eds), *Women, Social Science and Public Policy*, George Allen & Unwin, Sydney.
Grimshaw, P. 1988, 'Only the chains have changed', in V. Burgmann & J. Lee (eds), *Staining the Wattle*, McPhee Gribble, Melbourne.
Grimshaw, P. & Fahey, C. 1985, 'Family and community in nineteenth century Castlemaine', in P. Grimshaw, C. McConville & E. McEwen (eds), *Families in Colonial Australia*, George Allen & Unwin, Sydney.
Hicks, N. 1978, *This Sin and Scandal: Australia's Population Debate, 1891-1911*, Australian National University Press, Canberra.
Hyslop, A. 1976, 'Feminism, Christianity and temperance: The Women's Christian Temperance Union of Victoria 1887-97', *Historical Studies*, vol. 17, no. 66, pp. 27-49.
Jackson, R. V. 1987, *The Population History of Australia*, McPhee Gribble/Penguin, Melbourne.
Jones, F. L. 1987, 'Occupational statistics revisited: The female labour force in early British and Australian censuses', *Australian Economic History Review*, vol. 27, no. 2, pp. 56-76.
Jones, H. 1986, *In Her Own Name: Women in South Australian History*, Wakefield Press, Netley, SA.

Kingston, B. 1975, *My Wife, My Daughter and Poor Mary Ann: Women and Work in Australia*, Nelson, Melbourne.
Kingston, B. 1983, 'Golding, Annie MacKenzie (1855–1934), feminist teacher, and Isabella Theresa (1864–1940), public servant', in B. Nairn & G. Serle (eds), *Australian Dictionary of Biography*, vol. 9, *1891–1939, Gil–Las*, Melbourne University Press, Melbourne, pp. 41–2.
Kingston, B. R. 1986, 'The lady and the Australian girl: Some thoughts on nationalism and class', in N. Grieve & A. Burns (eds), *Australian Women: New Feminist Perspectives*, Oxford University Press, Melbourne, pp. 27–41.
Kingston, B. R. 1988, *The Oxford History of Australia*, vol. 3, *1860–1900: Glad Confident Morning*, Oxford University Press, Melbourne.
Knight, P. 1977, 'Women and abortion in Victorian and Edwardian England', *History Workshop*, no. 4, Autumn, pp. 51–79.
Lake, M. 1981, 'Building themselves up with Aspros: Pioneer women reassessed', *Hecate*, vol. 7, no. 2, pp. 7–19.
Lake, M. 1986a, 'The politics of respectability: Identifying the masculinist context', *Historical Studies*, vol. 22, no. 86, pp. 116–31.
Lake, M. 1986b, 'Socialism and manhood: The case of William Lane', *Labour History*, no. 50, May, pp. 54–72.
Lake, M. 1987, *The Limits of Hope: Soldier Settlement in Victoria 1915–38*, Oxford University Press, Melbourne.
Lake, M. 1988, 'Intimate strangers', in V. Burgmann & J. Lee (eds), *Making A Life*, McPhee Gribble, Melbourne, pp. 152–65.
McConville, C. 1987, 'Rough women, respectable men and social reform: A reply to Lake's "masculinism" ', *Historical Studies*, vol. 22, no. 88, pp. 432–40.
McLaren, A. L. 1978, *Birth Control in Nineteenth Century England*, Croom Helm, London.
Mackinolty, J. 1979, 'The Married Women's Property Acts', in J. Mackinolty & H. Radi (eds), *In Pursuit of Justice: Australian Women and the Law 1788–1979*, Hale & Iremonger, Sydney, pp. 66–74.
Magarey, S. 1985, *Unbridling the Tongues of Women: The Life of Catherine Helen Spence*, Hale & Iremonger, Sydney.
Matthews, J. J. 1984a, 'Deconstructing the masculine universe: The case of women's work', in Women and Labour Conference Collective (ed.), *All Her Labours: Working It Out*, Hale & Iremonger, Sydney, pp. 11–23.
Matthews, J. J. 1984b, *Good and Mad Women: The Historical Construction of Femininity in Twentieth Century Australia*, George Allen & Unwin, Sydney.
Merritt, A. 1982, 'Forgotten militants: Use of the New South Wales Masters and Servants Acts by and against female employees', in C. Tomlins & I. Duncanson (eds), *Law and History in Australia*, vol. I, May, pp. 54–104.
Modjeska, D. 1981, *Exiles at Home: Australian Women Writers 1925–1945*, Angus & Robertson, Sydney.
Morgan, R. (ed.) 1970, *Sisterhood is Powerful*, Vintage, New York.
Mulraney, J. 1988, 'When lovely woman stoops to lobby', *Australian Feminist Studies*, nos 7, 8, Summer, pp. 95–114.
Perrott, M. 1983, *A Tolerable Good Success: Economic Opportunities for Women in Australia 1788–1840*, Hale & Iremonger, Sydney.
Petchesky, R. P. 1985, *Abortion and Women's Choice: The State, Sexuality and Reproductive Freedom*, Verso, London.

Pringle, R. 1973, 'Octavius Beale and the ideology of the birthrate', *Refractory Girl*, no. 3, pp. 19–24.
Pringle, R. 1983, 'Rape: The other side of Anzac Day', *Refractory Girl*, no. 26, June, pp. 31–5.
Radi, H. 1979, 'Whose child?', in J. Mackinolty & H. Radi (eds), *In Pursuit of Justice*, Hale & Iremonger, Sydney, pp. 119–20.
Radi, H. (ed.) 1988, *200 Australian Women*, Redress Press, Sydney.
Reekie, G. 1983, 'Writing the history of rape in 1888', *Australia 1888 Bulletin*, no. 12, November, pp. 31–9.
Reiger, K. 1985, *The Disenchantment of the Home: Modernizing the Australian Family 1880–1940*, Oxford University Press, Melbourne.
Robinson, P. 1979, 'The first forty years', in J. Mackinolty & H. Radi (eds), *In Pursuit of Justice*, Hale & Iremonger, Sydney, pp. 1–16.
Roe, J. 1986, *Beyond Belief: Theosophy in Australia 1879–1939*, University of New South Wales Press, Kensington, NSW.
Roe, J. 1987, 'Chivalry and social policy in the antipodes', *Historical Studies*, vol. 22, no. 88, pp. 395–411.
Ryan, E. 1984, *Two Thirds of A Man: Women and Arbitration in New South Wales 1902–06*, Hale & Iremonger, Sydney.
Ryan, E. & Conlon, A. 1975, *Gentle Invaders: Australian Women at Work, 1788–1974*, Nelson, Melbourne.
Saunders, K. 1984, 'The study of domestic violence in colonial Queensland: Sources and problems', *Historical Studies*, vol. 21, no. 82, pp. 68–84.
Scutt, J. A. 1983, *Even in the Best of Homes: Violence in the Family*, Penguin, Ringwood.
Shaw, A. G. L. 1966, *Convicts and Colonies: A Study of Penal Transportation from Great Britain and Ireland to Australia and Other Parts of the British Empire*, Faber, London.
Sheridan, S. 1988, 'Louisa Lawson, Miles Franklin and Feminist Writing 1888–1901', *Australian Feminist Studies*, nos 7, 8, Summer, pp. 29–48.
Smith, F. B. 1979, *The People's Health 1830–1910*, Croom Helm, London.
Summers, A. 1975, *Damned Whores and God's Police: The Colonization of Women in Australia*, Penguin, Ringwood.
Walker, D. 1986, 'Youth on trial: The Mt Rennie Case', *Labour History*, no. 50, May, pp. 28–41.
Walkowitz, J. R. 1982, 'Jack the Ripper and the myth of male violence', *Feminist Studies*, vol. 8, no. 3, pp. 544–74.
Watson, S. (ed.) forthcoming, *Playing the State: Australian Feminist Interventions*, Verso, London.
Weeks, J. 1981, *Sex, Politics and Society: The Regulation of Sexuality Since 1800*, Routledge & Kegan Paul, London.
White, K. 1982, 'Bessie Rischbieth, Jessie Street and the end of first wave feminism in Australia', in M. Bevege, M. James & C. Shute (eds), *Worth Her Salt: Women at Work in Australia*, Hale & Iremonger, Sydney, pp. 319–29.
Windschuttle, E. 1980, 'Introduction', in E. Windschuttle (ed.), *Women, Class and History: Feminist Perspectives on Australia 1788–1979*, Fontana, Melbourne, pp. 1–29.
Woolf, V. (1938) 1977, *Three Guineas*, Penguin, Harmondsworth.

Wright, A. 1975, 'Jessie Street, feminist', in A. Curthoys *et al.* (eds), *Women at Work*, Australian Society for the Study of Labour History, Canberra, pp. 59–68.

13 Poverty in Paradise

Aitken-Swan, J. 1962, *Widows in Australia*, New South Wales Council of Social Services, Sydney.
Baldock, C. V. & Cass, B. (eds) 1983, *Women, Social Welfare and the State*, George Allen & Unwin, Sydney.
Brennan, D. & O'Donnell, C. 1986, *Caring for Australia's Children: Political and Industrial Issues in Child Care*, George Allen & Unwin, Sydney.
Broomhill, R. 1978, *Unemployed Workers: A Social History of the Great Depression in Adelaide*, University of Queensland Press, St Lucia, Qld.
Brown, J. C. 1972, *Poverty is not a Crime: The Development of Social Services in Tasmania 1803–1900*, Tasmanian Historical Research Association, Hobart.
Browne, P. 1987, '1981–1986: Poverty on the rise', *Australian Society*, April.
Buckley, K. & Wheelwright, E. 1988, *No Paradise for Workers: Capital and the Common People*, Oxford University Press, Melbourne.
Butlin, N. G. 1964, *Investment in Australian Economic Development 1861–1900*, Cambridge University Press, Cambridge.
Carter, J. 1981, *Nothing to Spare: Recollections of Australian Pioneering Women*, Penguin, Ringwood.
Castles, F. G. 1985, *The Working Class and Welfare: Reflections on the Political Development of the Welfare State in Australia and New Zealand 1890–1980*, George Allen & Unwin, Sydney.
Clark, D. 1978, 'Worse than physic: Sydney's water supply, 1798–1888', in M. Kelly (ed.), *Nineteenth Century Sydney*, Sydney University Press, Sydney.
Coghlan, T. A. (1918) 1969, *Labour and Industry in Australia*, Macmillan, Melbourne.
Connell, R. W. & Irving, T. H. 1980, *Class Structure in Australian History*, Longman, Melbourne.
Cottle, D. 1979, 'The rich in the Depression: Domestic service in Woollahra during the Depression years, 1928–1934', *Bowyang*, vol. 1, no. 1.
Crowley, F. (ed.) 1974, *A New History of Australia*, Heinemann, Melbourne.
Davison, G. *et al.* (eds) 1985, *The Outcasts of Melbourne: Essays in Social History*, George Allen & Unwin, Sydney.
Dickey, B. 1986, *Rations, Residence, Resources: A History of Social Welfare in South Australia Since 1836*, Wakefield Press, Cowandilla, SA.
Dickey, B. 1987a, *No Charity There: A Short History of Social Welfare in Australia*, 2nd edn, George Allen & Unwin, Sydney.
Dickey, B. 1987b, 'Problems in writing welfare history', *Journal of Australian Studies*, no. 21, pp. 80–95.
Eisenstein, H. 1984, *Contemporary Feminist Thought*, George Allen & Unwin, Sydney.
Evans, R. 1976, 'The hidden colonists: Deviance and social control in colonial Queensland', in J. Roe (ed.), *Social Policy in Australia: Some Perspectives 1901–75*, Cassell, Stanmore, NSW.
Facey, A. B. 1978, *A Fortunate Life*, Fremantle Arts Centre Press, Fremantle, WA.

Fisher, S. 1982, 'An accumulation of misery', in R. Kennedy (ed.), *Australian Welfare History: Critical Essays*, Macmillan, Melbourne.
Fitzgerald, S. 1987, *Rising Damp: Sydney 1870–90*, Oxford University Press, Melbourne.
Fitzpatrick, B. 1968, *A Short History of the Australian Labor Movement*, 2nd edn, Macmillan, Melbourne.
Fox, C. & Scates, B. 1988, 'The beat of weary feet', in V. Burgmann & J. Lee (eds), *Staining the Wattle*, McPhee Gribble/Penguin, Melbourne.
Francis, R. 1986, 'No more Amazons: Gender and work process in the Victorian clothing trades 1890–1939', *Labour History*, no. 50, pp. 95–112.
Fry, E. 1956, 'Out-work in the eighties: An examination of out-work in the infant industries of the eastern Australian colonies, 1880–1890', *University Studies in History and Economics*, vol. 2, no. 4.
Garton, S. 1987, 'Changing minds', in A. Curthoys et al. (eds), *Australians From 1939*, Fairfax, Syme & Weldon, Sydney.
Garton, S. 1988, *Medicine and Madness: A Social History of Insanity in New South Wales 1880–1940*, New South Wales University Press, Kensington, NSW.
Godden, J. 1982, 'The work for them and the glory for us! Sydney women's philanthropy 1880–1900', in R. Kennedy (ed.), *Australian Welfare History: Critical Essays*, Macmillan, Melbourne.
Gollan, R. 1960, *Radical and Working Class Politics: A Study of Eastern Australia 1850–1910*, Melbourne University Press, Melbourne.
Graycar, A. (ed.) 1978, *Perspectives in Australian Social Policy*, Macmillan, Melbourne.
Graycar, A. 1979, *Welfare Politics in Australia: A Study in Policy Analysis*, Macmillan, Melbourne.
Graycar, A. (ed.) 1983, *Retreat from the Welfare State: Australian Social Policy in the 1980s*, George Allen & Unwin, Sydney.
Green, D. G. & Cromwell, L. G. 1984, *Mutual Aid or Welfare State? Australia's Friendly Societies*, George Allen & Unwin, Sydney.
Henderson, R. F. et al. 1970, *People in Poverty: A Melbourne Survey*, Cheshire, Melbourne.
Henderson, R. F. 1975, *Commission of Inquiry Into Poverty: First Main Report*, Australian Government Publishing Service, Canberra.
Higgins, W. 1982, 'To him that hath . . . : The welfare state', in R. Kennedy (ed.), *Australian Welfare History: Critical Essays*, Macmillan, Melbourne.
Hollingworth, P. 1972, *The Powerless Poor: A Comprehensive Guide to Poverty in Australia*, Stockland, Melbourne.
Horne, D. 1964, *The Lucky Country*, Penguin, Ringwood.
Hutchinson, B. 1954, *Old People in a Modern Australian Community*, Melbourne University Press, Melbourne.
Jackson, R. V. 1977, *Australian Economic Development in the Nineteenth Century*, Australian National University Press, Canberra.
Jones, M. A. 1983, *The Australian Welfare State*, 2nd edn, George Allen & Unwin, Sydney.
Kelly, M. 1978, 'Picturesque and pestilential: The Sydney slum observed 1860–1900', in M. Kelly (ed.), *Nineteenth Century Sydney*, Sydney University Press, Sydney.

Kennedy, R. (ed.) 1982, *Australian Welfare History: Critical Essays*, Macmillan, Melbourne.
Kennedy, R. 1985, *Charity Warfare: The Charity Organisation Society in Colonial Melbourne*, Hyland House, Melbourne.
Kewley, T. H. 1973, *Social Security in Australia, 1900–1972*, 2nd edn, Sydney University Press, Sydney.
Kingston, B. 1975, *My Wife, My Daughter and Poor Mary Ann: Women and Work in Australia*, Nelson, Melbourne.
Kingston, B. 1988, *The Oxford History of Australia*, vol. 3, *1860–1900*, Oxford University Press, Melbourne.
Lack, J. 1985, 'Worst Smelbourne: Melbourne's noxious trades', in G. Davison et al. (eds), *The Outcasts of Melbourne*, George Allen & Unwin, Sydney.
Lake, M. 1981, 'Building themselves up with Aspros: Pioneer women reassessed', *Hecate*, vol. 7, no. 2.
Lake, M. 1986, 'The politics of respectability: Identifying the masculinist context', *Historical Studies*, vol. 22, no. 36.
Lake, M. 1987, *The Limits of Hope: Soldier Settlement in Victoria 1915–1938*, Oxford University Press, Melbourne.
Lee, J. & Fahey, C. 1986, 'A boom for whom? Some developments in the Australian labour market 1870–1891', *Labour History*, no. 50, pp. 1–27.
Lewis, M. & Macleod, R. 1987, 'A workingman's paradise? Reflections on urban mortality in colonial Australia, 1860–1900', *Medical History*, no. 31.
Lowenstein, W. 1978, *Weevils in the Flour: An Oral Record of the 1930s Depression in Australia*, Hyland House, Melbourne.
Lynzaat, A. 1979, 'Respectability and the outworker: Victorian Factory Acts 1885–1903', in J. Mackinolty & H. Radi (eds), *In Pursuit of Justice: Australian Women and the Law, 1788–1979*, Hale & Iremonger, Sydney.
Macintyre, S. 1985a, 'Australian responses to unemployment in the last Depression', in J. Roe (ed.), *Unemployment: Are There Lessons from History?*, Hale & Iremonger, Sydney.
Macintyre, S. 1985b, *Winners and Losers: The Pursuit of Social Justice in Australian History*, George Allen & Unwin, Sydney.
Mackinolty, J. 1981, *The Wasted Years? Australia's Great Depression*, George Allen & Unwin, Sydney.
Markey, R. 1988, *The Making of the Labor Party in New South Wales 1880–1900*, New South Wales University Press, Kensington, NSW.
Martin, E. 1964, *High Rents and Low Incomes: Housing Problems of Low Income Families*, Brotherhood of St Laurence, Melbourne.
Masterman, G. (ed.) 1969, *Poverty in Australia*, Angus & Robertson, Sydney.
Mayne, A. 1982, *Fever, Squalor and Vice: Sanitation and Social Policy in Victorian Sydney*, University of Queensland Press, St Lucia, Qld.
Mendelsohn, R. 1979, *The Condition of the People: Social Welfare in Australia, 1900–75*, George Allen & Unwin, Sydney.
O'Brien, A. 1979, 'Left in the lurch', in J. Mackinolty & H. Radi (eds), *In Pursuit of Justice: Australian Women and the Law, 1788–1979*, Hale & Iremonger, Sydney.
O'Brien, A. 1988, *Poverty's Prison: The Poor in New South Wales 1880–1918*, Melbourne University Press, Melbourne.
O'Donnell, C. & Craney, J. (eds) 1982, *Family Violence in Australia*, Longman, Melbourne.

Richardson, L. 1984, *The Bitter Years: Wollongong During the Great Depression*, Hale & Iremonger, Sydney.
Rickard, J. 1976, *Class and Politics: New South Wales, Victoria and the Early Commonwealth, 1890-1910*, Australian National University Press, Canberra.
Roe, J. (ed.) 1976, *Social Policy in Australia: Some Perspectives 1901-75*, Cassell, Stanmore, NSW.
Roe, J. 1987, 'Chivalry and social policy in the antipodes', *Historical Studies*, vol. 22, no. 88.
Rowley, C. D. 1972a, *The Destruction of Aboriginal Society*, Penguin, Ringwood.
Rowley, C. D. 1972b, *Outcasts in White Australia*, Penguin, Ringwood.
Ryan, E. & Conlon, A. 1975, *Gentle Invaders: Australian Women at Work, 1788-1974*, Nelson, Melbourne.
Sinclair, W. A. 1976, *The Process of Economic Development in Australia*, Cheshire, Melbourne.
Sinclair, W. A. 1981, 'Women at work in Melbourne and Adelaide since 1871', *Economic Record*, no. 57, December.
Spearritt, P. 1974, 'Sydney's slums: Middle class reformers and the Labor response', *Labour History*, no. 26.
Stannage, C. T. 1976, 'Uncovering poverty in Australian history', *Early Days*, no. 7.
Stubbs, J. 1966, *The Hidden People: Poverty in Australia*, Lansdowne, Melbourne.
Summers, A. 1975, *Damned Whores and God's Police: The Colonisation of Women in Australia*, Penguin, Ringwood.
Swain, S. 1980, 'Destitute and dependent: Case studies of poverty in Melbourne, 1890-1900', *Historical Studies*, vol. 19, no. 74.
Sydney Labour History Group (ed.) 1982, *What Rough Beast? The State and Social Order in Australian History*, George Allen & Unwin, Sydney.
Watts, R. 1987, *The Foundations of the National Welfare State*, George Allen & Unwin, Sydney.
Western, J. 1982, *Social Inequality in Australia*, Macmillan, Melbourne.
Wheatley, N. 1981, 'The disinherited of the earth?', in J. Mackinolty (ed.), *The Wasted Years? Australia's Great Depression*, George Allen & Unwin, Sydney.
Wheatley, N. 1988, 'All in the same boat?: Sydney's rich and poor in the Great Depression', in V. Burgmann & J. Lee (eds), *Making a Life*, McPhee Gribble/Penguin, Melbourne.
Wheelwright, E. L. & Buckley, K. 1988, *No Paradise for Workers: Capitalism and the Common People in Australia 1788-1914*, Oxford University Press, Melbourne.
White, R. 1981, *Inventing Australia: Images and Identity 1688-1980*, George Allen & Unwin, Sydney.
Wilson, R. (ed.) 1984, *Good Talk: The Extraordinary Lives of Ten Ordinary Australian Women*, McPhee Gribble/Penguin, Melbourne.
Windschuttle, E. 1980, 'Feeding the poor and sapping their strength: The public role of ruling class women in eastern Australia, 1788-1850', in E. Windschuttle (ed.), *Women, Class and History*, Fontana, Melbourne.
Windschuttle, K. 1979, *Unemployment: A Social and Political Analysis of the Economic Crisis in Australia*, Penguin, Ringwood.

PART V

POLITICAL IDEAS AND INSTITUTIONS

Brian Head

Introduction

Part V is concerned with three broad questions. First, how has Australia's historical experience of dependency affected the development of our political institutions and of our external relations with other nation–states? Secondly, how have the major political ideologies of modern western societies (liberalism, conservatism, socialism) been adapted to Australian conditions, and especially to the political party system? Thirdly, what have been the main features of state interventionism in Australia, and what, if anything, has been distinctive about the role of the state in Australian life? Is it true to say that Australia has been at the forefront of international experience of 'big government'? Discussion of these questions is intended to provide a critical account of the literature on Australian 'political culture', and to place Australian political experience in an appropriate comparative and theoretical context.

14 POLITICAL DEPENDENCY AND THE INSTITUTIONAL FRAMEWORK

Chapter 14 shows that the self-governing Australian colonies in the late nineteenth century borrowed a great deal from British political models but also from the institutions developed in other 'new' societies. The debate over federation is sketched as a case study in both innovation and imitation, though overlaid with political bargaining and compromise. The effects of dependency, or reliance on great powers, in Australia's foreign policy are noted, including a brief discussion of Australian involvement as an American ally in the containment of Asian communism.

15 POLITICAL IDEOLOGIES AND POLITICAL PARTIES

The place of liberalism, conservatism and socialism in Australian political history is examined in chapter 15. Emphasis is on the adaptation of these doctrines to local conditions, and the ways in which ideologies were reshaped by the political parties. Separate attention is given to each of the major ideologies in relation to the party system, including a discussion of which ideas have been regarded as constituting the mainstream Australian political culture.

16 THE ROLE OF STATE INTERVENTION

Building on discussions in part IV on welfare policies and the arbitration system, chapter 16 raises the issue of how and why the role of the state in Australia has been perceived as distinctive at key moments in Australia's history, for example at the turn of the century, in the inter-war period, and in the early 1970s (the Whitlam years of federal assertiveness). The chapter concludes by showing that the Australian experience of state interventionism and 'big government' has been exaggerated by the media commentators.

CHAPTER FOURTEEN

POLITICAL DEPENDENCY AND THE INSTITUTIONAL FRAMEWORK

The Australian colonists had already achieved a substantial degree of political independence from Britain before 1860. This was not only because of the logistic difficulties of imperial administration conducted over immense distance, but increasingly because the vast majority of colonists were free settlers and demanded self-government and civic rights. Moreover, the Colonial Office readily distinguished between the form of government and administration appropriate for a colonial dependency and that suitable for a free-settler colony; constitutional advancement in other parts of the 'white' Empire prefigured developments in Australia.

Achieving self-government on domestic matters was one thing; becoming an independent nation–state in the international system was another. Some writers have argued that political dependency continued, in two main senses: first, our political institutions and ideas were derived from Britain and created by British statutes; secondly, our foreign and defence policies remained securely tied to Britain's definition of imperial interests (McQueen 1970, 1973; Dunn 1984). This perspective is linked to the modern left-nationalist critique of Australia's dependent role in the international political economy and the power of transnational corporations (Crough & Wheelwright 1982). Other writers have suggested, however, that Australian political institutions and ideas were selected and adapted from a range of available models on the basis of locally perceived needs and interests, and that our foreign and trade policies evolved with a great deal of latitude *vis-à-vis* British preferences (Parker 1980; Miller 1980).

This chapter sketches the early development of political institutions, and more briefly foreign policy, in the light of these concerns with dependency and local innovations.

Self-government and federation

The Australian colonies in the nineteenth century did not share a single chronology of political and social evolution, owing to their different rates of population growth and their varied experiences with convict and other bonded labour. However, five colonies achieved a large measure of responsible government, each with a separate constitution, in the 1850s and the sixth (Western Australia) followed in 1890. This governmental structure was similar in most respects to that established in other British settler societies of that era, such as Canada and New Zealand, and was broadly modelled on Westminster conceptions of responsible government. The upper chambers of colonial parliaments were typically elected on a restrictive property franchise (or, in Queensland and New South Wales, appointed by the governor). The demand by landed proprietors for the creation of a colonial aristocracy, to provide stability and continuity in a hereditary upper chamber, was defeated by popular pressure in the 1840s and 1850s (Martin 1986).

Manhood suffrage for lower house elections was introduced in four mainland colonies in the 1850s, and forty years later in Western Australia and Tasmania. Women gained electoral rights around the turn of the century. The advent of manhood suffrage, and later of adult suffrage, occurred some decades in advance of political developments in Britain. In this sense, Australia's political dependency on Britain did not prove to be an obstacle to the relatively rapid evolution of citizenship rights. Indeed, it can be argued that the *absence* in Australia of traditional sources of resistance to democratic reformism facilitated the growth of a settler-democracy ideal of citizen rights to political participation and property ownership. (Citizenship, however, excluded Aborigines and Islanders.)

By 1901 the six colonial constitutions and systems of government were overlaid by a new superstructure of constitutional law, the Commonwealth of Australia Act of the British parliament, which created the basis for the federal system of government and law. Although the concept of inter-colonial federation had been suggested tentatively in the late 1840s by the British Colonial Secretary, it soon became clear that:

> no scheme of federal government would ever be imposed by Britain upon the Australian colonies: if they wanted one, they would have to work it out for themselves and the imperial Parliament would be convened only to give it legal sanction. [La Nauze 1972:4]

However there was no practical incentive for federation around the time the colonies gained responsible government. The free settlers were concerned to gain political democracy, at least for white males, and to encourage economic development within the context of the British Empire. Colonial governments expedited the inflows of British immigrants and capital, and the exports of primary industries. The isolation of the colonies from one another, together with the vested interests of political élites, tended to reinforce parochial and regional loyalties. Political rivalries and suspicions, and competing commercial interests, became obstacles to any form of unification. The existence of the American federal model, and of the Canadian federation from 1867, did little to spur emulation.

External events combined with shifts in political culture to change the outlook of colonial leaders. In the first place, the colonizing activities of other European powers in the Pacific region (for example France, Germany, and later Japan and Russia) became a source of concern. Fears of German expansion, for example, led directly to the annexation of New Guinea by Queensland in 1883 (Thompson 1980), and indirectly influenced the formation of a Federal Council of Australasia in 1885-6. British military advice urged that unification was essential for the defence of the continent. Secondly, the economic depression of the early 1890s convinced some business groups that co-ordination of banking and overseas borrowing, and the abolition of tariff barriers between the colonies, would provide better conditions for economic growth and a more attractive site for British investment. Some business leaders also viewed federation as a means of containing the rise of Labor political support (Crisp 1978:16). Thirdly, colonial political leaders, who in the 1890s drafted the terms of a proposed federal constitution, and who campaigned for its adoption in the referenda of 1898-99, were able to appeal to the symbols of national pride and national sentiment. Some regarded the federation proposal as enhancing British kinship and the 'glories of the Anglo-Saxon race', clearly signalling a desire to consolidate the exclusion of non-British immigrants from a White Australia, and even marking out Australia as an ascendant junior partner in a future imperial federation (Martin 1982; Bennett 1975). The achievement of federation was not simply a product of national identity. Nor was the desire for 'home rule' the major ideology underlying the federation movement.

Some republicans and labour populists saw constitutional innovation as providing an opportunity both for moving away from the British orbit and for enhancing democracy. However they were highly disappointed in the provisions which retained imperial links and which gave veto powers to the smaller states in the federation. Most Australians in 1901 were happy to feel integrated into the British Empire and had no desire for complete independence or for non-alignment:

The new Commonwealth was not sovereign: it had no power to declare war or peace; it could not make formal treaties with foreign powers and it had no diplomatic status abroad. The Head of State was the British monarch; the Governor-General, her representative, retained wide discretionary powers;

Commonwealth law could be invalidated by legislation of the British parliament; the highest court of appeal was the Privy Council in London; the national anthem was England's. In 1901 few Australians felt such restrictions to be onerous . . . Most would have seen them as reflecting the vulnerability of the new Commonwealth, and its necessary dependence for its security on the British Navy. But most would also have seen it more positively, as reflecting a natural, wider loyalty to the empire. Race and blood ran deeper than nationality. [White 1981:111]

At this time few Australians saw a paradox in their dual loyalties: a pride in Australia and a growing sense of Australian identity and maturity, alongside broader loyalties to the British Empire and the Anglo-Saxon inheritance. They did not have to make an exclusive choice between one or the other. Indeed, the dual loyalties persisted for several decades thereafter. The development, in settler societies like Australia, of a local identity within an imperial framework has been described by Eddy and Schreuder (1988) as 'the rise of colonial nationalism'. This contributed to the process of nation–state formation in Australia without, however, threatening to sever the bond between the former colony and the mother country. The maintenance of close ties with 'British civilization' helped to exclude Aborigines and other non-Europeans from the conception of Australian citizenship.

The form of federalism instituted in 1901 has usually been portrayed as a combination of elements from the British and American systems (Weller & Jaensch 1980:chs 1–4). The British contributions were: first, the Westminster conception of responsible Cabinet government, wherein the executive was drawn from and accountable to parliament (in particular the lower house); secondly, a political party system which gave shape to the electoral contests of parliamentary democracy; and thirdly, a continuing role for the monarch (through delegation to the governor-general) as head of state of the Commonwealth. The American system of federalism involved a written constitution (in which the federal government's powers were enumerated, leaving the residue to the states); an upper house (Senate) giving equal representation to each state; and judicial review.

The British and the American elements were necessarily in conflict, as some of the 'founding fathers' recognized, but most crucially in regard to a possible deadlock between the two houses of the federal parliament, where the so-called states house, the Senate, could obstruct the passage of supply for a government holding a majority in the lower house. Deadlocks were seen as resolvable either through practical good sense or through the time-consuming procedures of double dissolution and a joint sitting of both houses (s.57 of the Constitution); neither of these solutions proved adequate in 1975. The champions of federation understood that the Constitution would be a compromise; the federal elements such as the Senate were necessary to gain the approval of the smaller colonies. The Canadian federal model, which also combined federalism with the Westminster tradition, was seen by some as too centralist, and was thus less influential than the American model. Many elements of the American system were not, of course, adopted in Australia, most notably republicanism, a Bill of Rights, and a presidential chief executive whose cabinet was not accountable directly to the legislature. No one in the 1890s fully understood the extent to which the major political parties, with their internal discipline and control over legislation, would become central forces in the shaping of public policy and would turn the Senate into just another party house rather than a principled defender of the states.

The debate on constitutional design raised many issues about borrowing and selectively adopting overseas political models. Although there are obvious continuities between aspects of the Australian system and those of Britain and the United States, the new hybrid had particular local features and evolved in ways that differed from those other models. Moreover, the system developed in ways that were contrary to the intentions of the founders. (The growth of central power, in a constitution designed to limit centralism, is one instance. The federal government has collected 80 per cent of public revenues in the decades since 1945.) The British concept of responsible government, regarded by some as the foundation of parliamentary democracy, is heavily qualified in a federal system. Thus intergovernmental institutions (for example the Loan Council), federal–state agreements and overlapping jurisdictions mean that no minister is clearly responsible for policy at either the federal or state levels (Parker 1980). As Carl Friedrich has said, institutions seldom work in the same way in different contexts: 'particular features . . . torn from their context of living relations, rarely function in the same way within the new context to which they have been transplanted' (cited in Winterton 1988:7).

The debate on the Constitution was conducted mainly by 'men of property' and bourgeois politicians concerned to entrench the influence of political and economic élites in their own colonies. Some cynics viewed the constitutional proposal as by and for the politicians in the name of the people. The level of popular interest—as gauged by participation in the referenda—was low (45 per cent of eligible voters in 1898, 60 per cent in 1899). The labour movement regarded the Constitution as bolstering conservatism; working-class representatives having been excluded from the conventions which framed the proposal, the Constitution was seen as anti-democratic and a bulwark against radical change. For example, the labour journal *Tocsin*, co-edited by the poet and public servant Bernard O'Dowd, saw the constitutional proposal as a static and legalistic document, which entrenched the veto powers of small populations (via the Senate, and via the cumbersome mechanism for constitutional revision); which gave vague but sweeping powers to the governor-general; and which unduly involved the High Court in validating government initiatives (Anderson 1977; Bennett 1975). The labour movement was opposed more to the Constitution than to federation itself. Labour leaders and the labour press had attempted to promote a sharper break with Britain and a governmental system more open to reformist impulses. In this they were disappointed. However, the newly emergent labour parties were able to gain substantial electoral support, and in conjunction with liberal reformers were able to influence policy in the fields of wage-fixing and industrial arbitration, immigration, tariff protection and pensions. The nature of the policies and ideologies underlying twentieth-century political developments will be discussed further in later chapters.

External relations

The dependency theorists have portrayed Australian foreign policy (and international trade and investment) as subordinated to the powerful forces of imperial powers, namely Britain until about 1940 and the United States since the Second World War (Fitzpatrick 1941; Crough & Wheelwright 1982). Insofar as Australian-based trading companies became relatively significant economic forces in the South-West Pacific region by the late nineteenth century, they began to engage in their own forms of mini-imperialism and exploitation (McQueen 1970; Dunn 1984; Buckley & Wheelwright 1988). However, Australia's international weakness—small population, rural economy, lack of military capacity—led to its typical posture of sheltering from possible threats by falling in with the foreign policy priorities of a major protector. At the same time, Australia as a raw materials economy was opened up for foreign investment and structured as a specialist exporter of farm and mineral commodities. (This is linked to the explanation of Australia as a 'settler capitalist' society in chapter 2.) In short, according to dependency theory, Australia has remained under the wing of a great power in foreign policy, and under the thumb of foreign investors (see also Camilleri 1980).

A somewhat different picture of Australia's external relations has been advanced by other writers stressing the evolution of a capacity for realistically defining and pursuing Australia's own interests (Watt 1967) despite conflicts with major friendly powers (Miller 1980). This second interpretation emphasizes a growing maturity, the development of Australia's understanding of its position in the international system, but the continued necessity for close links to a major power (Millar 1978; Bull 1987; Hudson 1967; Hudson & Sharp 1988). Australia's relations with a protector, with or without a formal treaty, tend to be characterized in this view as partnerships of perceived mutual advantage rather than as relations of power and dependency.

The Australian colonies in the latter decades of the nineteenth century had gained substantial control over major issues, except negotiation with foreign nation-states. Immigration policy, nominally a local responsibility, was subject to British surveillance because the Australians proposed explicitly racist exclusion clauses, which would have offended nation-states (such as China and Japan) with which Britain had trading and diplomatic links. Defence forces became a colonial matter: the colonies established their own militias after 1870 but relied on Britain for naval protection, for which a financial contribution was levied. Even before federation the Australian colonies sent expeditionary forces to the Sudan (1885), South Africa (1899) and China (1900) to defend imperial interests. These were less a result of British pressure than of (some) colonists' patriotic and racist enthusiasms. There remained an undercurrent of anti-imperialist criticism, especially among the Irish and others who could see no justification for automatic involvement in British military affairs in remote lands (Millar 1978:ch. 3). After federation the Australian government lobbied unsuccessfully for greater influence over the deployment of British naval vessels in the South Pacific; it later gained approval for a separate navy, which was commissioned just before the First World War. Compulsory military training commenced in 1909, and conscription for overseas service became the subject of bitter dispute in the two referenda of 1916–17 which split the federal Labor government. In 1914 the Labor government of Prime Minister Andrew Fisher committed Australia to pursuing the war against Germany 'to the last man and last shilling'. Australia contributed 330 000 volunteers, who suffered immense casualties.

At the end of the war, Prime Minister W. M. Hughes gained for Australia its own membership of the League of Nations. In subsequent years, pressed in particular by Canada, the legal entitlement of the dominions to follow an independent foreign policy was gradually defined, culminating in the Statute of Westminster 1931 (not ratified by Australia, however, until 1942). Nevertheless, Australia under the conservative government of R. G. Menzies entered the Second World War in September 1939 on the same day as Britain, somewhat in the same spirit of automatic loyalty as Fisher's Labor government had displayed in 1914. The entry of Japan into the war in 1941, and rapid Japanese expansion through the Pacific islands, confronted Australia with the concrete embodiment of old fears of Asian invasion. The British military presence had been dissipated, and the United States became an indispensable ally in 1942. The federal Labor government, with H. V. Evatt as minister for external affairs, sought to protect Australia's trading and diplomatic interests in the post-war period during international discussions of global economic and political relations. However, Labor was drawn into active support of American and British foreign policy and intelligence networks in the early cold war years (Curthoys & Merritt 1984). The Menzies government capitalized on anti-communist fears in domestic politics, and cemented Australia's link to the American orbit by the ANZUS Pact (1951) and South-East Asia Treaty Organization (SEATO) (1954), and by sending Australian troops to fight communism in Korea (1950), Malaya (1950s) and Vietnam (1965).

The maturity/independence interpretation of Australia's external relations runs into great difficulty with the Vietnam war. Menzies's commitment of Australian forces was designed as downpayment on the American insurance policy for the defence of Australia, in the light of regional instabilities in the 1960s (including the Indonesia–Malaysia confrontation) and the great discretion for American action built into the ANZUS Pact (Sexton 1981; Pemberton 1987; King 1983). In the meantime, the American stance on the containment of Asian communism changed direction after the accession of Richard Nixon to the presidency in 1968. Nixon wished to avoid large-scale deployment of ground forces in Asia; he also sought closer trading ties with China. In the light of changing American policies, and strong domestic opposition to Australian military involvement in Vietnam, a gradual withdrawal of Australian forces commenced in the last two years of the Liberal–Country Party government.

The Whitlam Labor government (elected in December 1972) embarked on a more independent foreign policy, emphasizing regional issues, less reliance on American protection and better relations with non-aligned nations. The Fraser Liberal period in the late 1970s saw a swing back towards cold war ideology, blaming the Soviet Union for international tensions and the arms race; Fraser supported the American boycott of the Moscow Olympic Games in 1980, provoked by the Soviet military presence in Afghanistan. On the other hand, Fraser was also concerned to improve relations with Afro-Asian members of the Commonwealth. The Hawke Labor government adopted a safety-first attitude to preserving the American alliance when the New Zealand government effectively undermined the ANZUS Pact in 1984 owing to its opposition to port visits by nuclear-armed vessels. Defence strategy gradually changed in these years from a concept of fighting land wars overseas ('forward defence') to a greater emphasis on self-reliance.

In regard to external economic relations, the familiar pattern of semi-peripheral development continued: reliance on foreign investment to assist balance-of-payments deficits, export of raw materials, and imports of manufactured goods. Steps were taken in the 1970s and 1980s however to reduce tariff protection, encourage export of manufactured goods (especially high-technology products), and generally make the Australian economy more efficient and competitive internationally. 'Boom and bust' cycles in commodity prices, and export subsidy wars by major trading blocs, made Australia's external economic relations liable to rapid deterioration (Head 1986). Australia's vulnerability arose not so much from exploitation by transnational corporations as from structural economic dependence on primary production and inability to influence the major trends in world trade or the policies of major trading partners.

Having examined some aspects of dependency interpretations of Australia's political institutions and external relations, the discussion now turns to the development of major ideologies and their embodiment in the political party system. The treatment highlights conflicting interpretations rather than providing a narrative history.

CHAPTER FIFTEEN

POLITICAL IDEOLOGIES AND POLITICAL PARTIES

The conventional understanding of Australian political culture identifies two major traditions or currents of political discourse since the 1880s. A liberal–conservative tradition has contended with a social-democratic tradition, corresponding broadly to the contest between the champions of individualism and property and the defenders of the labour movement and collective rights (Connell & Irving 1980; Crisp 1978; Aitkin 1986; Kemp 1980). Each major tradition is given form and enduring influence through the work of intellectuals who shape values and priorities, and through organizational structures which mobilize resources to achieve specific objectives. The platforms of the major political parties, and the party system itself, have been regarded as the most lasting and concrete embodiment of this 'two traditions' approach to understanding Australian political culture. The party system, in turn, operates within the framework of the federal system of law and government and the parliamentary/electoral system of western liberal-democracies (Starr, Richmond & Maddox 1978; Maddox 1985; Jaensch 1983).

Contemporary liberal-conservatives and social-democrats have no difficulty in tracing their lineage back more than a century in Australian political history: to the debates on colonial constitutions and self-government; the debates on land reform; the growth of craft unions and industrial unions; the confrontations between labour and capital in the early 1890s; the federation movement; and the formation of the political party system in the national and state spheres by about 1910 (Loveday, Martin & Parker 1977). The two major traditions tend to emphasize their differences for reasons of political advantage and electoral persuasion. More radical currents, concerned to redirect or purify the ideology of the mainstream parties, seek to sharpen the polarities even further, and occasionally succeed in influencing the strategies and rhetoric of the key players on centre stage. The ideological heritage is contested both from within and outside each major party.

Some commentators have argued that, radical fringes aside, the major ideologies and established parties undergo a high degree of confluence and mutual permeation within the overall framework of the mainstream political culture. The boundaries of ideas are fluid, the packaging of policies is not subject to copyright. Not only do parties steal each other's clothes, they themselves have evolved new priorities and outlooks over time. Moreover, at a high level of abstraction it is possible to see that the major parties contribute to a specifically Australian mosaic of ideas and institutions which is different in important ways from the political culture of many other nations. The arguments emphasizing either the differences or the similarities between mainstream parties and their ideologies are complex and many-sided (Head 1985). Here, the discussion identifies four major variants of the 'integrated' political culture approach, before moving to a brief analysis of conservatism, liberalism and socialism.

The first version of the claim that Australia has a relatively integrated and distinctive political culture is based on historical interpretations of 'national character'. The labour historians of the 1940s and 1950s, the so-called Old Left (Wells 1988), presented an interpretation of Australian history in terms of progress and popular struggle. The Australian national character, forged in the harsh conditions of the rural industries of the nineteenth century (and enlivened by the dissenting voices of convicts, the Irish, Chartists and gold-diggers), developed a distinctive set of values, notably a commitment to democratic rights, and collective institutions to solve economic problems. This interpretation (for example Ward 1958) was adapted by other writers concerned with explaining differences between national cultures. Hartz (1964) and Rosecrance (1964) claimed that the Australian colonies' rapid achievement of democratic rights, welfare legislation and wages regulation was a result of a particular set of 'radical' ideas imported from Britain by the 1850s. In the absence of strong opposition from competing ideologies (such as aristocratic conservatism or urban liberal individualism), and following the political defeat of the 'squattocracy' by a coalition of the working class and the urban middle class, the political system quickly entrenched a mild, pragmatic and populist collectivism. This interpretation has been challenged forcibly by A. Martin (1973), who questions whether radicalism was ever dominant in the colonial period (let alone thereafter). Martin points to the real importance of urban liberal leaders (rather than working-class leaders) in all the important political issues of the colonial period. He also criticizes the static assumption of Hartz and Rosecrance that the early waves of immigration shaped the ethos to which later immigrants necessarily adapted. The 'radical fragment' interpretation of Australian political culture has also been criticized effectively by the New Left historians since the 1960s, arguing that the labour movement's achievements were more limited, that capital remained ascendant despite labour challenges, and that the working class was divided in terms of race and gender.

A second version of an 'integrated' political culture approach builds on this New Left perspective. Tim Rowse (1978b) has criticized the very concepts of 'political culture' and 'national character' as aspects of liberal–conservative ideology which disguise power relations and assume a natural harmony of individuals. However, Rowse argues that a particular social and political ideology—liberalism—has been dominant in Australian public life. In a major study of twentieth-century intellectual history, Rowse (1978a) attempts to demonstrate that a variety of Australian writers, educators and political reformers have worked within a 'liberal' framework marked by concerns about political and moral unity, progress, national identity and a defusing of class conflict. According to Rowse the labour movement's intellectuals have shared much of this outlook with more explicit defenders of the social order. In this sense liberalism has been a 'hegemonic' ideology, that is, widely diffused through most sections of society and setting the terms in which problems and solutions are identified. For example, the Workers' Educational Association leaders after 1914, including university teachers as well as trade unionists, offered a vision of social consensus through education and of prosperity through industrial harmony (for example, Northcott 1918; Atkinson 1919, 1920; Bourke 1982). Labor's post-war reconstruction intellectuals of the 1940s, according to Rowse, substituted a patriotic 'populism' for any class-based strategy. Labor's policies were primarily concerned not with equality, but with Keynesian notions of full employment, economic modernization and an alliance with American investors. By the 1940s both sides of party politics agreed that unregulated capitalism was indefensible; the ideology of *laissez-faire* (non-regulation) was in decline. This political accommodation defined a new era of social-liberal 'hegemony', centred on a mixed economy, state regulation, welfare measures and attempts to reduce industrial disputation (Rowse 1978a: ch. 4; Walter 1988). A similar interpretation of Labor and non-Labor ideologies of the 1930s and 1940s is also visible in a recent study of welfare state development by Watts (1987), who argues that Labor and conservative programmes for social insurance and pensions were shaped by similar concerns, namely a more systematic alleviation of poverty but without imposing higher rates of income tax to fund the welfare state.

A third version of an integrated political culture approach arises from the work of market-liberal critics of 'big government'. According to such writers, post-war Liberal governments (for example, those of Menzies, Gorton, Fraser) have been guilty of adopting Labor's social programmes and the bureaucratic apparatus of massive regulation and high taxation. This viewpoint (Kasper *et al.* 1980; Hyde 1982; James 1987) claims that widespread interventionism has become accepted practice in liberal capitalist societies since the 1940s. Interventionism is seen as economically disastrous, leading to inefficiency and low productivity. The steady encroachment of interventionism, according to the market-liberals, has been a product of affluence, expensive election promises, and misguided faith in the capacity of the state to solve problems. This perspective, as will be seen in chapter 16, leads to an urgent call for small government—low taxation, deregulation, and reliance on markets and family structures to deal with economic and social problems.

Finally, a fourth viewpoint which detects an underlying unity in Australian political culture is that which emphasizes bureaucratic and utilitarian processes. Collins (1985:154) claims that the major parties have exhibited a remarkable similarity of basic values and that this is explicable in terms of Australia's 'Benthamite' public sphere. By this term Collins draws attention to two key features. First, there is a *utilitarian* approach to institutional design and to policy priorities; decisions are justified by reference to majority interests, understood not in terms of classes or groups but 'the sum of individual interests' (Collins 1985:148). Secondly, Collins notes a *legalistic* approach to the structure and functions of government and administration; this is contrasted with some European and American political theories (e.g. 'natural law' theories of rights and consent) which provide a more exalted conception of citizenship and public purpose and are sometimes tied to a Bill of Rights. This interpretation builds on the classical account of state interventionism in Australia provided by W. K. Hancock in 1930:

Thus Australian democracy has come to look upon the State as a vast public utility, whose duty it is to provide the greatest happiness for the greatest number . . . Each of these individuals is a citizen, a fragment of the sovereign people; each of them is a subject who claims his rights . . . from the State and through the State . . . To the Australian, the State means collective power at the service of individualistic 'rights'. Therefore he sees no opposition between his individualism and his reliance upon Government [Hancock (1930) 1961:55]

These claims have been repeated so frequently as to be seen as obvious facts about Australian political culture, regardless of context and of social conflicts. In the remainder of this chapter some comments are made on the major ideologies themselves, before turning to a critical reconsideration of the debate about the role of the state in Australian life.

Conservatism and liberalism

Conservatism has an important place in any social and political order, in the sense that a continuity of institutions, processes and meaning-systems is valued by most citizens. This valuation is more explicit and defensive when the established order is threatened, and more implicit when the social order is seen as natural or taken for granted. Conservatism, as a general outlook, does not have a fixed set of policies; it is fundamentally a creature of time and place. However, there are a number of policies and processes which conservatism would typically oppose, namely the politics of utopianism, reconstructionism, perfectibility, rationalism and egalitarianism. Conservatism is generally sceptical of mass participation, preferring the stability of experienced élites. Conservatism does not seek to entrench a rigid status quo, but accepts that incremental adjustments are necessary. Moreover, the achievement of a particular objective by the radical reformers of one generation (for example universal suffrage) may become the basis for a conservative defence of past accomplishments by following generations.

Conservatism becomes tied in practice to specific policies or programmes. In Britain it became the name of a political party, the Conservative Party, which engaged successfully in electoral competition with both Liberal and Labour parties. In Australia the term has never been adopted by a major party, a fact which has been hastily seized upon by commentators to 'prove' that Australian political culture is inherently radical, reformist, liberal, and so on. This is to miss the point; what has been different in Australia is the absence of a strongly institutionalized link between conservative politics and specific features of Old World hierarchies: a propertied hereditary aristocracy, an established Church, a military establishment. Australian conservatism, lacking this definite social base, was much more socially and politically fluid and less constrained in its political rhetoric. However, British and Australian conservatism have both been marked by a significant degree of flexibility, adaptability and political expediency, including populist appeals for support. In Australian politics conservatism has usually been identified with the Liberal and Country parties (Hazlehurst 1979), though there are also many instances of conservative behaviour by incumbent Labor governments.

In a political system where the electoral laws tend to favour established major parties and where party discipline usually delivers bloc votes on the floor of parliament, the dynamics of party competition in Australia have produced basically a two-party system since the First World War. Labor has been one major player; the other has been the main anti-Labor party, whose name has varied considerably (Liberal 1909, Nationalist 1917, United Australia 1931, Liberal 1944 at the federal level). Country parties also emerged in the

1920s to defend the interests of small farmers (Graham 1966); their separate identity has been preserved despite changes of name (National since 1982) and despite a typical pattern of coalition arrangements with the Liberal Party (Barbalet 1975; Costar & Woodward 1985). Hostility to Labor 'socialism' has been one source of coherence in defining the identity of these parties. However, two notes of caution need to be made here. First, it is a mistake to regard the policies of conservative parties as merely 'reacting' to, or 'resisting', the reform initiatives of the labour movement (Mayer 1956). It is certainly true that mobilization against centralism and socialism have been important bases of political reorganization and electoral support; however, the conservative parties have their own 'business as usual' agenda in the absence of perceived socialist threats. Secondly, there is a gap between statements of principle (promoting individualism, markets, limited government) and the conduct of conservative governments. One example was Prime Minister S. M. Bruce's referendum in 1926 to increase federal power over arbitration; this failed, and Bruce later took the opposite position of wishing to abolish federal powers in this field.

Another example was Menzies's maintaining a number of public corporations and trading enterprises established by Labor governments (Simms 1982). A further example was Fraser's inability to restore substantial fiscal powers to the states as promised by his New Federalism policy in the late 1970s.

Federalism has been a key element of conservative doctrine since the 1890s, insofar as conservatives opposed the centralization of power implied by a unitary state and they endorsed the American concept of 'checks and balances'. At an ideal level this preference was justified in bringing government closer to, and making it more responsive to, the people. In practical terms, federalism lost this connection with democratic theory and became a matter of giving a veto power to the small states. Conservative rhetoric concerning the benefits of government close to the voters has never been translated into a desire to upgrade the resources and capacities of local government. The latter, created and restricted by state government legislation, continues to languish as the third tier of the federal system. Conservative leaders, with few exceptions, orchestrated a campaign to defeat a referendum (in September 1988) which sought to recognize local government in the federal Constitution. Conservative attitudes to the federal system have largely focused on a defence of state rights, seen as the bulwark against centralist expansion (Patience & Scott 1983).

Liberalism, the main version of conservative ideas and policies in Australia, should be understood as encompassing a range of positions (Tiver 1978; Kemp 1988). From the late colonial period there were important divisions between liberal leaders on issues such as free trade and protection, the use of 'coloured' labour in tropical industries, and forms of welfare assistance. In the years before 1909, politicians such as Alfred Deakin consolidated a programme which broadly can be termed 'social liberal' (Rickard 1976; Campbell 1975). This programme rejected the *laissez-faire* or market recipes of classical liberalism, instead requiring a 'positive' role for the state. The state was expected to provide economic and social security for its citizens, to induce co-operation between classes, and to promote national efficiency (Northcott 1918). Supported by the labour movement, Deakin's social liberalism included arbitration and conciliation, the basic wage, old-age pensions, protection of industry and restricted immigration (Markey 1982). Social liberalism was also tied in this period to progressivist movements in urban planning, public health and secular education (Roe 1984).

The social-liberal wing of Australian conservatism has been fiercely challenged in times of economic crisis and fiscal restraint, such as the Great Depression of 1929–34, when conservatives overwhelmingly supported cuts in real wages, pensions and public services. Similarly, in the years since the international recession of 1974, the ideology of free markets and deregulation ('market' liberalism) has successfully challenged the social-liberal orthodoxies which had become entrenched under conservative governments in the post-war decades of relative affluence. Social liberalism, after 1974, was effectively portrayed by its more free-market critics as tarred with the brush of Keynesian interventionism and a regime of high taxes and big government. Political leaders under the influence of market liberalism, and urged on by financial journalists and business lobbies, contested federal elections with the promise of cutting public spending (Sawer 1982). Social liberalism has underpinned some minor parties in recent years, such as the Democrats, who have resisted the trend among Liberal Party leaders to espouse market ideologies and champion the interests of large corporations.

Socialism and laborism

Discussions of socialism in Australia invariably disagree about the meaning of the key term (Irving 1983). Disputes are the more difficult to disentangle because the value perspectives of the commentators are often widely divergent. Four main lines of interpretation (see also Mark Finnane's discussion of labour historiography in chapter 11) may be distinguished.

The conventional view of early labour history by the Old Left tended to see labour ideology as a product of specific conflicts with the employer class in the second half of the nineteenth century (Gollan [1960] 1967), an ideology reinforced by an incipient nationalism which later contributed also to the success of the federation movement

(Ward 1958). The defeat of industrial strikes in the early 1890s led not only to the establishment of political labour parties to protect workers' interests through legislation, but also to labour's greater willingness to entrust the regulation of wages and conditions to state arbitration machinery (Macintyre 1985). A pragmatic defence of living standards, overlaid with organizational mateship, characterized the early labour movement. In conjunction with social-liberal politicians, significant economic and social measures were gained (Reeves [1902] 1969). 'Socialism' was a watchword of the movement, though it is not widely seen as indebted to European writers such as Marx. According to the French observer Albert Métin in 1901:

Labor parties in Australasia resemble the English movement in their trade union based structure, their exclusively practical nature, their pursuit of minor and immediately realisable reforms and the scarcity and vagueness of any declarations of socialist and other general principles to be found in their official publications . . . in practice they accept private ownership and the wages system, seeking simply to ensure good working conditions in the world as it is. [Métin (1901) 1977:51]

The word 'socialism' . . . displeases and perturbs Australasian workers by its very amplitude. One of them whom I asked to sum up his programme for me replied: 'My programme! Ten bob a day!' . . . Here, as throughout the English-speaking world, practical considerations are prized above everything else. Demands on government are for practical concessions rather than declarations of principle. Western Europe is richer in theory, Australasia in practice. [Métin (1901) 1977:180]

Whereas the above interpretation is celebratory of labour's triumphs, regardless of its alleged lack of 'theory', a second interpretation has undercut labour's early achievements as petty bourgeois, lacking a socialist critique of the capitalist order, and infected by racism. From a revolutionary Marxist perspective, Australian labour was obviously never genuinely socialist (McQueen 1970). Some of the New Left historians more cautiously drew a distinction between a 'laborist' outlook—centred on economic issues and the defence of unionism— and socialist perspectives which transcended capitalist social relations (Macintyre 1977).

A third approach to understanding socialism has been to document the extent of radical socialist impulses at various stages of the labour movement's evolution, showing their vitality but also the ways in which they were suppressed by careerist politicians and party bureaucrats. Burgmann (1985) traces the influence of European socialists (contrary to Métin's observations) in the period before 1905, and denounces the betrayal of socialist ideals by labour leaders in subsequent decades (Burgmann & Lee 1988:109–31). The judicial suppression of the Industrial Workers of the World in 1917–18, the political failure of the One Big Union concept (Childe [1923] 1964), the formation of the Communist Party in 1920, and the increasingly hostile relations between the Australian Labor Party (ALP) and the Communist Party in the 1920s and 1930s, have been well documented (Gollan 1985; Farrell 1981). The communist movement recruited strongly in the Depression years, and achieved leadership positions in some trade unions in the 1940s. By the 1950s, with the cold war and the split in the ALP, it was clear that the socialist left was politically isolated, and those remaining in the Communist Party were implicated in apologies for Stalinism. The New Left historians, twenty years later, had to re-think the issue of which radical socialist ideas were worth defending. Automatic support for existing parties and organizations might not always be the same thing as support for democratic freedoms and social equality—hence the New Left support for feminism, ethnic equality and participatory democracy.

A fourth approach to defining socialism has been to document the evolution of the 'socialisation objective' in the federal ALP since 1905, showing the broad ambit of the 1921 version as a highwater mark, detailing its subsequent revisions, and its virtual invisibility in recent years (Crisp 1955:ch. 14; Rawson 1966:ch. 5; Reeves & Evans 1980). Some have supported the dilution as realistic, others have seen this trend as further evidence of a sell-out by a party concerned above all with electoral success and ministerial leather.

The debates about whether Labor is really socialist are generally conducted among those who believe that Labor's mission should be some variety of socialism within a parliamentary system. Concern with redistribution, state controls over industry, and public trading enterprises have been among the key tests of democratic socialism. But not all regard socialism as the key issue. For example, the conservative Catholic strand of the labour movement has been the base for a very strong right-wing faction. The latter provided much of Labor's leadership, political and industrial, in the decades of competition against the Communist Party, and in the 1940s formed anti-communist groups to challenge communist leadership in trade union elections. An organization outside the ALP, the Catholic Social Studies Movement led by B. A. Santamaria, was prominent in assisting the 'groupers'. As the cold war deepened the ALP's anti-communism became more intense. In opposition after 1949, the federal ALP was under great pressure with a series of issues centring on the western alliance against communism and domestic issues of civil liberties, including Menzies's attempts to ban the Communist Party, and the Petrov spy case. Labor finally split in 1954–55 over the factionalism induced by these issues. A new conservative fragment, the Democratic Labor Party (DLP), became a significant electoral force for twenty years, directing its preferences to the conservatives and keeping the ALP out of office. The DLP was led and supported largely by conservative Catholics, though it was never a Catholic party and many Catholic labourites remained with the ALP. A number of right-wing trade unions disaffiliated from the ALP over the issue of anti-communism. The only parliamentary representation gained by the DLP was in the Senate, where the electoral system (proportional representation) assisted minor parties. By the mid-1970s, with the decline of communism as a key issue in domestic and international politics, the right-wing trade unions began to seek re-affiliation with the ALP, and the DLP lost its Senate seats.

The ALP is a labour party in the sense that it is one of a handful of political parties throughout the world which is built on the base of affiliated trade unions (Britain's Labour Party is another case). Trade unions have often been conservative or traditionalist on social and economic policy issues, however militant they may have been on matters of industrial disputation. Conservative labour intellectuals and supporters of the former DLP, such as B. A. Santamaria, have claimed that the ALP, following its grassroots traditions, should be promoting the economic and social needs of workers and their families, not the trendy libertarian issues of university graduates and hippies. The ALP, on this view, should be concerned with creating jobs, providing welfare support for children, keeping down interest rates, regulating monopolies, supporting the western alliance against communism, and resisting the breakdown of family structures (Santamaria 1987). Others, not all of them hippies, have argued that the ALP is the appropriate electoral machine to introduce modern concerns with conservation, peace, feminism and anti-discrimination. For social movement activists, much of Labor's traditional (white male) trade unionist ideological heritage lacks relevance (see McKnight 1986).

The ALP, like other parties nominally committed to certain political ideals, is always divided between those driven by 'principle' and those driven by the demands of political brokerage and compromise, between those who champion a class perspective and those who recognize a national responsibility. The ALP's appeal has been populist—directed at the interests of the common people, across lines of occupation—more than specifically class-based. In a parliamentary framework of competition for electoral support this populist element is inevitable. It is reinforced by calculated appeals to national sentiment, such as Curtin and Chifley's wartime calls for patriotic solidarity, or Hawke's rhetoric of consensus as a means of promoting industrial harmony in a period of economic recession (Alomes 1988). The other reason that the ALP is bound to disappoint many of its supporters is that governments cannot control many of the circumstances in which they operate, especially international finance and trade. It has also usually been the case that federal Labor governments have not enjoyed a majority of seats in the Senate, have failed to gain popular support for constitutional reforms to enhance their power, and have had ongoing conflicts with state governments.

Despite these difficulties the ALP has been regarded by some commentators as the principal cause of major policy changes in Australian politics. Before 1950 these included 'a much greater governmental role in economic affairs, a marked increase in social services and a somewhat more independent Australian position in international affairs' (Rawson 1966:5-6). With the Whitlam government of 1972-75 these trends were further developed, to a point where the succeeding conservative government felt obliged to reverse them. The Hawke government's major ventures both into market-based deregulation on the one hand, and closer consultation with labour and employers on wages and industry policy on the other hand, have again marked out policy innovations of significance (Head & Patience 1989).

The conservatives have portrayed recent Labor governments as centralist and expansionary, dedicated to big government and over-regulation, by contrast with a liberal concept of limited government and a narrower range of state intervention. The question arises: how have the two political traditions perceived the proper role of the state, and have they seen the conditions of life in Australia as requiring a different form or scale of state intervention from that in other countries?

CHAPTER SIXTEEN

THE ROLE OF STATE INTERVENTION

In European countries the doctrine of *laissez-faire* developed as a strong reaction to a historical experience of state regulation, patronage and mercantilism. *Laissez-faire* was a doctrine advocating the creation of wealth through market forces, unfettered by state restrictions. This doctrine in political economy was mirrored by liberal political philosophy, which championed civil freedoms and political participation. In Britain from 1840 to 1880 *laissez-faire* was in the ascendant, though increasingly challenged by social liberalism and labourism in later years. Given the waves of immigration of free settlers from Britain in these decades it might have been expected that liberal political economy would have had a dominant influence on colonial governments' behaviour. This was not the case. According to the leading authority on nineteenth-century public finance, the activities of the Australian colonial governments might be termed 'colonial socialism' (Butlin 1959).

Observers at the turn of the century noted the contrast between the relatively high level of public expenditure, borrowing, and employment in Australia, and the public sector profiles of other societies (Métin [1901] 1977; Reeves [1902] 1969). The scope and resources of the state in Australia clearly exceeded the experience of other New World societies such as the United States or of the mother country Britain. Why was this so? Is it true to say that Australia led the world in developing 'big government'?

Early state expansion

There are two main strategies for explaining the Australian experience of colonial socialism. One is to focus on the physical environment and the problems of settlement in a large continent. A second is to focus on ideologies and political struggles. A further essential distinction is to differentiate two main types of state activities: those which are concerned with establishing and extending the physical infrastructure required for industry, commerce and urban life; and those which are directed at the material and social welfare of workers, consumers and the general population.

The environmental explanation of early state action in Australia is widely shared. The theorist of free-settler colonization, E. G. Wakefield, wrote that new countries require 'ample government' (cited in Hancock [1930] 1961:52). Economic historians have pointed to the complete absence of transport networks and urban infrastructure in the new colonies. In the early convict period the state was the major centre of power in allocating resources and providing basic services. The free settlers brought very limited capital funds, perhaps sufficient for establishing a small business or farm, but not for investing in private companies to build roads, ports, railways and communications systems (Butlin 1959; Connell & Irving 1980). Private initiatives in railway infrastructure ended in failure. Business groups in both rural and urban industries demanded that the state take appropriate action to build transport systems, provide water supplies, service urban development and facilitate outflows of commodity exports and inflows of investment and immigrants.

Colonial governments began to borrow heavily on the London money market for public investment in infrastructure; this pattern was continued by the state governments after 1901, and eventually came under the co-ordination of a Loan Council established in 1926. (The experience in the United States, by contrast, was that a significant proportion of physical and urban infrastructure was funded by private corporations, made possible by large amounts of private capital, a proliferation of regional banks and a much larger population.) In short, the problems of development came to be seen in Australia as a governmental responsibility on behalf of business and citizens. By extension, the system of tariff protection established by the federal government was seen as a method of nurturing infant industries in a young country, shielding them from the competitive strength of more powerful overseas economies. Similarly, the various forms of subsidization, disaster relief and price stabilization guaranteed to sections of primary production can be seen as state action to reduce the risks inherent in exposure to the fluctuations of market forces and to the hazards of drought, fire and flood.

Public investment in infrastructure was seen as practical and nondoctrinaire, and was not very controversial so long as the fiscal burden of interest payments was not excessive and so long as loans could be arranged easily. But these problems did recur, especially in times of recession. State governments also heavily invested in 'closer settlement' schemes (small farming, mainly in poorly serviced areas) after the First World War, which turned out to be economically wasteful and badly planned. Public corporations and regulatory boards increasingly attracted ideological criticism in the inter-war years, when conservative liberals began to view the state's role as too paternalistic and almost certainly inefficient. Critics began to use the term 'state socialism' to describe the panoply of public utilities and commissions (Hancock [1930] 1961; Eggleston 1932; Osmond 1985).

The ideological explanation of early state action in Australia, on the other hand, is less concerned with pragmatic responses to the problems of settling and developing a large continent, and more attentive to the political demands of labour and of urban liberals. The mobilization of popular struggles around colonial constitutions and the issue of land reform led to the political defeat of rural landholders, though not curbing the economic power of export industries (Hirst 1988; Macintyre 1985). The temporary link between urban workers, small farmers and reforming liberal politicians was evidence that a populist-progressive alliance, based on hostility to (rural) 'plutocrats', could be mobilized as an alternative to conventional class conflict (Connell & Irving 1980:119-23). Hartz and Rosecrance, ever prone to exaggerated generalizations, claim somewhat differently that the dominant political ethos in Australia from the 1850s was 'radical', and that the 'labour spirit' had an easy triumph in the absence of both a feudal aristocracy and a powerful bourgeoisie (Hartz 1964:42). The mild and pragmatic socialism of the labour movement, based in their view on mateship more than militant doctrines, swept all before it but without seeking to abolish capitalism (Rosecrance 1964:304-9). Hartz and Rosecrance appear to believe that the line of causation begins with ideas (radical), which become embodied in policies requiring expansion of state action.

However, their explanation fails to provide detailed examples of how this process occurred. The nature of the link between labour and the reformist liberals is not discussed, leaving open the alternate reading, given by A. Martin (1973), that urban social liberalism was the leading edge of political change in the colonial period and early Commonwealth.

The relation between labour and social-liberal ideologies and platforms was very close at strategic points, such as 1895-1910, in the shaping of state action (Rickard 1976). However, the significant policy areas for state expansion at this time were focused not on infrastructure but on democratic rights, wages and working conditions, and welfare legislation. In many instances Liberal governments introduced such measures without pressure from a parliamentary Labor Party holding the balance of power. Liberal reformers were motivated by a desire for civilized standards of living, the abolition of pauperism and social harmony to replace class conflict. Connell and Irving (1980:211) regard this programme as a conscious policy of defusing working-class mobilization. Other writers see the reform programme as typical of social liberalism's ethical concept of the state having a broader responsibility for social problems (Dickey 1980).

What can be agreed upon is that the regulation of the labour market and the beginnings of state welfare had become well advanced in Australasia by the turn of the century. Australia and New Zealand were widely seen as 'the world's laboratories of social reform and democracy' (Farrell 1987:1). Against a background of economic crisis in the early 1890s and the political mobilization of labour, governments enacted a range of measures, including compulsory arbitration, wages boards, old-age pensions, unemployment relief work, labour bureaux, and women's enfranchisement (Métin [1901] 1977; Reeves [1902] 1969).

An argument has been developed by Francis Castles (1985) that the main thrust of the early welfare state was towards protecting the interests of those in the workforce (and of those temporarily unemployed) rather than the general social needs of all citizens. Preoccupation with working conditions, wages and industrial relations seems to bear out this interpretation. Castles (1985:87) further claims that welfare measures to protect the incomes of those outside the workforce (age pensions for example) constituted only a 'tenuous safety net'. Entitlements were restricted by means-testing and paid at a flat rate; welfare philosophy was 'residual and selectivist', providing state charity where the needs of the destitute could not be met by private charity (Castles 1985:16). The implication of this argument is that state interventionism in one field—the welfare state—bloomed early but failed to grow into more developed (universalist) forms because its priorities were with 'wage-earners' welfare'. This explains why public expenditure on welfare in Australia has not kept pace with Western European societies in the post-war period, because in those societies welfare provisions are more generally available as entitlements of citizenship, not as a badge of destitution. Popular mythology, however, spurred by conservative propaganda, continues to depict Australia as a big spender on welfare. Another illusion, perpetuated by federal Labor leaders, is that Australia has remained at the forefront of achievement regarding equity and social justice simply by virtue of Labor governments holding office in the 1940s and again in recent years.

The modern welfare state

Two crucial test cases concerning the nature of welfare state expansion in recent decades are first, the 'post-war reconstruction' Labor governments of Curtin and Chifley in the 1940s, and secondly the

Whitlam Labor government in the early 1970s. A brief account of the debates about the significance of these cases may be useful.

In 1942–43 the Labor government established a Department of Postwar Reconstruction and three investigatory commissions reporting on problems in rural industries, secondary industries and housing. Some of the leading social-democratic intellectuals in the federal bureaucracy (H. C. Coombs, L. Ross) participated in a conference outlining their programmes and objectives (Campbell 1944). In 1944 the government sought to increase federal constitutional powers in fourteen areas through a referendum, which was defeated. In the meantime Labor was pressing ahead under its defence power with extension of social security benefits and pharmaceutical benefits, confirmed as a peacetime federal power in a successful referendum in 1946. In 1943 a National Welfare Fund was established within the federal budget as a means of funding the increased costs of social security; funds were taken from taxation revenue after years of debate over the desirability and viability of 'contributory' schemes of social insurance (Watts 1987). Plans for a more comprehensive national health scheme were defeated by a combination of political pressure from medical practitioners and rulings of the High Court. In 1945 the government's White Paper on *Full Employment* outlined a commitment to high levels of public investment and a range of economic management techniques to combat problems of unemployment, inflation and recession. Labor also ventured into public ownership of airlines (TAA, QANTAS), and enhanced the central bank functions of the Commonwealth Bank, before being drawn into a politically disastrous attempt to nationalize the private banks when the latter challenged aspects of Labor's legislation regulating the banking sector.

What does this record of interventionism amount to? Some radical critics (Rowse 1978b; Connell & Irving 1980; Watts 1987) have argued that the main thrust of these policies was to promote economic growth, social stability, industrial harmony and a realignment towards encouraging American investors in manufacturing. In other words, Labor in the 1940s was *not* primarily concerned with a redistribution of wealth and power towards the working class, and was less committed to public ownership of key industries than was the Attlee Labour government in Britain (Catley & McFarlane 1981). A second, more positive, interpretation recognizes certain achievements of the Labor government as a social-democratic variant of 'liberal reformism' (Walter 1988). The concept of a partnership of capital and labour, facilitated by government economic and social policies, could satisfy demands for both economic productivity and social welfare and security. A business lobby, the Institute of Public Affairs, published a document, *Looking Forward*, in October 1944 outlining a social-liberal perspective on the proper role of government. While reiterating the virtues of private enterprise and opposing detailed central planning, the document supported a range of limited state interventionism in economic and social areas (Hay 1982). This perspective was also adopted by the newly formed Liberal Party. A third interpretation of Labor's post-war reconstruction programme is that of the hard-line conservatives, who attacked Labor as inherently centralist, socialist, seeking the indefinite expansion of government powers, and restricting freedom for entrepreneurs and citizens alike. These views were especially evident in the campaigns against the '14 Powers' constitutional referendum in 1944 (Waters 1969) and the bank nationalization issue of 1947–48.

The case of the Whitlam Labor government, between December 1972 and its demise in a constitutional crisis in November 1975, has been interpreted in similar ways. Labor undertook a wide range of inquiries, established many commissions, expanded the federal public service, and vastly increased federal spending on education, social security, health, urban development, and other areas. It espoused the view that the federal government should be concerned with national policy priorities, and should co-ordinate federal *and* state government solutions to national problems regardless of whether the Constitution clearly empowered the federal government to act in all these policy areas. The main device to assert federal influence was financial; the Whitlam government greatly increased the use of 'tied' (or specific-purpose) grants to the states, so that the latter became in effect the administrative agencies of federal policy in such areas as public health and education (Sawer 1977).

Interpretations of the Whitlam government varied widely. Radical critics claimed it was redefining labour egalitarianism to mean equal opportunity (a social-liberal concept), and that the middle class were the main beneficiaries of education and welfare spending (Catley & McFarlane 1974). Social-democratic sympathizers pointed to important gains in expanding public regulation, providing higher levels of social security, and giving a higher priority to economic and social planning (Patience & Head 1979; Whitlam 1985). Conservatives and liberals of many hues, including journals such as *Quadrant*, bitterly attacked the Labor government as unable to manage the economic problems of inflation and recession, as stifling the private sector by regulations and taxes, as wastefully spending too much on welfare, and as seeking to destroy states' rights through the ruthless assertion of federal financial power (O'Brien 1977).

It is clear from these cases that the major political traditions of social democracy and liberal conservatism have developed different emphases concerning the proper scope and forms of state interventionism in Australia. At a theoretical level of argument the traditions have tended to emphasize one side of a series of polarities: social *or* individual liberty, regulation *or* deregulation, public enterprise *or* private enterprise, egalitarianism *or* market outcomes. At a more practical level the traditions have focused on a few key issues, such as whether intergovernmental relations in a federal system should operate in ways which constrain or facilitate the central government's co-ordinating role, or whether health services are more efficient under a predominantly public or private system. For some commentators, however, defining the different emphases in party platforms is somewhat irrelevant if a governing party is unable to change the direction of established policies.

One of the key questions about state interventionism is whether the state is regarded as inherently enmeshed with the interests of a certain class (workers, capitalists, state bureaucrats) or a certain ideology (socialism, capitalist development, state expansion). The alternative position regards the state as a neutral apparatus which can be set in motion to achieve the objectives of the government of the day (Galligan 1984). For Hancock ([1930] 1961) the state seemed to be class-neutral, serving individual rights and collective needs as determined by the popular will. Similar assumptions are evident in the writings of those who see the state as utilitarian (Collins 1985; Loveday 1983; Encel 1960). The issue for such writers is which groups control the direction of state policy.

Liberals and conservatives, despite their frequent critiques of big government, have routinely resorted to state action in their quest for development, using various forms of state assistance for industries and state provision of infrastructure as techniques for encouraging entrepreneurs to create more wealth for the general good. State interventionism has been attacked, however, when industry assistance seems to breed inefficiency and dependence on subsidies—a common theme among economists and conservative liberals. State interventionism has also been strongly attacked when the target has been a federal Labor government apparently dedicated to expanding federal powers (the 1944 referenda), nationalizing industry (the banking issue of 1947), reducing the power of the states, restraining foreign investment (1973–75), or threatening the privileges of private medical practitioners by a national health scheme.

Marxist explanations of the capitalist state, on the other hand, have usually made two assumptions: first, that state action necessarily protects the long-term interests of business (even though in the short term specific sectors of business may suffer); and secondly, that state welfare is a strategic concession by the ruling class to defuse social conflict and political radicalism. Social democratic intellectuals (for example Stretton 1987) are more optimistic in arguing that genuine advances in welfare can be gained by increasing the quality and quantity of public expenditure, services and regulation—at the same time, however, seeking to retain individual choice in many spheres.

The social democratic position emphasizes that ordinary citizens are more likely to influence programmes debated in public forums and implemented through the state, than influence the outcomes of market forces.

I have suggested that Australia's reputation for a large degree of state action, in the years before the First World War, was justified by evidence of a wide range of commitments in welfare, industrial regulation and infrastructure services. Moreover, the public sector contributed half of total capital formation in most of the decades before 1950. What has happened to big government since 1950? The evidence points to increased social expenditures and broader categories of benefit, but a substantial decline in both public investment and in public spending as a proportion of gross domestic product (GDP) in Australia relative to the experience of other western societies since 1945 (Butlin, Barnard & Pincus 1982; Head 1983; Aitkin 1983; Withers 1983).

In the two decades from 1960 to 1980 governmental expenditures (not including public enterprises) in Australia increased from less than one-quarter of GDP to about one-third of GDP. In the same period, the *average* figure for the Organization for Economic Co-operation and Development (OECD) countries moved from 27 per cent to 43 per cent. At the top of the league, governmental expenditures in Sweden moved from 31 per cent in the early 1960s to over 60 per cent two decades later (Saunders 1987:35). So long as Australia remains below the OECD average it is difficult to accept the 'market' liberal and New Right claim that Australia has a major problem with excessive public spending and with high taxes to sustain such spending. The market-liberal and New Right critique of big government, however, is not solely concerned with cutting taxes and public expenditures. It is also concerned to promote deregulation of business activities. Regulations and legislative controls have compliance costs for those who are regulated (James 1987). But these same controls can be either expensive or cheap for governments, depending on the type of control, and thus do not always push up the level of government spending. Not all regulatory frameworks require, for example, the employment of large numbers of public servants, or the provision of subsidized services to clients, or the dispensing of transfer payments to disadvantaged groups. The New Right is also concerned to privatize public trading enterprises, that is, to sell commercially viable state enterprises to the private sector. The motives for privatization are twofold: to achieve greater efficiency in delivering services, and to reduce the overall size of the public sector (Abelson 1987).

The debate about whether big government is beneficial or harmful is largely pointless if the discussion remains at an aggregate level. How can we sensibly say whether 'big' means 30, 40 or 50 per cent of GDP? And when is big 'too big'? During wartime overall public spending greatly increased and priorities shifted dramatically towards defence. At other times (for example 1965-75) there was an expansion of education spending, which largely continued at the higher level thereafter. In periods of economic recession, spending on welfare payments increased substantially. Changes in spending priorities are just as important in understanding the significance of state intervention as changes in aggregate spending. Changes in forms of business regulation, or in co-ordination of inter-governmental relations, could also be significant without greatly affecting government budgets.

Conclusion

Part V has provided a brief survey of some key issues concerning the nature of the Australian political system and the role of the state. Much of the literature on these topics is enmeshed in the mythology of Australia's distinctive identity or in the mythologies of party ideologies. In seeking to go beyond these conventional forms of political understanding, part V has provided a broader range of perspectives. The questions raised are value-laden and difficult to resolve by any simple appeal to empirical evidence. The 'proper' limits of government, or the 'appropriate' scope of state interventionism, are topics which are embedded in different ways in competing ideological traditions. The attempt to document a 'distinctively Australian' political culture, including a set of assumptions about the norms of state intervention, is a dubious project. At best, a delineation of past practices can help to explain the pattern of present practices; but it is necessary to reject the notion that a specifically Australian political culture generates and determines policy options and patterns of state interventionism. Finally, it is worth reiterating that Australian political ideas and institutional developments have been rich in their variations and complexities, and not reducible to the clash of material interests. Ideas have been borrowed freely from diverse sources, international and domestic, in a continuing process of adaptation and renewal.

References

Abelson, P. (ed.) 1987, *Privatisation: An Australian Perspective*, Australian Professional Publications, Sydney.
Aitkin, D. 1982, *Stability and Change in Australian Politics*, 2nd edn, Australian National University Press, Canberra.
Aitkin, D. 1983, 'The Australian experience of big government', *Australian Quarterly*, vol. 55, no. 2, pp. 168-83.
Aitkin, D. 1986, 'Australian political culture', *Australian Cultural History*, no. 5, pp. 5-11.
Alomes, S. 1988, *A Nation at Last? The Changing Character of Australian Nationalism 1880-1988*, Angus & Robertson, Sydney.
Anderson, H. (ed.) 1977, *Toscin: Radical Arguments Against Federation, 1897-1900*, Drummond, Melbourne.
Atkinson, M. 1919, *The New Social Order: A Study of Postwar Reconstruction*, Workers' Educational Association, Sydney.
Atkinson, M. (ed.) 1920, *Australia: Economic and Political Studies*, Macmillan, London.
Barbalet, J. 1975, 'Tripartism in Australia: The role of the Australian Country Party', *Politics*, vol. 10, no. 1, pp. 1-14.
Bennett, S. (ed.) 1975, *Federation*, Cassell, Melbourne.
Bland, F. A. 1934, *Planning the Modern State*, Angus & Robertson, Sydney.
Bourke, H. 1982, 'Industrial unrest as social pathology: The Australian Writings of Elton Mayo', *Historical Studies*, vol. 20, no. 79, pp. 217-33.
Bourke, H. 1988, 'Social scientists as intellectuals', in B. Head & J. Walter (eds), *Intellectual Movements and Australian Society*, Oxford University Press, Melbourne, pp. 47-69.
Brugger, B. & Jaensch, D. 1985, *Australian Politics: Theory and Practice*, George Allen & Unwin, Sydney.
Buckley, K. & Wheelwright, E. L. 1988, *No Paradise for Workers: Capitalism and the Common People in Australia, 1788-1914*, Oxford University Press, Melbourne.
Bull, H. 1987, 'Britain and Australia in foreign policy', in J. D. B. Miller (ed.), *Australians and British: Social and Political Connections*, Methuen, Sydney, pp. 103-27.
Burgmann, V. 1985, *'In Our Time': Socialism and the Rise of Labor, 1885-1905*, George Allen & Unwin, Sydney.
Burgmann, V. & Lee, J. (eds) 1988, *Staining the Wattle: A People's History of Australia Since 1788*, vol. 4, McPhee Gribble/Penguin, Melbourne.
Butlin, N. G. 1959, 'Colonial socialism in Australia 1860-1900', in H. G. J. Aitken (ed.), *The State and Economic Growth*, Social Science Research Council, New York, pp. 26-78.
Butlin, N. G., Barnard, A. & Pincus, J. J. 1982, *Government and Capitalism*, George Allen & Unwin, Sydney.
Camilleri, J. A. 1980, *Australian-American Relations: The Web of Dependence*, Macmillan, Melbourne.
Campbell, C. 1975, 'Liberalism in Australian history, 1880-1920', in J. Roe (ed.), *Social Policy in Australia: Some Perspectives 1901-1975*, Cassell, Sydney, pp. 24-33.
Campbell, D. A. S. (ed.) 1944, *Postwar Reconstruction in Australia*, Australasian Publishing Co., Sydney.

References 305

Castles, F. G. 1985, *The Working Class and Welfare*, George Allen and Unwin, Sydney.

Catley, R. & McFarlane, B. 1974, *From Tweedledum to Tweedledee*, Australia & New Zealand Book Co., Sydney.

Catley, R. & McFarlane, B. 1981, *Australian Capitalism in Boom and Depression*, APCOL, Sydney.

Childe, V. G. (1923) 1964, *How Labour Governs*, Melbourne University Press, Melbourne (with intro. by F. B. Smith).

Collins, H. 1985, 'Political ideology in Australia: The distinctiveness of a Benthamite society', in S. R. Graubard (ed.), *Australia, The Daedalus Symposium*, Angus & Robertson, Sydney.

Connell, R. W. & Irving, T. H. 1980, *Class Structure in Australian History*, Longman Cheshire, Melbourne.

Costar, B. & Woodward, D. (eds) 1985, *Country to National*, George Allen & Unwin, Sydney.

Crisp, L. F. 1955, *The Australian Federal Labor Party 1901-1951*, Longman, London.

Crisp, L. F. 1978, *Australian National Government*, 4th edn, Longman Cheshire, Melbourne.

Crough, G. & Wheelwright, E. L. 1982, *Australia: A Client State*, Penguin, Ringwood.

Crowley, F. K. (ed.) 1974, *A New History of Australia*, Heinemann, Melbourne.

Curthoys, A. & Merritt, J. (eds) 1984, *Australia's First Cold War 1945-1953*, George Allen & Unwin, Sydney.

Dickey, B. 1980, *No Charity There: A Short History of Social Welfare in Australia*, Nelson, Melbourne.

Dunn, M. 1984, *Australia and the Empire: From 1788 to the Present*, Fontana, Sydney.

Eddy, J. J. & Schreuder, D. (eds) 1988, *The Rise of Colonial Nationalism: Australia, New Zealand, Canada and South Africa First Assert Their Nationalities, 1880-1914*, George Allen & Unwin, Sydney.

Eggleston, F. W. 1932, *State Socialism in Victoria*, King, London.

Encel, S. 1960, 'The concept of the state in Australian politics', *Australian Journal of Politics & History*, vol. 6, no. 1, pp. 62-76.

Encel, S. 1970, *Equality and Authority*, Cheshire, Melbourne.

Farrell, F. 1981, *International Socialism and Australian Labour: The Left in Australia 1919-1939*, Hale & Iremonger, Sydney.

Farrell, F. 1987, 'Australia: A laboratory of social reform', in Australian Labor Party (NSW Branch), *Traditions of Reform in New South Wales*, Pluto Press, Sydney, pp. 1-16.

Fitzpatrick, B. 1941, *The British Empire in Australia: An Economic History 1834-1939*, Melbourne University Press, Melbourne.

Foster, L. 1986, *High Hopes: The Men and Motives of the Australian Round Table*, Melbourne University Press, Melbourne.

Galligan, B. 1984, 'The state in Australian political thought', *Politics*, vol. 19, no. 2, pp. 82-92.

Gollan, R. (1960) 1967, *Radical and Working Class Politics: A Study of Eastern Australia 1850-1910*, Melbourne University Press, Melbourne.

Gollan, R. 1985, *Revolutionaries and Reformers*, George Allen & Unwin, Sydney.

Graham, B. D. 1966, *The Formation of the Australian Country Parties*, Australian National University Press, Canberra.
Hancock, W. K. (1930) 1961, *Australia*, Jacaranda, Brisbane.
Hartz, L. (ed.) 1964, *The Founding of New Societies*, Harcourt Brace & World, New York.
Hay, J. R. 1982, 'The Institute of Public Affairs and social policy in World War II', *Historical Studies*, vol. 20, no. 79, pp. 198–216.
Hazlehurst, C. (ed.) 1979, *Australian Conservatism*, Australian National University Press, Canberra.
Head, B. W. (ed.) 1983, *State and Economy in Australia*, Oxford University Press, Melbourne.
Head, B. W. 1985, 'The Australian party system', *Politics*, vol. 20, no. 2, pp. 89–94.
Head, B. W. (ed.) 1986, *The Politics of Development in Australia*, George Allen & Unwin, Sydney.
Head, B. W. & Patience, A. (eds) 1989, *From Fraser to Hawke*, Longman Cheshire, Melbourne.
Head, B. & Walter, J. (eds) 1988, *Intellectual Movements and Australian Society*, Oxford University Press, Melbourne.
Hirst, J. B. 1988, *The Strange Birth of Colonial Democracy*, George Allen & Unwin, Sydney.
Hudson, W. J. (ed.) 1967, *Towards a Foreign Policy, 1914–1941*, Cassell, Melbourne.
Hudson, W. J. & Sharp, M. 1988, *Australian Independence: Colony to Reluctant Kingdom*, Melbourne University Press, Melbourne.
Hughes, C. A. 1973, 'Political culture', in H. Mayer & H. Nelson (eds), *Australian Politics: A Third Reader*, Cheshire, Melbourne, pp. 133–46.
Hyde, J. 1982, *The Year 2000: A Radical Liberal Alternative*, the author, Canberra.
Irving, T. H., 1983, 'Socialism, working-class mobilisation and the origins of the Labor Party', in B. O'Meagher (ed.), *The Socialist Objective: Labor and Socialism*, Hale & Iremonger, Sydney, pp. 32–43.
Jaensch, D. 1983, *The Australian Party System*, George Allen & Unwin, Sydney.
James, M. (ed.), 1987, *Restraining Leviathan: Small Government in Practice*, Centre for Independent Studies, Sydney.
Kasper, W. et al. 1980, *Australia at the Crossroads*, Harcourt Brace Jovanovich, Sydney.
Kemp, D. A. 1980, 'Political parties and Australian culture', in H. Mayer & H. Nelson (eds), *Australian Politics: A Fifth Reader*, Longman Cheshire, Melbourne, pp. 413–25.
Kemp, D. A. 1988, 'Liberalism and conservatism in Australia since 1944', in B. Head & J. Walter (eds), *Intellectual Movements and Australian Society*, Oxford University Press, Melbourne, pp. 322–62.
Kennedy, R. (ed.) 1982, *Australian Welfare History: Critical Essays*, Macmillan, Melbourne.
King, P. (ed.) 1983, *Australia's Vietnam*, George Allen & Unwin, Sydney.
La Nauze, J. A. 1972, *The Making of the Australian Constitution*, Melbourne University Press, Melbourne.
Loveday, P. 1983, 'Australian political thought', in R. Lucy (ed.), *The Pieces of Politics*, 3rd edn, Macmillan, Melbourne, pp. 5–30.

Loveday, P., Martin, A. W. & Parker, R. S. (eds) 1977, *The Emergence of the Australian Party System*, Hale & Iremonger, Sydney.
Lucy, R. 1985, *The Australian Form of Government*, Macmillan, Melbourne.
Macintyre, S. 1977, 'Early socialism and Labor', *Intervention*, no. 7.
Macintyre, S. 1985, *Winners and Losers: The Pursuit of Social Justice in Australian History*, George Allen & Unwin, Sydney.
McKnight, D. (ed.) 1986, *Moving Left*, Pluto Press, Sydney.
McQueen, H. 1970, *A New Britannia: An Argument Concerning the Social Origins of Australian Radicalism and Nationalism*, Penguin, Ringwood.
McQueen, H. 1973, 'The suckling society', in H. Mayer & H. Nelson (eds), *Australian Politics: A Third Reader*, Cheshire, Melbourne, pp. 5–13.
Madden, A. F. & Morris-Jones, W. H. (eds) 1980, *Australia and Britain: Studies in a Changing Relationship*, Sydney University Press, Sydney.
Maddox, G. 1985, *Australian Democracy in Theory and Practice*, Longman Cheshire, Melbourne.
Markey, R. 1982, 'The ALP and the emergence of a national social policy, 1880–1910', in R. Kennedy (ed.), *Australian Welfare History: Critical Essays*, Macmillan, Melbourne, pp. 103–37.
Martin, A. W. 1973, 'Australia and the Hartz "Fragment" thesis', *Australian Economic History Review*, vol. 13, no. 2, pp. 131–47.
Martin, A. W. 1982, 'Australian federation and nationalism: Historical notes', in R. L. Mathews (ed.), *Public Policies in Two Federal Countries: Canada and Australia*, Centre for Research on Federal Financial Relations, Canberra, pp. 27–46.
Martin, G. 1986, *Bunyip Aristocracy: The New South Wales Constitution Debate of 1853 and Hereditary Institutions in the British Colonies*, Croom Helm, London.
Mayer, H. 1956, 'Some conceptions of the Australian party system 1910–1950', *Historical Studies*, vol. 7, no. 27, pp. 253–70.
Mayo, E. 1920, 'The Australian political consciousness', in M. Atkinson, *The New Social Order: A Study of Postwar Reconstruction*, Workers' Educational Association, Sydney, pp. 127–44.
Métin, A. (1901) 1977, *Socialism Without Doctrine*, tr. R. Ward, APCOL, Sydney.
Millar, T. B. 1978, *Australia in Peace and War: External Relations 1788–1977*, Australian National University Press, Canberra.
Miller, J. D. B. 1980, ' "An Empire that don't care what you do" . . . ' in A. F. Madden & W. H. Morris-Jones (eds), *Australia and Britain: Studies in a Changing Relationship*, Sydney University Press, Sydney, pp. 90–100.
Northcott, C. H. 1918, *Australian Social Development*, Columbia University Press, New York.
O'Brien, P. 1977, *The Saviours*, Drummond, Melbourne.
O'Meagher, B. (ed.) 1983, *The Socialist Objective: Labor and Socialism*, Hale & Iremonger, Sydney.
Osmond, W. G. 1985, *Frederic Eggleston: An Intellectual in Australian Politics*, George Allen & Unwin, Sydney.
Parker, R. S. 1980, 'The evolution of British political institutions in Australia', in A.F. Madden & W. H. Morris-Jones (eds), *Australia and Britain: Studies in a Changing Relationship*, Sydney University Press, Sydney, pp. 117–34.
Patience, A. & Head, B. W. (eds) 1979, *From Whitlam to Fraser*, Oxford University Press, Melbourne.

Patience, A. & Scott, J. (eds) 1983, *Australian Federalism: Future Tense*, Oxford University Press, Melbourne.
Pemberton, G. 1987, *All the Way: Australia's Road to Vietnam*, George Allen & Unwin, Sydney.
Rawson, D. W. 1966, *Labor in Vain?*, Longman, Melbourne.
Rawson, D. W. (ed.) 1986, *Blast, Budge or Bypass: Towards a Social Democratic Australia*, Academy of the Social Sciences, Canberra.
Reeves, J. & Evans, G. 1980, 'Two views of the socialist objective', in Evans & Reeves (eds), *Labor Essays 1980*, Drummond, Melbourne, pp. 155–81.
Reeves, W. Pember (1902) 1969, *State Experiments in Australia and New Zealand*, 2 vols, Macmillan, Melbourne (intro. by J. Child).
Rickard, J. 1976, *Class and Politics . . . 1890–1910*, Australian National University Press, Canberra.
Roe, J. (ed.) 1975, *Social Policy in Australia: Some Perspectives 1901–1975*, Cassell, Sydney.
Roe, M. 1984, *Nine Australian Progressives: Vitalism in Bourgeois Social Thought 1890–1960*, University of Queensland Press, St Lucia, Qld.
Rosecrance, R. N. 1964, 'The radical culture of Australia', in L. Hartz (ed.), *The Founding of New Societies*, Harcourt Brace & World, New York, pp. 275–318.
Rowse, T. 1978a, *Australian Liberalism and National Character*, Kibble Books, Malmsbury, Vic.
Rowse, T. 1978b, 'Political culture: A concept and its ideologues', in G. C. Duncan (ed.), *Critical Essays in Australian Politics*, Edward Arnold, Melbourne, pp. 5–27.
Santamaria, B. A. 1987, *Australia at the Crossroads: Reflections of an Outsider*, Melbourne University Press, Melbourne.
Saunders, P. 1987, 'Understanding government expenditure trends . . . ', *Australian Quarterly*, vol. 59, no. 1, pp. 34–42.
Sawer, G. 1977, *Federalism Under Strain*, Melbourne University Press, Melbourne.
Sawer, M. (ed.) 1982, *Australia and the New Right*, George Allen & Unwin, Sydney.
Sexton, M. 1979, *Illusions of Power: The Fate of a Reform Government*, George Allen & Unwin, Sydney.
Sexton, M. 1981, *War for the Asking: Australia's Vietnam Secrets*, Penguin, Ringwood.
Sheridan, K. (ed.) 1986, *The State as Developer: Public Enterprise in South Australia*, Wakefield Press & Royal Australian Institute of Public Administration, Adelaide.
Simms, M. 1982, *A Liberal Nation*, Hale & Iremonger, Sydney.
Starr, G., Richmond, K. & Maddox, G. 1978, *Political Parties in Australia*, Heinemann, Melbourne.
Stretton, H. 1987, *Political Essays*, Georgian House, Melbourne.
Sydney Labor History Group 1982, *What Rough Beast? The State and Social Order in Australian History*, George Allen & Unwin, Sydney.
Thompson, R. C. 1980, *Australian Imperialism in the Pacific: The Expansionist Era 1820–1920*, Melbourne University Press, Melbourne.
Tiver, P. G. 1978, *The Liberal Party: Principles and Performance*, Jacaranda, Brisbane.

Turner, I.A.H. 1965, *Industrial Labour and Politics . . . 1900-1921*, Australian National University Press, Canberra.
Walter, J. A. 1988, 'Intellectuals and the political culture', in B. Head & J. Walter (eds), *Intellectual Movements and Australian Society*, Oxford University Press, Melbourne, pp. 237-73.
Ward, R. 1958, *The Australian Legend*, Oxford University Press, Melbourne.
Waters, W. J. 1969, 'The opposition and the "Powers" referendum 1944', *Politics*, vol. 4, no. 1, pp. 42-56.
Watt, A. 1967, *The Evolution of Australian Foreign Policy 1938-1965*, Cambridge University Press, Cambridge.
Watts, R. 1987, *The Foundations of the National Welfare State*, George Allen & Unwin, Sydney.
Weller, P. & Jaensch, D. (eds) 1980, *Responsible Government in Australia*, Drummond & the Australasian Political Studies Association, Melbourne.
Wells, A. 1988, 'The old left intelligentsia', in B. Head & J. Walter, *Intellectual Movements and Australian Society*, Oxford University Press, Melbourne, pp. 214-34.
White, R. 1981, *Inventing Australia: Images and Identity 1688-1980*, George Allen & Unwin, Sydney.
Whitlam, E. G. 1985, *The Whitlam Government*, Penguin, Ringwood.
Winterton, G. 1988, 'Another Bicentenary: The influence of the United States Constitution in Australia', *Quadrant*, March, pp. 5-7.
Withers, G. (ed.) 1983, *Bigger or Smaller Government?*, Academy of the Social Sciences, Canberra.

INDEX

a'Beckett, William, Literary News, 110
ABC, television production, 168
Aboriginal culture, 199, 204; and European settlement 193-4; revisions in conceptualizations, 200-1
Aboriginal historians, 202-5 *passim*
Aboriginal history, 187-8, 202, 205; and chronology, 204-5; black responses to invasion, 198-9; challenge to, 198; pre-contact, 200
Aboriginal policy: and historiography, 205; *see* government policy, native policy
Aboriginal rights movement, 196, *see also* Aborigines, land rights
Aboriginal studies, 185
Aboriginal women, 228; labour in pastoral industry, 200; on frontier, 197
Aborigines Protection Association, 192
Aborigines, 243; 'doomed race theory', 191, 193; adaptation to environment, 200-1; and 'civilizing process', 191; and 1967 referendum, 196; and Australian history, 10, 12, 19; and celebration of Australia Day, 19; and Christianity, 191; Commonwealth and State Government Conference on, 1937, 193, 197 and paternalism, 198; and reformative institutions, 197; and statistics, 228; as first 'wave of immigration', 20; Bicentennial and symbolism, 204; biographies, 202; community, 70; Dreaming, 9; and agencies, 193; exclusion by radical nationalism, 13; exclusion from citizenship, 276, 278; in nineteenth-century histories, 190-1; in pastoral industry, 193, 200, 202; land rights 190, 196, 197, 205; language and traditional lands, 71; material life, 200-1; mining, 201; myth of Tasmanian extinction, 198; occupation and dispossession, 189-90; oral history, 202-3; paternalism, 195, 205; population, 189, 193, 200; resistance to dispossession, 198-9, 202; resistance to reform for, in 1960-70s, 196; segregation and protection, 187, 193, 194; self-determination, 196, 198; settler conflict, 54; social conflict, 185; squatters' view, 192; white invasion and settler society, 17
abortion, 236
academic debate, context and motive, 38-39
academics, 83, 110; liberal and *Meanjin*, 132
Actors' Equity, 163
actors, film disputes, 163
advertisements: *Bulletin*, 114, 125; *Meanjin*, 131
advertising, 110
Age Monthly Review, 133
Age, 116
agriculturalists, 54
agriculture, and pastoralism, different views of, 55
agriculture: investment, 53; production, 49
alienation, in nineteenth-century city, 72
ALP, 292-4, *see also* labour parties; Labor Party
American dominance and Australian nationalism, 22
American links, shift towards, 60
American literature, 110
Americanization, 73
Anderson, Benedict, 71-2
Anglo-Australian vision, 30, 51
Anglo-Saxon: race 58, 277; democracies,

Index 311

57; majority, 12, 14, 32, 68
Angry Penguins, 130
anthropologists, 200, 203
anthropology and 'native policy', 194
anti-authoritarianism and bush ethos, 120
anti-imperialist sentiment, 120
Anzac Day: as national day, 20; and women's protests, 238-39
ANZUS, 282
Arbitration Commission, 62
arbitration, 187, 188, 249; state intervention, 215-19
archaeologists, 200, 201
Archibald, J.F., 28, 112, 118, 119, 125
art cinema, Australian, 164
art: and criticism of cultural meanings, 238; as prose fiction, 127; colonial traditions, 33, 35; conventions, 33, 37; movements, influence on *Bulletin*, 125; *see also* European art movements
artisans, 54; and trade unions, 207
Asia, 66; and communism, 282
Asian conflicts, and Australian troops, 282
assimilation, 64; policy content, 194-5; rhetoric, 193
Astley, Thea, 74; 152-3 *passim*
asylums: and government de-institutionalization, 256; and immigrants, 246; and women, 239; government policies, 250
Attlee government (British), 299
audience, 119, 121, 128; *Meanjin*, 131; participation, 121
audience/implied audience, 123; 115-17 *passim*, 135; *Meanjin cf. Bulletin*, 133; *Meanjin*, 132
Australasian Post cf. Bulletin, 130
Australia Day Committee, emphases of, 20
Australia Day: and defining Australia, 18-20; debate over national celebration, 18-20; *see also* ceremonial moments
Australia: and radical nationalism, 15; as object, 3, 13; as outpost, 67; as problematic, 19; as social laboratory, 254, 298; different meanings, 3, 20; ethnic and linguistic diversity and film, 169-70
Australian Assistance Plan, 78
Australian Broadcasting Corporation, 158
Australian Bureau of Statistics, 71
Australian character: and radical nationalism, 12, 13; myth of, 6
Australian Council of Trade Unions (ACTU), 61
Australian culture, 110; and city, 92-3; and poetry, 142; misogynist, 227-8; politics and little magazines, 134
Australian economists, 61

Australian economy: and international capital, 78; vulnerability, 243
Australian film production, 158-9
Australian film, 107; film-makers, 163; as genre, approaches, 165
Australian frontier: and domestic violence, class-linked, 28; gender imbalance and misogynist culture, 28
Australian history: early courses, 10; place of European settlement, 12; sex blindness, 220, 222
Australian identity, 73; bush as symbol in, 35
Australian image: and colonial representatives, 59; and urbanization, 86
Australian Journal of Social Issues, 250
Australian Ladies Journal, 116
Australian legend, 3; and *Bulletin* writers, 118; and the city, 32-3; as bush ethos, 25; critiques of, 13; description of, 12-13; in 1890s, 25-5; role of *Bulletin* writers, 25
Australian literary criticism, 73
Australian literary tradition, 145
Australian literature, 110, 112, 124, 136; and education, 133; and nationality, 107; Australianness, 107; books written in Australia, 12; early courses, 10; in English departments, 11; in universities; institutions, 107; *Meanjin*, 131, 132
Australian natives: and *emigrés*, 57
Australian Society, 250
Australian society: 31-4; and immigrants, 68; conflicts, 186; critical analysis, 151; inequalities, 243; polarization, 250
Australian Studies Association, 5
Australian studies, 71; and community self-awareness, 3; and comparative studies, 14; and history of the sexes, 222; and periphery, 83; as a 'window onto the world', 8; as analysis of cultures, 15; as key questions 15-17; development of courses, 10-11; explanation of current popularity, 6; growth of, 5; how to approach, vii; humanities and social sciences, 17; misunderstanding of, 17; *see also* regional studies; spatial dimension, 84
Australian television: local and overseas material, 158; *see also* television
Australian universities, 11
Australian Workers Union, 206
Australian workers, 185
Australian writing, 74, 129; and cultural construction, 136
Australian: constructions of subjects as introduction to broader debates, vii; film and television, 156; perspective, vii

Australianism, 6
Australianist cycle, 5
Australianness, 109, 124; icons of, 138, 143; of Australian literature, 107; of cultural texts, 157–74; of film and television, 107
authors, 110
autonomy, as central to regional identification, 47
avant-garde, in films, 164–5 *passim*

balance of payments, 61, 63; 1980s economic crises, 62
banana republic, 61
banking and finance reform, in 1890s depression, 59
Barnard, Marjorie, 148
basic wage, 62
Bates, Daisy, 194
Baynton, Barbara, 28; 'Squeaker's Mate', 141–2
Benevolent Society (NSW), 247, 252
Bicentennial celebrations, 76
Bicentennial History Conference (1981), 204
Bicentennial: history project, 200–4; and national inventory, 148; as nationalist impulse, 5; debate on celebration, 19; role of historians, 203; symbolism and Aborigines, 204
big government: critics, 287, *see also* state intervention
black rights movement, in U.S., 195
black–white conflict, in films, 170
black–white relations, writing history of, 190, 197–8
Blainey, Geoffrey, on immigration, 212
Bleakley Report (1929), 196
Boer War, 59
bohemianism, 75
bohemians, 118–23 *passim*
books, 123; 1880s, 121, 188; 1940s, 130; production, Sydney and Melbourne, 74; publication: local, 116; reviewers, 109; trade, 135; and *Meanjin*, 132
booksellers, 109
boom periods, prosperity and growth, 52
Boomerang, 115, 129
boundary distinctions, 27; 'the literary', 112, 131; and community, 19; in *Bulletin* writing, 125
British character, racial purity of, and *Bulletin*, 58
British colonization: legitimacy, 201; legitimacy, and racial violence, 192, 194, 199
British dominance, and Australian nationalism, 22
British Empire, outpost, 49
British financial community, nineteenth century, 65
British influence, decline of, 60
British investment, 57, 60, 68, 277

British kinship, 277
British moral economists, 55, 57
British ruling élites, 50
British settlement: anniversary as national day, 19, 20; *see also* European settlement
British settlers: different visions of Australia, 19; *see also* European settlers
Britishness, as justification for policies, 57
broadcasting, regional, 73; Special Broadcasting Service (SBS), 170
Brown, Bryan, 144
Bruce–Page government, 60
Bulletin, 137, 142, 147, 253, 6, 107–29 *passim*; legend; and literary writing, 123–4; as 'Australian', 121; bush debate, 139–40; *cf. Meanjin*, 130, 131, 132; contributions to, 113–16, 120; critiques of, 124; legend, 114; literary editor, 111; racial purity and British character, 58; role of writers in Australian legend, 25; school of writers, 112; sense of literature, 125
bush ethos, 33; and national character, 25; challenge to, 26; debate, 120; *see also* Australian legend
bush imagery, in film, 165
bush images, in Depression fiction, 147
bush myth, 73
bush nostalgia, in poetry, 139
bush: as symbol in Australian identity, 35; moral and spiritual character, 140
bushman's Bible, 117
bushman, as cultural icon, 140
Butlin, N.G., 62; and urban concentration, 87

Cairns Group, 67
Cambridge, Ada, 116
Canadian federal model, 278–9
Canadian literary critics, 73
Canadian literature, 110
Canadian studies, argument for, 7
capital: accumulation, and urbanization, 91; foreign, and Queensland, 80; international, 78
capitalism, and urbanization differences, 91
careers, 1880s and 1890s, 118
Carey, P., *Oscar and Lucinda*, 148
Casey, G. 'Short-Shift Saturday', 147
Castles, F., 298
Catholic Social Studies Movement, 292
Catholics, and labour movement, 292–3
ceremonial moments: and local histories, 75; Australia Day, 3; *see also* symbolic action
ceremony, and meaning of 'Australia', 18–19
change, institutional, 65
charity: and self-help, 252; colonial, 251
Chifley government, 255

Index 313

child-care, 237
children's television, 162
Christianity, and Aborigines, 191, 197
cinemas, and film distribution, 157
cities: and newspapers, 73; colonial mortality rates, 247; commercial type, 86, distinctiveness, role, meaning, 85, *see also* urban; place in Australian history, 84; regional, 70; rivalry between, 14
citizenship rights, 276
city–country debate, 96
city–country opposition, 70
city: and Australian culture, 92–3; and Australian legend, 32–3; and *Bulletin*, 118; and country, in bush ethos, 120; as a social construct, 93; as collection of facts, 87–8; communication with country, 116–18 *passim*; demography and literary conventions, 32–3, 37; different meanings, 95; representations of, 93; significance, determining factors, 47; slums, 185
class conflict, 254; in Australian history, 206
class consciousness, in late 19th century, 29
class formation, national culture and state intervention, 188
class relations, and urbanization, 91
class struggle, 185; and arbitration, 216
class: and Australian films, 168; and urban experience, 94; as concept in historiography, 206–11; critiques in Australian historiography, 209; in Australian film, 107
Coghlan, T.A., 86; *Labour and Industry in Australia*, 242
cold war, 282; and communism, 292
collectivist institution, 68
colonial era: governments, 62, 296; health, 247; innovations, British disapproval of, 58; period, 17; philanthropists, 251; reforms, and new liberalism, 59; representatives, and Australian image, 59; self-image, and boosterism, 57; socialism, 62, 295; society, 54, 66;
colonialism, 50, 68, 69; racism debate, 196
colonies: and British political models, 273; and common identity, 57; and military expeditions, 281; different social and political evolution, 276; images and myths, 53
colonists, and self-government, 275
colony, and metropolis, in *Bulletin*, 122
comedy: and national differences, 167; film, 166, 167
commodity boom, 1970–71, inflationary pressures, 61
common man, and radical nationalism, 25, 31
Commonwealth Australian studies project, 5; CRASTE report, on contextual self-awareness, 6
Commonwealth bank, 299
Commonwealth Grants Commission, 77
Commonwealth powers, 76
communication: Aboriginal, 204; between country and city, 116–18 *passim*; process of, as community, 7
communist movement: rise and decline, 292
Communist Party, 292
community, 47; 'true' and cities, 72; and horizontal comradeship, 72; and language, 24; *Bulletin*, 118, 122; construction of, 19; of *Bulletin* story, 128; pioneering, and sense of inferiority, 27; process of, as communication, 7; *see also* print community
community life, 107
community studies, 83; and sociology, 72
comparative approach, and urbanization, 90, 96
comparative studies, 11; and national identities, 14; and settler societies, 50; critiques of, 14; in Australian studies, 14
competency, literary, 133
conflicts: and depressions, 244; and history, 222; and nation-state, 6; and order, themes in Australia, 187; and the labour movement, 206, 209; and women, 234; containment by the welfare state, 251; economic, 215; frontier, 192, 195, 197; frontier, 47, 59; horizontal and vertical dimensions, 70; in Australian federalism, 278; in films, 170; reality of, 49; social, 54, 185–6; state–federal, 47 conformity, 72
conscription, 281
consensus, and ALP, 293
conservatism, 285, 299–90; agendas, policies *vs* conduct, 289; and rural towns, 72; British *cf.* Australian, 288
Conservative Party (British), 288
Constitution, 277, 278; and labour movement, 280; design debates, 279
convict: culture, 143; image, functions of, 146; legacy, in NSW and Tas, 55; literature, 145; system, 54; policy and theory concerns, 55
convictism: and sex imbalance, 223; legacies, 224

convicts: and administrators, 19; understandings of Australia, 19
conventions, literary, 33, 37, 74
country: and city, in bush ethos, 120; as origin of myths, 14; communication with city, 116–18 *passim*; differences from city, 14
Coombs, H.C., 299
CRASTE, viii; *see also* Commonwealth Australian studies project
crime, 234
criticism: academic, 125; *Bulletin*, 112; essentialist, 136; as institution, 135; literary, 110, 129
critics, 110, 133; literary, 73, 74, 109; radical nationalist, 12
Crocodile Dundee (film), 68, 69
Crown land, revenue and social engineering, 54
cultural construction, and Australian writing, 136
cultural cringe, 3, 67, 144
cultural discourses, nineteenth century, 230
cultural distinctiveness, and urban nation, 96
cultural formation, 120, 124, 135; and *Bulletin*, 117, 119; and regional studies, 15; *Meanjin* writers, 132; of writers and intellectuals, 115
cultural generation gap, in 1880s and 1890s, 118
cultural icons, 140
cultural industries, 156
cultural institutions, 107
cultural maturity, 109–10
cultural mythologies, 152
cultural politics: and dissident women, 235; formation, *Meanjin*, 131, 133
cultural production: and academic writers, 39; and colonial reactions, 27; and culture, 3; and women, 238; in settler society, 36; model of, 34–9 *passim*; of national identity, 18–36; processes in versions of Australia, 38; *see also* 'imagined community'; symbolism
culture: and cultural production, 3; literary, of rural areas, 116; Australian, 130; *Bulletin*, 114
currency, symbolic importance defined, 61
curricula, 110
Curtin government, 255
Cusack, D. and James, F., *Come In, Spinner*, 148

Dark, Eleanor, 28, 48
Darwin, Charles, 58
Deakin, Alfred, 28, 290
democracy, 51, 68
democratic attitudes, 120, 122; indigenous, 112

Democratic Labor Party (DLP), 292
democratic politics, and realism, 127
Democrats, 290
Denoon, Donald, 50
Department of Postwar Reconstruction, 299
Department of Urban and Regional Development, 78
dependence, 66
dependency theorists; and foreign policy, 280
dependency: and Australian historical development, 273; benefit to Australia, 50; Latin America and Australia, 50; of Australian society, 31–2
dependent development: and urbanization, 91; in Australian economic history, 50
depression: 1890s 33, 49, 53, 55–60 *passim*, 277; 1890s and labour movement, 254; 1929–34, and challenge to social liberalism, 290; 1930s, 60, 243–4; and bush ethos, 120; and communism, 292; debates, 6; fiction, 146; and social conflict, 244; diverse experiences, 244
development, 62, 72; nineteenth century, 65
Dickens, Charles, 33
disciplinary approaches, 11–14; determination of regionalism, 47
disciplines: analyses of social conflicts, 186; methods of study, 7, 17
discourse, in film and television, 165, 166
divorce, 237; and colonial women, 232
Docker, J., 137
documentary, series and class, 169
domestic servants, 213
domestic violence, 232, 237; and working-class oppression, on Australian frontier, 28
domestic work, and colonial wives, 229
domestic *vs.* public, in nation-building agenda, 29
domesticity, rejection of cult of, 28
doomed race theory, 191, 193
drama, regional broadcasting, 73
dualism, in Australian settler society, 57, 66, 67
Dyson, E.D., 'Blind Love', 125

Ealing films, 160
economic analyses, 64
economic and social policy, 1890s, 53
economic base, vulnerability of, 49
economic boom, 60–2 *passim*, 68–9; post World War II, 243, 250
economic co-operation, regional, 66
economic conflict, and arbitration, 215
economic contributions, and women, 230
economic crises: 1970s and 1980s, 49, 61;

1980s, balance of payments, 62; and debates about society, 47; and economic vulnerability, 50; and national values, 95; 1974, and challenge to social liberalism, 290
economic development pattern, 64
economic development: and boom conditions, 59-60; Australian, and settler society, 51; nineteenth century, 68; semi-peripheral, 282
economic diversification, 59
economic downturn, and welfare net, 256
economic factors, and urbanization, 89
economic fluctuations, inter-war period, 60
economic growth, 243; 50-53 passim
economic historians, 242; and poverty, 245
economic management, Eurocentric criteria, 201
economic policy: and arbitration, 217; restructuring, 61, 66
economic relations, semi-peripheral development, 282
economic stability: and international relations, 53
economic strategies, 66
economic structure, 49, 61, 63
economic vulnerability, 283
economics: Keynesian, 60; transnational, 31-2, 37
economy: 47, 49; Aborigines' part in, 200; conglomerate structure, 62; pastoral, and frontier conflict, 197; plantation, 54; primary based, 79; primary export based, 244
editorial; *Bulletin*, 113-19 passim, 121, 124; *Meanjin*, 131, 132
editors, 109, 110, 116, 129; literary, of *Bulletin*, 111, 127; of *Meanjin*, 131; role in literary periodicals, 133
Education Acts, 121
education: and Australian literature, 133; and social order, 186; literary, 135; public, 121
educational institutions, 67
egalitarianism, 25, 243; sexual, and colonial male domination, 226
Eggleton, T., 137
electorate, 65, 66
Empire 'kinship', 64
entrepreneurs, 14; and urbanization, 94
environment, 74; Aboriginal adaptation, and management, 200-1; conflict, 186, 187; invasion metaphor, 190; reactions to, 26-7, 37; strangeness in settler society, 17, 27
epitome: definition, 154; rhetoric of, 140; and diverse social meanings, 142; and national values, 148; as tools for critical analysis, 151; linguistic, 147
Esson, Louis, 28

Establishment; and *Bulletin*, 115-19 passim, 123
ethnic communities, 64, 71; conflict, 186; equality, and New Left, 292; ghettos, in American suburbs, 72
ethnicity, 70; and films, 169; in Australian film, 107
Europe, 66
European: art movements, 33, 35; colonizing activities, 277; expansion, 68; heritage, 26; legacies, in Australian economy and society, 53
European perspectives, 9-10; cf. Aboriginal, 19
European settlement: and Aboriginal culture, 193; and pre-contact history, 200; colonial policy, 190, 205; place in 'Australian' history, 12; see also British; social order and conflict, 187
European settlers, 9-10; see also British
Evatt, H.V., 281
export diversification, 56; and structure, 62-3
external affairs; post-war, 281

factory and shop legislation, 249
family economy, contribution of women, 95
family wage, 231, 249
family: and arbitration, 218; and social order, 186; and women, 213
federal government, divisions in national policies, 51
federal influence, and Whitlam government, 300
federal system, 70, 301; anomalies, 279
federal-state conflicts, 47; and Labor, 293-4
federalism: and conservative doctrine, 289; elements, 278
Federal Council of Australia, 277
Federation Day; as national day, 20
federation, 29-30, 59; and defence, 281; British moral economists, 57; history, 276-8
feminism: 1890s, 28, 29; and New Left, 292; *Bulletin*, 117; critiques of labour history, 212-14; impact on frontier conflict, 197
feminists: activism, 238; campaigns, 235; historians, 28, 39
femocrat, 238
fertility: rates, colonial, 229; control, 234, 235-7; strategies and debates, 235-6
fiction, 115-34 passim
film: and television: as industries, 156
film production, 158; and government subsidies, 159-60; key roles and Australianness, 163
film, 107; audience and Australianness, 161-2; Australianness, different views of, 164; Australian genre, approaches

to, 165; Australian subject-matter, 164; avant-garde, 164–65 *passim*; certification of, Australian factors, 164; and class, 168; comedy, 166, 167; as cultural text, 157; distribution, history of, 157; 166, 167; hallmarks of Hollywood, 159; historical period, 166; location and Australianness, 161; production, subsidies for, 159–60; and market considerations, 162; social realist, 164
film and television; as industries, 156; production in Sydney, 168
Financial Assistance Grants, 77
fiscal policy, Commonwealth government control, 60
Fisher government, 281
Fitzpatrick, Brian, 12
Flaus, John, 165
Forshaw, T., 'The Mateship Syndrome', 147
Foucault, M., 238
fragment thesis, critiques of, 285–6
Franklin, M., 28; *All That Swagger*, 143
Fraser government, 65; and cold war ideology, 282
free settlers, 296
free trade, challenges to, 59
freedom rides, 196
friendly societies, exclusion of women, 247
frontier, 54–7 *passim*; in Aboriginal dispossession, 189–90; conflict, 47, 59, 192, 195; inter-racial relations, 198; heritage, 68
Froude, J.A., 242
Furphy, Joseph, *Such is Life*, 25

gender: Australian frontier, 28; in Australian film, 107; and *Bulletin* audience, 123; and films, 169; relations, ordering of, 220; and nationalism debates, 27; and urban experience, 94
gentry, colonial and English, 54
geographers, and urbanization, 89
geopolitical thinking, 66
gold-rushes, 252; effects in families, 247
Government Destitute Board (SA), 252
government institutions, welfare, 252
government: intervention, 65; and borrowing, 57; spending, 65; government: regulation, 303; spending priorities, 303
Gramsci, A., on hegemony, 211
group identification; and *Bulletin*, 119–20
Guam doctrine, 67
Hancock, W.K., 287, 301
Hardy, Frank, 148
Harpur, Charles, 5

Harrower, E., *The Watch Tower*, 147
Hartz, L., 285–6, 297
Harvester judgement, 62, 217–18, 249
Hawke government, 61, 282; and policy innovations, 294
hegemonic ideology, and liberalism, 286
Heidelberg school, 6, 33, 138; and 'city bushmen', 35
Henderson Poverty Inquiry, 243, 250
Higgins, Justice H.B., 217, 249
'high' culture, 127
historians: radical nationalist, 12; women, 221
historical and literary studies; central role of, in examining Australia, 3, 11; *see also* radical nationalism
historical canon, representation of women, 221
historical enquiry, and masculinist closure, 227
historical period film, 166
historiography: Aborigines and policy, 205; and class, 206–11; contradiction in, 247; Australian, critiques of, 209; gap in urban labour history, 206, 207; nationalist 26–8; *see also* history
history: black-white relations, 190, 197; of labour movement, 188; of sexes, 188; and nationalism, 203; and nationhood in film, 166; newspapers and publishing, 112–13; nineteenth century, 190; oral, and Aborigines, 202; oral, methodological problems in, 202–4 *passim*; order and conflict, key areas of, 240–1; pre-contact, 200; regional, 74; and women, 220; writing, and radical nationalism, 6; urban themes, reasons for neglect of, 87–8
Hobart, images of, 93–4
Hogan, Paul, 144
Hollywood film: 158; hallmarks, 159
Holmes, Cecil, 157
homogeneity: as central to regional identification, 47
Horne, Donald, 67, 86; *The Lucky Country*, 242
housing, 299
housing schemes, government, 249
Hughes, R., *The Fatal Shore*, 145
Hughes, W.M., 281
humanities and social sciences: and Australian studies, viii, 16; methods of analysis, 3; *see also* Australian studies
icons: of Australianness, 138; and ideological disturbance, 143; and thematic intersections, 143
ideas: frameworks, 22, 34–7 *passim*; history of, 32–7

identity, 47, 50, 57, 71–4 *passim, see also* national identity
ideology, nationalist, 24
imagery, in films and television, 165–6
images: battle of, 67; and meaning, 107; nationalist, 34–5
images, of Australia: 68; British, 57–60; in policy debates, 57; as socially cohesive, 49
imagined community, 71, 72, 76, 122; and academic writers, 39; and Australian legend, 25; and contending groups, 27; in cultural production, 15; as more than invention, 35; as nation, 23; and radical nationalism, 25; and regions, 82; understanding of, 17
immigrants, 5, 19–21; and asylums, 246; conflict, 186; cultural differences between, 14; non-British, 12, 14, 19, 60; and poverty, 246; in social relations, 36
immigration policy: and British surveillance, 281
immigration, 60, 62, 64; and growth, 49; as indicator of economic expansion, 52; policy, and British surveillance, 281; programmes, 187; and racism, 212: and settler society, 17; 'three big waves', 20
imperial federation movement, 57, 59
imperialism, 23, 50, 57–9, 67–8, 120, 196; anti, 281; and labour movement, 211
import-substitution, 56
independence, and bush ethos, 120
indigenous culture, 22
indigenous peoples, 17, 50, 55, 58, 64, 68
industrial base, 64
industrial expansion, 1950s and 1960s, 49
industrial logic, 62
industrial productivity, and economic growth, 68
Industrial Revolution, 189, 201
industrial sector, 62
Industrial Workers of the World, 291
industrialization, 62; and world wars, 60
industries, sweated, 216
infants: deaths, colonial, 229; mortality rates, 94–5
inflation, 243; pressures towards, 1970–1, 61
Ingamells, Rex, 145
Inglis Moore, Tom, 12
Institute for Aboriginal Studies, 196
Institute of Family Studies, 237
Institute of Public Affairs, 299
institutions: innate conflict, 186; differences, 63; reformative principles, and Aborigines, 197

intellectuals: 130, 132; movements; and formation of *Meanjin*, 133; literary, 130; 1940s and populism, 286; and political traditions, 284; traditions, and bush ethos, 120
intelligentsia, 24, 33–5, 38, 118
interdependency, 70
investment: informed controls on British, 60; foreign, 280; in Australian resources, 61; public, in infrastructure, 296
Island Magazine, 134

Japan, 69
Jenks, F., *A History of the Australasian Colonies*, 192
Jindyworobaks, 145
journalism, 76; *Bulletin*, 11, 115; in colonial literary production, 116; 'higher', 131; and realism, 123–9; literary, 113; professionalization, 118, 119
journalists, 110, 116–18 *passim*, 123, 125; and *Meanjin*, 132

Keynesian economics, 60, 286
kinship, and Aboriginal history, 203; Empire, 64; links, 69
knowledge, production of, 190

Labor 'socialism', 289
Labor governments, conservative portrayal of, 294 *see also* ALP, labour
Labor Party, emergence of, 30; and labour movement, 209, 210; and welfare, 255
Labor split, 1916–17, 281
Labor, and federal-state conflicts, 293–4; and welfare, 298
Laborisms, history, 210
laborist outlook, and socialist perspectives, 291
labour history, and historiography, 206, 207; and radical nationalism, 188; Old Left, 290; and the state, 244
labour ideology, and nationalism, 290
labour market, 54, 213, 217
labour movement: and Catholics, 292–3; and Constitution, 280; and socialism, 291; in government, 206; and state, 208; and social order, 214; social reforms and 1890s, 254
labour parties, and policy reforms, 280; emergence of, 291
labour populists, 277
labour productivity, 62
labourism, *laissez-faire*, 286, 295
land: boom, 57; dispensation of, 54; legislation, 56; ownership, and urbanization, 90; policy, 58; SA and Vic as 'free' colonies, 55; reform, 297; rights, 70

Lang government, 65
language: *Bulletin*, 113, 121, 124, 128; and community, 24; and construction of identity, 71; and dependency, 32
Lawrence, D.H., *Kangaroo*, 12
Lawson, Henry, 6, 28, 114–21 *passim*; 'The Union Buries Its Dead', 141
Lawson, Louisa, 28
League of Nations, 281
legacies: of boom and contraction, 53; convictism, 224; nineteenth-century development, 59; settler society, 63, 64, 66
leisure, and colonial women, 229
liberal hegemony, 286
Liberal Party, 64, 300
liberals: political philosophy, 295; reforms, and welfare state, 255; reformers, 55; and policy reforms, 280; and welfare, 297; social justice, 255
Liberal–Country parties, and conservatism, 288
liberalism, 285, 286; divisions, 289–90; *Meanjin*, 132, 133
libertarianism, 75
literature, 37, 73–4, 100, 110–12, 118, 130; 1950s and 1960s, preoccupations, 147; and national agendas, 147; and social issues, 147; rhetorical approach, 137; structuralist/semiotic approach, 137
living wage, 218
Loan Council, 296
local councils, 74–5; regional identity and state governments, 77
local government, lack of power, 78
local histories, 74; within national history, 47
local production, 66
localism: and corruption in America, 65; disappearance of in television, 73; in Australian film, 107; in film and television, 168
London money market, 296

Métin, Albert, 291
Macquarie, Governor, 191
macro-economic regulation, 62
macro-economic strategy, 61
magazines, 116; literary, 74, 107, 110, 129, 133, 134; nineteenth century, 128–9; relations with audience defined, 129; role in defining audience, 119; tones and styles, 129, 131, 133
Malouf, D., 152–3 *passim*
manufacturers, 14, 34; development of, 1920s Melbourne, 76; industry, 60, 250
marginalization: of Australia, 63; of Australian exports, 69
markets, foreign, 64

market considerations, and film, 162
market-liberals, 287
marriage: ages and women, 224; and alternatives, 228–9; in colonial Australia, 223; and colonial males, 226; as compulsory for Australian women, 228; as focus of conflicts, 234; and men, 241; and protection, 226; social mobility and critiques, 225; urban/rural distinction, 223–4; as women's trade, 225
Marx, Karl, 17
Marxism: accounts of Australian society, 185; and labour history, 207, 209, 211; state explanations, 301
masculinism and quest for identity, 27; 1890s conflict with feminism, 29; context of *Bulletin*, 117
masculinist: closure, and historical enquiry, 227; national culture and identity, 238
masculinity, and *Bulletin* advertisements, 114
mateship, 25, 26, 120, 142; in literature, 147; and misogynist culture, 28
McCarty, J., 75
meaning: and literature, 115; cultural construction of, 107
Meanjin, 71; 129–33 *passim*
media: and regional identity, 72; and social order, 186
Melbourne Charity Organisation Society, 252
Melbourne, 71, 72, 75–6; land boom, 57; development of, 55; images, 93; and British moral economists, 55
Melbourne–Sydney rivalry, 15, 94
men: privilege of, and philanthropy, 254; sexuality of, hydraulic notions about, 226–7; as workers, and reforms, 254;
male–female relations, structural asymmetry of, 225
Menzies government, 281–2 *passim*
mercantilism, 295
merchants, 54
metropolis, 3; and colony, in *Bulletin*, 122; communication with regions, 118; parent culture, in viewing subjects, vii
Miles, Bea, 239
military, 186; 'vulnerability', 64
mining, 74; Aborigines, 201
misogyny: Australian culture, 227; in *Bulletin* humour, 128; and nineteenth century; popular culture, 225; and gender imbalance, 28; and urban intellectuals, 33, 35
missionaries, 191–2, 197
modernity, 66
modernization: urban, 57
money market, international, 61
moral economy, 65

Index 319

Morant, H., 'The Austral Light', 138
mortality rates: in colonial cities, 247; maternal, 229
Moubray, Philip, 118
multiculturalism, 64, 68; and Australian film, 167
Murray, Les, 'The Quality of the Sprawl', 144
Murray-Smith, Stephen, 12
music, 121
mutual aid funds, 247
myth-making: and Australian films, 160; and Australian nationalism, 58; and imperial expansion, 57-8
mythology, popular, 68
Myths of Oz, 136
myths: Aboriginal historians, 204; and images of Australian colonies, 53; founding, and rhetoric in self-image, 15; of Oz, 109; of Tasmanian Aborigines' extinction, 198

narrative: voice, 128; in film, 165
nation, 3, 18, 70; and internal diversity, 167, and film, 168; and rhetoric, 19; appeal of, 24; arguments in *Bulletin*, 123; as 'whole people', 22; as intellectual construct, 37; as political mobilization, 22-3; definition of, 71; epitomes, 148; origin of, 20-1, 24; *versus* states' rights, 22
nation-state: as legitimate international norm, 24; as site of conflict, 6; differences within, 14
national agendas, and literature, 147
national anthems, 24
national arts organizations, in Sydney and Melbourne, 76
national character, 109, 111, 285; and bush ethos, 25; and convict images, 146; and urban milieu, 95; criticism, 107; in films, 167
national characteristics: in poetry, 141; literature, 74
national chauvinism, 72
national cultural agenda, and realism, 149
national culture: 1950s realism, 150; and literature, 110; and magazines, periodicals, 129; 131; and urbanization, 84; class formation and state intervention, 188; masculinist, 238
national cultures, explanations for differences, 285
national day, 19-20, 36; *see* ceremonial moments, symbolism
national distinctiveness, notion of, deployment in poetry, 142
national economy, 59, 72; fragmentation, 79
national epitomes: and satire, 152
national goals, 72

national history, 75
national icons, 142, 151
national identity, 47, 70; and convictism, 145; and epitomes, 144; and political literature, 303; and social criticism, 151; and system of ideas, 72; and urbanization, 86; appearance of singular, 49; *Bulletin*, 112; cultural production of, 18-36; dual loyalties, 278; exclusion of women from, 28; in comparative studies, 14; in historical and literary works, 109; inhibition of regionalism, 83; masculinist, 238
national image, 'workingman's paradise', 242
national inventory, and Bicentennial, 148; and contemporary writers, 152; and regional writing, 153; and women's writing, 152; as agenda, 154; of epitomes, 147; rhetorical function, 153-4
national literary tradition, exclusion of regional variations, 73
national media networks, 72
national mind, 110
national minorities, 68
national networks, television, 168
national questions, and films, 167
national self-confidence, response to crisis, 146
national self-definition, 6; by posing questions, 16
national self-determination, 68
national sentiment, and ALP, 293
national symbols, 76, 143; and federation, 277
national transport systems, 72
national type, 37, 38, 57, 58; in films, 167
national values, and economic crises, 95; and epitomes, 148
National Welfare Fund, 299
nationalism, 6, 18, 66, 21-4, 26, 153; 1890s images, 137-8; and *Bulletin*, 122; and history, 203; and labour ideology, 290; and peripheral areas, 83; and political economy, 29; and urban contribution, 95; Australian, and myth-making, 58; Australian, nineteenth century, 210; construction in poetry, 139; cultural, and *Meanjin*, 130; egalitarian, 30; feminist interpretations of, 28; literary, 107; new liberalism, and social reforms, 254; New Zealand, 83
nationalist attitudes, 120, 122
nationalist challenge, to colonial ideas, 195
nationalist critique, of *Bulletin*, 124
nationalist historiography, 26, 27-8
nationalist ideology, 24
nationalist image, role of intelligentsia, 34-5
nationalist movements, indigenous, 195

nationalist politics: and convict images, 146; and realism, 127; pre-federation, 112
nationality: 71, 107; 'epitomes of', 107; and Australian epitomes, 153; epitomized in gestures, 144; rhetoric of, 137
nationalization, banks, 299–300 *passim*
nationbuilding, agenda, 29
nationhood: and 'coming of age', 20; and contending groups, 24; and continuity, 36; and federation, 30; and history, in film, 166; and literature, 110; independent, 5
Native Police, 192, 196
native policy, 193–4, 205; failure of reform, 197; social history, 203; *see also* government policy
native-born: and colonial careers, 27; and nationalism, 21; in debate over 'national type', 38; in social relations, 36; understandings of Australia, 19
nativist intelligentsias, 24
nativist moderate vision, 30
nativist vogue, 142–3
natural scientists, early interest in studying Australia, 9
neo-classicism, 127
New Federalism, 77, 289
New Guinea: annexation, 277
new journalism, 118, 127
New Left historians, 209–11, 214, 286, 291–2
new liberalism: and colonial reforms, 59; and social reforms, 254
new literature, 111; and literary periodical, 133
New Protection, 217
New Right, 215, 302; challenge to welfare system, 251
new social history, and politics, 221
new societies, institutions, 273
new society, 3, 57–8, 64, 111, 118; attention to formation, vii; Australia as, 68; social conflicts, 185
New South Wales: regional diversity, 81; self-image, 81
new unionism, 207, 214
New Zealand literature, 110
newspapers, 73, 107, 116, 121; 1940s, 130; advertisements, 125; and radical nationalism, 5; and urban intellectuals, 33; as mediators, 111; Australia Day 1988, 19; in literary production, 110; national, 76; nineteenth century, 128–9
Nixon, Richard, 282
nostalgia, in poetry, 139
novelists, 6, 117
novels, serialization in *Bulletin*, 116

ocker, origin of style, 27
oil production, and prices, 61

Old Left, 210, 211; labour historians, 285; labour history, 290
Old World hierarchies, absence in Australia, 288
Old World privilege, radical rejection of, 50–1
One Big Union, 291
OPEC, 61
order, and conflict, themes in Australia, 187
Organisation for Economic Co-operation and Development (OECD), 302
orphanages, 247
Overland, 134
overseas writing, 130; *Scripsi*, 134

Pacific, Australia's role in, 69
painting, 121; professionalization, 118
Palmer, Nettie, 12, 28; Vance, 12, 28
pamphlets and books, about Australia, 58
parent culture, 64; 'metropolis' and 'periphery', in viewing subjects, vii; and settler societies, 17; Australia's difference from Britain, 51; *cf.* colonial society, 36–7; colonial relationship, 10
parochial loyalties, 277
parochialism, 73–4
Partisan Review, 131
party platforms, and established policies, 301
party system, 273; Labor and anti-Labor, 288
pastoral boom, 75
pastoral expansion, 1820s and 1830s, 65
pastoral industry, 49, and steam power, 56; Aboriginal labour, 193, 200, 202
pastoralism, 55, 74; and Aboriginal culture, 194
pastoralists, 34, 54–6 *passim*
paternalism: and Aborigines, 198; and histories of Aborigines, 205; liberal-inspired, and Aborigines, 195, 197
Paterson, Banjo, 6, 120, 121; 'Clancy of the Overflow', 140
patriarchy, 186
patronage, 295; and public service reform, 59; and regional histories, 75; of intelligentsia, 35, 38; state, 135
penal authorities, and male sexual access, 227
pensions, 249
Penton, B., *Landtakers*, 146
periodicals: and urban intellectuals, 33; as mediators, 11; twentieth century, 107, 110 *see also* magazines, literary

periphery, vii, 3
Perkins, Charles, 196
philanthropists, and Christian ideals, 253
philanthropy, and sex conflict, 254
Phillips, A.A., 12, 144, 189
Pike, Douglas, 185
pioneer achievement, 49
pioneer women, 248
pioneering society, 143
plantation economies, 54
poetry, 124, 129, 134; Australian, 130; in *Bulletin*, 116, 124; irony in (Lawson), 141; *Meanjin*, 131, 132; and nationalism, 139
poets, 6, 117
police, 186, 244
policies, and rural poverty, 248
policy: Aborigines, 192–4; economic, 61, 66; fiscal, 60; government, 66; imperial, 50, 68; 1890s, 53; foreign, 275; 'maturity view', 280, 282; and dependency theorists, 280; and Whitlam government, 282; land, 55, 58; metropolitan, 66; and political culture, 303; protests against, 186; rural poverty, 248; tariff, 58; national economic, and arbitration, 217; reforms in Britain and Australia, 59; thinking; reorientation of, 62
policy innovations, and ALP, 294
policy reforms: and liberal reformers, 280; liberal and labour influence, 280
political élites, 56
political control, 74
political corruption: and public service reform, 59
political culture, 303; and arbitration, 216; and regional diversities, 15; Australian, 273; utilitarian and legalistic approaches, 287
political culture approach, variants, 285
political dependency, features and critiques, 275
political discourse, traditions, 284
political economy, and nationalism, 29; and regional studies, 79
political factionalism, and *Bulletin*, 121
political history, 284; and political ideologies, 273
political ideologies: and Australian political history, 273; fluid boundaries, 285
political institutions, 275
political left, and realism, 150
political mobilization, and nationalism, 22–3
political models, British, 273
political movements, influences on *Bulletin*, 125
political opinion, in nineteenth-century Australia, 29–30
political parties, central role in government, 279

political resistance, and fertility control, 236
political struggles, and women, 234
political system, 303
political traditions: and key issues, 300; and state intervention, 300; polarities, 300
politics: Australian culture and little magazines, 134; *Bulletin*, 114–15, 122, class, and labour history, 206–9; democratic, nationalist and realism, 127; radical, 219
Poor Law, 251
poor relief, 252
poor, deserving and undeserving, 251–2 *passim*
popular culture: and film, 174; and misogyny, 225
popular struggles, 297
population growth, 62: 1850s, 235; and settler society, 64; as indicator of economic expansion, 52
populism, 65; and 1940s intellectuals, 286; and ALP, 293; and Queensland politics, 81
populist attitudes, 122
populist collectivism, 285
populist-progressive alliance, 297
Port Adelaide, 70
Port Phillip Protectorate, 196
post-war economy, and America, 66
post-war reconstruction, 60, 64, 298–300; interpretations of, 299–300
post-war trends, 68
poverty, 188; and depressions, 244; and economic historians, 245; and immigrants, 246; and inequalities, 257; and prosperity, 246; and women, 246; dimensions, 250; feminization of since 1945, 257; rural, 248; urban, 247; vulnerable groups, 250
power, 54, and resistance, and women, 238
pre-industrial urbanization, 85–6
Pre-Raphaelitism, 127
press, popular, 118
Preston, Margaret, 28
Prichard, Katharine Susannah, 28
primary production, subsidies, 296
primary-based economy, 280 *see also* economy
print circus, *Bulletin*, 113–16
print community, 122
print community/imagined community, 135
print economy, 107, 110, 113, 115, 129–35 *passim*
print media, and urban intellectuals, 33
private benevolence, 251–2
problem-oriented approaches, 11, 14–17
professionalism, and intelligentsia, 118–20, 132

prose fiction, as art, 127
prose sketches, 114, 116, 124
prosperity: 1920s, 60; and poverty, 246
prostitutes, 227, 240–1
provincial areas, 123
pseudonyms, in *Bulletin*, 128
psyche, and environment, 74
psychological realism, 150
public investment: and infrastructure, 296; criticism, 297
public finance, 58
public institutions, 69
public service reform, 59
public sphere, women's representation by men, 231–2
public: *vs.* domestic in nationbuilding agenda, 29
publishers, 109, 110, 133; and Aborigines, 202
publishing industry, local, absence of, 133

QANTAS, 299
Quadrant, 134, 300
Queensland: and foreign capital, 80; as case study of regional analysis, 80; aspects of difference, 80; characteristics, 153; economic differences, 80; late nineteenth century, 224; political culture, 15; politics, 81; towns, and locality-based newspapers, 73; literature, 74

race: and *Bulletin* audience, 123; critiques in Australian historiography, 209–12
racial purity, 58, 68
racial purity, British character and *Bulletin*, 58
racial stock, 64
racial types, 58
racism: 50, 69, 197; and histories of Aborigines, 205; and immigration, 212; and nationalism, 22–3; and sexism, 197; *Bulletin*, 115; debate, 195–6, 205; working class, 211–12
racist assumptions, *see* Aboriginal history
radical attitudes, 120
radical fragment, interpretation, 285–6, 297
radical ideology, and state action, 297
radical nationalism, 5, 6, 12–13, 25–8, 31, 37, 67, 124, 146, 188; and labour history, 207–9; exponents, 12; influence on polity, 3
radical political ethos, 297
radical populist vision, 30
radical socialism, 291–2
radicalism, 68
radicalism, Australian, nineteenth century, 210
railway and urban infrastructure, 57
rape, 226, 232

rationalism, *cf.* Aboriginal history, 204
readers, 129–30
readership, and Aborigines, 202; *Bulletin* 113–17 *passim*, 120–3 *passim*
reading and writing, structured activities, 134
reading public, 110
realism, 148–51; *cf.* Aboriginal history, 204; debates, 149; definition, 149; European theories, 127; and journalism, 123–9; literary, 148–9
realist fiction, 127
realist tradition, 150
recession, 61
reciprocity, 198, 199
Red Page, *Bulletin* reviews, 130
Redfern, 70
redistribution, 65
referenda: 1926, 289; 1944, 299–300 *passim*; 1946, 299; 1967 and Aborigines, 196; 1988, 289
reform programme, 298
reform, obstacles to welfare, 255
reformatories, 251
reformers: and liberal framework, 286; liberal, 55
reformism, democratic, 276
reforms, in women's legal position, 232
region: and environment, 78; as imagined community, 82; as synonymous with state, 76
regional diversity, and New South Wales, 81
regional history, versions of, 75
regional loyalty, and Tasmania, 81
regional studies, 11, 14, 15; and political economy, 79; and women's life course, 224; international comparisons, 79–80
regional writing, 153
regionalism, 47, 53, 56–7, 66, 70–4 *passim*; and national identity, 83; as voice of periphery, 83; key problems, 82
regions and relationships, 75
regions: and economic identity, 79; competing definitions, 75; definition and local councils, 77; functionalist histories, 75–6; problems of definition, 82; social and cultural dimensions, 82; territorial and political aspects, 82; ways of defining, 74
regulation, macro-economic, 62
religion, decline of authority, and rise of nationalism, 23
reorientation, 66; economic dreams, 63; policy-thinking, 62; social and economic, 69
representation of women, challenges to, 234
reproduction, 213; state incentives, 187

republican sentiment, 120
republicans, 277
reserves movement, 193, 196
resistance, and women, 233
resources boom: 1979-81, 65; effect on economic development, 51
resources: economic growth, 62; global, European appropriation, 50, colonial exploitation, 189
respectability, and social reform, 29 *see also* ultrarespectability
reviewers, 110, 133
reviews: *Bulletin* Red Page, 130; *Meanjin*, 131; *Scripsi*, 134
revolution: and nationalism, 24; and twentieth-century workers, 210
rhetoric: of epitomes, 140, 142; in *Bulletin*, 125; invention of, and self image, 15; of 'the nation', 19
Roberts, S.H., *History of Australian Land Settlement*, 192
Roberts, Tom, 119
Roberts, Violet, 240
Robinson, George Augustus, 191, 196
romance fiction, 127
Ross, L., 299
Rowse, T., 286
Royal Commission into the Decline of the Birthrate (1903—NSW), 236
Royal Commission into the Moving Picture Industry (1927), 157
Rudd, Steele, 6, 128
rural areas, 123; literary culture, 116
rural crisis, 250
rural industries, 299
rural labourers, and technological change, 248
rural poverty, 248
rural sector, 62
rural technological improvements, 56
rural towns, conservatism, 72
Rusden, G.W., *History of Australia*, 192, 197

Sala, George Augustus, 55
Santamaria, B.A., 292-3 *passim*
satellite society, 66
satire, and national epitomes, 152
Schedvin, Boris, 62
Scott, E., *A Short History of Australia*, 192
Scripsi, 133, 134
SEATO, 282
secondary industries, 299
sectarianism, conflict, 186, 187
sectional needs, 72
segregation, policy, 194-5
Selection Acts, 248
selectors, 56
self-government, 56, 275
self-help, 252
self-image, 63-68 *passim*; invention of, 15
Serle, Geoffrey, 12; *From Deserts the Prophets Come*, 109-10
settlement patterns, 84
settlement schemes, 296-7 *see also* soldier settlement schemes
settlement, 54; and development, 47 *see also* European settlement
settler dependency, Australia, 50 *see also* dependency
settler expansion, 49
settler power, and imperial concerns, 60
settler societies: and government structure, 276; and urbanization, 90
settler society, 14, 27, 47-53 *passim*, 56-69 *passim*; and indigenous peoples, 17; and literatures, 110; social relations in, 36
settlers, 64
sex conflict, 186
sex, critiques in Australian historiography, 209, 212-14
sex imbalance: and female distribution, 223; inter-racial relations on frontier, 198
sex ratio, colonial, 222-3
sexes, and history, 222
sexism, and racism, 197
sexist attitudes, 186
sexual abuse, 237; legacies, 227
sexual access, and penal authorities, 227
sexual division of labour, 188; and urbanization, 95; Harvester judgement, 218; state sanctioned, 214, 215
sexual harassment, 239
sexual violence, 226
shearers, 123, 207
shearers' strikes, 216
short stories, 124, 125; *Bulletin*, 114, 116
Sinclair, Frederick, 28
slum clearance programmes, 249
Smith's Weekly, 147
Smith, James: *Melbourne Review*, 110
soap operas, 165
social élite, and depressions, 244
social and economic change, debates, 63
social attitudes, 63, 69
social contract, 194
social control, interpretation of welfare, critiques, 253
social Darwinism: and Aboriginal marginality in history, 191; and British 'racial stock', 51; and indigenous elimination, 58
social discipline, 245; and urbanization, 94
social engineering, Crown land and revenue, 54
social equality, 68-9
social experiments, 254
social formation, levels of analysis, 47
social groupings, writers and intellectuals, 110; *see also* cultural formation

social historians, and urbanization, 90
social history, new, and politics, 221
social inequalities, failure of welfare state to address, 255
social inequality, 54, 250–1 *passim*; and sex conflict in Australian society, 185
social insurance, 255
social issues, and literature, 147
social justice, 54; and liberals, 255
social legislation, 254
social liberal programme, 290
social liberalism, 295; policies and challenges, 290
social meanings: and convicts, 145; diversity, and epitomes, 142
social networks, 72
social order, 186, 215; and labour market, 214; and women in colonial culture and politics, 220; effects of gold, 58; moulding of women's existences, 240; nature of Australian, 49; threat by male predominance, 223
social power, 54
social realism, 150
social realism: and radical nationalism, 13; novelists and artists, 6
social reform, and respectability, 29
social reforms, 254
social relations, in settler society, 36
social sciences, *see* humanities and social sciences
social structure, 54
social welfare advocates, 243
social-democratic intellectuals, 299, 301
social-democratic, discourse tradition, 284
socialisation objective, and ALP, 292
socialism, 285, 289; interpretations, 290; and Labor, debates, 292
socialist, accounts of Australian society, 185
socio-economic factors: in analysing Australia, 30–1, 37
sociology, community studies, 72
soldier settlement schemes, 230, 249
South Africa, 68
South Australian Film Corporation, 168
South-East Asia, 70
South-West Pacific, 66, 69
Southerly, 131, 134
Spence, W.G., *Australia's Awakening*, 206
squatters, 54, 56, 192, 248
squattocracy, 285
stagflation, 61
Stalinism, 292
staple industries, 59
state action, 302; environmental interpretation, 296; ideological explanation, 297
state anomalies, and women, 232
state assistance, 201, *see also* subsidies
state autonomy, 76
state debates, 301

state expansion, policy areas, 297
state intervention, 188; agendas for decline, 256; and interests (class/ideology), 301; and political culture, 303, and political traditions, 300; arbitration, 215–19; Australian features, 273; critics, 287
state power, 54
state regulation, 295
state role, 303
state socialism, 215, 297
state sovereignty, 68
state–Commonwealth relations, 76–7
State–federal conflicts, 47
state: activities, 296; and labour history, 244; and labour movement, 208; as neutral, utilitarian, 301; as unit of regional study, 79; dual role, 215; in Australia, 294; Marxist explanations, 301; role; and purpose in social order, 186
states' rights: and conservatism, 289; as antagonistic to 'the nation', 22; Qld versus Canberra, 22
states: and regional diversities, 15, 70; core and periphery studies, 79; differences in economies, Qld *cf*. Vic., N.S.W., 14; identification of differences, 81; Qld's demographic differences, 15
statistical tables and divisions, 71
Statute of Westminster, 281
steam power, effect on pastoral industry, 56
Stephens, A.G., 111, 118, 119, 127
Stivens, Dal, *Jimmy Brockett*, 148
strikes, 185, 216; 1890s, 244, 291
structural change, 65; and world wars, 60
structuralist, semiotic, definition, 154
structuralist/semiotic approach: to literature, 137
Stubbs, J., *The Hidden People*, 250
subsidies, primary production, 296
suburbanization, 86
suffrage, manhood, 276
Swan River settlement, 55
Sydney Harbour Bridge, 76
Sydney Mail, 116
Sydney Morning Herald, 129
Sydney, 71, 76, 95; and television production, 73; film and television production, 168
symbolism: and Bicentennial, 204; and cultural production, 15–17 *passim*; and currency, 61; of bush in Australian identity, 35
system of ideas: and national identity, 72

Toënnies, F., 72
TAA, 299
tariff policy, 58
tariff protection, 62, 282, 296

Tasmania, and regional loyalty, 81
teachers, 109, 110; and *Meanjin*, 132, 133
technological change: and rural labourers, 248
technologies: print, 123; publication and distribution, 110
television stations, and localism, 168
television: and working-class milieux, 169; Australian content, 73; Australian, 107; children's 162; national networks, 168; programme production, 74, 168; soap operas, 165
temperance movement, women's 234
The Man From Snowy River (film), 107, 170–4
The Overlanders (film), 161
The Return of Captain Invincible (film), 163
theatre, 121
They're a Weird Mob (film), 170
Third World, 61; activism, 68; collective identity, 50
Threlkeld, Reverend L.E., 191
tied grants, 300
Tocsin, 279
totalizing approach, 112, 129, 134; to Australian literature and literary history; defined, 109
Town and Country Journal, 116
town planning, 78
trade unions, and ALP, 293
trade unions, and artisans, 207
trade, terms of, 61
tradition, 3; Australian literature, 130–1
traditions, ideological, 303
traditional societies, their inattention to formation, vii, 17
transport, 76; decentralized in Queensland, 80
Trollope, A., 242
Turner, G., *National Fictions*, 136
Turner, H.G., *A History of the Colony of Victoria*, 192
Turner, Ian, 12
Twopeny, R., 242

ultrarespectability, colonial women's refuge in cult of, 29
unemployment, 243; protests, 245; relief, 245; rural crisis, 250; rural, 248
union movement, 61; and welfare state, 255–6; and women, 231
unions, skilled and unskilled workers, 245
United Nations, racism resolutions, 196
United States investment, 60
unity: and Bicentennial, 203–4; false imposed on past, 75; in defining Australia, 19; in meaning of national day, 19–20, 22
universalism, 74
universalist, critique of *Bulletin*, 124
urban areas, differences from country, 14
urban biography approach, 88–9

urban bohemianism, 120
urban construction, 59
urban development, 47, 58; images of, 57
urban dwellers, exclusion by radical nationalism, 13
urban experience: and class, 94; and gender, 94
urban growth, developmental model, 92
urban historians, and poverty, 248
urban history: and disciplines, 85; growth of, 87; problems, 85
urban imagery, in television, 165–6
urban industrial economy, 60
urban industrial growth, 53
urban infrastructure, and railway, 57
urban intellectuals, 125; and bush ethos, 120; and print media, 33; in radical nationalism, 32–33
urban liberals, ascendancy of, 56
urban modernization, 57
urban nation, and cultural distinctiveness, 96
urban poverty, 247
urban professionals, 54
urban revisionists, 96
urban sociology, 88
urban–rural paradox, 47, 95, 96, 139
urbanization, 47, 90; and economic factors, 89; and entrepreneurs, 94; and environmental factors, 87–9 *passim*; and human agency, 89–90; and national identity, 86; and social historians, 90; Australian, 84, uniqueness, 85; central questions, 85; distinctive process, 96; gap in historiography, 87; limitations of models, 92; pre-industrial, 85–6; process of, 87; theories of, 88–92
utilitarian approach: to political culture: 287

value conflicts, 65
Victoria, regional study of, 75
Vietnam war, 282
Vietnam, 67

wage-labourers, 14
wages, 231
wages boards: and sweated industries, 216
Wakefield, E.G., 296
Wakefield's theory, 54
Wall Street, 66
Ward, Russel, 12, 57, 73, 285; responses to critics, 96; *The Australian Legend*, 6, 12,120
Waterside Workers Film Unit, 168
Weber, Adna, 86
welfare, 188
welfare: and economic recession, 303; and Labor, 298; and liberal reformers, 287; and women, 29; colonial, private, 251; limitations of, 257; obstacles to reform, 255; policing, 250; selective

and universal criteria, 254
welfare cutbacks, and non-organized groups, 256
welfare debates, competing interests, 257
welfare decline, post World War I, 254
welfare finance, 255
welfare net, and economic downturn, 256
welfare recipients, stigmatization, 256
welfare reforms, and workers, 249
welfare state expansion: test cases, 298–300; and liberal hegemony, 286; and social order, 186; and union movement, 255–6; Australian image, 298; containment of conflict, 251; debate dimensions, 256; development, 254; foundations in the 1940s, 255; interpretations, 252–7; residual nature, 256; retreat, 256; theory inadequacies, 257
welfare system: challenge from 'new right', 251; inadequacies, 250
Wentworth, W.C., *A Statistical, Historical and Political Description of New South Wales*, 10
West, Morris, 12
Westerly, 74, 134
Western Australia, and literary production, 74
Western Europeans, 63
wheat-growing, new techniques, 56
White Australia, 277
White Australia Policy, 214
white invasion, 17, 19, 190
White Paper on Full Employment, 299
White, Patrick, 148–51
White, R., 72: *Inventing Australia*, 136
Whitlam government, 6, 61, 78, 294, 300; and foreign policy, 282; interpretations of, 300
Wilmot, Frank, 28
Wollongong, 70
'Women of the Sun' (TV series), 170
women writers, 6
Woman's Day, 134
women's fiction, nineteenth century, 116
women's films, 169
women's health, 237
women's history, 188; and happiness, 233; context of emergence, 221
Women's Liberation Movement, 221
women's pay rates, 231
women's studies, 185
women's temperance movement, 234
Women's Weekly, 130
women's writing, 152
women: Aboriginal, labour in pastoral industry, 200; Aboriginal, on frontier, 197; and 'enforced whoredom', 226; and asylums, 239; and contraception, 235; and cultural production, 238; and dissident cultural politics, 235; and divorce, 237; and domestic work, 229; and experts, 233; and factory and shop legislation, 249; and family, 212, 213; and forms of resistance, 233–40; and homicide, 240; and hotels, 238; and male protectors, 226; and marriage, 223–4; and philanthropy, 253; and political struggles, 234; and poverty, 246; and social mobility, 225; and social order, 233; and social order in Australian colonial culture and politics, 220; and state anomalies, 232; and union movement, 231; and urban life, 94–5; and welfare, 257; and workforce participation, 234; as moral sex, 226; as sexual commodities, 227; *Bulletin* column, 114; *Bulletin*, 117; contribution to family economy, 95; exclusion by radical nationalism, 13, 27–8; exclusion from friendly societies, 247; historical interrogations, 220; impact on urbanization, 92; individual rebellions, 239–40; legal identities, 231; marginalization in history, 222; pioneer, 248; reforms in legal position, 232; social identities, 230; social order and challenges, 240; statistics, and economic contributions, 230; work options, 223, 228; work, 188, 212–14; working-class oppression, 147
wool production: 53–4, 59, 62
work: definition, exclusion of women, 230; sex segmentation, 231
Worker, 115, 116, 137
workers' compensation, 249
Workers' Educational Association, 286
workers, docile, 253
workforce, structure, 213
working class racism, 211–12
working class radicalism, 254–5 *passim*
working class, 207–8; and radical nationalism, 13; divisions within, 249
working-class oppression, and domestic violence, on Australian frontier, 28
working-class suburbs, 70
workingman's paradise, 188, 189
world economic system, 70, and regions, 47
world trade, 283
World War II, 60; and Australia, 281
world wars, and economic changes, 60
writers, 123, 129; and national inventory, 152; and urban contribution to nationalism, 95; and urbanization, 86; Australian, 130; contemporary, 152; *Meanjin*, 131, 132; regional, 74
writing: 1890s, 143, 148–9, 153; 1930s and 1940s, 143; and realism, 148; Australian, 74, 129; genres, *Meanjin*, 131; humorous, 128, regional studies, 15; overseas, 130, 134; and reading as structured activities, 134

yeoman-farmers, 248
yeomanry, 54

Zola, E., 149